MURDER, HONOR, AND LAW

The American South Series
Edward L. Ayers, Editor

MURDER
HONOR
AND LAW

4 Virginia Homicides

FROM RECONSTRUCTION TO
THE GREAT DEPRESSION

Richard F. Hamm

University of Virginia Press
Charlottesville and London

UNIVERSITY OF VIRGINIA PRESS
© 2003 by the Rector and Visitors of the University of Virginia
Printed in the United States of America on acid-free paper

First published 2003

1   3   5   7   9   8   6   4   2

LIBRARY OF CONGRESS CATALOGING-IN-PUBLICATION DATA

Hamm, Richard F.
  Murder, honor, and law / four Virginia homicides from Reconstruction to the Great
Depression / Richard F. Hamm.
     p. cm. — (The American South series)
Includes bibliographical references and index.
  ISBN 0-8139-2207-0 (cloth) — ISBN 0-8139-2208-09 (paper)
  1. Murder—Virginia. 2. Murder—Press coverage—United States. 3. Virginia—Social
life and customs. 4. Southern States—Social life and customs. I. Title. II. Series.
  HV6533.V8 H356 2003
  364.15'23'09755—dc21
                                                                        2002153614

Dedicated to Francis R. Hamm

Contents

Illustrations

Preface

THIS BOOK IS AN EXAMPLE of how teaching improves scholarship. It began in 1985, when as a graduate student, I taught a undergraduate research seminar: Notable American Trials. To aid my students I outlined a dozen trials suitable for study, including some cases from Virginia. Unknowingly I had done my first research on this book. In the following years, while I finished my dissertation and turned it into a book, and while I searched for and found secure academic employment, I continued working on some of these cases. My work on these crimes and trials intensified when, after coming to the University at Albany, I revived a once popular course, Trials in History. I worked my research on these cases into lectures. How my students reacted to what I presented shaped my subsequent work on each case. Moreover, preparing the course compelled me to examine and read many books and articles about historic trials, allowing me to refine my ideas by learning from what other scholars have done with similar topics.

The rhythms of academic life set the pace for the creation of this book. Most of it was researched and written during the breaks and summers. Chapters were written in the summers, and during a one-semester sabbatical leave the entire manuscript was reconceptionalized, reorganized, and rewritten. Then it was subjected to readers, revised, rejected, and so forth. This prolonged process of gestation and birth has resulted in a far different (and I think better) work than I set out to write. Besides discarded versions, I have accumulated many debts, and the least I can do is thank the people and institutions instrumental in the making of this book.

The research for this work was supported through a Mellon research grant from the Virginia Historical Society, a Princeton University faculty support award, and a State University of New York and United University Profession joint faculty development award. Alice McShane, an expert tracker of obscure references, was indispensable in the completion of the research and the location of several of the illustrations.

The research was made far more pleasant and productive by the staffs of the Virginia Historical Society, the Albert and Shirley Small Special Collections Library of the University of Virginia Library, the Virginia Baptist Historical Society, the Library of Virginia, the Franklin D. Roosevelt Library, the Library of Congress, the Wise County Historical Society, the Clinch Valley College Library, and the Lonesome Pine Regional Library. I am very thankful for the hospitality, far exceeding even the extravagant levels of Virginians, offered by Betsy and Howson Cole, Mary Hill Cole, Newby Day, Richard Fiesta, Chuck and Sharon McCurdy, and David McKinney. In addition, I thank Candice Bredbenner, Elaine Cascio, Jane Dailey, Leland Estes, Richard Felson, Stephanie Jarrach, John Kneebone, William Rainbolt, Richard Sherman, Gregory Stanley, and Bill Statzer for sharing specialized knowledge, insights, or materials.

My thinking and the writing about these crimes and trials benefited from encouragement from Lewis Bateman, Nelson Lankford, Christopher Lee, Jean Lee, Harriet Temps, Dan S. White, and Ann Withington. In conversation, both Allen Ballard and Gerry Zahavi made important suggestions that shaped the work. Fred Adler, Richard Holway, Amy Murrell, and Julian Zelizer all offered constructive advice on what they read of the work. The trenchant comments of Edward L. Ayers and Mark Wahlgren Summers were critical in making this book what it is. An early and perceptive reading by Reid Mitchell greatly improved this work. A late and far-reaching critique by Anette Lippold worked wonders; she, as much as anyone, is responsible for the final form of the introduction.

I am very grateful for the editorial assistance this work has received. Debbie Neuls, queen of the comma, graciously corrected hundreds of niggling problems. I thank the Virginia Historical Society for giving its permission to reprint, as chapter 2 of this book, a different version of "The Killing of John R. Moffett and the Trial of J. T. Clark: Race, Prohibition, and Politics in Danville, 1887–1893," *Virginia Magazine of History and Biography* 101 (1993): 375-404.

Finally, I would like to close where I began, with teaching. I would like to thank my students (from the University of Virginia, Princeton University, the University of New Hampshire, the University at Albany—State University of

New York, and the Bethlehem Humanities Institute for Life Long Learning), who showed great interest in these cases and who raised many questions that it took me years to answer. The very methods I used to answer those questions I learned from my father. My one regret in finishing this book is that he did not get to read the final version.

MURDER, HONOR, AND LAW

INTRODUCTION

IN 1868 A SCION of one of Richmond's leading families ambushed and killed the city's most controversial journalist over an article that had dishonored the killer's family. In 1892 a Democratic politician killed a crusading Danville minister after a dispute at the polls. In 1907 a former judge shot to death the son of the Nelson county sheriff for what was alleged to be an attempted rape. And in 1935 an Appalachian schoolteacher stood accused of killing her father by beating him with a shoe. All of these killers stood trial; two were convicted, and two were acquitted. These cases attracted extensive press coverage; journalists became not only recorders of the stories but an integral part of them, constructing the meaning of the events as they occurred. Besides journalists, these cases drew the attention of other people and groups outside the state. The comments and actions of these outsiders provoked Virginians to explain the interaction of their social values and legal system. Many of these exchanges occurred in the press and so also became woven into the stories.

The cases detailed in each of this book's chapters explore the press's perception of Virginia law and custom while illuminating the functioning of law and custom in the courts of the state. Each killing and trial show the interplay of the national media and culture with southern law, values, and culture. Each highlights how newspapers accepted, produced, altered, and disseminated ideas of

southern exceptionalism, especially ideas about honor and chivalry. Taken together, the cases show a pattern of complex interchange between outsiders and
Virginians over time. First, the character of northern criticism of the South
changed, starting as a strong critique of the barbarism and backwardness of the
region, passing through a period of reconciliation that muted the criticism, and
reemerging as an indictment of the South as retarded economically and socially.
Second, white Virginians in responding to outsider criticism went from defending the South's separate civilization as superior to that of the North to defending
it from claims that it was distinctive from the rest of the nation. In the course of
these exchanges, the culture of honor lost its place as the centerpiece of southern
distinctiveness in newspaper (and popular) conceptions of the South.[1]

This book's focus on press coverage of a number of crimes and trials over
seventy years allows it to develop a full picture of the development of southern exceptionalism. Looking at more than one incident helps to illuminate the
distinctions between the particulars of a case and the general features of a society. Examining more than one case sheds more light and increases the number of vantage points. The trials covered in this work were chosen to reflect the
social, economic, and geographic diversity of Virginia. Yet limiting the study
to one state reduces the number of variables among the individual cases, thus
avoiding the problem of comparing cases stemming from entirely dissimilar
circumstances.[2]

It is important in the comparison of these four cases that the Virginia law of
homicide remained essentially static. Virginia shared with most American states
a legal tradition of homicide law inherited from England which separated homicide into three distinct categories: murder (itself divided into first and second
degrees), manslaughter, and justifiable homicide. Murder was the killing of a
person when the killer was animated by malice, often with planning; it was punished the most harshly, with death or long imprisonment. Manslaughter was a
killing motivated by passion or anger but lacking the premeditation of murder; it
was punished with imprisonment. Justifiable homicide was a killing that was not
a crime and was not punished. One key issue in determining whether a homicide
was murder, manslaughter, or justifiable homicide was the idea of provocation
of the killer; killing to stop a crime, in defense of the home, or in the heat of passion could mitigate or excuse the crime. To constitute provocation the law required an act; legally, mere words by the victim could never mitigate murder
to manslaughter or justify a homicide. Despite sharing a common legal definition of homicide, Virginia, and the South as a whole, differed from the rest of the

nation in that the honor culture sanctioned certain killings. Thus many killers were brought to trial whom southerners thought justified in their homicide because they were acting out of honor. Often juries would acquit such individuals, overriding the requirements of the law.[3]

Not only was the law of homicide similar in the cases covered here, but each case captured the interest of the public and newspapers from inside and outside the state. For newspapers, any notable case was newsworthy because it contained elements sure to attract readers. As Clarence Darrow observed, "A murder that seemed especially brutal, as all killings do; a case growing out of sex relations; the weird, the salacious, the painful, the seemingly mysterious—all especially appeal to the crowd." Legal historians Lawrence Friedman and Robert Percival point out that criminal trials which received extensive press coverage and public attention functioned as "powerful teachers and preachers of conventional morality" and customs. The trials were public theater, presenting the mores of society to an audience larger than that in the courtroom. Such trials, in the words of Friedman, could "lay bare the soul of a given society." As Jake Lule shows in his study of the mythological elements of modern journalism, trial stories conveyed some of society's "eternal stories," exhibiting the society's "archetypal figures and forms." They offered "dramas of order and disorder, of justice affirmed and justice denied."[4]

In addition, each of these cases was marked by the presence of groups and individuals from outside Virginia society. Their criticisms provoked Virginians to explain or justify the criticized aspects of their society. Indeed, these exchanges between outsider critics and Virginia defenders often occurred in the pages of the Virginia and national press. Also, the coverage of each of these cases by out-of-state reporters is especially revealing of the different perceptions of Virginians and outsiders. As they were strangers in this land, their observations can help outsiders from a different time understand Virginia society better. Thus, despite their inherent differences, the four killings and murder trials covered in this book are tied together through their revelations about Virginian— and southern—society as portrayed in the press and, by extension, debated by the public.[5]

As the press helped to construct an image of Virginia and southern culture from Reconstruction through the Great Depression through the coverage of these four murder cases, it underwent dramatic changes itself. This seventy-year period, which begins with the reintegration of the nation's cooperative news system after the Civil War and ends with the emergence of radio as alternative to print, was a period when daily newspapers dominated news coverage. Then, as now, news was an assemblage of facts and interpretations designed to appeal to a large audience. And more than their rivals—weekly papers, magazines, and later radio—newspapers predominated in explicating and explaining events to the great mass of the American people. Typically, newspapers were produced in towns and cities. As the nation's urban population increased dramatically, the daily papers (as an aggregate) were well placed to reach a large part of the American people. Because a chief goal of the proprietors of daily newspapers was to increase their circulation, newspapers reached a great proportion of the nation's city and town dwellers and, after the rise of truck transportation systems, suburban and rural people, making papers a daily fixture in their lives.[6]

For those who did not live in cities or towns, the daily papers managed to exercise great hegemony over the news through the various mechanisms of cooperative news gathering. The oldest forms of news sharing, exchanging papers through the mail and sharing correspondents, favored the larger urban papers over the smaller rural ones because they had both more stories and more reporters. And while news (like stories of Virginia homicides) continued to be shared through the venerable practices of press exchanges or special correspondents, most news was transmitted through wire services. A wire service, or syndicate, supplied all the member papers with stories, gathered cooperatively, and they in turn sent in their stories. The number of major wire services grew from one to four in the seventy years covered by this book, and they were always dominated by the urban dailies. Similarly, the emergence of newspaper chains, anchored by flagship urban papers, cemented the dailies' domination of news.[7]

During this period of city papers' predominance, there were three distinct periods of press development. In the first period, during middle decades of the nineteenth century, the partisan tradition dominated the press. Newspapers blended news and editorial commentary together and slanted it in favor of their party. In the second period, from 1890 through 1920, sensational and independent journalism eclipsed partisan journalism. Independent journalism promoted "objective" news and separated out its political and editorial opinions from "news." Sensational newspapers engaged in spectacular stunts and used simple language and prolific illustrations to attract readers. The final period, beginning in the 1920s and extending through the 1930s, saw convergence in coverage. The idea of objective reporting was now used to tone down the sensational press, while at the same time daily newspapers assimilated the former hallmarks of the sensational press.[8]

In the period from Reconstruction through the Great Depression, the southern press followed the pattern of the history of the nation's press, with variations. During Reconstruction the partisan tradition was basically unchallenged in the South by the rise of either sensational or independent papers. In the 1880s and 1890s, the newspapers of the South promoted the idea of "the New South," drifted away from political partisanship, and embraced both independence and sensationalism. By the 1930s the southern press resembled the rest of the nation's newspapers in style and substance. The only exception was that in the South weeklies continued to be an important source of news for small agricultural and extractive communities.[9]

No matter what the shape of the press, in every period covered by this book, newspapers were eager to cover criminal trials. For the newspapers trials had many advantages. First, they could be covered cheaply, often with a single reporter or in later years with a reporter and a photographer. Second, they had inherent drama and form that was familiar to most readers. The components of a trial—opening statements, prosecution case, defense case, cross-examination, closing statements, judge's instructions, and jury verdict—were equivalent to the acts of a play or the chapters of a novel. Third, trials were venues for the kind of stories on which the press thrived. Curtis MacDougall captured this fundamental fact when he observed, in a 1938 textbook on reporting, that "there is . . . no more potent source of human interest material than the average court room." Finally, and most importantly, trials promised repeat business. Daily newspapers were always starved for copy, and trials virtually guaranteed that a story would run for more than a single issue. Thus, in the late nineteenth and early twentieth centuries, trial coverage provided the same form of social melodrama that made serialized novels the reading sensation of the early nineteenth century.[10]

In many ways the manner in which newspapers throughout this period covered crime and trials resembled fiction. Their emphasis was on telling stories of universal interest. Helen MacGill Hughes, a daughter of "newspaper people," called such stories human-interest stories. Using an event to evoke "the common fortunes, fears, and fates of mankind," human-interest tales asked readers to ponder how they "would feel in like circumstances." In order to be successful, human-interest stories had to summon the "stresses and temptations" common across the society; thus they tended to become "perennial stories," which repeated the same themes. Although the human-interest theme was pivotal, dressing the basic story in sensational or lurid detail added to the appeal. The sensational press specialized in human-interest stories, but the partisan, independent, and every other sort of newspaper also produced them.[11]

Throughout this period working conditions contributed to newspapers' tendency to produce human-interest stories. Reporters basically were trained on the job, learning quickly the conventions of the craft, especially how to cast a story which would appeal to the greatest number of readers. Because newspapers did not just follow the events but fabricated and enhanced stories, they reveal the perception of reporters (and by extension the larger public) about those events. Reporters were common people who were trained to write what the public wanted to read. Stories about the four trials, therefore, highlight contemporary assumptions about the South and southern distinctiveness from both insider and outsider perspectives. Nevertheless, despite the importance of reflecting existing notions, newspapers also set agendas and framed public debates through what they presented and what they emphasized. As a result, in their reports about the cases and trials, newspapers helped shape the debate over the North-South dichotomy and reveal how perceptions of southern culture changed between Reconstruction and the Great Depression.[12]

Like papers everywhere, the Virginia papers in this period covered stories of crime, and often their coverage raised issues of southern exceptionalism. Postbellum Virginia journalism reflected southerners' strong tendency to define their region as the opposite of what they saw as northern values. In essence, the press was constructing an oppositional culture, defining its own region in reference to its rejection of the North. Indeed, the Virginia press routinely used stories from northern papers to attack the culture of the North. In this trait Virginia papers typified post–Civil War southern journalism. The war supplied the region with a unified experience of struggle, suffering, and loss which prompted southern journalists into expressions of southern exceptionalism. Reconstruction, according to Carl Osthaus, intensified this exceptionalist stance as "Southern editors scoured the Northern Radical Press for prejudicial charges and indignantly rebutted them almost daily." For the next two generations, southern newspapermen would use such attacks on the North to define southern exceptionalism. What Osthaus characterized as the stance of the major editors of the New South was true of the newspapermen in the larger period from Reconstruction through the Great Depression: "all were *southern* journalists sensitive to Northern slights and Yankee criticism."[13]

Southern exceptionalism has long been one of the major themes of southern history, reflecting the reality that the South was different. Virginia typified the

South, a region that was distinct from other parts of the Union. How the South was different has long defied easy explanation; as Paul Escott and David Goldfield observe, "The South, less a geographical region than a state of mind, is a fickle place, and writers have grasped it about as well as they might a greased pig." Moreover, the South was never a uniform and static place; there were regional differences within the South, and vast changes occurred over time within the section. Nevertheless, southern distinctiveness had hallmarks that were not just metaphysical. The South had a distinct economic base, and its population had different racial, ethnic, and religious proportions than the North and the West. The region's politics were strikingly divergent from what prevailed in other areas. And the South possessed a culture which was oppositional to that of the rest of the nation.[14]

Different economy and demography helped to define the South. Although the rest of the nation industrialized during the late nineteenth and early twentieth centuries, agriculture predominated in the South. As a result, the South was comparatively poorer than other parts of the nation, and more of its people lived on farms than in other regions. Few immigrants from Europe went to the South, and through the Great Depression the largest concentrations of African Americans were found in the South. Moreover, the South remained the most violent part of the nation. It is easy to overdraw the distinctions, for industry existed in the South, much of it directly tied to the region's agricultural economy. Mill towns like Danville and cities like Richmond dotted the landscape. There were immigrants in the South and African Americans in the North. The South became part of the modern market economy. Even so, the South lacked the ethnic and religious divisions and sharp rural-urban conflicts that informed so much of the rest of the nation's political culture. Rather, the dichotomy of racial divisions shaped the South's politics. After a period of experimentation with biracial politics, the region disfranchised blacks, transforming southern politics into a system of one-party, white rule. From roughly the turn of the century to World War II, conservative Democrats controlled the South. And they ruled a region which was culturally different.

The loss of the Civil War helped to make the white South's culture distinctive. It gave rise to the cult of the Lost Cause and contributed to the perpetuation of honor in the region. Beginning in Reconstruction, the notion of the Lost Cause helped to define the region's culture. Southerners had a different nationalism (that of the Confederacy), a different history (that of defeat), and even different heroes (like Robert E. Lee) than people in other areas.[15] At the same time white southerners continued to proclaim their adherence to the codes of manly honor and ladylike womanhood.

Honor, as Edward L. Ayers has remarked, "remains, after many studies, an elusive, complex, and problematic concept." The work of Bertram Wyatt-Brown and Ayers revitalized the concept of honor as an important facet in the southern historical experience. According to Ayers, "Southern honor . . . grew out a historical conjunction of economic system and received culture." After the war, I believe, honor was less an intrinsic standard that continuously shaped southern life than a useful tool for men. It helped define manhood in a way that cushioned and protected men from the vicissitudes of social and economic change. Honor also helped to define the color line in the era of black voting. But honor was under attack at the same time. As the southern economy became more integrated into the national economy of modern market capitalism, honor slowly declined. Thus for the elite of southern society honor lost its social purpose. Because, as Edward L. Ayers notes, "the men who steered the South into 'progress' tended to have little use for old-fashioned honor," it "died from the top down in the New South." [16]

But one of honor's persistent social purposes was defining gender relations. The cult of the lady flourished in the late nineteenth- and early twentieth-century South, even if it did not correspond with the realities of most women's lives in the region. No part of the nation was more resistant to the emancipation of women than the South. The idea of the lady shaped how white, male southerners saw and treated their women. Womanhood was revered, and the sexes were separated into their respective spheres. Moreover, men sought to keep women in this position because they felt their own position and masculinity encroached upon by the economic changes that occurred in southern society after the Civil War. Under such pressure the role of men as the protector of women, part of the honor culture, was often violently enforced. Indeed, conceptions of gender relations, the culture of honor, and the use of force to preserve white power made the South the most violent region within the nation. [17]

Virginia shared these hallmarks of distinct southern regionalism. Its racial makeup may not have been that of Georgia or Mississippi, but the African-American population was considerable. The state's largest cities, Richmond and Norfolk, were urban industrial centers that attracted immigrants and their children, but the overwhelming majority of Virginians were native-born Protestants who lived on farms or in farm towns. Virginia was comparatively wealthy in contrast to Alabama but lagged far behind industrial states like New York. And like

other southern states, the political system in Virginia went from the uneasy bira-
cialism of Reconstruction to one-party, white rule. Moreover, Virginia fully embraced the oppositional culture of the South. The creation of Monument Avenue
in Richmond, with its statutes of Confederate figures, neatly symbolized Virginia's adherence to the Lost Cause. One historian asserts that "most of the white
citizenry" was "involved in transporting the" first statute, that of Robert E. Lee,
"through the streets. Infants and toddlers were taken from the nursery to touch
the ropes that pulled the statute; one in four ropes was especially for young
ladies." The leading role of society ladies in creating Monument Avenue epitomized the ideals of a society of genteel and proper women complemented by
chivalrous and honorable men.[18]

The perception and presentation of the differences between the North and
the South and the unique nature of southern culture often differed from the actual differences. Nonsoutherners often portrayed society and life in the South as
different from the rest of the United States. Similarly, from the early days of the
Republic, southerners sought to distinguish their society from that of the rest of
the Union. Following the Civil War the tendency to see the South as separate
grew, both within the South and outside it. In the region, even as southerners
propounded a "New South creed," striving to remake the South in the image of
the rest of the nation, their foundation was the idea that the South was different.
As the nineteenth century turned to the twentieth, historians, writers, intellec-
tuals, and others (both North and South) sought to isolate and identify the very
essence of the South. Although differing over exactly what traits were important,
southern regionalists tended to define the South as the antithesis of the North;
whatever else the South may have been, it was not the North. Using the newspaper coverage as a source for public opinion and influence, this book examines
popular conceptions of specific aspects of southern distinctiveness. It shows
how outsiders constructed an exceptionalist image of the South and how southerners' tendency to define themselves in opposition to the North was manifested
in Virginians' reactions both to the cases themselves and to outsider comments
and criticism of their legal system. Significantly these exchanges constructed the
meaning of southern exceptionalism and did so in a medium that reached nearly
every American.[19]

Typically, northern newspapers raised southern exceptionalism as a critique of some aspect of southern society, and Virginian newspapers responded
by reasserting southern exceptionalism as a constituent of the superiority of
the South. Through the give-and-take between papers outside the state and in

Virginia, southern exceptionalism was defined and constructed in a continuous process. Honor and three other major topics that were part of the debate over southern exceptionalism emerged in the press coverage of these cases. It is important to note that although honor was the chief way that Virginia papers expressed southern exceptionalism, it was never the only expression of southern exceptionalism.

The press asserted that honor pervaded southern life. According to both critics and defenders, honor required men to take action (often violent action) against slights to their reputations or in defense of their women's reputations. For northern papers, critical of the South, honor was a vestige of barbarism and just another sign that the South was backward. For Virginia newspapers their state was better because its men were honorable; unlike men in the North, they did not prey upon women or lust after money. While honor remained a functioning system, it was the chief way that Virginia papers expressed southern exceptionalism. Thus when northern papers asserted that the South was socially retarded, Virginia papers asserted that honor showed the region's superior social system. But when honor declined as a functioning system, it lost it salience in press accounts.

Journalists also portrayed the South as socially and economically different. Depending on whether one was a critic or a defender of the region, either the South was a backwater area that had not embraced the nation's progress, or it was the repository of the nation's traditional economy and society. To many northern papers the South was a place that had not fully embraced modern industrial and commercial ways, and for Virginia papers the South was the area where virtues of self-sufficiency and simplicity still prevailed.

Beyond honor and social differences, Virginia journalists often declared that southern white women were refined and ladylike. In part, this assertion was an outgrowth of the culture of honor, as the journalistic defenders of the South often declared that as a result of honor, southern white women were treated more chivalrously than women elsewhere. And while the journalists never mentioned it, the elevation of white womanhood had much to do with the construction and maintenance of racial hierarchy in the South. Indeed, the exulting of white womanhood was tied to other aspects of southern exceptionalism. Significantly, this debate over womanhood was usually only one-sided; Virginia journalists prompted by criticism that their state was socially or economically backward responded by asserting the superiority of southern womanhood.

And finally, newspapermen described the South's unique form of politics in the coverage of these cases. At first the Virginia press was caught up in the political struggles of Reconstruction that were purely sectional in nature because of the South's large number of black voters. Later, both in-state and out-of-state newspapers recognized the development of the one-party South, based on the disfranchisement of African Americans. Depending on their political stand (not where they were published), papers either accepted or condemned the nature of Radical Reconstruction, Redemption, and one-party, Democratic rule. Although it was implicit in their accounts, journalists seldom asserted that the region's politics had been shaped by issues of race.

Indeed, race, perhaps the most prominent topic of southern exceptionalism for scholars, did not enter directly into most notable trial stories in the southern press. Southern newspapers, with the exception of the Republican papers of the Reconstruction era, did not seek an audience among blacks. Therefore they had difficulties covering homicides and subsequent trials as human-interest stories when a defendant was black. Because the purpose of human-interest stories was to have the reader identify with the protagonist, and because racial stereotyping blocked easy (or any) identification with a black defendant by the white readers, black killers put on trial were not judged newsworthy, except as examples of black inferiority or viciousness. Prominent headlines like "Black Murderer Pays Penalty on Scaffold" typified the region's treatment of blacks and crime. Homicide among blacks did not constitute human-interest news for the region's papers.[20]

In contrast, homicide among Virginia whites, especially when it could invoke human-interest themes, was news. Initially, such stories were covered by local reporters, who brought into their stories internalized assumptions about southern life. But these stories did not stay local news; rather, they moved out into the national arena. And in the national setting the assumptions and presuppositions that informed the interaction of law and society were questioned, debated, and examined. So when the Virginia press broadcast news of local trials, the regional standards of custom and law became part of the story and made these cases perfect venues to explore the interplay of society, law, and the press.[21]

One

"A GOOD AND EFFICIENT REMEDY FOR LIBEL"

ON NOVEMBER 24, 1868, Henry Rives Pollard, the publisher and editor of the Richmond weekly *Southern Opinion,* was shot from ambush as he neared the office of his paper. James Grant, the son of one of Richmond's reportedly richest men, was arrested for the killing. It was widely assumed that Grant killed Pollard over a matter of honor, for Pollard had published an article which was construed as an attack on the virtue of Grant's sister. According to a later account, "For weeks and weeks the murder of Pollard was the subject of conversation—on the streets, in the hotels, in the places of business, and in the home." Although the case had nothing to do with the policies and politics of Reconstruction, it nevertheless became a battleground between officials of the Reconstruction government intent on prosecuting Grant and former Confederates who defended him. Virginia papers and leading urban dailies in the North extensively covered the story. The Associated Press (the only wire service in operation) broadcast the story's details across the nation, highlighting how they related to Reconstruction issues. This killing presented outsiders determined to change Virginia society with a chance to decry its lawlessness, which they saw as symptomatic of the backwardness of southern society. The crime and trial also gave Virginians an opportunity to defend their system of honor, even though the circumstances of the killing made such a defense difficult. Thus, in both Virginian and out-of-state papers, the reports of the events leading up to the crime, of the killing, and of the subsequent legal proceedings became infused with debates over the merits of northern versus southern civilization.[1]

At the time of the Pollard killing, a revolution was just beginning in the American press. The trade was dominated by partisan newspapers, which were confronting the rise of the independent press and the sensational press. During Reconstruction and well into the 1880s, most newspapers were openly partisan. Although not organs of political parties, they claimed loyalty to one party and slanted both news and editorials toward their partisan goals. But beginning in this period, and accelerating as the century wore on, the partisan press was challenged by other forms of reporting: sensational newspapers and the self-styled "independent journalism." The sensational papers, which deliberately aimed at reaching a broad audience, grew out of the urban penny press of the 1830s and the *National Police Gazette* that was founded in 1845. Often moralistic and always lurid, they eschewed the standard political topics of the partisan press to focus on personality, crime, and sex. Independent journalism, a conscious movement of publishers and editors, sought to sever the formal ties between political parties and newspapers. The goal of independent journalism was to create papers with appeal to the better parts of people's natures and the "better sort" of people. Although still focused on political issues, the independent papers separated reporting from editorials, popularizing the notion of objective reporting. Both new forms of journalism affected partisan papers. The partisan papers, lured by the potential for greater readership, sought both to include more sensational materials in their columns and to make their news reportage look more objective in form. Despite these changes, strong partisanship—which presented editorial and news as a seamless product—remained the norm in this period.[2]

During Reconstruction the South's press lagged behind the changes that were taking place in the rest of the nation. In the South the partisan tradition was basically unchallenged by the rise of either sensational or independent papers. Because the South had fewer cities than other regions of the nation, it failed to develop successful sensational papers. And only limited sensationalism was imported over the telegraph wires into the South because the southern papers received only half the news the Associated Press sent to wealthier papers in the North and Midwest. On another front, the deep divisions between Republicans and Democrats retarded the development of the independent press; papers were either Republican or Democrat/Conservative. Thus partisanship tied to issues of Reconstruction was the lens through which newspapers reported this Richmond crime.[3]

In the decade before Grant shot Pollard, continuity marked Richmond's experience. Richmond, a city spread out along the north bank of the James River, was a growing manufacturing and commercial city in the 1850s. During the war years and the years up to the panic of 1873, it saw continued population growth. Tobacco-manufacturing factories, making products from bright leaf, dominated the city's industry before the war, and though reduced in number and value, they continued to predominate until the geographical center of the crop moved southward in the 1870s. Before and after the war, industry lined the river, while government buildings and commercial offices surrounded the Capitol, which dominated Shockoe Hill overlooking the bridges across the James. Residences fanned out along a grid pattern from these two districts. In Richmond the rich tended to build their mansions either on Shockoe Hill or Church Hill. The entrepreneurial rich joined with the old elite of the city in living on the hills, creating a new social grouping by the 1850s, the "upper tendom." Accustomed to ruling their city, after the war this economic and political elite "preferred to model the future on the past and to continue social relations and industrial growth on their antebellum basis."[4]

The maintenance of the old order was not easy in the period of Reconstruction as the political landscape had dramatically changed. At first, under Presidential Reconstruction directed by President Andrew Johnson, the old order — minus slavery — seemed restored. The military and the president recognized Francis Pierpont as the governor of Virginia, and Pierpont, in June 1865, appointed as mayor Joseph Mayo, who had been mayor of Richmond from 1853 but was briefly out of power in the earliest period of Reconstruction. "This reinstatement of Confederate city officials made it appear as if nothing changed in the social and political relations between the races." The city instituted a pass system for blacks and punished violators — through the mayor's court — with sentences of thirty-nine lashes. Complaints and petitions led to a change in military leadership, and Mayo was removed. But under the lenient terms of Reconstruction proposed by President Johnson, in the elections of 1866 Mayo again became mayor.[5]

Before the old order could consolidate its power at the local level, the rules shifted nationally. In March 1867 Congress took control of Reconstruction, cutting the former Confederate states into military districts and requiring each state

Editor H. Rives
Pollard, from
Harper's Weekly,
December 12,
1868, 788

head of the *Southern Opinion.* (Courtesy of the Valentine Museum / Richmond History Center)

to hold a new constitutional convention in which freedmen were entitled to vote. In Virginia such a convention, chaired by federal district judge John Underwood, drew up a constitution which transformed the nature of the political system by enfranchising African-American men. In 1868, while this constitution was waiting for approval by the United States Congress, the military removed Governor Pierpont and replaced him with Henry Wells, a New York native and former Union infantry general. In April 1868 Wells removed Joseph Mayo as mayor of Richmond and named a fellow New Yorker, George Chahoon, the new mayor. Wells, Chahoon, and many others engaged in building a biracial Republican Party which sought to remake the state by building public schools, guaranteeing civil equality for African Americans, and fostering economic growth. Those in the state who wished to maintain of the old order formed the Conservative Party and pledged to stop this reconstruction. Thus in 1868 and early 1869, the political and social direction of the city and state remained uncertain.[6]

The symbol of the uncertainty that loomed over former supporters of the Confederacy was the pending Richmond trial of former Confederate president Jefferson Davis. Davis, jailed since his capture in May 1865, was arraigned before a federal grand jury composed of white and black men. After hearing a strident jury charge from Judge Underwood, the grand jury indicted Davis for treason. Then the case bogged down in delays, and the trial was postponed. Finally in February 1869 a *nolle prosequi* was entered, terminating the possibility of trial. Until the indictment was disposed of, the possibility remained that the victors of the war and the long dispossessed members of southern society could use the legal system to punish the leaders, and by inference the supporters of the Confederacy. For those Virginians seeking to restore the Union much as it had been, the threat clouded their hopes of retaining southern civilization.[7]

Faced with social and political change and uncertainty, Virginia newspapers that supported the Conservative Party—which was virtually every newspaper not linked to the Republican Party—took up the defense of southern civilization against the union of "the carpet-bag gentry" (northerners who had come South), their white southern sympathizers, and freed people. The creation of Military Reconstruction, the adoption of the 1868 constitution (which enfranchised blacks), and the proposed Fifteenth Amendment prompted one paper to denounce "the scheming interlopers who are now attempting to perpetuate their power by the help of ignorant negro voters." Officials under the Reconstruction regimes were marked as illegitimate. Governor Wells was "the so called Governor of Virginia," while others—like George Chahoon—had their titles enclosed in quotation marks. Revealing of the extent of Virginia press opposition to the remaking of Virginia society was a comment by one paper praising Governor Wells for not issuing a Thanksgiving Day proclamation. The paper explained that such a proclamation would be inappropriate as "we have very little to be thankful for in our political relations" and because "Virginian people" were "utterly opposed to . . . puritanical fashions." Such foreign habits were fit only for New Englanders, who had been "oppressed and subjected to a yoke such as our colonial ancestors never felt." Neatly summarizing its determination to preserve southern distinctiveness, the paper concluded, "Down with baked beans and pumpkin pies!"[8]

While this antinorthern and anti-Reconstruction attitude in the press cut across all topics, it was particularly strong in stories about crime and justice. In Virginia papers' crime articles, the resistance to imposed change took two main forms: attacking "northern civilization" by recounting horrific crimes in northern states and criticizing the loss of social order (especially as it related to race) caused by Reconstruction. It was common for the non-Republican papers in the state to run articles that reported sensational crimes from northern states. Sometimes these stories ran as regular features under a headline "Northern Civilization." A typical story detailed how a father in an Illinois town, having intercepted a letter from his daughter's suitor setting out plans for an elopement, shot the young man and seriously wounded him. Sensational crime stories made good copy and sold papers, but they also served a didactic point in the resistance to the reconstruction—or rather, remolding—of southern civilization. They intimated that before northerners sought to remove the mote from southerners' eyes, they should remove the beam from their own. Although such stories reflected the strategic maxim that the best defense was an offense, they had limits. They merely put the two regions in a race for degrees of depravity in crime. But to white Virginians enduring the uncertainty of potential radical change of their society, any means to deflect attention away from the deficiencies of southern civilization were probably welcome.[9]

Moreover, the Virginia press thought that the attempts to remake southern society had made things worse, especially on the issue of race. Typical of the treatment of the race issue was an article in one Richmond paper in 1868. It reported that since a black man had been tried in the mayor's court for bigamy, "every day or two there is one or two arraigned before the Mayor by their wives." Sarcastically the paper commented, "It has become fashionable for negro women to have their liege lords arrested for committing that offense," implying that the freed people were not yet ready for the responsibilities of marriage. Similarly, some papers portrayed black criminals differently from white criminals. One issue described five different people arrested in Norfolk as "a dark brown Negress, wall-eyed, sullen, and dirty-looking"; "a bullet headed, surly looking Negro, black as a tar bucket"; "a jet black, rowdyish Negro"; "another Negro, dandy, beetle-browed, and scowling"; and "a white man." By sheer weight of description, this paper conveyed the impression that the freed people constituted a dangerous criminal class. Hammering home that view, the papers extensively covered crimes by blacks against whites, especially rape and robbery. Indeed, the papers asserted that under the new order black criminals were emboldened and unrestrained, eroding the social order.[10]

A controversy that overlapped with legal proceedings arising from Grant's killing of Pollard epitomized how the complications of Reconstruction fueled the perception that the Virginia Reconstruction regime was unable to preserve social order. The Sally Anderson case arose in Henrico County, the county surrounding Richmond. Her "brutal crime" was that she burned the fine "suburban residence of Mr. Richard Margruder," for whom she worked, and unsuccessfully attempted to kill his infant daughter in the fire. In August 1868 Anderson, a black woman, was convicted of arson and sentenced to death by the Henrico County court. Before emancipation, when the defendant was black, arson had been one of the most severely punished crimes in the state. Thus the Henrico court sentence was consistent with past practice and represented continuity in the social and legal order. In November, Anderson's counsel sought a writ of habeas corpus to the United States circuit court alleging that the court that condemned her was illegally composed because it contained individuals barred under the Fourteenth Amendment from holding office. Judge Underwood, for the court, agreed with this reasoning and ordered Anderson released. Mayor Chahoon, under his "sense of official duty to apprehend all persons at large within this city who are charged with crime," quickly had her arrested again. He informed the Henrico court that he was holding her for it, but that if it did not claim her, he would release her. Unwilling to admit that their previous action was "illegal and nugatory," the Henrico justices refused to take further action, and Chahoon set her free.

The state's conservative newspapers placed all blame on outsiders for Anderson's release. Even though it was the refusal of the Henrico officials to take up her case again—thereby proclaiming their contempt for the restrictions imposed on former Confederates in the Fourteenth Amendment—that compelled Mayor

Chahoon to release Anderson, the papers saw only an "assault upon the [state] judiciary." Underwood's continuing to hear more habeas corpus petitions with similar pedigrees prompted some Virginia papers to call his actions "jail delivery" and "Underwood's General jail delivery," making ironic references to the old practice of a traveling court processing all the inmates held in jail since its last visit. The papers overlooked that one solution was to comply with Judge Underwood's interpretation of the Fourteenth Amendment "by convening a court composed of men not subject" to the restrictions on former Confederates. Instead, the papers pointed out that other criminals would be released under similar actions, endangering public safety. Conservative Virginians thus showed a determination to control their own justice system, even if it led to the absurdity of felons being released, and to run it according to their own social notions.[11]

Honor was one of those social notions. Honor had once been present all across the nation, but by the middle of the nineteenth century, it was increasingly being seen as a distinctive aspect of southern society. Honor was brought to all the American colonies by Europeans and flourished in public life across the nation in the late eighteenth and early nineteenth centuries. The Declaration of Independence's closing lines ("our sacred Honor") and the practice of dueling among elites—as evidenced by the Hamilton-Burr duel—show that public figures took honor's precepts seriously. Two other examples show that honor was still functioning across the nation in the mid-nineteenth century. In 1842 the rising politician Abraham Lincoln nearly fought a duel; "major political figures fought duels at least once a year in San Francisco from 1852 through 1861." Clearly, not only southerners valued honor. Across the nation—until the Civil War—editors, politicians, and lawyers were particularly known for their propensity for dueling, a reflection of the nationwide prevalence of honor.[12]

Honor was well rooted in southern and Virginian life. It came to the tidewater in the seventeenth century, was refreshed by new influxes of immigrants to the backcountry in the eighteenth century, and survived the evangelical challenges of the late eighteenth and early nineteenth centuries. By the antebellum period honor became intertwined with the culture of slaveholding. To quote one scholar, "In the South the concept of personal honor was intimately wrapped up with ideas about the manly republican independence and liberty of free citizens, as opposed to the submission and degradation associated with slavery." In the Old South honor was a gender- and race-specific system of belief and behavior. It did not extend to blacks or women. Blacks, because they were not permitted to be social equals, were dismissed from the system. Women, seen basically as domestic beings who were dependent on men, could not have honor. Rather, they possessed virtue, a trait nearly synonymous with sexual purity. Honor was for white men alone.[13]

In the society of the Old South, honor was quite broadly distributed among white men. In the words of Bertram Wyatt-Brown, "In the American South before the Civil War, those belonging to the circle of honor were much greater in number than in any other traditional society. [Political] Democracy . . . made that possible." Those other honor societies exhibited strong social hierarchies, and in them only those of high status could have honor. Because men were on the make in the booming economy of the cotton lands and because most white men there could vote, the boundary of who could be among the honorable was far lower and was relatively open in the American South. As one scholar noted in comparing dueling in the South with dueling in Prussia, when a clerk in a land office and a sugar broker dueled in Louisiana in 1842, it meant that the term *gentleman* was "fast losing its elitist connotations and becoming applicable to all respectable citizens." This trend "was encouraged by the widely perceived necessity to promote the unity of white southerners in support of black bondage. . . . In other words, the traditional prerogatives of a superior class in Europe had become those of the superior race in the American South."[14]

There were limits to the democratization of honor before the Civil War. Status distinctions remained key in the vesting of honor. Wealth, individual and family, was important in establishing a man's status as a gentlemen (and all gentlemen were presumed to be honorable); and given the economic realities of the antebellum era, it is not surprising that most gentlemen were slaveholders. Honor thus came to be closely associated with the slaveholding planters and other leaders of the society. "White southerners" were "highly conscious of even the subtlest distinctions in rank among themselves." Although honor "in the Old South" "applied to all white classes," it did so with "manifestations appropriate to each ranking." Thus prominent men, like Andrew Jackson, would refuse to duel with someone whom he "knew not as a gentleman." In general, "poor whites in the Old South were subject to the ancient prejudice against menials, swineherds, peddlers, and beggars." And "vigorous traces of the archaic stigma against the honorless could be found, particularly in the animadversions against slaves and white 'tackeys' or 'crackers.'" Indeed, as Wyatt-Brown noted, "if there had been a rankless democracy in the Old South, honor would soon have become irrelevant, its ubiquity cheapening its value."[15]

In antebellum southern society honor was a public commodity, conferred upon its recipient by the community and internalized by its holder. Honor was related to individual character: a liar or a coward could not be honorable. Society sought to dictate the terms of honor, declaring that honorable men be honest, brave, and protective of women's virtue. Men who claimed honor were required to act honestly, bravely, and virtuously. Any statement or action that implied a man who claimed honor was not honest or brave or that women "under his protection" were not virtuous was perceived as an insult. For any insult an honorable man could, at the least, demand an apology from the transgressor. If the transgressor did not mollify the man who was wronged (thereby acknowledging his honor), that individual would prove his honor by employing violence against the transgressor. An honorable man could also skip the step of seeking an apology and move directly to force. Such violence could range from a simple blow, to a whipping or caning, or to a prearranged duel under elaborate rules. Honor helped to make the South the most violent part of the nation immediately before and after the Civil War.[16]

The connection of slaveholding to honor and of honor to violence became the basis for the perception that honor was somehow distinctive to the South. A famous incident underscores this point. In 1856 Congressman Preston Brooks of South Carolina caned Senator Charles Sumner of Massachusetts for a speech Sumner had delivered on the question of slavery in Kansas. Sumner was sitting at his Senate desk when Brooks struck without warning and continued to beat him after his chair collapsed and he lay trapped by the wreckage. Brooks was widely hailed as a hero across the South. "For many white southerners during the 1850s" such honorable violence "could and did become intertwined with their prideful search for a regional cultural identity. . . . This seems particularly true of those southerners who defended Preston Brooks' caning of Charles Sumner." Antislavery northerners also focused on the connection between honor, violence, and southern identity. They widely used Brooks's act to claim that southerners' code of honor merely veiled their determination to preserve slavery by any means. A particularly revealing statement of this idea came following Brooks's return to Congress. Massachusetts representative Anson Burlingame attacked Brooks's and the South's claim to honor: "What! Strike a man when he is pinioned—when he cannot respond to a blow! Call you that chivalry? In what code of honour did you get your authority for that?" Significantly, Burlingame's speech "served its turn many years thereafter as a favorite piece for declamation in the schools of the North." Thus for both southerners and northerners, honor (interpreted in widely different ways) became linked with the culture of the Old South.[17]

The growth of the national news network affected the functioning of honor. Honor always had two parts, community conferral and individual assertion. In the antebellum rural South, because of the spread-out and hierarchical nature of the society, the community that vested honor often could be quite small. Recognition that a man used violence to expiate an affront to honor was often confined to the community. Yet even in the Old South the public prints had served as forums for claiming and resolving affairs of honor. The widespread tradition of newspapers publishing a gentleman's letter (in the language of honor, "a card") voicing a grievance or offering an explanation illustrated how the press expanded the community. As the press broadcast outward the process of claiming and recognizing honor, the means used to judge honor changed from a focus on the character of the individual to the deed performed by the individual. After all, editors hundreds of miles away always knew the act but may not have known the man. This focus on the deed made it more likely that there would be disagreements over what constituted honorable violence. In the press-created community, honorable violence was often judged by standards of proportionality and fair play. Thanks to the functioning of the national news-gathering system, any violent assertion of honor could be broadcast to a national community; this was a community with members who saw honorable violence as a violation of law.[18]

The mid-nineteenth-century Anglo-American legal tradition was mostly hostile toward honorable violence. Its doctrine of provocation had, long before, put law on a collision course with honor, for one of the basic precepts of honor was that a man must respond to a verbal insult by seeking an apology or, if necessary, by violence. This disparity between law and honor was papered over by the jury, which often refused to convict men who had acted out of honor. Moreover, in much of the nation, the governments' desire to limit extralegal violence, whether it be mobbing or duels, made honor's relationship with the law "uneasy." In the northern states social condemnations and laws limited the practice in the years before the Civil War. Such developments did not occur at the same time in the South.[19]

Honor, the war, and Reconstruction shaped the journalistic career of Rives Pollard. One of six children, Henry Rives Pollard was born in Nelson County, Virginia, in 1832. After attending the Virginia Military Institute and the University of Virginia, he began his newspaper work as editor of a paper in

Leavenworth, Kansas. In the 1850s he moved to work on various Baltimore newspapers, and with the outbreak of the war, with his elder brother, he joined the staff of John M. Daniel's *Richmond Examiner.*[20]

During the war Rives and his brother Edward A. Pollard were two of the leading journalists of the South. While Edward has gained a measure of fame through his history of the Civil War, Rives Pollard has fallen into obscurity. Both Pollards as journalists were slashing and vicious in their style. Politicians and the socially prominent felt the sting of their pens. Jefferson Davis was a target of the two; indeed, Edward Pollard was the coiner of the phrase "the Lost Cause," the idea that the noble armies of the Confederacy had been let down by the politicians' leadership. After the war Edward migrated to New York while Rives remained in Richmond.

Rives Pollard continued on as he had before, a fine example of what Carl R. Osthaus has called a "battling southern editor." Before the fall of Richmond, Daniel died (willing Pollard his dueling pistols), and during the fall of the city, the plant of the *Examiner* burned, prompting Pollard to become editor of another paper. He left it, "in consequence of a disagreement with the part proprietor of the paper," to start yet another paper. At first he tried unsuccessfully to revive "the old *Examiner,*" promising it would take no political stands except "to preserve southern language and chivalry" against the "Malignants of the North."

In 1866 he announced the creation of the *Southern Opinion,* with himself as editor and proprietor. In a broadside announcing the new project, Pollard wrote that his action was "prompted by a love for a free and independent press" and promised that his paper would "characterize men and measures as they deserve." Moreover, he proposed to make the paper "a true exponent of southern thought and sentiment," predicated on the belief of the "mutual hate of Yankees and southerners." Pollard's paper was part and parcel of a common movement in this period to stake out a southern stance based on both differences with the North and the experience of the Confederacy. *Harper's Weekly* characterized Pollard's paper as "representing the extreme political sentiments of the South." A Baltimore Republican newspaper said Pollard's paper resembled, "so far as illustrations and filth are concerned, both the *La Crosse Democrat* and the *Police Gazette,* and is weekly embellished with caricatures of prominent friends of the Union and denunciation of their course, in many instances going into the private life of those it seeks to misrepresent." The *Police Gazette* was one of the first mass-market papers to specialize in sensationalistic coverage of crime, while

Mark "Brick" Pomeroy's *Democrat* was the most violent of the nation's copper-head papers. It had urged that Lincoln's tenure be abbreviated by assassination and fixed the label of "Spoons" to General Benjamin F. Butler for his supposed robbing of those utensils from southern households. The characterization of the *Southern Opinion* was close to the mark; although few copies of the paper survive, an article reprinted in another paper gives some idea of where and how Pollard positioned his paper on the issues of Reconstruction. The article attacked Reconstruction as a program designed to undermine American liberty, called military control despotism, and decried the debasement of the suffrage by its extension to black men. The paper reflected Pollard's views; he repeatedly announced, despite the Confederacy's defeat, that he was an unreconstructed Rebel: "I am for the South. I make no pretensions to an affection for a Union that is both false and hateful." [21]

The war seems to have intensified Pollard's self-conscious southernness. The masthead of the *Southern Opinion* glorified the southern cause of the Civil War. On the left it showed Confederate troops going into battle, with flags flying. The center, cluttered by the accoutrements of war, was dominated by an imposing military leader on a horse and a woman scribe in classical garb. On the right a weeping widow and two small children mourn at a tombstone. Underneath it all ran a banner, "My country may she always be right, but right or wrong my country." Not surprisingly, the paper was suppressed by military authorities at least once. Similar in tone to his paper was Pollard's lecture on the chivalry of the South. In an 1867 broadside he promised that his talk would show how the war illustrated the people's chivalry, would justify the code of honor, and would denounce the men now courting "the clatter and dirt of Yankee civilization." [22]

Rives Pollard's support of chivalry extended beyond the theoretical, for he participated in many affairs of honor. During the war he stood in as second in a duel between Daniel and a Confederate official. In one wartime duel Pollard maimed his opponent, while during another between Pollard and an "officer of the Confederate navy" resulted in no harm. In 1868 Rives Pollard participated in a shooting affray between rival newspapermen on the grounds of the state Capitol. A reporter's humorous account of the subsequent legal proceedings prompted Pollard to try and whip him. The style of journalism he practiced and his support of the system of honor in both idea and action make it no surprise that Pollard structured his paper to accommodate the social mores of honor. [23]

In Pollard's *Southern Opinion* all of the articles appeared without a byline. The articles appeared unsigned because being a newspaper writer in the nineteenth-century South could be a dangerous business. In a society that prized personal honor, that required people to be deferential and polite to those with honor, to cast aspirations on someone was dangerous. The party slighted could not take insults lying down; he had to respond. Men did not protect honor by filing a lawsuit but by personal means. As Virginius Dabney later wrote, when an editor "took pen in hand," he was "risking life." Outraged readers could challenge him to a duel. Or the wronged could forgo formalities and upon next seeing the newspaperman attack him, with a cane, a whip, a fist, or a gun. By leaving the articles in his paper unsigned, Pollard indicated that he, as editor, bore the responsibility for everything printed, conferring a limited protection on his writers but increasing the likelihood that the aggrieved would seek satisfaction from him. Thus it is no surprise that Rives Pollard routinely went about "well armed"; indeed, "he was always a sort of walking arsenal." A close associate said at the trial that "Mr. Pollard was armed as usual" on the day he was shot. "He had . . . a revolver . . . in his belt and a Derringer on either side." [24]

Considering the nature of the *Southern Opinion,* it was probably prudent for Pollard to carry three guns. By all accounts the *Southern Opinion* was a scandal sheet. A Virginia Republican paper said Pollard's paper published "the scandals of the town" and that he had made "his paper a vehicle for abusing private character and attacking private virtue." Edward Pollard in the last issue of the *Southern Opinion,* published in his brother's memory, quoted a letter he had written to a New York paper just after the killing, in which he confessed, "His paper some times fell into a style of personalities that I greatly deprecated." It was Rives Pollard's penchant for personalities and scandal that led him to publish an article about the Grant family.[25]

The Grants were one of the elite families of Richmond. William H. Grant was a rich tobacco manufacturer, who had made a fortune in processing and reselling tobacco. He was reputed to have been the richest man in the city before the war. Suitably, he had built a mansion in 1857 on Clay Street where it ran up Shockoe Hill. Before the war the house was assessed at $20,000 for taxes and had a staff of twelve. The one Grant daughter, Mary, and her brothers circulated in the highest of social circles. As members of the upper crust, they embraced the romanticism so common to southern society. Marie Tyler-McCraw has captured the tone of this circle when she writes that the young ladies of Richmond favored "the romance novels of Sir Walter Scott" and were entranced with the idea of the "'reigning belle' whose very presence drew all the swains of the region." One of the Grant children's friends completed the manuscript of a "romantic novel" called "Clover Nook" in May 1860. Its 176 handwritten pages feature all of the author's social set, including James Grant. According to one account William's eldest son was "the fiery, poetic, aesthete of the family" who adhered to the code of chivalrous honor. James had a fine bass voice and had served in the Confederate cavalry during the war. He was, in short, a gentleman, excelling at horse riding, scholarship, and shooting. Not surprisingly, because they were so frivolous and socially prominent, any gossip about the Grants was news.[26]

On Saturday, November 21, 1868, an article appeared in the *Southern Opinion,* under the headline "An Elopement (So Called) on Clay Street—An Upper-Ten Family Concerned—Dreadful Denouement," which reported upon the doings of Mary Grant. The story, written in an ironic mode, decried the thwarting of true love, detailing a secret engagement (or marriage) and flight of Mary to join (or in company with) Horace Ford. Although the Grants were not named, they were described with enough specificity to identify them. Mary was the "fair and radiant daughter of one of our first citizens (a nabob of Clay Street), a gentleman who, suffice it to say, holds the very first position in the wealthy and fashionable circles of the city." Horace Ford, of Goochland County, was described as "an orphan, just plunging into teens," who had converted his family's wealth "into ready rhino [cash]" and "ventured for a swim in the sea of gay life and love." Ford "some months ago" secretly "plighted his troth and accepted the tiny hand, grasping it within his own." No one, "much less the father," suspected "a mesalliance" until "the daughter . . . fled to parts unknown, or at least only guessed in the company with one (a masculine) who should ere then have been proclaimed his son-in-law." According to the article, Ford had left Richmond for New Orleans but continued to communicate with Mary. "And when he announced . . . that he was off for Texas right away, and couldn't stop for trifles like an affianced," Mary decided to follow him. "Being of age, and no longer the slave of parental control, Miss Mary . . . having habilimented herself becomingly deserted the palatial mansion of Clay Street . . . casting behind her wealth, society, and friends." She was reported to have been crying bitterly on the train and to have arranged to meet Ford in New York. "Her departure created, of course, a hubbub . . . and, amid the wringing of hands and loud expressions of distress, the telegraph was invoked, and parties sent in hot pursuit." The article left the ending of the story open; in the last paragraph it declared that "Miss Mary has been heard from; that she is now in Philadelphia, and that, upon the whole, there is a very sorry family history connected with the case, which is not within our province to reveal." But earlier the piece had asserted that the "runaway parties have been heard from, and it is now said that the lady proclaims herself a wife of some six months." Thus the article left the readers to draw their own conclusions from the events.[27]

The openendedness did not offer the Grant family any relief from dishonor. Although the article contained enough detail for interested Richmonders to verify (for instance, Ford had gone to Texas by way of New Orleans), it remained unclear as to exactly what had transpired between Horace Ford and Mary Grant. Each possible explanation for the events raised questions either about Mary's virtue or the Grant men's ability to protect her. If there was a secret marriage of six months' standing, then William Grant was a false patriarch. If there was a secret engagement and planned elopement as hinted by Mary's traveling alone, then the Grant men had not sufficiently protected their home. Her crying could be interpreted in two ways: either her father had banned her marriage to Ford and she had defied him, or Ford had loved and left her and she was desperately pursuing him before it became widely known. But if Mary had traveled with a male companion, as the article also said, then it was a presumption of nineteenth-century American society that her virtue was lost. For the Grant family honor, each permutation was damning. And the vagaries of the article were designed to stimulate discussion. If enough gossip and interest were generated, then perhaps it would be "within the province" of the *Southern Opinion* to reveal the "very sorry family history" in another article.[28]

By one account this edition of the *Southern Opinion* "was in great demand." It promptly sold out and apparently generated much comment. Some people "after reading and gloating over the article" said that the "man who would publish such a thing . . . ought to be killed." Indeed, *Harper's Weekly* later asserted that "the article was purposely insolent; and it is certain that Mr. Pollard would have shot at sight the editor of any journal which had thus shamefully insulted his own sister." It was rumored that the Grants would seek satisfaction. On the Monday after the publication, Rives Pollard "was in his office all day." But "as neither of the young Grants had called on Pollard, or sent anybody to see him, as required by the code," public expectations of an incident dwindled. Yet some "sharp-witted reporters kept on the constant watch for a sensation—and their vigilance was well repaid."[29]

On Tuesday, November 24, three days after the publication of the "elopement" article, Pollard went by carriage from his suburban home to his office. He was accompanied by reporter J. Marshall Hanna who had stayed with Pollard the previous night. They arrived at the office of the paper, near the intersection of

Fourteenth and Main Street, around 9:30 A.M. After they alighted, Hanna lagged behind Pollard, and as Pollard approached the door, "a loud report was heard, and almost instantaneously Mr. Pollard fell flat upon his face, uttering only a groan of pain." Hanna, "expecting another shot" and looking for where the first had come from, "drew his pistol almost involuntarily." A number of uniformed police officers and plainclothes detectives who saw Pollard fall came quickly. Some, with the aid of bystanders, picked up Pollard and carried him into the *Southern Opinion*. He expired before they got him into the office. Because Hanna was standing over the body with a gun, the police promptly arrested him. When the wounds to Pollard's head and chest proved to have come from buckshot, and Hanna's pistol showed no signs of having been fired, he was discharged.[30]

"With swift wings the news" spread, and within minutes "a crowd of several hundred in number" blocked "the streets in the vicinity" while the police investigated. Under the direction of Captain Edwin H. Chalkly, the police decided "that the shot had been fired from an upper window of the building opposite" and centered their search there. Detective William Knox searched all the unlocked rooms, returned to the street, and then, joined by detective Robert B. Craddock (who had helped carry Pollard off the street), resumed searching the building. Soon Craddock and Knox (as well as the reporters who had followed them) heard a voice from a locked room on the third floor say, "Is that you Bob? It's all right. You'll have to break the door open it is locked." In the room the officers found James Grant with four guns, including a double-barreled shotgun resting against the wall in the corner. One of the shotgun's barrels was loaded with buckshot, but the other one had recently been fired. The window of the room facing the office of the *Southern Opinion* and near the shotgun was, in Craddock's words, "partly hoisted," perhaps held open with a shoe brush. Moreover, "the sill was blackened as if by burnt powder."[31]

When they arrived, Grant asked, "You'll see me protected?" Upon receiving assurances, he was arrested and taken through the crowded streets to the nearby police station. Perhaps Grant feared retaliation from a friend of Pollard in the crowd. Events soon showed that he had nothing to fear from this crowd. According to "Kappa," the correspondent of the *New York Times,* when Grant "made his appearance" before this "crowd of the best people of the city," voices cried, "'Three cheers for Grant.'" Some congratulated him as he passed. Putting the best face on the onlookers' deportment, the radical

Richmond State Journal wrote, "The crowd thoughtlessly cheered him." Moreover, as a conservative Richmond paper put it, "Everybody in Richmond knows James Grant, and there are not many young men more popular." The *Times* correspondent declared, "All the city are his friends—because perhaps, everybody was Mr. Pollard's enemy." Grant was treated like a respected guest at the police station. He was jailed in the office of the chief, where a mattress was brought to the room for his comfort. While there, he spent time with a "number of his friends. . . . He was in good spirits, and passed the time in smoking and lively conversation." He also "was well provided for from Zetelle's coffee house." At no time after his arrest did Grant admit to shooting Pollard.[32]

Within three hours of Rives Pollard's death, a coroner's jury convened over his body in the office of the *Southern Opinion.* Coroner Dr. J. P. Little examined the body and determined that pellets of buckshot had caused Pollard's death. The jury visited the site where Grant surrendered and heard testimony from the witnesses, including Hanna, about the shooting. The jurymen heard a black man who, from the sound, thought the shot "was fired from the corner window of a building across the street." They also heard various policemen tell of the arrest of Grant with a shotgun in the room. The jury learned that Grant had recently bought two derringer pistols. From the regular occupant of the room the members learned that James Grant had spent the evening in the room where he was found. They were not the only ones investigating the shooting; on the day of the killing former governor Henry A. Wise visited the sites to take measurements. Grant's motive was, by nearly all accounts, the chief topic of public debate. For those who had not heard it by the time the jury finished its meeting, in the morning after the killing, anyone who could read one of the city's newspapers could have read of the elopement article and thus learned a motive for Grant to kill Pollard. The circumstantial evidence pointed strongly at Grant's being Pollard's killer.[33]

The jury, however, disregarded that evidence. From the questions put to witnesses by members of the coroner's jury, they seem to have been reluctant to put the blame on Grant. For instance, they asked Craddock if the killer had time to escape while the policemen were carrying the body into the *Southern Opinion.* After less than an hour for consultation, the jury of Coroner Little returned a verdict that Pollard "came to his death by a gun-shot fired on the 24th of November . . . from an elevated position, by some person unknown to the jury." The jury's verdict and the crowd's reaction indicate that white public opinion in

Richmond saw Grant's action as acceptable. Some Virginians, left to their own devices, were willing to accept assassination from ambush as an honorable act under these circumstances. But they would not be left to their own devices.[34]

The nation's press and two individuals, Edward Pollard and George Chahoon, insisted on further action. Chahoon and Pollard acted out of different motives and in different ways, but the upshot of their intervention was to add new layers of complexity to an already involved story. Their actions became grist for the mills of Richmond's gossips and ink for the pages of the city's papers. And from there, the telegraph carried the news north. This combination of action, reportage, and commentary made the aftermath of the killing almost as sensational as the killing itself. In this coverage some northern papers used the crime and later events to show the deficiencies of Virginia society, while other papers (both in and out of the state) focused on the sensational.

In Richmond—and the rest of the state, if the coverage in the state's papers is any indication—the appetite for information on the case continued unabated. It remained "the talk of the week" for a public "ever ready to feast on gory banquets and on the recital of horrid crimes." Apparently among the gossip was a rumor that Grant had not shot the true author of the article. The day after the killing, Hanna received an anonymous letter saying, "You are known to be the author of 'that piece. . . .' You must and shall retract every word of that article or abide the consequences." Rumors also surfaced in the press that Hanna was going to be driven out of town. Hanna, who had considered publishing the *Southern Opinion* and printing an article of retraction, announced that he would do neither until after conferring with Edward Pollard.[35]

Edward Pollard lived in New York, where he held a patronage job in the customhouse while trying to advance his literary career. He learned of his brother's death from the daily presses of New York that carried telegraphed stories from Richmond. The story of the killing of Rives Pollard by Grant was quickly disseminated across the nation. Reconstruction was a central news story of the day, and so a killing in the former Confederate capital was worthy of coverage in both major and minor papers. The nature of the newspaper business in the 1860s contributed to the spreading of the tale. Extensive clippings from other papers, the cooperative news gathering of the Associated Press, and the presence in Richmond of Kappa, a *New York Times* correspondent (who wrote the Associated Press version and a more detailed version for the *Times*), allowed the story to circulate throughout the nation.[36]

Beyond the circumstances of his killing, Edward also read in the early reports attacks on Rives's character. For example, the *New York Times* story on November 25 contained the statements that "public sympathy is with Grant," that the "excited crowds" cheered him, and that in Richmond "the universal remark is that Pollard's terrible death was deserved." Correspondent Kappa attacked both Pollard's character and the *Southern Opinion.* Pollard had "been a thorn in the side of Reconstruction, and done much harm as a publisher." As a newspaperman, "he lacked ballast and carried too much topsail." Moreover, his paper recently published "in rapid succession" articles that were "outrageously slanderous and scandalous." On November 25, before he left to go to Richmond, Edward Pollard responded by sending a letter, his card, to the leading papers.[37]

In his letter Edward criticized the press for printing the "brutal telegrams" from Richmond "announcing 'joy'" over Rives's assassination. Edward thought that the editors "might have perceived that" the telegrams "came from enemies of my brother" seeking to sway public opinion in favor of "the hideous interest of the assassin," who was "the son of a rich man." The editors should have refused to print the telegraphed reports. He defended his brother's honor as journalist by blaming the Grant article on a "disreputable" reporter on the paper (Hanna), who was "in the habit of smuggling into the paper" out of "depraved ambition" articles that contained "gossip." In this letter Edward Pollard also denounced the behavior of the crowds in Richmond, the character of James Grant, and the actions of the police after his brother's killing. Pollard asserted that a crowd that cheered "a murderer who had shot his victim with buckshot from a second story window, and from a room in which he had locked himself" could logically be "imagined" as "partners in the infernal deed of cowardice." Moreover, that Grant was "unconfined, unconcerned, and allowed to remain in the open office of the Police Chief, 'receiving the congratulations of his friends,'" made the police accessories to his crime. Pollard saved his strongest words for Grant. According to Pollard, Grant had not asked for an explanation from Rives Pollard, thus confronting him honorably, but instead "took precautions for his miserable safety — and murdered . . . an unsuspecting and perhaps wholly innocent person."[38]

When Pollard reached Virginia, he no doubt discovered that the papers there carried stories similar to the telegrams sent North. Most of the Virginia papers that reported the killing attacked Rives Pollard's character and his journalism. One exception was the *Richmond Daily Dispatch.* Admitting that despite his skills as a journalist, Pollard was not a popular man, that paper added, "Of his private life this is not the place nor the time to speak." At the same time the paper left little doubt that he had deficiencies in character, but it was "not the temper of charity to speak evil of the spirit just ushered into the presence of its God." Most papers were more direct. The radical *Richmond State Journal* was among the kindest, merely admitting that Pollard was a man of "rude nature" with "many enemies." On the other hand, the *Norfolk Virginian*'s editorial of November 25 asserted that Pollard in "temper and judgment . . . evidently lacked the coolness of the one and the soundness of the other necessary to fit discharge of the responsible duties of a public journalist." It denounced his tendency to cross the "broad line of demarcation between criticisms" of public figures and "the invasion of the domestic circle, or delineation of the habits of private persons." Another paper argued that Pollard "belonged to a class who have wrought irreparable injury to our people." Now that he was dead, it hoped "God may have for him a more befitting and congenial duty than kindling the base passions of an evil and gainsaying age." A Warrenton newspaper thought Pollard's article in the *Southern Opinion* was "one of the most brutal attacks upon the character of Miss Grant and the peace of her family that ever blackened the columns of any journal." Thus "Pollard richly deserved death, and met with a fate that should befall all others" who engaged in the same sort of "slanderous and envenomed" journalism. Pollard had become so odious that when the *Baltimore Sun* reprinted a story which detailed Pollard's biography, mentioning that Pollard had worked as "news editor of the *Baltimore Sun*," it added a note that "such connection as Mr. Pollard had with *The Sun* office was very temporary." His employment there lasted only "some three weeks, during the indisposition of one of our regular news editors."[39]

Faced with a barrage of attacks on his brother's character, Edward Pollard, soon after arriving in Richmond, issued another card, repeating his earlier condemnations and attacking the coroner's jury. "They shame not me; they shame not the dead"; rather, they shamed Richmond and showed it had no "chivalry." He repeated his charge in stronger language that the assassin was a coward, asserting that there was no equal to his deed "in all the black achievements and crooked paths of crime." Moreover, he restated his claims that Rives had not written the article and that the killer "took not one single measure which the brave man, no matter how wronged, always takes before he comes to the last resource of blood." Thus while Pollard was arranging his brother's funeral, seeking to employ counsel to assist in the prosecution of the killer, and planning to stop publication of the *Southern Opinion,* he also saw fit to try to defend Rives's reputation in the press.[40]

Rives Pollard's character mattered little to the mayor of Richmond, George Chahoon. He had little sympathy with the code of honor; for instance, he used the power of his court to try and stop dueling by binding over to keep the peace (under heavy bond) those caught preparing to duel. Also, as mayor he had a great interest in keeping order in the city. For nearly a year Chahoon kept the same police chief—a noted champion of order—who had served Mayor Mayo, despite that man's unpopularity with Republicans, white and black. Thus while Edward Pollard was traveling to the city, and while the coroner's jury was still in session, the mayor convened his court to investigate the killing of Rives Pollard. The mayor's court had the power to make a recommendation to send an individual before the grand jury when it next met.[41]

The mayor's action prompted the Grant family to hire some of the best-respected lawyers in the city and the state. Before the hearing the Grants retained one of Jefferson Davis's lawyers, Robert Ould, noted advocate Marmaduke Johnson, and John S. Wise, a son of the former governor. The addition of Wise increased the enmity between Edward and the defense. Governor Wise had been a particular target of the Pollards' pens; in response, earlier that year in Maryland, two cousins of John Wise had been involved in a shooting affray with Edward. When Mayor Chahoon held his court, charges against them were still pending, but they soon would be dropped by Edward's refusal to prosecute.[42]

On Friday, November 25, the mayor heard testimony of the major witnesses from the inquest, including Hanna, as well as the coroner, Dr. Little. They testified "substantially" as they had at the coroner's inquest. Grant's lawyers declined to call witnesses or to make any statements. At the end of the testimony, Mayor Chahoon "announced that he would send Mr. Grant on to the grand jury" that would meet in late February. At the conclusion of the hearing, perhaps with the memory of how Jefferson Davis's imprisonment had built public sentiment in his favor, the mayor released Grant on $10,000 bond. Grant went home in a carriage, and soon after Edward Pollard appeared before the court to ask for reconsideration of Grant's bail.[43]

Edward, in trying to block Grant's bail, sought to undermine the presumed claim to honorable vengeance by the Grants. He said to the mayor's court that two witnesses could tell of a conversation between Rives Pollard and "Mr. Stover, a friend of the Grant family." William Stover had visited Pollard at home the night before publication and asked him "not to publish the article."

According to the witnesses, his brother replied that "the press had never felt the least delicacy about publishing anything in regard to members of his family" (or "female members of his family" in some versions) based on rumors, so "he had determined to spare none in the future who should lay themselves liable to public censure." On the question of satisfaction, he offered his paper to William Grant, saying "that I will publish any explanation he may choose to make, without a single alteration no matter what he may say." Edward Pollard's broadcasting of this statement raised the possibility that the Grants used violence because they could not refute the charges.[44]

The state did take advantage of Edward's work among the witnesses and added Stover's name to the list of witnesses for the grand jury, but he had to retreat on a number of fronts in his campaign to bring Rives's killer to justice. The next day Pollard retracted his request to reconsider Grant's bail. Edward had been rebuffed by at least two lawyers he approached to act as counsel to assist the Commonwealth in prosecuting Grant. Also, the commonwealth's attorney had explained to Pollard that the law did not favor his motion to revoke bail. Furthermore, Edward retracted his statements concerning the origins of the elopement article. Papers in the city, across the state, and even in New York carried cards from Hanna and Pollard concerning the article. In his card Hanna said that he wrote the article at Pollard's direction. Moreover, he had asked Pollard before it was published that it be "modified, expunged altogether, or the names left blank, or filled with initials that would have left the case without a 'local habitation,'" but Pollard refused. Pollard took responsibility for the article, said Hanna, and "always assumed, and never evaded the responsibility of every line and paragraph printed." Edward Pollard published his card at the request of Hanna, admitting that "I must say that I am satisfied that Mr. Hanna did not promote the publication of it, but wrote it as an . . . employee."[45]

Having cleared the air between them, Hanna and Edward Pollard collaborated on burying Rives and agreed that Edward alone would bring out the last issue of the *Southern Opinion*. Edward and Hanna accompanied the body by train to Nelson County. They went by way of Charlottesville, where Edward told several people that he did not plan on taking "any revenge on Grant other than that obtained from his legal prosecution, but he condemns severely, as all other men should, the cowardly way in which Grant committed the assassination." Pollard was buried at Oak Ridge, once the property of the Rives family. Within a week of his interment, the last issue of the *Southern Opinion,* devoted totally to his assassination, was printed.[46]

On December 5, 1868, this issue of the *Southern Opinion*, shrouded in black borders, appeared. Its headlines revealed its sentimental and accusatory thrusts; among them: "Mockery of Justice in Richmond," "The Neglected Corpse," "Refusal of Richmond Lawyers to Appear against the Murderer," "Extraordinary and Horrible Experience of the Brother of the Deceased," "Misrepresentations of the Newspapers," "The Feast of the Assassin," and "Touching Story of Fidelity—The Grave at Oak Ridge." Beyond trying to elicit sympathy for Pollard and outrage toward Grant, the issue also included three sensational bits of news. First, Edward alleged that Rives's death was a result of a conspiracy, that the enemies of his brother and the friends of James Grant collaborated on planning and executing the killing. Second, the issue contained an article that essentially retracted the elopement article. It accepted the version of events circulated by the Grant family, that Mary Grant had gone to Philadelphia to visit friends and her brother retrieved her after she fell ill. And third, it contained a long account detailing the origins of the article and how the Grant family through Stover attempted to negotiate with Rives Pollard for suppression of the article.[47]

The story on the elopement article, along with three columns of excerpts from various papers, undermined the notion that Grant's action was honorable. The press clippings, many of them from northern papers but also a fair sampling of Virginia ones, were focused on the means—"bushwhacking" as one paper put it—used by the assassin. The history of the elopement article reached the same goal by detailing the events that led to the shooting. On November 19, 1868, Hanna heard gossip of an elopement of Mary Grant. He communicated this information to Pollard, who already knew of the scandal. He gave Hanna another source to use and told him to pursue the story. Pollard directed it be written "in the old style," the sarcastic manner popular in Richmond during the war. Hanna showed a draft to Pollard, suggesting that "it would be best to suppress names, as the parties stood high," but Pollard refused to delete the names. After the proof was printed, Hanna again unsuccessfully urged the article be toned down.[48]

At this stage Stover spoke to Hanna at the office, asserting that the rumors were false and asking to have the article suppressed and replaced with a paid advertisement. Hanna, unable to make such a decision, sent Stover to Pollard's home. After that visit Pollard had Hanna hold the completed article from the typesetters until the day before publication. On Thursday night Stover again visited the office, assuring Pollard that the reports of an elopement were false, that the article would do much harm, and asking if there was any way to prevent its publication. Pollard replied with several options. He was willing to let Grant buy every copy of the paper containing the article. Or he would sell more than half—or all—of the business to Grant. After all, as he said, "I publish my paper to sell." He also offered to "print line for line and word for word whatever he [Grant] may write in contradiction of the article." Stover asked to see the article. Pollard showed him the proof sheet, and Stover remarked, "Well, that is not so bad as I expected." Stover left, coming back the next day to say that Pollard's terms were rejected. The article was published, and the Grants did not follow any of the honorable options available. No member of the family sought Pollard at his office, even though he was there on Sunday and Monday. On Tuesday morning Pollard was shot from ambush.[49]

Edward Pollard's intentions in publishing the last issue of the *Southern Opinion,* to arouse sympathy for his brother and marshal outrage against his killer, may have failed. The *Bristol News* contended in an editorial that Edward's role as "calumniator of Mr. Davis" in his publications, his "inken stain of malignity on the tomb of Jackson," and his attacks on the character of Mrs. Davis made him "ill selected as the one to bring to rectitude the public sentiment at the death of his brother." While Edward's own reputation hurt his brother's cause, the details he released of the events about publication of the article raised questions about Rives's motives. The *New York Times* in a long editorial denied that Pollard could have been motivated by principle. "The only principle involved was the right to print any attack on private character—of man or woman—true or false, which he might *choose* to print." Only by buying the edition or the paper could the slander be suppressed, "as Mr. Pollard 'printed his paper to sell.'" If the Grants had bought out the issue, Pollard could have in turn reprinted the article "in every successive issue of his paper" to even greater profit. The *Times* called it "plain, barefaced black-mail." Certainly, as the *Times* knew, the newspaper business in the 1860s could easily slide into such actions. Many reporters were nothing more than hired pens for various private concerns planting stories that favored their clients' interests. Moreover, newspapers could be bought wholesale through advertisement purchases. If some newspapermen were willing to print stories for payment, surely some were willing to suppress stories for the same reason. Even so, most newspapers admitted that Grant's offense in shooting Pollard amounted to murder.[50]

A Richmond grand jury of Judge Horace B. Burnham's hustings court agreed. The court met as usual in Richmond City Hall, which had been completed in 1818. But little else about the proceedings followed Virginia traditions, because Judge Burnham, a former Union officer who had been appointed to the bench by the military authorities in July 1868, knew little of those traditions. On February 17, 1869, the grand jury indicted James Grant for murdering Pollard. Grant, who looked "well, and not at all abashed," was represented by Robert Ould and upon arraignment to this indictment pleaded not guilty. Commonwealth's Attorney C. S. Bundy, assisted by J. Harmer Gilmer (a lawyer retained by Edward Pollard), urged after the indictment that Grant's bail be revoked. Bundy implied that Grant had been allowed bail "merely because he was able to give any amount required."[51]

A debate ensued between the prosecution and defense which carried undertones of Reconstruction politics. Ould, and others in the court, treated Bundy as an outsider, and indeed he had been appointed to his position by the military authorities a month earlier. Charles Smith Bundy (1831-1928), born in Chenango County, New York, served in a Wisconsin-raised regiment for part of the war and practiced law in the District of Columbia late in the war and again in the 1880s, when he became both a United States commissioner of claims and judge. The Richmond 1869 city directory contains an advertisement announcing C. S. Bundy's practice, implying that he was new to Richmond; it also lists him as boarding at the Spotswood Hotel. Bundy did not seem familiar with Virginia law, relying on Gilmer for assistance. Ould said that Bundy's motion (made by an officeholder in what many Virginians called the "military government") "was unheard of in the practice of this court" and violated an 1866 law passed during Presidential Reconstruction. He cited several precedents in which bail had been permitted. Bundy replied that the statute gave the judge a discretionary power and argued that Ould's precedents did not fit the current case. Moreover, he stressed that in the annals of American justice — citing infamous cases from New York, Massachusetts, and Washington — never was an indicted murderer allowed bail. (The reference to the Washington case was a subtle dig at Ould, who had prosecuted the case of Congressman Daniel Sickles for killing Philip Barton Key.) Gilmer supported the motion, asserting that "in all his experience of thirty-five years in Virginia courts he had never heard nor read of a case in which, after an indictment for murder in the first degree bail had been allowed." Judge Burnham agreed with the prosecution's positions. He stressed the seriousness of the act of which Grant was accused, violating "the most sacred right of a human being in a civilized community . . . the right to life unmolested." He committed Grant to jail and set trial for the next week.[52]

The opening of the trial bogged down in jury selection. On opening day the court interviewed 23 veniremen or talesmen (potential jurors in what we now call the jury pool but was then called a venire or tales) and rejected 22 of them. Judge Burnham called for the court officers to procure, as was the custom, talesmen (who needed to be freeholders) "from the street, office, store, and workshop." On the second day of the trial, the court interviewed 96 more men and accepted only one as a juror. On the third day a tales of 150 produced no jurors. On the fourth day a tales of 118 produced no seatable jurors. Commonwealth's Attorney Bundy declared that "at this rate it would take thirty-five days and forty-eight hundred men" to fill a jury. Part of the problem was that the venire came from the same social circle as James Grant, embracing "substantial worth, intellect, high character and influence." The practice of drawing men from public areas only intensified the problem, because it was there that much of the talk about the killing occurred. Many of the men also had read the newspapers and had made up their minds. Most Richmond talesmen, when asked "had they formed or expressed any opinion as to the guilt or innocence" of Grant, responded they had and were excused.[53]

Many talesmen seem to have thought like one potential juror who wanted to serve. He said, "Assuming that Grant killed Pollard, . . . I think he was justified." When pressed with further questions by the defense, who wished to seat him, this man added, "If Grant had made up his mind to kill him the mode of doing it which he selected was about as good as any other." Another said his "sympathies are too much with the prisoner." And yet another said that "I would sooner hang the jury than the prisoner." At the end of the fourth day, the judge ordered tales to be brought from other cities.[54]

An "unusual amount of wrangling among the counsel" also marked the opening of the trial. The state was represented by C. S. Bundy, assisted by J. Harmer Gilmer, while Grant utilized temporarily a fourth lawyer along with the three who had already been retained. Reconstruction tensions lay behind many of the wrangles. At one point Ould referred to "the gentleman representing the outside part of the Commonwealth," thus virtually calling Bundy a carpetbagger. Gilmer deflected Ould's suggestion by acting as if Ould had referred to him, interrupting him to say, "No sir, I am not an outsider." Ould also clashed with both prosecutors over whether the prosecution could ask a talesman who said he had not expressed an opinion on the case whether he had read the city newspaper stories on the crime. Ould called the question an "impertinent inquiry," implying that it questioned the honor of the venireman. Ould denied Bundy's contention "that this class of questions were allowed by the courts in

Virginia," again insinuating that Bundy was an outsider. Gilmer produced the precedents that swayed Judge Burnham to allow the question. Ould, Johnson, and Wise all argued strongly against calling veniremen from other jurisdictions. They challenged the assertions of court officials who told the court that they thought no jury could be obtained, showing that some of them were unfamiliar with the city. They also insisted that the court call former Richmond officials as they were "perfectly familiar with the city from . . . long official acquaintance with it." In the end, the judge ruled against their arguments for another tales from the city and summoned thirty-six men each from Alexandria and Norfolk.[55]

From the venires brought in from those cities, the remainder of the jury was formed. These men too were "men of intelligence and great respectability"; indeed, some of them had previously served as jurors in the Sally Anderson trial. The seventy-two talesmen brought from out of town underwent the same scrutiny that the Richmond residents had endured. Testifying to how far the news of the case had spread, many of them asserted that they had formed a decided opinion on the case. From them, twenty-two more men were added to the body of jurymen. The defense exercised its peremptory challenges in striking off seven men; the rest drew lots, and the five who drew blanks were excused. The jury of twelve contained ten from outside Richmond.[56]

In its elicitation of testimony from its witnesses begun on March 1, 1869, the prosecution developed a strong circumstantial case. Various white and black witnesses—mostly bystanders, but also Hanna—spoke about Pollard's shooting and the nature of his wounds. Through the evidence of the occupier of the room—a friend of Grant's—the prosecution showed that Grant had obtained a key to the room (which functioned as a private social club for the younger elite men of the city) the day before and that guns were not kept there. Moreover, the room's tenant, who had not spent the night there, testified that he had met Grant there that morning at seven and drunk a glass of wine with him. Through the testimony of the police and various reporters, it detailed the discovery of Grant in the locked room surrounded by guns. A local gunsmith testified that he sold Grant, on either November 17 or 18, two "dueling pistols" found with him when he was arrested. A member of the coroner's jury, John S. Stubbs, testified about the partially open window with its black mark on the sill that "was elongated in form of about one inch in width." Stubbs had laid his cane in line over the mark, determining that it was on line to the place where Pollard was shot. Apparently, central to the prosecution's strategy was a studied avoidance of motive. After all, the examination of talesmen had shown that knowledge of the motive tended to prompt Virginians to exculpate Grant. So, on direct examination Hanna never mentioned the Grant family, the newspaper article, or the attempts to suppress it.[57]

The defense did not let the prosecution develop its case uncontested; it tried to introduce motive and to rebut various parts of the circumstantial case, prompting much "sharpshooting between counsel." When Hanna, during cross-examination, referred to "the article" (quickly correcting himself to "or the matter"), Ould (and later Johnson) attempted to force him to testify about the article or identify it in the paper. The prosecution objected to these attempts "to introduce the defense of the prisoner at a wrong time and in an improper manner." In cross-examination the defense attempted to discredit witnesses' testimony, especially concerning the nature of the mark on the sill and whether the mark lined up with the site where Pollard was struck by buckshot. At the conclusion of the prosecution's case, returning to the issue of motive, Ould attempted unsuccessfully to force the court to follow the old English rule requiring the prosecution to call all of the witnesses whose names were appended to the indictment. The most important dropped witness was William Stover, who could only testify as to motive.[58]

Beyond motive, the defense cast doubt on the Commonwealth's circumstantial case that James Grant fired the fatal shot from the window in the locked room. The defense called several witnesses who testified as to the lack of gunpowder smell in the room soon after the shooting. This evidence was of questionable value, as the smell might have quickly have dissipated, depending on the variety of powder and the flow of air in and out of the room. To buttress its point about the shot, the defense called former governor and Confederate general Henry A. Wise. Wise, father and law partner of defense counsel John Wise, had visited where Pollard fell and the room where Grant was found on the day of the shooting. From the measurements he took, Wise testified that the shot if fired along the line on the mark on the sill would strike eighteen feet from where Pollard fell. He also asserted that the mark was not made by muzzle flash. The defense sought to use this evidence to show that the shot may not have come from the room where Grant was found but another in the building. It also called police detective James M. Tyler to say that given the configuration of the rooms and the building, someone who had shot Pollard from these nearby unlocked rooms could have easily escaped unobserved. But this development of reasonable doubt was a minor part of the defense's case.[59]

The defense revolved around the elopement article and attempts to stop its publication. The defense, as Johnson said, "held that Mr. Grant did not kill Mr. Pollard," but "as some minds might be so curiously constructed as to believe" that he had, "it was thought best to show" that if he did do it, "he was perfectly justifiable." The article, which he characterized as an "attack" on that "which every woman holds most dear, and which every man stands ready to defend—female virtue," was "the fortification behind which his client was entrenched." Getting the article, and the attempts to suppress it by Stover for the Grants, into the trial was a legal problem. The article and Stover's intercession had to be connected to James Grant to be admissible evidence. Although the prosecution "had signified their entire willingness to let" the article "be introduced by the defense" to "prove the provocation," it objected to Hanna's testifying as to what passed between him and Pollard over the article (and by implication to Stover's proposed testimony) as "entirely irrelevant, of which the accused knew nothing." The judge agreed, saying that the article and its suppression would be good evidence "if the deceased were on trial for libel" but not in a murder trial of his killer, unless "the accused was informed of the results of the interviews." He ruled that Hanna and Stover could testify to these issues only if it could be shown that James Grant knew of what had transpired. If the defense failed to connect their testimony to Grant, then the judge would "instruct the jury to disregard it."[60]

Hanna and Stover were called to develop this facet of the defense's strategy. They were buttressed by the article itself, which Johnson read to the jury. Hanna testified to his writing the article in "the old style" under Pollard's direction. He told of his conversations with Pollard, revealing his own reluctance to have the article contain identifying details but Pollard's insistence that it carry them. He spoke of Stover's dickering with Pollard to keep the story from being printed and of Pollard's willingness to delay publication of the piece. Stover picked up the tale, telling of his unsuccessful efforts to discover from Pollard who had given him the information, to persuade him that it was false, and to keep him from publishing it. He detailed that he raised the issue of paying to stop the printing, at first by taking an advertisement, but that Pollard upped the price significantly by offering to sell the edition or even the paper. He said that William Grant refused Pollard's terms. He also told how James Grant visited him the evening that the *Southern Opinion* was published to discuss the matter. At the end of his testimony, after a question from the judge, Stover said: "I gave James Grant a very minute statement of the circumstance of my interviews with Mr. Pollard. His response was that he should hold him personally responsive."

The defense also attempted to imply through Stover's and Hanna's testimony that Pollard was a blackmailer. Stover in recounting his conversation with James Grant after the article had been published said Grant remarked that "he had hoped I would have been able to prevent its publication." Stover said he told Grant that he "could have done so with money," relating the details of the negotiations with Pollard. Asked directly, Hanna denied that Pollard was a blackmailer, asserting that he did "not know of any case where money was paid to prevent an article from going" into the *Southern Opinion*. In response, the defense produced in court a version of the November 21 *Southern Opinion* that did not contain an article which appeared in most of the edition. Hanna admitted that in this case Pollard "thought better of it, and after two or three hundred copies . . . [of a press run of 2,000 or more] had been issued took the article out." Combined with the testimony about the negotiations between Stover and Pollard over buying the edition, this admission supported the idea that Pollard was a blackmailer, prepared to drop the article once his price was met. Thus the testimony of Hanna and Stover was used by the defense both to attack Pollard's character and to focus the case on his publication of the elopement article.[61]

The defense also tried to introduce evidence to show that the article was untrue, producing a clash between it and the prosecution and it and the judge. First, in examining Hanna when he testified that Pollard had said that the facts in it were true, Johnson attempted to determine what facts were true. Bundy objected, and when Johnson repeated his question, he apparently told Hanna not to answer. Johnson retorted that the judge controlled the courtroom and "that the gentlemen on the other side were too much in the habit of speaking in this dictatorial manner." He quoted Shakespeare, "Upon what meat doth this our Caesar feed that he has grown so great." Although Bundy lost the rhetorical duel, he won the legal point when the judge sustained his objection. The issue reemerged when the defense put on a witness from Philadelphia to testify about Mary's visit. Judge Burnham raised a question as to the pertinence of such testimony. In arguing for the admission, Ould said the defense "wished to prove . . . that there was nothing in this visit to excite even the gossip of a tea-table." Along the same lines Johnson said "that common humanity demanded that they should be allowed to prove" the falsity of the article. Not to be trumped in the defense of female virtue, "the prosecution attorney both explained that it was not their intention to throw the most remote discreditable reflection upon Miss Mary Grant, or upon any other young lady whose character, like hers, was above suspicion." Disregarding honor, the judge ruled that the falsity of the article was immaterial, that it "did not aggravate the provocation" for a killing. He added, "Ordinarily, a man would be excessively angry if he knew such a publication to be true; but if he knew it to be false, he would treat it with contempt." After the judge said this, Ould replied, "Would your Honor be thus influenced if the libel affected your wife, your daughter, or sister?" Burnham answered, "Yes sir; its influence would be just the same." The ruling stood, and the defense filed an exception and after a brief consultation rested. In the next phase of the trial, closing statements and the judge's jury charge, this conflict between honor and law became more exaggerated.[62]

Bundy began the prosecution's closing arguments by focusing on the facts of the case and the law of homicide. He chronicled the "naked, hideous facts" that pointed to James Grant's having shot Pollard. As to motive, he said, the defense finished the prosecution's case when they had "thought proper to disclose in the fullest manner the motive of the accused." He stressed that after the publication of the article, Grant had said he would hold Pollard "responsible." After reading it to the jury, Bundy contended that there was nothing in its words that impugned the virtue of Mary Grant. Rather, he asserted that the Grant family had misconstrued the article, causing James Grant to kill Pollard. And not satisfied at his death, the counsel for the defendant had then sullied the dead man's reputation portraying him as an extortionist seeking "hush-money." In any case, defense of a sister's virtue or attempted blackmailing did not legally give James Grant sufficient provocation, three days after the publication, to mitigate his crime to less than murder. Bundy left undermining a defense based on honor to Gilmer, who would speak after the defense attorneys.[63]

Although they would try to rebut the prosecution's circumstantial case, pleading honor and attacking Pollard's character dominated the defense attorneys' speeches, which were sandwiched between Bundy's and Gilmer's efforts. John Wise, the youngest of the speakers (and who had questioned no witnesses), introduced the themes, and Johnson and Ould built on his foundation. Wise's argument was crafted as a point-by-point refutation of Bundy's statement. He reviewed the facts raised by Bundy, asserting that taken together they did not "prove" murder. In particular, he turned Bundy's question of motive on its head by saying that in this community "outraged and vilified" by Pollard, it would have been better to ask, "Who had not a motive?" Similarly, Wise dismissed the prosecution's assertion that the article was not an attack on female virtue. Wise said, "Where does a gentleman come from that he could get up before a jury of Virginians and say that there was nothing in the article that could be construed as an assault on female virtue?" Wise savaged Pollard's character, calling him a blackmailer and invoked the cheers of the crowd on hearing his death to demonstrate his reputation. Moreover, Wise claimed Pollard's publication of the article left the Grants no other recourse but that of blood. Law was useless: "Suppose he had entered a suit, how would it have looked upon the record, 'James Grant vs. Henry Rives Pollard—action for one virtue *in detenu*'?" He concluded by asking the jury "to first ascertain whether or not" Grant did it and, if he did do it, "to ask themselves if he was not right."[64]

Johnson's closing statement followed lines similar to Wise's opening speech for the defense. In dealing with the circumstantial case, Johnson relied on the concept of reasonable doubt, telling the jury that "the circumstances must be of the most conclusive nature." The thrust of his speech turned on the provocation of Pollard's publication. Johnson underscored that Pollard, by commanding the article be written in "the old style," engaged in a deliberate attempt "to ruin the character of one of the best established families in the city." While admitting that common law and Virginia law made it a crime for a man to kill his wife's or daughter's seducer if it was done after the fact, Johnson said that there was "not a man on the jury who has not seen this ignored." He denied knowing of a guilty verdict "in a case where the provocation even approached that in this case." Indeed, "the law of nature and the human heart" commanded the killing of a defiler, and "all the legislation on God's earth" could not alter that impulse. Protection of the family was "the foundation of society itself."

Ould, like Johnson and Wise, also attacked the circumstantial case, vilified "the gross licentiousness of the press," and extolled honor. He contended that the prosecution's case was not proven and lambasted the idea that Pollard by offering to open his paper to the Grants removed their need to seek satisfaction. To "enter upon a controversy with a newspaper" was a futile, unequal battle. The individual "might be a Titan, hurling rocks . . . but the editor . . . was a Jupiter . . . controlling the very air through which they flew." Thus Pollard's offer to open his column was not an offer worth considering and his publication of the story was an affront requiring action. Indeed, the major part of Ould's argument was directed at proving that James Grant's killing of Pollard was "fully justifiable." Ould portrayed Grant's action as honorable and necessary. James Grant, "acting upon the first impulse of a sensitive and honorable heart, . . . had done no more than was his duty in visiting swift vengeance upon the libeler of" his sister. Ould asserted, ignoring the facts of the shooting, that no Virginian "would brand" as a felon one who "dared to step forth and defend, at the risk of life itself, the reputation of the helpless ones whom God has committed to his charge." In short, the thrust of Ould's and the defense's arguments was that a man's chivalric duty to protect his family's women overrode the formal demands of the law.[65]

Gilmer closed the case for the Commonwealth, and his speech attempted to overcome the defense's appeal to honor by invoking both the principles of law and the concepts of honor. He appealed to the known law, calling it "the sheet-anchor of all that is dear or worth preserving." Law protected "property, honor, lives, and character." Its "stern integrity" and "fixed inviolability" upheld "the social structure." If the jurors, moved by "prejudice — the whim of fancy — or the higher impulses of sympathy," ignored the law, they would "reduce society to chaos" and "expose the honor of your sons and the virtue of your daughters to the brutal passions of all bad men." The jurors must then follow their oaths to be bound by the law.[66]

Gilmer's speech also focused on turning honor against the defense. First, Gilmer mocked the defense's portrayal of Grant's act as honorable, pointing out that if he killed Pollard, he fired from a locked "third story room, where no eye could see him, no hand reach him, no weapon be fired at him, no danger assail him." Second, Gilmer asserted that the defense committed the dishonorable act of staining "the memory of the dead as the only means of surely screening the guilt of the living." Third, he appealed to the "manly sympathies" of the jury to leave Mary Grant out of this case. He urged them not to dwell on "the publication of the libel." And contrasting himself with all three defense attorneys, he said "I have never read" to the jury the elopement story for "I have no taste for such productions." He reminded the jury that woman "in her purity" should be respected and "in her fall" contemplated "in silence." The jury should do the honorable thing and "throw around that young lady the mantle of a lofty chivalry." And fourth and finally, he repeatedly hammered on the idea that assassination was by its very nature distinctly dishonorable. Gilmer asserted that this case was the "first instance in which a Virginia jury" had been asked "to justify a cold-blooded, premeditated assassination." That such a request had been made was "an outrage upon the manhood of Virginians!" He told the jury to "guard the honor, preserve the manhood, rescue the personal character of every Virginian from even the implied imputation of countenancing, encouraging, sustaining, honoring the assassin." Thus the Commonwealth gained the advantage of having its invocation of honor in the last lawyer's speech, where the other side could not assail it.[67]

Beyond being favored by delivering the last argument, the prosecution in

Grant's case gained the advantage of having the judge side with it in his delivery of the jury charge. Over the objections of the defense, the commonwealth's attorney asked for six jury instructions, and Judge Burnham delivered all of them. The first charge explained the concept of premeditation while the remaining five focused on the issues of provocation and "sufficient cooling time." The Commonwealth's instructions as delivered by Judge Burnham eviscerated the legal basis of the defense. They underscored that the circumstances of lying in wait and securing a room pointed toward premeditation; also, while they admitted that setting the cooling period for the passions raised by provocation was a question for the jury, they emphasized that a long period of three days passed between the provocation and the act. And most strongly, the instructions told the jury that if there had been sufficient cooling time, the provocation "as the moving cause to the act" was to be "disregarded." Moreover, the judge in explaining the instructions informed the jury that Johnson's position on the interpretation of provocation was incorrect. The "atrocity of a libel" could not "take away from the homicide" the attributes of murder if the killing "was done by lying in wait, or willfully, deliberately, and premeditatedly." Burnham emphasized that no "principle of law . . . justified the commission of murder in answer to a libel or slander." [68]

Indeed, Judge Burnham tried to make law the touchstone for the jury in deciding its verdict. Again and again he emphasized that the jury was duty bound, indeed oath bound, to try the case "under the law *as it is*—not as you interpret it, but as you find it." Courts and juries administered law; they did "not invent or evade it." And law was central to society, as the "very foundations of free government are based upon a reverence for and recognition of the supremacy of the law." Any "denial" of its "binding obligation" was destructive of free government and returned society "to red-handed anarchy." Burnham closed by explaining the presumption of innocence and reasonable doubt and commended "this cause and all its important issues to society" to the jury's "deliberate and just finding." The jury remained in deliberations for about forty minutes while the large crowd in the courtroom whispered its speculations as to their decision. It hushed upon their return to hear their verdict of not guilty. [69]

The reaction of the spectators in the courtroom and the two leading daily papers of the city revealed where the community's collective sympathies rested. When the verdict was announced, "there was a manifestation of applause among the spectators by way of the clapping of hands and the stamping of feet." Also reporters sketched in sympathetic terms the Grants' and their friends' reactions to the end of the trial. The *Dispatch* noted that when the jury returned, the "prisoner's demeanor remained unchanged save for a slight tinge of anxiety which seemed to overspread his countenance." His face "grew a shade paler, made . . . more so by contrast with the dark shadows underneath the eyes." This account underscored the stress of the trial on Grant, asking the readers to sympathize with him. This positive portrayal of him was extended by showing that he was a man of many friends. After the verdict Grant could not leave the courtroom because "the rush of friends towards" him "to extend their congratulations was so great." The *Whig*, on the other hand, focused on William Grant's and William Stover's reactions. "The gray-haired father stood by with a feeling which no words can express, and beheld friends . . . around his boy who four minutes before stood arraigned as a felon before the bar of justice." It reported that tears flowed down "the cheeks of his firm fast friend, Stover, who throughout the trial had shown for him a brother's affection." James Grant, "now free by the decision of a sworn jury of his countrymen," left with his father "and quietly repaired to his residence"—to the private world—from where Rives Pollard had pulled them with his article in November.[70]

In view of the strong circumstantial case against Grant and that much of his defense rested on the assertion that the killing was justifiable, the verdict in the case threatened Virginians' belief in a system of law. The *Richmond Whig* directly confronted this problem by saying that the jury's decision was law based. Citing an "undeniable source," it declared that the jury's verdict "was not founded in the slightest degree upon the plea of provocation." Law, as embodied in the "instructions of the Judge," precluded consideration of provocation "and brought the issue to one of life and death." The jury then was unwilling "to say positively, upon the evidence adduced, that the accused was guilty of murder." That is, the prosecution had not proved its case beyond a reasonable doubt. This was a strange conclusion to draw as the defense had virtually admitted that James Grant did shoot Rives Pollard. If Grant was responsible for the shooting, then the verdict turned not on law but on honor. The system of honor that characterized Virginia society, even after the war, subverted the formal rules of the legal system and substituted its own rules.[71]

The newspaper accounts of the killing and trial reveal that much of the nation's press saw the case as a triumph of honor over law. For instance, the *New York Times* was uncomfortable with Richmond's refusal to act decisively against the accused killer of Pollard. When the coroner's jury came to its "lame conclusion," the *Times* warned Virginians of the "consequences of such a line of conduct." If one man could do it, so could others. Thus "John Smith's name appears in the Police reports," so he "quietly loads his guns and lies in wait till the gentleman whose name stands at the head of the paper—Mr. Horace Greeley, or somebody else—" comes along "and deliberately shoots him down." Later, when Grant's trial bogged down in trying to impanel a jury, the *Times* presumed "the difficulty in getting a jury" came from "the fact that nearly all the citizens of Richmond justify the killing on" the grounds that Pollard had violated the Grant family's honor. "If so, this fact is not creditable to Richmond as a city pretending to be governed by law, and generally supposed to belong to a civilized rather than half civilized or barbarous state of society." The *Times* thought that in civilized communities crimes were "punished by the state, as offenses against the general good" under "laws made for the common safety . . . whereas in a savage state, each person takes the redress of his own wrongs into his own hands and inflicts upon the offender such penalties as his own passions may prompt." In the *Times*'s formulation of the social order, there was no room for a system of honor. Thus according to the *Times* it mattered that the law punished Grant; if it did not, the lives and property of Richmond's citizens would be "at the mercy of the outlaws who recognize no law but their own selfish passions." But honor and its deficiencies constituted just one way for papers to interpret the meaning of the crime.[72]

Northern papers' stance on the crime and trial followed established political lines and reflected their stands on Reconstruction. Some northern papers did not comment on the case. For instance, the conservative Republican Illinois *Oquawaka Spectator*, determined to minimize divisions in Republican ranks, did not write editorials on the case but merely ran it as a news story. Silence avoided problems, for to comment on the case might exacerbate differences over Reconstruction policy between Republican factions in their state. Other papers more concerned about the national policies of Reconstruction wrote articles about the case. They used the Grant affair to assess the progress of Reconstruction in the South. Their articles and editorials reflected their stances on remaking southern society.[73]

In an editorial the day after the "barbarous deed," the *New York Daily Tribune* attacked both Pollard and Grant but presumed that the law would take its proper course and punish the assassin. The *Tribune* declared that "the Virginia capital" would be "better off" rid "of the person who prostituted a noble profession to publish the scurrilous gossip concerning a lady" and "the person who in a civilized (or semi-civilized) country could find no better way to honor his sister's name than to lie in wait at a second story window and shoot her defamer in the back." Initially the editorialist of the *Tribune* assumed that the law, even in a semicivilized country, would automatically convict and execute James Grant. After news of cheering crowds, of the coroner's jury refusing to name Grant, and of Grant's release on bail, the *Tribune*'s editorialist decried that a man who "brings down his man, as he would a turkey, is held, in Richmond, to be an offender of so mild a type that he only needs to give ten thousand dollars bail." Criticizing "the first families" of Richmond, the paper declared "that their action in this case is as yet painfully inadequate." The editorial intimated that Grant would jump bail and sarcastically called for "a public meeting in his honor, and a Corporation dinner."[74]

The *Tribune* used the killing to explain verities of the human condition and the failings of Virginian (and southern) society. Its last editorial on the case asserted that this assassination "proves, however luxuriantly chivalry may once have flourished in Richmond, that it bears but a starved and stinted life in the present state of Virginian civilization." The circumstances mocked the old code; "firing from a window makes a duel, by comparison, seem actually virtuous and a street assault respectable." Society and law in Virginia failed to control human nature. Man was "unregenerate," and thus "murder will always be." But "the peculiarity of this Richmond felony is that the culprit, after his slaughterous work" was done, made "no attempt either to conceal himself or to abscond. He was afraid of Mr. Pollard, but not at all of the public, and not overmuch, as it would appear of the police." The *Tribune* thought Grant "probably has but slight apprehension that any jury of the vicinage will be inexorably severe." The *Tribune* then compared Virginia to a known savage land where vendetta, not law, ruled. "How much better is the condition of the public conscience" of Richmond "than that which existed in Corsica when it was not unusual there for an avenger of a family wrong to tear out the heart of his victim and devour it raw?"[75]

The *Tribune*'s interest in the killing of Pollard by Grant did not extend to the trial. From the point of view of its editorial page, coverage of the trial was unnecessary because the social conditions of Virginia predetermined the outcome. Symbolic of its treatment of the killing was the prominent use of the word *assassination* in the headlines and lead sentences in both its news and editorial articles. Less than four years after the Lincoln assassination, after the violence of the 1868 elections in the South, its use of the term and its hammering away on the failings of southern civilization placed the Pollard-Grant killing into the maelstrom of Reconstruction policy. The assassination was another reason why the nation needed to remake southern society.[76]

Other northern papers, unfavorable to extensive Reconstruction, looked at the killing differently. Two examples show the range of possibilities. First, soon after the killing a conservative paper published in Harrisburg, Pennsylvania, decried the killing. It found particularly disturbing the report in the Associated Press dispatch that the "sympathy of the public is almost universally with" Grant. "The public evidently meant here is the new society of negroes and adventurers; for surely no public with any humanity, or pride or honor could sympathize with a base wretch" who killed from ambush. The paper's commentary, while showing that it did not have a good grasp on the local conditions, revealed its predisposition to assume that anything that blacks and carpetbaggers did were the cause of the problems in the South.[77]

Second, James Gordon Bennett's *New York Herald* portrayed "the shooting of Pollard by young Grant" as both an illustration of the state of southern society and a lesson in journalistic standards. According to a November 26 editorial, the killing "was doubtless in accordance with the universal unwritten law by which, throughout the South, every man feels compelled to avenge such insinuations against a lady relative as were contained in the article." According to the editorial, the killing showed "that the traditional habit of taking the law into one's own hands, which was prevalent during the old slave holding days in the South, has survived all the changes wrought by our great civil war." The solution was evolutionary change: "more than one generation must yet pass away before the spirit which originated and fostered this habit shall become utterly extinct." Even if Grant chose "an extraordinary mode of revenge," Pollard was at fault. The article "should not have been published. Every journalist ought to have blood as well as ink in his views. One should never write what as a gentleman, he cannot properly say about the private life of individuals of every sex." Even after Grant's acquittal the *Herald* persisted in seeing Pollard as in the wrong. The verdict should not be regarded as "approval of a dangerous and too frequent practice in this country—that of seeking to redress grievances by taking the law into one's own hands." Rather, the outcome of the trial revealed "the feeling with which an entire community indignantly protests against anything like 'blackmailing,' and worse than murderous attacks, under shelter of laws never intended to protect the guilty, upon the privacy and peace of families." In the *Herald*'s view the South was shown not to be a lawless and violent part of the land needing active remaking. By focusing on the sins of Pollard, the *Herald* over-looked the sins of the South.[78]

On the other hand, other northern newspapers were unwilling to see the killing as anything but the manifestation of all of the evils of southern "chivalry." For example, the *Albany Evening Journal* took its facts of the killing from Kappa but put its own stamp on the meaning of the crime. In two editorials published soon after the events, the *Evening Journal* argued that the killing furnished "a suggestive commentary upon that sort of chivalry which it was the mission of slavery to foster and encourage." The paper found all participants in the killing to be tainted by the social pathology of the South. Grant was particularly guilty; "a more fiendish and dastardly crime" would "be impossible to conceive" than Grant's act. By firing from ambush Grant "proved himself cowardly, despicable, mean—a very natural product of that unmitigated barbarism which so long dominated southern society." Grant was a perfect example of "the southern bred gentlemen" who would "brook no insult, tolerate no opposition. . . . They are tyrants in nature and act. . . . Their social life is repulsive and their history full of warning." Pollard was equally tainted, as he had "been a champion of chivalry. He inculcated its ideas, sounded its praises, empathized its theories by his own acts." The paper found it fitting that Pollard fell "a sacrifice to the very spirit he has created." But before he died, he had already done damage to others by spreading the ideas of chivalry. Focusing on the crowd that cheered Grant, the paper noted "its first impulse was to cheer the murderer." They were "forgetful of the dreadful character of his crime." Their reaction "was the instinctive one—and the instinct from which it sprung was the same that moved Grant to do his bloody and unpardonable deed." In short, Pollard fell victim "to that arrogant, domineering and vindictive spirit, reckless of statutory law or personal right . . . Chivalry."[79]

To the Albany paper the crime and Virginia's reaction to it had implications for Reconstruction and the reform of southern society. The paper tied the killing of Pollard to attempts by conservative forces in the South to muzzle the radical press in the region. "There is no difference between the man who would kill an editor because his paper contained a reported elopement, and the one who would destroy his property and hang him because of obnoxious political senti-ments." The paper linked the crime to reinstitution of the whipping post in Del-aware and to riots in Louisiana against a radical newspaper for asserting freed-men's rights. The *Journal* assumed these crimes stemmed from desire of the "lords of the soil[,] who hold by a diabolic right the disposition of all things within the States lately in rebellion," to return "millions of human beings" to slavery. To stop such outrages the *Evening Journal* urged greater reconstruction of southern society. "No reform in this matter can be expected, until the sentiment of the community upon the subject [of chivalry] has been changed." Ideas about honor and personal vengeance for acts needed to be replaced "in a civilized community" with the notion "that the laws should govern." While the paper doubted that Grant would hang, it would "be a good day for society" when gallows was erected "for some such murderer." But that would require a complete reordering of southern society; "if the South desires peace, it must eradicate its chivalric notions, and substitute instead respect for law and courts as the only arbiters between men." [80]

In a similar view, the opinion magazine the *Nation* saw the Pollard murder as evidence of "the provincialism of southerners." The touchstone of its comment on the case was that "in several of its details" the crime was "a curiously exact reproduction of a famous historical murder," the assassination of Scottish regent James Stewart, earl of Moray, in 1570. Moray was shot from ambush as he rode by on the street, but his killer escaped. Part of the explanation for the similarity, the *Nation* thought, lay in southerners' "childish love" for the "melodramatic" and the romantic as exhibited in Walter Scott's novels. It explained Grant's not escaping by declaring it would not be surprised "if it should turn out that this Grant when he laid his seemingly cowardly plan was thinking less of saving his own skin than of the notes to Scott's novels." For "people who had been indulging a hope that the South had got into the neighborhood of the nineteenth century must have been shocked . . . to find the southern people applauding a crime obsolete throughout the rest of civilized Christendom." The *Nation* then asserted that in sports, literature, oratory, philosophy, and other areas, the southerner was "a long, long way behind the age." In the *Nation*'s view slavery produced this provincialism which had survived its death. The paper found nothing redeeming in the circumstances of the killing. "It is pushing provincialism to excess when people" disregard "the opinion of mankind as to tolerate for months a most scurrilous slanderer, and then cheer his cowardly murder." [81]

A week later the *Nation* published a letter from Baltimore written by "Tertullian" challenging its assertions. Tertullian saw the killing of Pollard by Grant as the logical solution to the problem of "Pollard's paper," which was "an intolerable nuisance" to "which no remedy was provided either by law or society." Tertullian asked his readers to cast themselves in the place of a man like Grant when Pollard had "blackened the character of your wife or daughter, and made your home wretched." Pollard, "who went constantly armed, was doubtless a practiced shot," and to seek redress "in accordance with what is call 'the code'" made it likely "he would have killed you in addition to libeling you." Prosecuting him for libel would result in trials and delays, keeping "your name . . . before the public . . . besmirched with the Pollard filth" while he "enjoyed the notoriety." Therefore, it was "allowable" to kill in such circumstances. And in two jumps of logic, Tertullian added, "It is ridiculous to ask the injured man to risk his own life in doing it. The crowd in Richmond who cheered Grant felt all this."[82]

The *Nation*'s comments on the letter passed over the obvious point that if Tertullian's argument was a sample, the "provincialism of southerners" extended to syllogistic reasoning. Instead, it focused on "the practical question . . . whether murder is a good and efficient remedy for libel?" It argued that it was not, on the grounds "that a public which enjoys seeing a man like Pollard assassinated . . . is just the kind of public which enjoys reading" the kind of "scurrilous attacks on private character" in which Pollard specialized. The "bloody retribution" only heightened "the excitement." Thus Tertullian's solution would merely increase "the number of Pollards, inasmuch as it helps to perpetuate the low civilization of which men like Pollard are the natural product." If Virginia wished to be rid of Pollard's kind, it must practice "self-purification." The magazine included all of American society, North and South, in its prescription: it faulted the South for its patronage of intemperate papers like Mark "Brick" Pomeroy's *La Crosse Democrat* and northerners for listening to "Republican agitators" whose writings contained equal amounts of "foulmouthedness and unscrupulousness." The nation's newspapers should lead the way in trying to make "readers calmer, wiser, more reasonable, and more refined." In other words, the South and the nation needed to reconstruct themselves.[83]

Tertullian's tortured response to the northern criticism of the Pollard killing underscored how difficult it was for southerners to excuse Grant's act. To defend Grant mocked the very code of honor, for Grant had followed none of the common steps in seeking satisfaction. But Virginia papers refused to see Grant as a symptom of the ills of southern society. Thus, for example, the *Norfolk Virginian* portrayed the killing as part of a national crime wave. "Our columns for the last few weeks have virtually reeked with blood." The paper listed the killing of a New York politician in a street attack and a brutal Thanksgiving murder in Philadelphia and then noted that "in Richmond a man is assassinated in a dastardly manner by a concealed foe." Thus Grant's killing of Pollard was balanced by northern crimes; all sections were suffering from the social ill of violent crime.[84]

Similarly, Virginians could go further in defending their society from the outside criticism prompted by Grant's killing of Pollard by denying the criticizing locale's implicit claim to the moral high ground. The *Richmond Daily Dispatch* made that point without mentioning the case's name in an editorial entitled "Northern Horrors." It asserted that "from the time of the 'pretty cigar girl' and 'Helen Jewett'"—two of the first crimes in the United States to receive nationwide and sensational coverage in the press—through the present day, "the great metropolis of this continent" presented "one continual narration of horrible outrages and murders." The editorial was calculated to inflame sectional animosities. Focusing on the cities and towns of New York, Pennsylvania, and New England, the *Dispatch* recounted recent "shocking outrages." Its list included murders and rapes, but the paper asserted that "these deeds and scenes involve less of real wickedness . . . than the swindling operations of Wall Street." Indeed, the *Daily Dispatch* asserted that many of these crimes were motivated "all for money." Beyond evoking the images of evil Wall Street and northerners as money-grubbing wretches, the paper sought to show that northern society lacked loyalty to the race by comparing Philadelphia's treatment of two criminals. One was a woman convicted of infanticide and sentenced to hang, while the other, a black man, was condemned to death for seducing and murdering another man's wife. "More than twenty thousand" people petitioned the governor to pardon or commute his sentence while "no one puts in a plea for the poor white English girl." The "neglect" of the woman was "so marked" that "even New York is excited to sympathy." But being New York, it merely made "a sensation and parade over it." The editorial concluded by calling for the hypocrites of the North to tend their own gardens. "Yet from these whited sepulchres pour forth streams of virtuous indignation with regard to the recent tragedy in this city." Instead of criticizing Richmond, they should direct their attentions "upon their own abominations." [85]

In case readers had missed the point about northerners' right to criticize Richmond over the Grant case, the *Richmond Daily Dispatch* on December 4, 1868, repackaged its editorial of the previous day as a news article, "More of Northern Civilization." The article detailed a story that came to Richmond via Chicago about an attack on a pregnant woman on a ship off Milwaukee. The captain of the ship "after angry words between his wife and himself knocked her down and stamped on and kicked her," bringing about a "premature birth to a child, which he seized and threw overboard." The paper drew the sectional point from this tragic tale: "And Chicago groans over the state of society in Richmond." The weight of such articles was that northern civilization lacked a monopoly on virtue and had no basis to find fault with the South over the Pollard and Grant affair.[86]

Direct attacks on Richmond by northern newspapers for its treatment of Pollard's killer brought forth rebuttal articles. In a direct response to comments that the people of Richmond had disgraced themselves "by their outspoken sympathy" with Grant and by the mayor's action in releasing him under bail, the *Daily Dispatch* added to the hypocrisy defense two other defenses. The first was a bare assertion that the people of Richmond had "wisely refrained from any expression of opinion" because they believed in the workings of the legal system and the presumption of innocence. The second was that Richmond was not responsible for Mayor Chahoon's actions. After all, he was "a Republican and a military appointee—not elected by the people, and not a representative man in this city." Perhaps, because Grant's actions seemed so lacking in honor, Virginians were forced to skirt the main facts and focus on side issues.[87]

Virginian defensiveness extended to the terminology used to describe the crime. While papers outside of Virginia tended to call the crime a homicide, a murder, or an assassination, Virginia papers tended to be more circumspect. Some employed those terms, but others used less-loaded language. The Richmond papers used the term *tragedy* to describe the killing and its attendant circumstances. The vagueness of the term proved useful, because by the end of the trial many of the state's newspapers had come to see the Grants as sympathetic figures, and at least one paper saw the outcome of the trial as the fair workings of the legal system.

But another Virginia paper was not so sure. A March 11, 1869, comment in the *Virginia Gazette* saw the case as an attack on the dead and as a failure of Virginia justice. Concerning the victim of the crime, the *Gazette* noted that "had the people of Virginia been asked before the death of Pollard, what superscription, directed by the hand of affection, should be put upon his slab they would have said, as Emmet said for himself, 'Let no man write his (my) epitaph but wait till other men and other times can do justice to his (my) memory.'" But the epitaph was written in the courtroom where Pollard's name was sullied by the defendant's lawyers. And while the verdict ended the "Richmond chapter," it also was "a picture for universal commiseration." Continuing in a style congenial to Rives Pollard, the paper asserted that "Pollard has met his Appomattox. . . . If the jury, or Grant, or both, don't know who killed 'poor cock robin' (no reflection), Almighty does. The edict has gone forth, the murderer will reap his reward in

the torrid zones of the regions of Tartarus. 'Vengeance is mine,' saith the Lord."
The conditional phrasing of its assessment coupled with the invoking of the
vengeful God of the Old Testament indicated the paper's doubt that the verdict
in the trial was a fair one. It also revealed the failure of Virginia justice, for without a doubt whoever killed Pollard went unpunished. The power of the law
proved insufficient, and Virginia would have to rely on God's vengeance to punish the killer of Pollard.[88]

Perhaps a vengeful God shaped the destinies of many of the protagonists in
this trial. Most of those who continued to surface in the historical records soon
tasted despair, defeat, and death. Whether from changes in the tobacco market,
the effects of the panic of 1873, or the high costs of defending his son, William
Grant's wealth declined. He sold the house on Clay Street and died soon after.
His son James predeceased him. Edward Pollard renounced his old views and
retired to Lynchburg where he died in 1873. On the other hand, John Wise lived
a long life following the trial. He became a successful lawyer in his own right and
a prominent politician. But political success equal to that of his father eluded him
as Wise took the very unusual step, for a son of Virginia's aristocracy, of embracing the Republican Party. No doubt had he stayed in the Conservative/Demo-
cratic fold, his fame and power would have been greater, for soon after the trial
the opponents of Reconstruction began to capture control of the state.[89]

The later years of George Chahoon in Virginia epitomized what happened
to supporters of a reconstructed Virginia in the following years. Chahoon allied
himself even closer to Richmond's blacks as his term matured, eventually hiring
black men to work for the city police. While he and other radical Republicans
were cementing their connections with the black population of the state, other
Republicans were allying themselves with Conservative/Democrats. In the election of 1869, Virginia's Conservative Party cut a deal with conservatives in the
Republican Party to accept the Underwood Constitution and to elect a conservative carpetbagger, Gilbert Walker, as governor. Walker won office and, taking
advantage of an 1870 act, dismissed the city council of Richmond, appointing
men sympathetic to the old order in their stead. They in turn selected a new
mayor, but Chahoon and his white and black allies refused to yield the office. After a few violent confrontations, both sides turned to the courts; the trial held
in the Capitol was interrupted when the gallery collapsed, killing sixty spectators. The court ruled in favor of Walker's appointees, and they solidified their
power by stealing ballot boxes from the pro-Chahoon ward in the next election.
What happened in Richmond was symbolic of the whole state: Reconstruction

was over in Virginia by 1870. With the return of the unreconstructed to power, men who valued honor regained control of the legal system. But the failure of Reconstruction did not mean the end of outsider scrutiny of the state's legal processes.[90]

The journalistic accounts of Pollard's death and the trial of his accused killer underscored the strong hold that the system of honor had on Virginia society soon after the war. The press stories also showed the dynamic that connects the cases in this volume: the interaction of outsider criticisms of Virginia practices and local responses to outsider comments and actions. Even though the case had little to do with Reconstruction, northern partisan and independent papers were willing to slant the story in ways that connected it to their stands on Reconstruction. Some southerners and conservative Virginia newspapers — even those for whom the facts of the case caused problems — defended their social and legal system from these attacks. In doing so they typified southern journalists of their time, who presented "a united front against perceived revolutionary change" by "celebrating the superiority of a southern way of life."[91]

A generation after Pollard's death, another homicide would occur in a Virginia city. Like the Pollard shooting and the Grant trial, this later killing would resonate with the political strife of the day. Like the Grant trial, honor would be raised as a defense. And like the earlier affair, this new trial would also prompt outsiders to question Virginia justice and Virginians to respond.

Two

"A DANVILLE
DIFFICULTY"

TWENTY-FOUR YEARS after the Pollard case, on November 11, 1892, Baptist minister John R. Moffett was killed. Moffett, a prominent prohibitionist crusader on his way to the annual Virginia Baptist Convention, was gunned down during a scuffle with J. T. Clark, a fellow Baptist, an attorney, and a minor Democratic Party political operative. The events leading up to the killing of Moffett and the trial of Clark illuminate aspects of the interaction of the local Virginia culture and a small part of the national media in the 1890s. It is important to note that the national media in this case were not the major urban dailies but rather the *Voice*. This New York–based Prohibition Party newspaper (with nationwide circulation through the mails) was an exemplar of the specialized, issue-oriented press proliferating in this period. Like much of the media at this time, the *Voice* did not cover the story as a southern story; indeed, this story came at a time when sectional tensions between North and South were suppressed by a deep and broad movement of national reconciliation. At the same time, the local papers were strong Democratic partisan papers. Thus, although there was a strong convergence between national and local media both in presenting the news through an ideological filter and in their becoming directly involved in the story, there was wide divergence over what they published about the case. The local press tended to play up the role of honor in the case, while the out-of-state press focused on the political dimensions of the case. In the 1890s notions of honor were very much alive. The forms of the code of honor played a role in the events leading up to the killing; Clark's attorneys strongly invoked concepts of honor during the trial; the Virginia press utilized tropes of honor to explain the case. Moreover, politics was an important part of the story, as prohibitionists claimed Moffett's threat to the political order—which required white Virginians to conform to the color line that the Democratic Party drew in the state's politics—prompted Clark to act in defense of Democratic hegemony and kill Moffett.[1]

By the time of Clark's trial for killing Moffett, the further development of sensational and independent journalism had transformed the nation's newspapers. Improvements in printing techniques, the move to pulpwood newsprint, and population growth led to an increase both in the ranks of newspapers and in the number of newspapers in circulation. Joseph Pulitzer's *New York World* and William R. Hearst's newspapers set the pace for change. The two publishers invested heavily in new technology to add illustrations to their newspapers. They avidly sought the broadest possible audience, wooing them with spectacular stunts, simple language, lurid stories, and prolific illustrations. At the same time the independent papers shifted to giving more space to news stories as opposed to editorial commentary, thereby sharpening the distinctions between them. This trend was balanced by two others that preserved editorial content in news stories. The first was the rise of muckraking—journalism that moralistically exposed public wrongdoings—in the growing numbers of magazines. The second was a proliferation of smaller single-issue papers (such as socialist or prohibitionist papers) which continued the old traditions of seamlessly presenting point-of-view news. Faced with competition from these new forms, waning partisan journals tended to adopt the methods of their successful commercial rivals, isolating news from opinion and devoting more attention to muckraking and sensationalism.[2]

The contours of the press were different in the South. In the 1860s and 1870s the deep divisions between Republicans and Democrats retarded the development of the independent press. When Reconstruction ended, the Southern Republican press died, beginning a process in which the South's newspapers began to abandon partisanship. Yet through the 1890s the partisan tradition predominated in the South as its major rivals, the independent and sensational papers, were still rarities in the region. Less rare in the South and reflecting the national trends were small issue-oriented newspapers, such as papers focused on temperance or other reforms. The convergence of the region's newspapers with those of the rest of the country underscored what many scholars have noted about the period from 1890 to 1920: that sectional reconciliation was particularly strong. In particular, the rest of the Union was less likely to see the South as different, partly because of the rebuilding of intersectional organizations and the acceptance of white supremacy in much of the nation. However, this reconciliation did not mean that southerners abandoned assertions of exceptionalism; indeed, their newspapers, whatever their stripe, tended to define themselves consciously as southern, and often part of that identification was a revitalization of the concept of honor.[3]

In the South, as a number of historians have shown, honor survived the Civil War. Cultural psychologists Richard E. Nisbett and Dov Cohen—using both survey data and controlled laboratory experiments—show that even today a culture of honor exists among some American southerners. But honor did not survive unchanged or unchallenged in southern states like Virginia. As the nineteenth century wore on, honor lost some of its earlier characteristics in Virginia life. Most dramatically, as across the South, formal dueling disappeared. This was a trend that began in the Civil War, when prominent military men, most notably Robert E. Lee and Thomas Stonewall Jackson, avoided duels. Their undoubted bravery and gentlemanly reputation (especially as enshrined in later remembrances) built a space for other men to eschew the duel. By the 1880s and beyond, prominent politicians and newspaper editors, such as William Mahone, John S. Wise, and Joseph Bryan, when challenged refused to duel. Significantly, their refusal to duel was not condemned in the press, and each man maintained his social and political standing after refusing to engage in combat on the field of honor. This antidueling stance was ratified by new state laws across the South, which replicated the legislation adopted before the Civil War in northern states. The 1882 Virginia law was typical. It required state officials to take an oath that they would not duel; violators would lose their offices and be banned from future state offices. The law mixed a potent punishment, loss of office, with honorable sanctions: a state official who dueled violated his oath—his word—something that all honorable men felt bound to protect. Similarly, as Kenneth Greenberg has observed, other laws struck against honor among those who would seek office by banning duelers from office: "To withhold office from a statesman is to prevent the public from confirming his vision of himself." Thus the very legislation that sought to control the duel underscored the vitality of the idea of honor in the state

Rev. John R. Moffett, from
Rev. S. H. Thompson,
*The Life of John R.
Moffett* (Salem, Va., 1895)

Danville City Hall (1873–c. 1890),
site of the Clark trial. (Courtesy of
the Virginia Historical Society)

and region. Even as the duel disappeared, the lure of honor grew stronger for many white southern men.[4]

The work of legal anthropologist Frank H. Stewart is particularly useful in explaining the expansion of honor in the South during the late nineteenth and early twentieth centuries. The fundamental fact about this honor system was that despite the similarities, it was different from the prewar era's system of honor. In Stewart's terms the system of honor that characterized the antebellum era South was a vertical honor system, in which the honorable man demanded and received filial-like respect from subordinates in society. Even though the Old South's system of honor was more democratic than most other honor societies, it was less democratic than what later emerged in the region. Beyond such vertical systems of honor, Stewart's work shows the existence of horizontal systems of honor. In such systems honor extends among the members of a large group, giving its members the right to claim to be treated as full and equal members of the group. Such a horizontal type of honor more accurately describes the social situation of the postbellum South, where the category of gentleman expanded while distinctions along gender and race lines were maintained. It is suggestive to compare the course of honor in the American South with that in Latin America where the democratizing of social relationships occurred later. As in the American South, honorable violence's relationship with the law was uneasy, and men in the public arena were particularly prone to follow honor's precepts. Unlike in the South, in the Latin countries formal dueling lasted well into the twentieth century and was socially sanctioned among the elites. In any case, it is clear that the honor systems were functional adaptations within particular societies. Thus honor did not die with the plantation social order but survived to become even more democratic in form, even as the economy and society continued to change. Indeed, the culture of honor became more deadly as guns became more widely available.[5]

Moreover, this system of honor was not a cultural holdover but a functioning part of the social and legal system. Obviously its sustaining social forces were different from those that had existed in the antebellum period and those which sustained honor in European countries like Prussia. For example, the connection between slavery and honor had been severed by abolition, and the republican political culture of America gave no room for honor to root in an aristocratic class. Similarly, institutions like colleges and universities did not foster honor as they did in the German states. Rather, the public institutions of press and politics called for honor among all white men. Honor "was not some naive hold-over from a 'traditional' culture. Instead it was something that had to be self-con-sciously constructed and maintained." And it needed to have a function. Thus this more democratic system of honor was most vital in the postwar period when it helped to build white unity before disfranchisement and segregation were es-tablished. This system of honor in many ways functioned exactly like the earlier, far more studied system of honor prevalent in the antebellum South. And like that system, this system of honor's legitimacy was being challenged in southern society.[6]

For example, in the neighboring state of Kentucky, a spectacular affair of honor among officeholders in 1883 led to challenges to honor's hegemony over behavior among white men. Richard Reid, a candidate for the Court of Appeals, refused to resort to honorable violence against a fellow lawyer, John J. Corneli-son, who had beaten him publicly with a cane and a whip. Reid justified his course as a manifestation of his "dedication to Christian principles and the rule of law." And during the campaign he, his wife, and their supporters attacked the code of honor. But his stance did not resonate with the voters, and with his elec-toral hopes dimming, Reid committed suicide. In the wake of his death, his po-litical allies charged that Cornelison's attack had been orchestrated to promote the electoral chances of another candidate for the office. Moreover, the newspa-pers attacked the code of honor. Indeed, in the words of historian Robert M. Ire-land, "No other single episode in the history of Kentucky had produced so many criticisms of the doctrine of manly honor." Yet although promoting "reassess-ment," the affair "did not signal the end of" honor in Kentucky or the South.[7]

In Virginia honor persisted as a social fact in homicide trials and thereby showed the existence of honor among white men who were not socially promi-nent. Indeed, the categories of men who could be seen as proper recipients of honor had moved down the social ladder. For instance, the two 1879 trials of John E. Poindexter for the shooting of Charles C. Curtis revolved around the ideas of honor among office workers. Poindexter, a bookkeeper at a Richmond tobacco factory, whipped Curtis, a clerk at a store, for his alleged insult to a lady. After the whipping Curtis denied the insult, promised to apologize to the lady "if he had unwittingly" insulted her, and shook hands with Poindexter. Later that day Curtis, threatening to cane Poindexter, demanded an apology. Poindexter, refusing to apologize, drew a gun and, when Curtis hit him, shot him. The de-fense, including John S. Wise, kept the issue of honorable violence before each jury, bringing about a hung jury in the first case and a verdict of involuntary manslaughter in the second trial. Clearly, among social equals some aspects of honor existed in the state's public culture.[8]

But Virginia's public affairs were not restricted only to social equals. Blacks, whom most white Virginians presumed their social inferiors, were guaranteed the right to vote. From their restoration to power in 1869 to their disfranchisement of blacks in 1902, white Virginians in the Conservative Party, and later the Democratic Party, confronted the reality of black political participation. Both the federal Fifteenth Amendment and the state's Underwood Constitution recognized black suffrage. Thus for Democrats, Virginia was a particularly difficult state to hold. According to J. Morgan Kousser, "Since Negroes made up more than 40 percent of Virginia's populace in the 1870s and since a goodly number of white mountain folk translated their Unionist sympathies into membership in the Republican Party after the War, the Virginia Conservative-Democratic Party was fortunate that it did not lose a statewide contest during the decade." The party kept its hold by levying a poll tax and by staying unified. When the party divided over the questions of funding or adjusting the state debt, it lost its hold on the state. Those who bolted from the party joined forces with some Republicans to form the Readjuster Party; led by William Mahone and embracing blacks as political partners, the Readjusters gained control of the state. In the course of three years, 1879-82, the Readjusters captured the legislature twice, the governorship, the two national Senate seats, and a majority of the state's delegation to Congress.[9]

In response, the Democratic Party became openly white supremacist, and this stance helped restore it to power. Party leaders publicly drew a color line in politics; in 1883 a former Democratic candidate for governor said, "I am a Democrat because I am a white man and a Virginian." This stand had echoes of the old system of honor because the party also was attempting to "reinstitutionalize hierarchy and rerank society." But it was a simpler ranking of society than that which had characterized antebellum society; honor was racially democratized, available to all white men who claimed it and denied to all black men. The race issue and a brilliant tactical campaign managed by John S. Barbour allowed the Democrats to recapture the state in 1883. Once they gained control, they showed fierce determination to retain it. Immediately following the election the *Richmond State* editorialized, "We have Virginia once more in our possession, and we will keep her this time, be sure of that."[10]

As across all the South, electoral fraud and intimidation became one of the ways that the Democrats kept the state. A prominent Funder/Democrat admitted that the party amended the election laws to permit voter fraud and intimidation. The most important act passed by the legislature in this regard was the 1884 Anderson-McCormick election law, which gave the Democratic Party control over the election machinery. At the time the *Richmond Dispatch* said it was "passed in the interest of the white people of Virginia. . . . It operates to perpetuate the rule of the white man in Virginia." Barbour summed up the party's position: "We have the power and we must win." And they did, as the law, according to historian Allen W. Moger, "made possible a system of election control and election frauds by the Democrats." In the words of another historian, the 1884 law "marked the beginning of the wholesale ballot-box stuffing." In 1885, the first year of the new law, the Democrats swept the state, winning the office of governor and consolidating their hold on the assembly. But according to Kousser the "tenure of the dominant party was not as secure as it appeared on the surface." Its hold was precarious, resting on the foundations of manipulation of the suffrage and assertions that all whites should vote Democratic. Any issue that divided the white Democratic vote could bring about a Democratic disaster.[11]

In the 1880s the liquor issue threatened to do just that. The Virginia Democratic Party contained both liquor dealers and temperance advocates. The party seldom supported reform and had developed strong links with wet urban machines across the state. But at this time temperance and prohibition emerged as powerful concerns among many churchgoing Democrats. Under the pressure of their dry constituents, the party pushed through a local-option law in 1886. The law codified the existing practice of letting a community go "no license," that is, refuse to grant liquor licenses. Going "no license" effectively ended the legal selling of spirits in the community. The 1886 local-option law replaced the county court as the agency of this decision with a vote of the electorate (prompted by a petition of one-fourth of the voters), which could be held only once in two years. The measure was an adroit compromise that took the prohibition issue out of statewide politics. But it transferred the conflict over wet and dry—and to Democrats, dangerous divisions in white ranks—to the localities, such as Danville.[12]

Site of the 1883 race riot that marked the return of the Democrats to power in the state, Danville was no stranger to Virginia's racially tinged politics. Located in the Southside—an area defined by being geographically south of the James River and demographically by having a large black population—Danville was a prospering community in the late nineteenth century. The small mill cities of Danville and North Danville had grown up separately, connected by bridges across the Dan River. Not until well after this killing and trial were the two communities consolidated under one government. In the early nineteenth century the two Danvilles had been the center of a major tobacco producing and processing area, but later in the century a new industry arrived. In 1883 the first textile mill opened, drawing its power from the Dan River. Through 1895 there was steady expansion of the cotton mills. Danville boomed, fortunes were made, and mansions were built. Workers and others flocked to boardinghouses in the two cities.

As befitting a mill and market town, Danville had a thriving liquor trade. The city had at least one wholesaler, who specialized in sales to the country, and at least one brewery, which ran its own saloon. Liquor was sold at dry-goods stores throughout the town. At the same time, the growing Baptist and Methodist congregations became strong supporters of temperance. Indeed, North Danville had "many churches" but "no saloons," which deepened the divisions in the community. From 1877, the Roanoke Baptist Association, which included the local churches, banned liquor sellers from its membership. Thus the liquor issue divided the cities; moreover, race split Danville and North Danville to an even greater degree.[13]

Until the later years of the textile boom, Danville and North Danville had African-American majorities, and this fact was a constant in the cities' politics until disfranchisement. In 1880 Danville's population was 4,397 blacks and 3,129 whites. A decade later Danville was still 54 percent black. For a number of years, the Republican Party and the Readjuster Party, many of whose main supporters and officeholders were black, controlled the cities. Danville elected a carpetbagger mayor, J. H. Johnston, who appointed blacks to city offices, including the police force. Blacks remained the key voting bloc until 1883, when a group of Democratic business leaders capitalized on a violent event to redeem the cities.[14]

Before the 1883 election the Democratic Party, in an effort to draw a color line in politics, distributed a circular throughout the state. It cited testimony of leading white Danville citizens describing the abuses of "black rule" there. When Readjusters raised doubts about the accuracy of the circular, Danville's Democrats met to reaffirm it. On November 3, 1883, they gathered at the Opera House to sign the circular again. While they were meeting, a street fight between a black man and a white man escalated into the white man shooting at the black man, which drew some of the Democrats to the scene. A large crowd of blacks also congregated there, demanding that the police arrest the white man who had fired his gun. When the black crowd refused to disperse at the orders of the whites, Democrats started shooting indiscriminately, killing five people. Blacks fled while armed whites filled the town. The city was put under martial law, enforced by the white county militia. Because the ensuing election was marked by the absence of blacks at the polls, the Democrats swept back into office in both Danvilles. The new government condemned the previous regime and justified the violence. It portrayed the previous government as corrupt, declaring that its indulgence of blacks had encouraged them to become "rude, insolent and intolerant" to white citizens. The new Democratic government sent the message that it was acceptable that Danville had been redeemed for whites through violence.[15]

The cities' Democrats stayed in power by making it difficult for blacks to vote and encouraging all whites to support the party's candidates. However, to maintain its control of the cities, the party had to make sure that the white vote did not divide. It did so by catering to all white factions in the community. One late nineteenth-century observer of Danville politics reported that "as far as possible every interest is sought to be presented." Beyond such inclusiveness, Democrats, as they did across Virginia, built a tight political machine. This machine reached from the counting rooms of major businesses, including railroads, through the small respectable stores, down to groceries that were part store, part hangout, and part saloon. The Danville newspapers—the daily *Register* and the weekly *Times*—dominated communication among all elements of the white Democratic political system. Typical of the papers in the partisan tradition, these newspapers published strong editorials supporting local, state, and national Democratic positions and assailing the opponents of those positions. They also presented their news stories with a clear Democratic slant, seeking to maintain their party's control of office. Their news stories and editorials were one of the staples of talk in the local groceries.[16]

Until the 1902 suffrage restrictions, the Democrats needed a solid white vote to win in the Danville towns. To achieve this goal, they engaged in a system of overt manipulation of the voting process. Under the Anderson-McCormick Act, a voter had to cast his vote using a party's ticket. This ticket (or ballot) was inserted into the ballot box to register a vote. In theory, this was a form of secret ballot. In practice, the Democratic Party in the cities subverted it. To vote Democratic a voter had to ask for the party's ticket from the single party worker assigned to dispense them at each polling place. No other Democratic tickets were available. If a voter entered the polling place with his own ticket, the party knew that he was likely not voting Democratic. It could use this knowledge to pressure and punish such voters. Or it could throw out such voters' ballots after the voting ended. This voting system helped the Democrats maintain power.[17]

This was the political landscape when John R. Moffett became the new minister of the North Danville Baptist church. Moffett, born in 1858, the youngest son of a Culpeper County farming family, was self-consciously southern. In a brief autobiographic fragment, he claimed the Civil War left a mark on his character; he wrote that his family had "often gone out on the hills to listen to the booming of the cannon on some hard fought field." With typical childish regard for soldiers, the five-year-old boy adored the heroes of the southern cause. He recalled seeing the army pass by the family's gate on its way to Gettysburg. He revered the soldiers, their uniforms, and their horses. Moffett was crestfallen that he missed sight of General Robert E. Lee. When the retreating troops came back, he romanticized his mother's nursing of the sick and wounded. Beyond devotion to the Lost Cause, Moffett as a young boy accepted the lessons of honorable manhood. He learned how to be brave to deserve honor. Thus when he reminisced about a friend being whipped at school for some infraction, Moffett wrote that he "acted bravely. . . . He took his whipping like a man and didn't blab a word." Moffett's outlook was "wholly southern," despite the religious leanings that shaped his life.[18]

Moffett's religious views, indeed his whole view of the world, were encapsulated in his recollection of one of his first religious experiences. He had a dream that his family home was divided into heaven and hell; the "backroom at home seemed to be the abode of misery" while the front was heaven, and he felt driven to be in the front. This simple dichotomy, and the assurance that he belonged in the good, marked his life. At age fourteen Moffett converted at a Methodist camp meeting and soon after joined the Baptist church. He was not just a member but a crusader for the church; he became a prayer leader and proselytizer. Educated first at home, then at Washington Academy (headed by Landon C. Berkeley) in neighboring Rappahannock County, he excelled at his studies. After schooling, Moffett managed the family farm for four years. He continued to study and was elected minister. Typical of his drive and ambition, he decided that to perform his duties well, he needed to go to seminary. In 1881 he graduated from Southern Baptist Theological Seminary in Louisville, Kentucky. At the same time Moffett began his lifelong association with temperance. He joined the Independent Order of Good Templars, a fraternal and international society founded in 1851 and very strong in Kentucky. The Templars preached total abstinence and prohibition. Moffett moved from pastorate to pastorate, steadily called to larger and larger congregations; he was, by all accounts, a rising star of the Baptist Church.[19]

On July 1, 1887, Moffett became the minister of the Missionary Baptist congregation in North Danville. His first two years there were a record of achievement and acceptance by his congregation and community. In 1889, marking his determination to settle in Danville, he married Pearl Bruce, a Halifax woman educated at the Danville College for Young Ladies. He renewed his ties with his former tutor L. C. Berkeley (whom he had not seen in fifteen years) and with his cousins. He also formed friendships with a number of members of his church, especially with J. H. Hill, who would be instrumental in prosecuting Clark. Moffett likely also made enemies; his manner was assertive, and as later events showed, he had a short temper. Moffett's ambition made him a dynamo as minister; he increased the size of his congregation fivefold in two years, while raising the money to build a new chapel in the town. Another Baptist minister wrote that Moffett worked "like a beaver, always on the outlook for new comers, with a happy faculty for recognizing people and for putting them to work. He is bound to succeed. He is making occasional excursions into the country round about collecting money for the new church."[20]

He was also traveling throughout the surrounding region to deliver temperance addresses. Within a month of settling in town, Moffett was speaking to Good Templar (he would rise to the rank of grand lecturer in the order) and Baptist meetings about the evils of drink. Like many prohibitionists, Moffett believed that liquor caused much of the evil and suffering in his society. He saw evidence of it daily during his ministerial duties. In September 1887 he was summoned to the bedside of a woman who had been beaten by her drunken husband, who stripped her of her clothes and "turned her out of doors." Another time he visited a woman "awaiting the trial of her son indicted for killing his best friend while under the influence of liquor." Once while he was visiting the sick, a drunken doctor came up and dragged "up a dying girl from her bed and fill[ed] the [room] with his oaths." On still another occasion he saw "Dr. Edmunds, a man of intellect and culture, lying on a pallet in a corner, drunk, without strength and without hope." Moffett wanted to save these people, and their society, from this evil. He intended to do so whatever the personal cost; reflecting on the horrors of liquor, he asked himself, "Shall I stop preaching temperance for fear of being called fanatic?" At this point Moffett was not a party prohibitionist.

Formed in 1869, the Prohibition Party preached that only through election of its slate could the nation be freed from drink. The party was strongest in the Northeast, though in the 1880s it began to attempt to organize in the South. In 1888 Moffett voted for the Democratic ticket, but he wrote in his diary that he wanted the prohibition candidate "to have [a] fair chance . . . next time."[21]

Prohibition became the cause that carried him into politics, in dramatic fashion. On August 23, 1889, Moffett gave a speech in the nearby town of Chatham, where he mixed the politics of prohibition with the race issue. In this speech Moffett said, "I would rather have good Negro rule than the rule of the alcoholic devil." Considering his personal attitudes and the view of the Prohibition Party toward blacks, it is doubtful that Moffett intended his speech to attract black voters to his cause. Some idea of Moffett's views toward blacks can be found in a March 1, 1888, diary entry. Moffett wrote that he attended a lecture by "Page, the already famous delineator of Negro character. Enjoyed him very much." Thomas Nelson Page was a prominent late nineteenth-century southern writer who disseminated the plantation myth of the Old South. His short stories, poems, essays, and novels portray blacks as a simple and humble people happy with their place in southern society. A man who would enjoy Page's delineation of "Negro character" was unlikely to seek their political support. Moreover, by 1889 the experience of the Prohibition Party with black voters in the South had proved dismal. For instance, in Atlanta black voters were an important part of the electorate that made the city dry in 1885, but they were equally important in making the city wet two years later. Leaders of the Prohibition Party tended to blame their defeats in the South on the fickleness of black voters. And Moffett's phrasing was not directed to appeal to the black electorate but to the white voters. His words sought to dramatize the evils of liquor in politics by comparing it to the favorite demon of the day, "Negro rule."[22]

Reaction to his speech from the local Democratic papers was swift and pointed; the *Danville Times* printed editorials asking Moffett to explain his speech. "Good Negro rule! Where did you get such an idea? Who ever heard of, read of, or even dreamed of such a thing. We are sorry to hear such an expression coming from such a respectable source, just on the eve of a great battle for the supremacy of the white race." The *Times* was referring to Mahone's running for governor against Philip W. McKinney, a political battle which Democrats portrayed as a struggle to maintain white rule. Historian Allen W. Moger later called this campaign "the most bitter" electoral conflict "in the history of Virginia politics," during which the "most effective argument the Democrats had for winning votes was that Democratic solidarity was necessary to save white civ-ilization from Negro-Republican domination." Thus, Moffett's ideas had to be repudiated by the Democratic papers. The editorial writer of the *Register* (prob-ably the editor William Copeland) twisted his words, denouncing Moffett's "modern utopia where 'good Negroes' hold the sway of government and white men and white women are peaceful and happy under the dark regime." Refer-ring to the Republican-Readjuster coalition rule that had ended a mere six years earlier, the *Register* continued, "The people of Danville and North Danville, who have tasted the bitter fruits of Negro rule, . . . fear it and fight it as they do small pox, yellow fever, or leprosy." The *Register* warned Moffett that such views wounded the temperance cause "to the heart." The Democratic papers assured him that they would welcome him back into the fold, that he was one of them. They were certain he did not believe in black supremacy, "for it is a sentiment that cannot live in the heart of any honest white man, and we have no doubt that in his own way he will set himself right before the people."[23]

Moffett spent the better part of a day writing a reply to the charges of "hot headed Democrats mad because I chose [to] set whisky worse than the Negro." Reflecting his ambition to rise in his denomination, and seemingly blind to the larger political context, he attributed the *Register*'s attacks on him to a man "whom I had given a drubbing in the [Baptist General] Association." He dis-missed the editor of the *Times* as a tool of the liquor interests, declaring that "the author . . . has a paper which is liberally supported by the liquor men of Danville, and we have it from good authority that his rent has been paid by subscriptions from liquor men." Moffett's printed reply asserted that as a man of the South, of Anglo-Saxon blood, he had his share of race pride and horror of "Negro domination." He then compared the expenses of the Republican Party, "which I use here as the standard of good Negro rule," against the much larger bill presented by the alcohol devil through its creation of addiction, poverty, and crime. He then recast the phrase so inflammatory to Democrats in stronger lan-guage: "I would rather be governed by a good Negro than by a drunken white man." He was sure that his explanation would silence his critics: "Everybody will see however who reads the piece calmly that I am right." He was wrong. Calm reflection was notably absent from the 1889 campaign. As a result Moffett's reply only made the Democratic papers more virulent in their attacks on him.[24]

The *Times* ran a series of articles on this crusading prohibitionist while the *Register* apparently kept silent. The *Times* called his reply "worse and worse." It told the minister to get back in "his sphere" and out of "ours," implying that ministers, like women (who the prevailing ideology said lived in a separate sphere), had no place in the manly world of politics. The *Times* questioned whether he had enough race pride, raised the specter of "Negro rule," and pointed out the danger of dividing the white vote. It predicted confidently that "every white Democrat is going to get into line on the day of the election and vote solidly for McKinney." The *Times* could not believe that a white man would think the "liquor question was a bigger question than the Negro question." It styled Moffett "the champion of good Negro rule of North Danville" and denounced his "injurious political advice." The paper even accused Moffett of supporting Mahone, running that year as a Republican, and said that he was backed by Republican money. The paper left a vague threat hanging in the air: "Woe be unto you Mr. Moffett, if McKinney should be defeated by votes taken from white ranks and thrown away on [Thomas] Taylor," candidate of the Prohibition Party. McKinney won, but Moffett continued his agitation unabated. He received great support in his church; his congregation voted 110 to 3 to back his stand on temperance.[25]

Moffett expanded and intensified his temperance activities. He dismissed the *Times* as a one-horse newspaper, and on election day he refused to give in to the "tremendous pressure" and voted the prohibition ticket. This vote was a public act, and it prompted gossip. Following his vote, a fellow Baptist minister refused Moffett's request to preach in his North Danville church. Such actions did not deter him. Moffett led the dry effort in trying to bring local-option prohibition to Danville in 1889. When that failed, he helped to found a temperance newspaper. In May 1890, with a group of temperance men, he began publishing the *Anti-Liquor* first as a monthly, then a weekly. Under community pressure the other founders of the paper abandoned it, making Moffett the body and soul of this paper. Typical of reform-minded papers in the late nineteenth century, the *Anti-Liquor* exposed minor corruption in the operation of the Danville jail. Moffett also turned the *Anti-Liquor* into a Prohibition Party newspaper, and it endorsed an independent Republican for Congress in 1890. Moffett, through his paper, opposed the Democratic nominees for various offices because they did not measure up to his moral standards.[26]

As it did in many cities of the state, the Democratic Party responded forcefully to the emergence of the liquor issue in Danville. The party's papers set the tone. The *Register* ignored the minister's work among his congregation but, according to one of Moffett's supporters, made sure that Moffett's "sermons were watched, and every utterance that could be twisted from its place and made to serve as a blow at him was taken down and so used." Most significantly, the *Register* kept the other papers of the state informed through its membership in the AP. "The Associated Press dispatches to the great dailies in Richmond, helped the work of misrepresentation." The *Times* became "the organ of 'personal liberty,'" that is antiprohibition, and therefore anti-Moffett. Indeed, Moffett's politics were, as J. H. Hill later admitted, "vigorous and offensive to many of his former friends." The contests over the liquor issue were bitter. J. T. Clark, a former storekeeper, a Democrat, and an attorney, became Moffett's nemesis. During the 1891 local-option election campaign in North Danville, Clark circulated a petition "to buy a lot and build a house for a Negro by Moffett's home." Clark's action can be interpreted in two ways. It could have been intended to show that Moffett did not understand white southern values, or it could have been designed to trap Moffett into revealing himself a hypocrite on the race issue. In any case, nothing came of the subscription effort but talk. Yet the talk did have consequences for Moffett; he had become identified as an enemy of the political order. Thus, during a rally during the 1891 local-option election, a man placed a pistol against Moffett's chest and pulled the trigger. The gun misfired. The town went wet by eighteen votes. Undaunted, Moffett continued his prohibition agitation. In 1891 he was instrumental in using the Baptist Association to call a statewide temperance and prohibition convention. The following year he endorsed the Prohibition Party candidate for president.[27]

In October 1892 Moffett preached a sermon explaining his political position. In this sermon he told his congregation why he was a party prohibitionist and why he used his pulpit to discuss political questions. Moffett held the liquor traffic to be a sin and therefore felt compelled to speak out against any institution, including a political party, that supported it. He rejected expediency and compromise positions on the liquor question. Nor would he permit "the RACE PROBLEM" to deter his activism. "I want to say right here that I have as much horror as any one of a government ruled by a semi-civilized, superstitious, improvident, uneducated, often brutal, recently liberated set of slaves." Moffett maintained that the two major parties "have been trying to settle this race question for nearly thirty years and according to the assertions of their brightest political minds *the danger is supremely* greater to-day than ever before." Expediency, which led to this state of affairs, needed to be rejected and replaced with God's "method of *right*." Moffett denounced "our plan for controlling the colored man" as "contrary to God's plan, ... founded on hate, and ... on corruption and dishonesty at the ballot box." He proposed instead to focus on killing "the liquor serpent" because it caused "nine-tenths of the difficulties between white and black." According to Moffett, liquor led to black crime and corrupt black voting, so adopting prohibition would *"settle the Negro question."* Moffett, in taking this line, was echoing the views of Rev. A. E. Dickinson, the senior editor of the Baptist *Religious Herald.* In 1891 Dickinson lambasted the major parties for ignoring the "far greater calamities" caused by liquor to focus on the race issue. The "threat of Negro domination has been handled for all it is worth; we are no longer called upon to pray one way and vote the other way." [28]

It is important to note that Moffett, while sharing Democratic racist assumptions about blacks, rejected Democratic means of controlling politics. His acceptance of their fundamental beliefs about race could have been of little comfort to Democrats who maintained their control through electoral manipulation because he questioned the very means they used to stay in power. Moreover, Moffett was willing to do more than simply speak out against the electoral system. One of the impediments to Prohibition Party progress in Danville, Moffett knew, was the ticket-holder system of the Democratic Party. In search of a solution to this problem, he consulted with his eldest brother. William Walter Moffett, also a Baptist who shared many of John's attributes, had entered the legal profession and had become a Democratic politician and state judge. Even though he was a Democrat, W. W. Moffett denounced the Danville system to his brother as "cowardly" and "fraudulent." He suggested that it could be broken if someone scattered Democratic ballots throughout the community so that any Democrat could get a ticket without going to the man at the polling place.[29]

Following his brother's advice, John Moffett had "Regular Democratic Tickets" printed, copying a nearby newspaper's slate of candidates. These tickets — distributed by the printer before Moffett could check them — did not match the ones produced by the city's Democratic machine. On November 8, 1892, Democratic politicians and newspapers charged that Moffett was scattering bogus tickets. Clark warned voters against the tickets, asserting that they were frauds, designed to get their votes thrown out. These fears were realistic; the *Roanoke Times* had recently reported that in South Carolina many Democratic electoral tickets were found illegal for similar printing errors. Clark accosted Moffett on a North Danville street as the minister was passing a public meeting and accused him of fraud. In reply, Moffett struck Clark with a "stunning blow." When a police officer intervened, Moffett accidentally delivered a "severe blow" to the top of his head. After the fray both men were arrested for fighting. And though both men were fined for fighting, that did not end their dispute.³⁰

Neither man was willing to let the matter drop, and their responses reveal the range of options open to men having a public dispute in Virginia during the last decade of the nineteenth century. Before being removed from the scene, Moffett and Clark continued to exchange bitter words, and Moffett sought to use the language of honor to best Clark. At one point, as Moffett addressed the crowd, assuring them his intentions were only to break the voting system, not to defraud anyone of their votes, Clark tried to ask him a question, to which Moffett replied with a blatant insult: "I don't propose to answer any questions you ask. I only converse with gentlemen." After the street exchange Moffett took advantage of the conventions that allowed parties to a controversy to print a "card" in the local paper, to counter Clark's charges. In his card in the *Register,* which appeared on the day after he was shot, Moffett defended his honor against the charges raised on the street and in the press. "I believe in a manly ballot, and always vote an open one myself, but there are persons, peculiarly situated, to whom it is not only a privilege and right, but a duty to vote the secret ballot. Our aim was simply to secure to such persons . . . that right." In print, Moffett showed every determination to continue to attack his accuser. Moffett lashed out at Clark in the November 10, 1892, issue of the *Anti-Liquor.* "This is the same one-horse lawyer that has been doing the dirty work of the liquorites for about two years, who had a subscription circulated among the liquor men during a wet and dry campaign, to buy a lot to settle a 'nigger' on it next to Mr. Moffett," he wrote. He called Clark a "contemptible whiskeyite" and gloated over having "banged him in the face." He continued by publicly insulting Clark again, saying of the incident in the street, "Mr. Clark was completely squelched, and subsided amid the yells of the crowd."³¹

Clark, on the other hand, did not invoke the system of honor against Moffett. Rather he sought to use the legal system against him. Clark later testified that he consulted with his friends about this "difficulty with Mr. Moffett" and decided to "let the matter drop . . . and to let the law take its course." Indeed, the day after the exchange on the street, he sought advice from among the town's leading lawyers concerning the affray with Moffett. (Ironically, although Clark sought advice from men who later represented him, they were not in their offices, and instead he received advice from N. H. Massie, who would later prosecute him for killing Moffett.) Clark may have thought he could have Moffett charged with assault, and he pondered not paying his fine as a protest. In any case, following the first insult, Clark did not seek redress through violence. It remained a point of contention in his trial whether he sought violent redress after he learned of Moffett's printed attack on his character.[32]

When Moffett's paper was distributed on November 11, Clark—who only boarded at his sister's in the city—was out of town and did not know of Moffett's attack on him in the *Anti-Liquor*. When he returned, he went to work for his party, visiting various stores and public places and talking politics. On election night Clark was lionized before a Democratic meeting by many of those present as the man who "exposed Moffett." Sometime during the night he heard about the article in the *Anti-Liquor*. Clark began wandering about town, looking either for a copy or for Moffett.[33]

In the meantime, after the election Moffett turned his attention to his religious duties. He attended the annual meeting of the Baptist General Association, which was held that year in Danville at the First Baptist Church. Moffett walked to the meeting from his home in North Danville, stopping by the office of the *Danville Register* to drop off his card. He went into the printshop and spoke with the printer in an inner office which was visible to the outer room. Clark entered the outer office, saw Moffett (though Moffett did not see him, according to witnesses), turned, and left. Moffett soon followed, and the two men met on the street. Then "a difficulty at once ensued to which four shots were fired from a pistol, one of which took effect in Mr. Moffett's abdomen."[34]

Two men—Green Williams (chief of police), and Peyton B. Gravely (a prominent citizen)—who had seen the struggle ran up and restrained Clark. Williams arrested both Moffett and Clark, relieving Clark of a pistol. Moffett was taken to a nearby doctor's office, and Clark was escorted to jail. Clark was released on bail thirty minutes after the shooting, though he was subsequently recommitted. The news of the shooting spread quickly through the town, and some Democrats rejoiced. When the news reached a Democratic meeting, one speaker declared: "The damned rascal! Clark ought to have killed him." As W. W. Moffett hastened from the First Baptist Church, accompanying his sister to their brother's side, he ran across crowds of carousing, victorious Democrats. He later compared them to "Devils" at "carnival upon the streets of Danville. There were huzzas for the Democracy" while Moffett was denounced as "a damned black hearted Republican; others said that Clark had shot a dog. One demon named three other ministers who should also be 'dispatched' in the same manner."[35]

Other Democrats rallied to the wounded preacher as doctors ministered to him. Most notably, William Copeland, editor of the *Register,* came to see Moffett while he was at the doctor's office. In the presence of Moffett's brother, Copeland expressed "in the sincerest and warmest manner" his desire to mend their differences created by political disputes. The two men "had a complete reconciliation." Later that night three doctors probed the wound—which lay about three inches above his navel—for the bullet. When it could not be found, they performed a laporotomy, or coeliotomy, which entails cutting open the abdomen to take a look at the organs and includes temporarily removing the intestines and the colon from the body cavity. As the doctors began, Moffett fainted from the chloroform, and they revived him with an enema of whiskey mixed with strychnine. Again, partway through the procedure, as the doctors were running his intestines through their hands looking for holes, Moffett reacted to the chloroform. They stopped the operation, replaced his innards, and sewed him up. Because they felt some roughness on the liver, the doctors were sure that it was damaged and that Moffett was bleeding internally. When he revived, they told him he would soon die. Within twenty-eight hours of the shooting, Moffett was dead, probably from the combination of shock and what the doctors called "immediate peritonitis," infection resulting from the bullet wound and subsequent operation.[36]

Moffett before his death spoke to his gathered family, friends, and government officers. The mayor of Danville visited him, and Moffett recounted the events of the shooting. At law, upon Moffett's death this statement became a dying declaration, which would be admissible in court. It carried extra weight because a professing Christian made the statement right before his meeting with God; presumably Moffett would not wish to face God with one of his last living acts being a lie. Moffett asserted that as he was walking up Main Street, he "met a man, . . . so I stepped aside to give room. He was four or five yards from me. At that time he commence[d] firing upon me. I endeavored to secure his weapon, but was not successful in so doing until Mr. Green Williams . . . came up." Moffett named Clark as his attacker, saying he shot without warning. Moffett also declared that he was not carrying a pistol and did not physically attack Clark until after Clark had fired.[37]

Although Moffett's death became national news in prohibitionist circles, it did not interest the mainstream press. The story lacked the key ingredients of human-interest themes or sexual titillation that sensational and independent press craved. The death of Moffett was not a tale of universal interest, especially given the complicated political nature of his dispute with Clark. Also, for the major surviving partisan papers outside of the South, the killing was essentially an unattractive story. Northern and western Democratic papers probably saw no advantage in covering the killing as it raised difficult questions about their southern allies. Republican papers, also, probably had little stake in covering the story as the victim was not a Republican and as the party no longer had a significant presence in the South. Furthermore, the Virginia papers played the gatekeeping role in the commercial cooperative news-sharing contacts, and thus their take on the story was what papers outside the state learned of the crime. So, only reform-minded, muckraking publications, like those of the Prohibition Party, paid attention to the story outside Virginia.

In the six weeks following Moffett's death, the national prohibition press portrayed it as part of the drys' struggle against the liquor interests. The *Voice,* the New York–based Prohibition Party weekly, headlined its November 17, 1892, story, "A Democratic Ex-Rumseller Takes the Life of Rev. J. R. Moffett." The *Voice* did not have a reporter in Danville and for its story relied on a fellow prohibitionist who worked with Moffett at the *Anti-Liquor.* This article reviewed the accusation of ballot fraud, saying that the *Anti-Liquor* had "proven" it "to be absolutely groundless." It reported the shooting with embellishments likely to appeal to a prohibitionist audience, asserting that Clark, "an ex-barkeeper," after being exposed for a liar, "became enraged and arming himself, lay in wait for his victim in an alley, and without a word of warning fired upon him." The paper denounced Clark and Danville in the strongest of terms. "Clark was prompted by a vicious politico-whisky sentiment. As yet the daily papers of the city have expressed no condemnation of the crime."[38]

A week after the killing, the *Voice,* under the headline "Clark Has Shot a Dog" and bylined "special Correspondence," reported the story in great detail, reviewing the ballot controversy, Moffett's life and career, Clark's character, and what the liquor interests did after the shooting. It took its facts from various sources, including Moffett's dying declaration. Like the previous story, it contained material sure to capture the attention of political prohibitionists. For example, it reported that on the night of the election, Clark at a public meeting had "repeatedly charged Moffett with being criminally intimate with a woman in North Danville while the crowd laughed and jeered" and that "on the night of the murder, one of Clark's heelers went into a saloon and mockingly remarked that Clark 'had shot a dog on the street.'" Clark was described as having a "vicious, cunning face" and being "until recently . . . a whisky-seller at Fall Creek, from which place he is said to have been driven by the citizens owing to the vile reputation of the resort which he maintained." It concluded by maintaining that whiskey men would "combine to secure his acquittal, and they are already bragging that they have many thousands of dollars at their command for that purpose." The accompanying editorial contended that "there are strong indications that this assassination is the result of a dark and wide-spread conspiracy." The *Voice* speculated that the whiskey Democratic element, led by Clark, was working to form a mob that very night to drive Moffett out of town. The paper thought there was "little likelihood in this case that justice will be meted out to the murderers unless the people of Virginia mete it out at the ballot-box by a decree of death to the lawless traffic."[39]

In a series of stories and one letter printed in three different December issues of the *Voice,* the paper put Moffett's death in the context of the crusade to bring about prohibition by the election of the Prohibition Party. One article blamed the slow dry progress in the state to the "well-known and plainly-recognized fact that the dominate political party of the State is under the thumb of the saloonkeepers." Another explained the low vote totals for the Prohibition Party's presidential candidate in 1892 on the "partisan Anderson-McCormick election law" which "gives the Democrats . . . full capacity" to undercount Prohibition Party votes. A letter linked political obstacles to Moffett's assassination, asserting that his martyrdom would permit the Prohibition Party to unite with the Republicans and the Populists to overcome "the Democratic Party and party papers," which constantly raised the cry of "'Negro supremacy' in order to save whisky." The longest of the articles attacked the "strange apathy on the part of the politicians and newspapers in denouncing the act of Clark," implying that Moffett's death, if not a conspiracy, was "at least a determination" by "saloonkeepers and liquor politicians" to rid the cities of Moffett. The article denounced the two Democratic Danville papers for their "persistent attack upon Moffett" in an attempt to "prejudice public opinion against him." Moreover, indicative of their stand, prohibitionists charged that "not one Democratic paper of any importance has said a single word of condemnation of the murder, and most of them simply made a three or four line notice of it as a news item"; the Democratic *Richmond Dispatch* gave Moffett's death "only an inch of space." Nothing in the *Voice*'s coverage of Moffett's killing indicated that his was a southern story. The attacks that the paper leveled on Danville's political leaders and the state's newspapers were the same as those it leveled at politicians and press in the Northeast or Midwest.[40]

Although most Virginians disagreed with the *Voice*'s interpretation of Moffett's killing, the Virginia Baptists shared similar sentiments. At his funeral, in their meetings, and in their press the Baptists called Moffett a martyr, implied that his death was the result of a conspiracy, and decried the silence of the state's Democratic press. Like the national prohibitionists, the Virginia Baptists never portrayed the killing as linked to the values of honor. In this, they stood in contrast to the representatives of the Democratic Party in Danville. The Democratic papers portrayed the killing as a private affair, asserting that Moffett "was not slain because of his convictions." In response to a letter by a local dry stating that Moffett's death "was the unfortunate outcome" of the bitter fights over local option, the *Register* on November 15, 1892, published an editorial asserting that "his unfortunate taking off was the result of personal difficulty." Moffett's death had, according to the Democrats, no greater meaning.[41]

While the press was expressing these differing explanations for Moffett's death, the Virginia legal system prepared to try his killer. Clark was indicted by a grand jury, and he remained in jail until his trial at the local hustings court. His trial began on February 6, 1893, before Judge Archer M. Aiken and lasted for ten days. Many of the differences that separated the Danville Democrats from prohibitionists and Baptists in interpreting Moffett's death reemerged during the trial. Thus Clark's lawyers would use the ideas of honor to explain the event, while the prohibitionists and the prosecution denied its applicability to the case. The press coverage of the trial reflected this division as the Virginia newspapers, unlike the prohibitionist paper, invoked chivalric images.

Clark was represented by five of the best lawyers in Danville. His counsel included the partners from the firms of Harris & Peatross and Berkeley & Harrison. A former city attorney, R. W. Peatross was, according to the *Register,* "too well known to require an introduction," and his legal skills were considered "second to none in this part of the state." Peatross's partner, W. T. Harris, was an "earnest pleader." The firm of Landon C. Berkeley (who had been Moffett's friend) and James P. Harrison specialized in business law and was well connected to the local Democratic Party. Rounding out the defense team was John D. Blackwell, a former judge of the hustings court. It is unlikely that Clark, who was not wealthy, paid for his representation. Perhaps the Danville Democrats paid for Clark's counsel, for Clark had been a loyal Democrat, and Moffett had threatened the voting system. Such an action would have been consistent with the Danville Democratic Party's record toward violence; after the 1883 riot the party justified the violence as the means necessary to restore white rule. As Kenneth C. Barnes has shown in his study of an 1888 killing in Arkansas, "Democratic elites used violence to end any aspirations to power by poor white and black farmers" and to seize political power. Apparently the Danville Democrats were also willing to countenance violence in maintaining their power.[42]

Clark's array of legal talent surely dismayed Moffett's family, his church, and the national prohibitionists, and they took steps to strengthen the prosecution. They probably feared that the inexperienced county attorney, N. H. Massie, was not up to the task of convicting Clark. Although Massie had practiced law since 1885, he had been in office for less than a year. The case of J. T. Clark would be his first big criminal trial. Moreover, he was a good machine Democrat; in the next congressional election, Massie would be accused of trying to scare black voters away from the polls. So W. W. Moffett and J. H. Hill contacted a friend of the Moffett family, Colonel William R. Aylett. A lawyer before the Civil War, Aylett worked as a newspaper writer until the lifting of restrictions on former Confederates allowed him to return to the law. He served as commonwealth's attorney in King William County and soon became one of the state's leading advocates. His addition also balanced the political scales between defense and prosecution, for Aylett was being promoted as a candidate for lieutenant governor on the Democratic ticket. Aylett and Massie were assisted by Moffett's brother. Indeed, the prosecution soon had more help than it wanted.[43]

The prosecution found it had to stave off the assistance of the out-of-state prohibitionists. Temperance advocates in Ohio hired Olin J. Ross (a Hillsboro, Ohio, lawyer) to assist the prosecution. Massie, Aylett, and W. W. Moffett thought it unwise for Ross to participate. He would bring several problems to the prosecution team. Not only was Ross an outsider and a northerner, but he was a representative of the Prohibition Party. W. W. Moffett, Aylett, and Massie feared that "his appearance would afford the defense an opportunity, greatly desired by them, of introducing politics into the case." Massie wrote Ross telling him not to come. When Ross arrived and was welcomed by Moffett's temperance friends, the lawyers persuaded him not to participate directly in Clark's prosecution. Still this was only a partial victory as Ross stayed in Danville to be an observer for the prohibitionists. The *Richmond Times* reported, "He now says he is here merely to watch the trial and decide for himself if the killing . . . was the result of a conspiracy on the part of whisky men or was merely the result of a personal difficulty between two men."[44]

Ross's staying as an observer underscored one of the features of the specialized press: it could not rely on the commercial press's collective news-gathering. The specialized papers could seldom afford the costs of membership in the AP or other wire services, and by their nature they tended to see the stories that came over the wire as lacking the point of view that characterized their publications. Thus the specialized press needed their own agents on site to cover stories. Ross, who had been sent as lawyer, was probably then converted into a reporter. He may have written or assisted in writing the dispatches about the trial that appeared in the *Voice*. Even as an observer Ross embodied the outside forces that threatened the political order of the community, so keeping Ross from the counsel's table did not keep politics out of the case.[45]

Political feeling was so strong in the community that the court had difficulty in finding a jury in the town. On the first day Judge Aiken summoned 118 veniremen from Danville but impaneled only three men for the jury. As the *Danville Register* put it, although some were surprised that a jury could not be obtained in Danville, "a great many more expressed surprise that even three jurors" could be found "who had not formed or expressed an opinion" on the case. Failing to find men to fill the jury locally, the court sent to Lynchburg for a panel of 24 men from which to complete the jury. Securing additional venireman from out of town took an extra day, and the delay resulted in the loss of two of the three previously accepted Danville men. One of them, J. H. Vernon, claimed to have become sick. Also, local temperance advocates, led by J. H. Hill, were unhappy the selection of Vernon and another juror, H. Hirsh. Hirsh was a brewer and saloonkeeper who had been denounced by Moffett in the *Anti-Liquor*. The drys' objections to his presence on the jury made Hirsh angry; as he put it, "he had learned that a feature had been lugged in[to] this case which made it impossible for him" to render a fair verdict. He successfully requested to be removed. The defense fought to keep every Danville man on the jury. Vernon was visited by a doctor who pronounced him well, and he was dragged into court. But the prosecution trumped this move by showing that he had expressed an opinion favoring Clark, and he was dismissed. The next day, seeking to avoid jurors presumed to be sympathetic to Moffett, the defense struck off three prohibitionists and one Baptist from the Lynchburg panel. The jury finally consisted of one Danville resident and eleven Lynchburg men.[46]

The prosecution presented a classic case of act, motive, and opportunity. Setting the scene, it began by introducing a map of the area of the crime drawn by the city engineer. Lengthy testimony by the doctors followed, pointing out that the bullet which entered Moffett's abdomen "occasioned" his death. After establishing how Moffett died, the prosecution turned to Clark's actions, reviewing his long and acrimonious history with Moffett. It showed through a number of witnesses that Clark saw Moffett at the *Register,* went out, and waited on the street. From the various places that Clark had stopped during his wanderings around Danville that night, the prosecution called a number of witnesses who said that Clark was looking for a copy of the *Anti-Liquor* and that he threatened Moffett. One witness said that Clark asserted that he would get even with Moffett and that both of them "couldn't live in the same town for twenty-four hours longer." At another location, according to a witness, Clark declared he would go to jail before paying his fine from the first fracas, and it would be "a d—d dark day for North Danville when they send me to jail for that fine." Further, he denounced Moffett as a "damned scoundrel" who had tried to "perpetuate a fraud" and warned "the sooner he leaves North Danville the better for him, for I have held my friends back from him about as long as I can." According to another witness, Clark swore that "he held the life of Moffett in the hollow of his hand" and could bring a thousand men from the country to mob him. This was damaging testimony, and the prosecution capped it by having the mayor present Moffett's dying declaration.[47]

Surprisingly, although the prosecution called approximately half a dozen witnesses who rushed to the scene after hearing the gunshots, it neglected to call the two eye witnesses to the fray, Chief of Police Green Williams and Peyton B. Gravely. Perhaps it feared that these two stalwarts of the Democratic organization would be unfavorable witnesses. Williams had come to Danville in 1872 and became chief of police in 1873. He lost this office when the Readjusters gained power; but after the events of 1883, he was elected to the position again as a Democrat. Gravely was a partner in a plug tobacco business and a prominent Democrat. The defense tried to force the Commonwealth to call them, and the prosecution strongly resisted this move. If they were Commonwealth witnesses, the defense would gain an advantage because the prosecution could not contradict their testimony. Judge Aiken denied each side the advantage by announcing that he would place the two men on the stand.[48]

Williams and Gravely testified to essentially the same set of facts. Williams said he and a number of other men were near the *Register* when Clark came up and asked for a copy of the *Anti-Liquor;* Williams directed him to the newspaper's office. Clark went in and came out of the office. Williams waited, fearing trouble because he had learned after directing Clark to the paper's office that Moffett had gone into the *Register.* When Gravely came up, they drifted toward the Masonic Hall. Upon returning toward the *Register,* Williams heard voices ahead in the dark and then saw two men struggling with each other. He ran toward them and before he got there heard a pistol shot, then two or three more. He and Gravely, when they reached the men, tried to separate them, and Clark again fired at Moffett. Moffett fell, and Clark made several attempts to shoot him after he had fallen. Williams grabbed Clark's pistol and arrested both men. Clark at that time said Moffett had shot him and pointed to a wound on his wrist. In reply, Moffett said he had no pistol and asked to be searched. No pistol was found. Gravely interpreted this exchange to favor Clark by saying Clark may have thought Moffett was armed. Gravely added that Clark insisted Moffett had attacked him and he acted to defend himself. After this testimony the defense opened.[49]

While the prosecution had presented a narrowly focused case, Clark's lawyers put forth a very broad effort. They developed five different lines of defense. On the legal front the defense tried to establish self-defense on the part of Clark and offered rebuttal testimony to the prosecution's case. Beyond law, the defense blamed Moffett's death on the doctors, asserted that the code of honor sanctioned the killing, and put temperance politics on trial. Some of the defense's theories conflicted because it seemed intent on presenting to the jury all the reasons that could excuse the killing or mitigate the crime from murder to manslaughter.[50]

In building an argument for self-defense or manslaughter, the defense focused on Clark's perceptions. It sought to establish that the shooting occurred during a scuffle and that Clark was the smaller and weaker of the two men and thus fired his gun out of fear for his life. From the first day of the trial, defense attorneys asked cross-examination questions about Moffett's size and strength. To bolster the idea that Clark feared Moffett because of his short temper, the defense pointed to the street brawl on election day when Moffett had hit both Clark and the constable. When he took the stand, Clark testified that when he saw Moffett at the *Register* office, "I had reason to believe that Mr. Moffett was seeking a difficulty with me," so he went away and remained long enough, he thought, for Moffett to finish his business. When he started to return, he claimed, he was assaulted by a man who seized him, drew a pistol and shot, striking him in the wrist. He fired at his attacker after that. Further, the defense established that Clark habitually carried a gun and therefore had not armed himself to take vengeance on Moffett.[51]

To support its arguments for self-defense or manslaughter, the defense tried to refute the version of events put forth by the prosecution. The defense attacked two key prosecution points. First, it called a number of witnesses who also saw Clark on the night of the shooting who contradicted the prosecution witnesses' testimony that Clark had threatened Moffett. Moreover, when Clark took the stand, he denied all but one threat. He explained away that one—the statement that Moffett ought to be driven from town—by saying he thought he was only echoing the views of all the people. Second, the defense attacked the veracity of Moffett's dying declaration. Clark's counsel pointed out that Moffett's statement varied from the testimony of two eyewitnesses—Gravely and Williams—and was therefore unreliable. It also questioned whether Moffett was in his right mind when he gave it. Because peritonitis causes fever, and the doctors had given him painkillers, they asserted that his statement was the product of hallucinations.[52]

In fact, blaming the doctors was a key part of the defense's strategy. As one paper put it, "Much of the day was taken up in the examination of physicians introduced by the defense to show that the operation performed on Moffett . . . was wrong, dangerous, and fatal." One doctor testified that the procedure was malpractice. Indeed, the defense laid the groundwork for this testimony during cross-examinations of the prosecution's physicians. However, even if the doctors' actions brought about Moffett's death, at law the shooting was the event that started the process. Clark was responsible for that and, therefore, the resulting death. Despite the questionable legal status of this line of defense, it was one the jury might accept.[53]

A Virginia jury presumably was also susceptible to the argument that Clark acted out of a call to honor. Thus the defense showed that Moffett had ridiculed Clark in the press, belittled him in person, and attacked him in the street. The defense contended that this treatment prompted Clark to shoot Moffett. In closing arguments Harrison asserted that it was a worse crime than rape for "an editor to stab the character of a fellow-man through his newspaper" and that juries "invariably said by their verdicts that a man was justified for shooting down the editor who had ruthlessly assaulted his character." In other words, the defense kept trying to build a case for socially, not legally, justifiable homicide. Clark's attorneys shrewdly married honor to undercutting Moffett's dying statement by saying that because it varied from testimony of Gravely and Williams, it was likely that Moffett struck first. If he had done so, honor demanded that Clark reply.[54]

Beyond honor, the defense made the case into a struggle between fanatic prohibitionists and good Democrats. Before testimony began, the defense began this tack by questioning potential jurors, asking: "Are you a Baptist? Are you a Prohibitionist?" Those who answered yes to either query were struck off the jury until the defense ran out of challenges. During the examination of witnesses and in closing statements, Clark's lawyers returned to this theme by rebutting (and thereby injecting prohibition politics into the trial) the idea that Moffett's death was the result of a conspiracy. They denounced the theory advanced by both national prohibitionists and Virginia Baptists. The incident, they said, was nothing more than "a personal affair between two men." Peatross in his summation said, "Clark had been slandered, insulted and hunted down, not by the preacher Moffett, but by Moffett the political leader." Drawing a distinction between the sphere of politics and the sphere of religion, Peatross asserted that Christian morality could not shield a preacher from the requirements of honor. "Preachers have a right to go into the political arena if they so elect but when they get there they must stand on the footing of a politician and not claim . . . preacher's rights. In the law the preacher is only a man." He denounced the efforts of church and prohibition papers to make Moffett's "death chargeable to this community." Blackwell tied the prosecution to the prohibitionists, asserting that Aylett had come to Danville "at the call of and representing the Prohibition faction." Similarly, Harrison asserted that the defense was "the weak side, because against the prisoner were arrayed the church and all the prejudices of a political party, a party of one idea; one idea parties were always prejudiced and oppressive."[55]

The closing arguments replayed the strategies of the two sides. Clark's lawyers utilized all five of their lines of defense in closing, while the prosecution focused on only two points. Aylett made a tremendous effort to separate the crime from the prohibition and church press cries of conspiracy. Massie, on the other hand, closed the case by detailing a clear narrative explaining the events, relying on Moffett's dying declaration for his account of how the shooting occurred. He theorized that Clark came to Danville to look for a copy of the *Anti-Liquor*. When he unexpectedly spied Moffett at the *Register*, he suddenly saw how to kill him. Clark left the office and loitered on the street, lurking in shadows, then rushed upon Moffett and shot him. Under the instructions given to the jury, this would be first-degree murder.[56]

Judge Aiken's instructions, delivered both orally and in writing, set out the conditions of first-degree murder, second-degree murder, voluntary manslaughter, and justifiable homicide and applied them to the case. The Commonwealth sought a first-degree murder conviction. Willful, deliberate, and premeditated killing without provocation constituted first-degree murder. Malice, and degree of penalty, distinguished first- and second-degree murder. All killings in the state were presumed to be second-degree murder, and the Commonwealth had to prove premeditation and malice to gain a conviction for first-degree murder. Premeditation, Aiken told the jury, did not necessarily imply a long period, just enough time for reflection. Hence, in Massie's narrative of the killing, the loitering established enough time for premeditation. On the other hand, to reduce a second-degree murder to voluntary manslaughter or involuntary homicide the defense had to prove a provocation that deprived a person of self-control; mere published words or speech would not be sufficient to justify a killing. Moreover, Aiken's instructions clearly pointed out that if Clark "inflicted" a wound "calculated to endanger and destroy life" and Moffett died within a year and day afterward, even if the doctors had aggravated the wound "by unskillful or improper treatment," Clark remained legally responsible. The Virginia press, which had covered all aspects of the trial, reported that the case went to the jury at 3:00 P.M. on February 16, 1893.[57]

As the trial progressed the Virginia daily papers and the weekly Prohibition Party newspaper wrote accounts of it; these reports followed the pattern that had emerged earlier in the coverage of the killing. Both groups' accounts reported the basic facts of the trial, such as the difficulty of impaneling a jury, but their interpretation differed. The prohibition press saw the trial as a struggle between the virtuous, church-going prohibitionists and the unscrupulous "whisky ring." In contrast, the Virginia papers tended to cover the trial not as a political morality play but as a human-interest story and notable local event which revealed the chivalric nature of Virginia society. This difference in coverage was clearly shown in their treatment of Clark and his family.

For the prohibition paper Clark became a caricature of the evil men who made up the whiskey ring. According to the *Voice*, he was "a large man" with "a sly vicious countenance." The paper employed the notion of facial slope as indicative of intellectual and moral inferiority when it wrote that his "forehead falls back on a straight line with his nose at an angle of about 45 degrees." The shape of his head indicated that Clark was stupid and that his moral sense was underdeveloped. In short, his "countenance clearly indicates him as a suitable tool of the whisky men." The *Voice* concluded its description of his character by saying that in his community "his reputation is exceedingly bad and he is one of the last men around whom friends would ordinarily gather in time of trouble." In the dry account Clark had no family, and his supporters were not friends but hirelings of the whiskey ring.[58]

Because most Virginia papers apparently composed their stories on the trial from the stories in the *Danville Daily Register,* and because it saw no need to describe Clark, who was well known in Danville, there was no Virginia paper that physically described Clark. But in their treatment of the trial, the Virginia papers stressed Clark's humanity by showing both the devotion of his family and Clark's emotional responses to events in the courtroom, stock-in-trade techniques of the human-interest story. They mentioned that his sister, his uncle, and his wife all sat with him during the trial. The papers left a good impression of the family. Mrs. Clark was described by one as "a handsome little woman" and by another as "a woman of refinement and handsome appearance." Beyond description, the press detailed how Clark reacted to his family's presence. At least three Virginia papers told of his six-year-old daughter's first visit to the court. When she climbed on to his lap, Clark, according to one account, kissed her "tenderly and wept as if his heart would break." In another account "Clark broke down and sobbed like a woman," while in yet another version Clark "wept bitterly." Although the coverage of the trial in the Virginia papers did not descend to the level of the later overwrought sob-sister style, it was clearly aimed at showing the human drama of the trial.[59]

In general, the Virginia papers presented the trial as a public event that reflected Virginian society, especially ideas of honor. The papers noted that the trial's sessions usually were "thronged" with a "dense crowd," and that on the day closing arguments began the room "was packed to suffocation." The press portrayed this interest not as morbid fascination with the spectacle of crime but as part of the fabric of daily life. The papers noted the attendance of women at the trial and the public's willingness to eat in the courtroom to avoid losing their seats or missing some development. According to one account, the people came "prepared to make a day of it, bringing picnic baskets," whose contents "they demolished during" pauses in the trial. Beyond providing what could be called local color, the Virginia press often, as was the tendency in Virginian society, presented events as embodying chivalric significance. For instance, a dogfight that broke out during closing speeches was characterized as an affair "between a blooded canine owned by Judge Aiken and foreign cur, which had invaded the halls of justice."[60]

Ideas of honor and the human-interest aspect of the trial emerged clearly in the Virginia press's reporting of an incident during Aylett's closing arguments for the prosecution. About fifteen minutes into his speech, "several ladies," relations of counsel, "were escorted through the crowd" to seats set aside for them by the clerk's desk. Aylett "stopped to pay a handsome tribute to" womanhood, saying that "he was glad to see them here. They came like a band of angels to grace the halls of stern justice." Aylett could see these women coming down the left aisle of the court room, but he did not see that Clark's wife and sister had entered the room and were making their way down the right side of the court. Mrs. Clark reached her husband and embraced him just as Aylett concluded his remarks with the phrase "stern justice." The papers noted that "this created quite a sensation and many spectators drew their handkerchiefs to wipe away a tear."[61]

The jury apparently did not share in this emotional and chivalric view of the trial. It deliberated in two sessions stretched over two days and arrived at a compromise verdict. According to the *Roanoke Times,* on their first informal ballot some voted for acquittal and some for murder in the first degree. But these votes were considered "feelers," and on the first formal ballot, five jurymen voted for second-degree murder and a short prison term, and seven for manslaughter. When they returned to the court, the jury found Clark guilty of manslaughter and committed him to prison for five years.[62]

The jury's decision avoided the stark dramas of conviction for murder or acquittal. By not convicting Clark of murder, the jury dismissed much of the prosecution's case. Stripped to its essentials, the prosecution alleged that a political worker shot and killed a prominent minister. The prosecution developed evidence of bad blood and of loitering with intent. It also introduced the victim's statement that he was unarmed, and from witnesses called by the judge, it showed the jury that the killer had shot at a victim already on the ground. The jury apparently did not put much stock in Moffett's dying declaration. Perhaps Moffett's controversial public career as a political prohibitionist, with all that it implied for white Democratic hegemony, undercut his credibility with the jury, even one composed mostly of men from a different city, and to that extent one of the defense's strategies may have worked.

On the other hand, by not acquitting Clark, the jury discounted much of the defense's contradictory evidence and alternative theories of the killing. By convicting Clark of manslaughter, it discounted his claim that he acted in self-defense. The jury apparently ignored the defense's contention that the doctors' malpractice caused the death. It may be that the judge's clear instructions on the issue or that the trial testimony overwhelmingly showed that Clark shot Moffett precluded the jury from basing a verdict on this point. Most significantly, given how often it usually carried the day in Virginia courts, the jury failed to see Moffett's killing by Clark as an affair of honor beyond the realm of law.

There were structural weaknesses to the defense's appeal to honor. The multiplicity of strategies (which forced Clark into playing the fool on the witness stand) weakened the claim of honor and ultimately may have given the jury too many options. One part of the defense was to ascribe the shooting to self-defense. To support this line of defense, Clark said on direct examination that he shot "to defend my life. I thought it was in imminent danger." The prosecution then used this testimony to weaken the honor defense. Building on this statement, the prosecution, in cross-examination, tried to elicit Clark's admission that he was afraid, something no honorable man should admit. Massie, when questioning Clark about firing the gun, asked, "Were you excited, or frightened?" Clark parried the question, replying that there was no difference between the two states and "it all has about the same effect upon me." Following up, Massie asked, "You were very much frightened then?" Clark replied, "I mean that I was very much excited." After several more similar exchanges, Harris interrupted the cross-examination to say to Clark, "You ain't much of a lexicographer?" His counsel's attempt to rescue him underlined Clark's evasive replies and thus weakened the lawyers' claim that he was an honorable man. In addition, multiple defense strategies may have given the jury too many choices. If the defense had left it at honor or conviction of first-degree murder, the jury might have selected honor.[63]

As his evasiveness showed, Clark himself proved to be a serious impediment to the development of the idea that the killing could be excused because of honor. In several ways he emerged on the witness stand as a man who may not have deserved honor. If the jury clung to prewar notions that social status was important in vesting honor, Clark weakened his claim to honor by revealing that he was a marginal man. He admitted to having kept a store before becoming a "practicing attorney." And though a lawyer for two years or three years, he had no office but made a drugstore his "headquarters." Moreover, it emerged in the trial that Clark did not own a home in the city but boarded with his sister; and apparently he could not afford new clothes for his trial, for his hat and suit were the same as those he wore on the night of the shooting. His elocution may have reinforced the image of him as a poor man. Clark misspoke when testifying, calling one landmark in town the "Persian Dye Works" instead of the "Paresian Dye Works." Significantly, W. W. Moffett later claimed that all the older Lynchburg jurors, who were more likely to adhere to the older forms of honor, were initially disposed to convict Clark of murder. In the postwar era social standing did not determine honor, but even on the more democratic field of the period, Clark did not emerge as a good candidate for honor.[64]

Clark revealed patterns of behavior on the witness stand that undercut his lawyers' claim that he was acting out of honor. He did not speak forthrightly as an honorable man should but played verbal games in an attempt to deflect questions. For instance, when presented with a discrepancy between his comments at his bail hearing that Moffett had tried to shoot him and at the trial that he thought Moffett had tried to shoot him, Clark hedged his replies with qualifiers including "I think," "I may be wrong about that," and "I may be mistaken about it." Also, when Massie questioned him about what advice he received concerning the fine for fighting with Moffett, Clark successfully derailed the inquiry by saying that Massie himself had advised him to "get a stick and give" Moffett "a good caning" to "learn him sense." Similarly, Clark denied that the gun admitted into evidence was his gun and said that he could remember firing only one shot, even though investigation on the scene showed that four shots had been fired from the five-shot revolver Williams took from his hand. He also showed that he was not the patriarch of his family. On cross-examination he admitted that his "wife objects to town life, and I haven't been able to persuade her to come to town yet." His failure as a patriarch may have caused the jury to doubt that he had the proper character to claim honor.[65]

Beyond these obstacles to the jury's acceptance of the honor defense loomed larger ones. First, Clark never explicitly claimed to have taken vengeance against Moffett for his insults. Although his lawyers asserted that he acted as an honorable man, Clark did not. Indeed, in his testimony he said that he sought to avoid a "difficulty" with Moffett on the night of the shooting. He also said that he shot Moffett in defense of his life. In short, nothing Clark said advanced a claim of honor. Second, the jury would have had to be willing to overlook an act that was not usually considered honorable. Gravely and Williams testified that Clark attempted to shoot Moffett after he had fallen. To strike a man when he could not defend himself, was the act of a coward, not the act of an honorable man. Juries had been proved willing to go that far in the past (as in the case of James Grant), but they had to be given good reason to overlook a cowardly act. Clark gave them little reason to do so.[66]

The evidence of Gravely and Williams may have weighed most heavily with the jury. Certainly the jury's verdict fit their testimony. Their evidence weakened Clark's self-defense claim: because others had arrived and Moffett was down, Clark had little reason to fear for his life. Indeed, Clark's shooting looked like malice. However, Williams and Gravely weakened the prosecution's case when they implied that Moffett and Clark exchanged words before the fight and that Moffett was struggling with Clark before the first shot was fired. These facts contradicted Moffett's dying declaration, one of the strongest aspects of the prosecution's case. Apparently Believing Gravely and Williams, the jury picked a middle course between the case presented by the prosecution and that of the defense.

The jury's verdict of manslaughter further polarized views of the case. The Moffett family, the Baptists, and the prohibitionists were outraged by the decision. W. W. Moffett was so angry that he apparently paid to have the whole transcript printed to show that the jury had misjudged the case. The Baptists expressed "our disappointment and dissatisfaction with the verdict found and the penalty fixed by the jury," as Clark "waylaid, assaulted and shot" Moffett "in the dark of the night and with malice aforethought." They thought it "much more easy to believe that the two witnesses, for the sake of whose testimony all other testimony seems to have been liberally brushed aside and count for nothing, were mistaken than to believe that" Moffett's deathbed statement was untrue. The verdict was, in short, a "grave and serious miscarriage of justice." Similarly, the prohibitionists called the verdict "virtually an acquittal for the murderer." They feared it would be easy "for the whisky ring" to secure Clark's pardon. Apparently with no evidence the *Voice* asserted that "already some Democratic politicians have boasted that they will have the murderer out in time to take part in the next election."[67]

The verdict gave the Virginia press, on the other hand, another chance to humanize Clark and to promote the Democratic version of the killing as a personal affair. One Richmond paper described Clark rising to hear the verdict, mentioning his "powerful effort to control" his "great nervousness." After the verdict Clark "sat down and looked steadily on to vacancy. It was plain that he was making a desperate effort not to show by his face the emotion that was moving his breast." His expression and demeanor returned to normal after a whispered conversation with his uncle. Another Richmond newspaper, in reporting the verdict, dismissed the claims of conspiracy and focused on Moffett's character as the source for his death. Although admitting "that he was as brave as any man who ever espoused a cause," the paper saw him as an extremist in his "misguided" prohibition views and so "intolerant" that he made for himself personal "enemies." No matter what the disagreements over the meaning of the verdict, the jury's decision turned out to be final. The processes of the law continued as Clark's attorneys worked for an appeal; it failed, and Clark apparently served his sentence.[68]

The disparity between Democratic and prohibitionist accounts underscores the division caused by the liquor issue in the South. In the late nineteenth century, the nature of southern politics retarded the development of prohibition. When the Democrats were engaged in their struggle to win control of states, the prohibition issue threatened to sidetrack their efforts. After the Democrats' victory and prior to disfranchisement of blacks, prohibition threatened white solidarity. As Howard N. Rabinowitz showed in his study of southern capitals, "Prohibition divided communities and parties nearly down the middle and thus encouraged pursuit of the black vote." The local-option campaigns "several years before the Populist-Bourbon split, commonly cited as the reason for Negro disfranchisement," according to Rabinowitz, "convinced whites of the need to eliminate black suffrage." After the removal of blacks from politics, the prohibition issue lost much of its divisiveness and could be voted on without threatening the political order.[69]

The state of Virginia shows a similar pattern. Prohibition, even local-option prohibition, made little headway in the state before black disfranchisement. Moffett worked when the color line was not fully drawn and division over the liquor issue threatened the white political order. Blacks had not been disfranchised fully, and a unified white vote was required for the Democratic Party to maintain power. Moffett, in his zeal for temperance, attacked the electoral system used to enforce white conformity. His activism led directly to the disputes that prompted his death, a fact which the partisan press of Virginia steadfastly ignored.[70]

A decade after Moffet's death, the political terrain changed. In the face of constant calls for cleaning up elections and with Populism threatening to seduce away part of the white vote, Virginia Democrats passed a new election law, the Walton Act of 1894. This act was a secret-ballot law, "probably written by the head of the Democratic organization Senator Thomas S. Martin" and characterized by "another Democratic leader, Richard E. Byrd," as "the Democratic salvation." The effect of the law is shown most clearly by the change in the percentage of black adult males who cast ballots in gubernatorial elections before and after the act. In 1893, 35 percent of adult black males did not vote; in 1897 the figure rose to 78 percent. Moreover, according to J. Morgan Kousser, most of the black votes recorded for the 1897 Democratic candidate "probably existed only in the minds of election officials. The Walton Law ended most actual black voting in Virginia." In 1902 the Democratic Party completed the process of disfranchising much of the black population through the adoption of a new constitution with various restrictions on suffrage.[71]

As shown by the subsequent history of Danville, once the new constitution went into effect, the transformation of the political landscape was completed. White Virginians could now debate prohibition without the specter of black voting. For a decade after Moffett's death but before the constitutional disfranchisement, the prohibitionists—despite repeated efforts—were unable to move Danville into the dry ranks. Immediately after the new constitution took effect, in 1903, and again in 1907, the city voted dry.[72]

A clear indication of the changed political climate can be seen in the strange echo to the debate on the meaning of Moffett's death that swirled around at the time of the killing and Clark's trial. In April 1903, after a local-option campaign in Danville in which there had been "several references" to the Moffett "affair," the *Richmond Times-Dispatch* published a letter by local-optionist John Moncure Jr. asserting that John Moffett had died as a martyr for his cause. Moncure's views clearly had been shaped by the prohibitionist press; in 1900 the Anti-Saloon League's national newspaper had included Moffett's case in the column of "liquor murders." He even repeated the assertions that Moffett had been shot by a barkeeper. In its accompanying commentary the paper denied the claim that Clark was a saloonkeeper, pointing out that that he was a lawyer. Furthermore, Moffett had not died for his cause; the commentary declared "in the interest of truth it must be further said that Mr. Moffett was not killed because he was a prohibitionist" but because of personal difficulties between him and Clark. "The two men had a difficulty at the polls, but there would in all probability have been no further trouble if Mr. Moffett had let the affair rest there." But instead "he denounced this man in unstinted terms and subsequently there was another personal encounter between him and the lawyer in which Mr. Moffett was shot to death." Moffett died, "not through his advocacy of prohibition, but because he deliberately and fearlessly and we might almost say recklessly denounced in print a man whom he knew to be his enemy." The *Times-Dispatch* thus reprised the party line of the Democratic papers from a decade earlier.[73]

The assertion that Moffett did not die for his convictions prompted W. W. Moffett to write several letters calling for a retraction from Joseph Bryan, publisher of the *Times-Dispatch,* and William Copeland, editor of the *Times-Dispatch,* who had been editor of the Danville paper when Moffett died. Moffett's letters—all couched in the terms of superpoliteness that characterized honorable communications—claimed his brother was an honorable man, that Clark was not honorable, and that the killing was a direct result of John Moffett's political agitation. On the topic of honor, he defended his brother's editorial attack on Clark as the response of honorable man, asking: "Mr. Copeland, how could any true, brave, honest man let the matter rest after the difficulty at the polls? . . . Put any other good man loving honor more than life in his place." He portrayed Clark as a contemptible ex-barkeeper, returning to the original assertions of the *Voice.* Moffett averred that Clark's "reputation was most unsavory," so much so that "there was not a gentleman . . . who would have received him socially in his parlor" and no lawyer would move his admission to the bar. Most importantly, Moffett wrote that his brother "was regarded as the embodiment of the prohibition movement" and his work was construed as an attack on the Democratic Party by men like Clark. His death thus stemmed directly from his principles.[74]

These letters caused the paper to print another editorial, entitled "Justice to the Dead," which aimed "to clear up possible doubts" concerning the meaning of Moffett's death. This editorial asserted that Moffett did not seek personal difficulties with Clark but only acted as any honorable man would. It praised Moffett's adherence to his cause and judged his article written in *Anti-Liquor,* which "incidentally" denounced Clark, as Moffett's defense of himself from the charge of ballot fraud, one which persuaded "all fair minded men" of his innocence of the charge. It also called Clark "a lawyer of no enviable reputation" and indicated that he lied when he testified that Moffett began the fight that culminated in the shooting. Although not retracting its earlier statement, the paper modified it, concluding, "We do not believe that Mr. Moffett was killed simply because he was a prohibitionist." Even so, the paper had come a long way in admitting that Moffett's death did have political dimensions. The switch of emphasis is important, for as Linda Gordon has noted in another context, "every town has its unique stories, personalities, and local politics" that are significant because "it is through these local particularities that social systems get constructed." When the story changed, it reflected the changed political circumstances in the state. The *Times-Dispatch* could now afford to make such admissions. The 1902 constitution entrenched the political power of the Democratic

Party, enabling it to build a statewide machine which exercised political hegemony. Thus the issue of prohibition and ministers like Moffett no longer threatened the political order or prompted the specialized press to examine Virginia
justice.[75]

Just four years after these *Times-Dispatch* editorials on the meaning of Moffett's
death, the killing of another Virginian captured the attention of journalists from
out of the state. This later killing and subsequent trial differed from the earlier
Pollard and Moffett affairs in that the crime sprang from private, not public, actions. But this crime and trial revealed that the ideas about honor which had
been so important to the earlier cases had begun to lose their grip on Virginia
society during the opening decade of the new century. As in the earlier trials,
there would be differences in how the national and the Virginia press treated the
case, and outsider attention of Virginia's legal system would provoke the Virginia
press to explain the workings of the Commonwealth's justice system and society.

Three

"GIRL WHOSE STORY CAUSED FATHER TO KILL"

ON APRIL 22, 1907, in Nelson County, former judge W. G. Loving killed the son of the county's sheriff. Judge Loving shot Theodore Estes because he had taken Loving's daughter, Elizabeth, for a buggy ride from which she returned incapacitated. The next day Loving shot and killed Estes inside a freight car as Estes supervised the unloading of a supply of fertilizer. The homicide, which took place fifteen years after the Moffett killing and almost forty years after the Pollard affair, generated statewide and national press interest. Focusing on the lurid cause of the killing, the Virginia and national press portrayed the killing as an example of the so-called unwritten law in action. While ostensibly mounting an insanity defense, Loving's lawyers also portrayed his action as an unwritten-law killing. Both the defense and the prosecution conducted press campaigns about the unwritten-law aspects of the case. Similarly, because the killing took place among Virginia's governing elite, politics wove itself into the state's newspaper coverage. Also, as in the earlier cases, the trial was marked by entry of outsiders into a Virginia courtroom. Loving shot Estes near the estate of one of the nation's richest men, Thomas Fortune Ryan, for whom Loving served as estate manager. The Ryan connection and the lurid details of the case lured reporters from Pulitzer and Hearst newspapers to Virginia.[1]

In 1907 the sensational dailies were in full flower, the partisan papers were continuing to decline, and the independents were shifting their emphasis. The slow death of partisan journalism left the independent papers without a defining foe, prompting them to elevate objective reporting to a near fetish. Drawing upon their antipolitical heritage, the independents also experimented with muckraking against urban evils to boost circulation. The sensational dailies, called the yellow press, searched assiduously for stories with lurid details, sending reporters to obscure corners of the nation to cover them. The resulting coverage was filled with details designed to reach the emotions of readers and illustrated with photographs and drawings. The style was so successful that almost all parts of the news industry were touched by it. Even socialist and Yiddish-language newspapers adopted it. The publishers and editors of the yellow press encouraged a special version of sensationalism in trial coverage, denounced by critics as "sob-sister journalism." Written by both men and women reporters, it was aimed at women readers, telling stories in a heavily sentimental style which invited them to empathize with the person the reporter chose to romanticize. Sob-sister journalism, like the yellow press in general, had enormous appeal.[2]

By the first decade of the twentieth century, the newspapers of the South embraced the idea of "the New South" and began drifting away from political partisanship. Under the leadership of dynamic editors like Henry Watterson of the Louisville *Courier-Journal* and Henry Grady of the *Atlanta Constitution,* some papers remade the southern image into the New South, an image that romanticized the Old South while seeking to replace it with a South devoted to commerce and progress. These New South editors pushed to make their papers resemble the nation's leading urban dailies; they consciously adopted and promoted independence from party as an ideal for their papers even while remaining Democratic papers. They tended to separate firmly their editorial pages' party advocacy from the regular pages' news reporting. Also, leading southern newspapers subscribed to the wire services and from them imbibed some of the independence and sensationalism of early twentieth-century journalism. In addition, during the first decade of the new century, the sensational chains, like the Hearst interests, purchased southern papers, imbuing them with their sensationalist style. Established southern papers followed their lead. For example, the *Richmond News Leader* in tone and coverage looked remarkably like the sensational papers of any northern city.[3]

The convergence between northern and southern papers reflected the cultural forces at work in the era of reconciliation that was strongest in the two

Judge William Loving and his daughter, Elizabeth Loving, from the *New York World*, June 30, 1907. (Courtesy of the Judge Aubrey E. Strode Papers, the Albert and Shirley Small Special Collections Library, University of Virginia Library)

JUDGE LOVING COMFORTING HIS DAUGHTER WHILE TRIAL WAS GOIN

EX-JUDGE LOVING'S VICTIM

THEODORE I. ESTES
Whose drive with Miss Loving led to his death.

Theodore Estes, from the *Baltimore Sun*, June 27, 1907. (Courtesy of the Judge Aubrey E. Strode Papers, the Albert and Shirley Small Special Collections Library, University of Virginia Library) decades surrounding the turn of the century. The treatment of the pre-Civil War South became one important area of convergence between the press of the nation and the South. Journalists and others across the nation romanticized the Old South. Among the many representations of the Old South perpetuated in this period was that of honor. As journalists and others looked back at the Old South, they no longer presented honor and dueling as evidence of the deficiencies of a barbaric civilization rejecting progress (as they had been portrayed by some northern papers in 1868) but rather as a part of the nature of simpler days. Their construction necessarily presumed that honor was no longer so prevalent in the modern South, which was true because the rise of urbanism, commercialism, and changes in law had worked to weaken the system. Typical of this new treatment of honor was the work of Richmond journalist Evan Chesterman, a reporter for various Virginia papers who specialized in crime and trial stories. When there were no current crimes to cover, Chesterman wrote articles on antebellum affairs of honor for the *Richmond Evening Journal.* His thinly researched pieces always had a romantic, if not elegiac, cast; his work celebrated the world of honor while admitting that its time had passed.[4]

Because honor had declined even as it became part of the myth of the Old South, it did not emerge as the chief social construct in the coverage of the Loving case. Rather, the related idea of the unwritten law—which had a currency far outside the South—replaced honor as the main trope in the press coverage of the case. The unwritten law was, in the words of historian Robert M. Ireland, the recognition by "American juries" that "an outraged husband, father, or brother could justifiably kill the alleged libertine who had been sexually intimate with the defendant's wife, daughter, or sisters." Although rooted in the society's view of the proper roles of the sexes and popularized when marriage law was being liberalized, the custom derived from the "complex of self-defense rights" that existed in law to protect the home (which allowed a man to kill a burglar) and from the law of provocation in homicide. As historian Hendrick Hartog points out, a husband who "found his wife in the arms of another man" and "killed the other man on the spot" would "never be convicted of murder." The sight of the adultery was presumed to be sufficient provocation to excuse the killing. From this narrow legal definition, the idea of the unwritten law—as a jury appeal, not a matter of law—was extended to include other men beyond the husband and situations other than the unlikely catching of the "wife and her lover together, in a seriously and unquestionably compromising position."[5]

It is important to note that the unwritten law was not honor but rather a closely related idea with similarities and differences. There were two important differences between the concepts. First, honor was comprehensive, while the unwritten law was limited only to cases of violation of close female relatives. Second, honor was claimed by the individual and conferred by the community; to hold honor a man needed to follow its precepts and have a reputation for morality, bravery, and honesty. But any man who faced this certain situation, regardless of reputation, could invoke the unwritten law. Nevertheless, honor and the unwritten law also had similarities. Each extended a social sanction to violence, and each exalted the ideal of womanly purity and virtue. And the worthiness of each was established in public debates, usually in the press. Thus the unwritten law, like honor, when linked with a crime had the necessary ingredients to be news.

This unwritten-law killing in an out-of-the-way Virginia community brought reporters from outside the state to Virginia to cover the trial in detail. Yet this outsider scrutiny did not result in the articulation of deep resentment by Virginians over what they would characterize as misrepresentation of their society and justice system. In part this occurred because the outside press, reflecting the national mood of reconciliation and reunion, did not criticize Virginia society. Also, in part, the lack of resentment of the role of outsiders stems from the nature of the state's press coverage and the trial itself. From the beginning the Virginia press tended to sensationalize and romanticize the story. Thus the national chains' typical exaggerations and distortions were consistent with what many Virginians were reading in their own newspapers. Similarly, while the press reportage focused especially on the issue of the unwritten law, this idea was not unique to the South. Indeed, earlier in the year the unwritten law had been the center of one of the most famous trials in American history, the first Harry Thaw trial. As a result, the critics of the outcome in the Nelson County trial were not seen as outsiders attacking Virginia justice and society but as critics of all of American society and justice. Indeed, the strongest critiques of the application of the unwritten law to the facts of this case came from within Virginia. This fact underscored the sectional convergence of the early twentieth century.

The facts of the Loving trial also included the insanity defense. By the early twentieth century, this defense was an established part of American jurisprudence but in practice was used mostly as a defense of last resort. The insanity defense is a species of the broad category of diminished criminal capacity. Central to the idea of Anglo-American criminal law is the idea that a defendant, to be culpable, must have a *mens rea,* a guilty mind. If the defendant is somehow diminished in capacity, through idiocy or mental illness, then that defendant cannot have a *mens rea*—cannot have the capability to know what they did was wrong—and cannot be guilty of crime. For a defendant there were many reasons why an insanity defense was risky. American courts and legislatures had borrowed or formulated a number of restrictive doctrines, setting very difficult standards for defendants to meet. Moreover, there was much popular sentiment against the plea, and juries had to be persuaded that the defendant was insane. And winning a case on the insanity plea meant the defendant, at the least, would be labeled insane. On the other hand, there were good reasons for a defendant to use such a defense. The insanity defense allowed defense lawyers to escape the confining rules of evidence and to bring up materials that had a direct relation to the criminal act or to bring in social questions that might sway the jury. Also, it gave juries a pretext not to convict if they were so inclined, allowing other considerations—like a sympathetic defendant or circumstances that marked socially accepted crime—to enter into their deliberations through a legal side door.[6]

This is the course that Harry Thaw's lawyers followed in his trials for the murder of Stanford White. Thaw shot White during the performance of a musical review held on the roof of Madison Square Garden in New York. Thaw claimed at the time that he did it for his wife, Evelyn Nesbit, a famous beauty. Thaw's lawyers presented an insanity defense, arguing that the knowledge that White, five years before, had debauched Evelyn Nesbit drove Thaw insane. This defense enabled Thaw's lawyers to appeal to (while extending it almost unbelievably) the unwritten law. The trial turned on Nesbit's tearful testimony, detailing what she had told Thaw about her sexual encounters with White. Legally this testimony was aimed at showing the effect of her story on his mind, but socially it was pointed at painting White as a libertine who deserved the sanction of the unwritten law. The first trial ended in a hung jury, and the second resulted in Thaw's acquittal on the grounds of insanity. William Loving's legal defense and the course of his trial paralleled the Thaw cases.[7]

The killing of Estes took place at the village of Shipman in Nelson County, near the county seat of Lovingston. Shipman, which previously had been known as Oak Ridge, was "an unpicturesque hamlet which nestles garishly and self-assertively" along the Southern rail line. Nelson County, at the western edge of the piedmont up against the Blue Ridge Mountains, is a rural county of rolling hills and some mountains. The last decade of the nineteenth century had seen the emergence of apples as its key money crop. Most of the county's people lived on small farms, but a number of rich people resided on large estates there. The county had few towns and little industry, typical of much of the rural upland South. Like most of Virginia, it was connected to the rest of the nation by railroads, telegraph lines, and phone wires. Thus a homicide story in the state's newspapers quickly became national news. In telling the tale, these newspapers focused on the personal, introducing to the nation each of the principals.[8]

William G. Loving emerged from the press accounts as a leading citizen, "one of the most widely known men in the piedmont section." He was born into a prominent Amherst County family in 1858. His father had represented the county in the legislature and had also been a commission merchant in Richmond. Loving followed his father into the legislature and practiced law in Richmond. In 1893 Loving relocated to his wife's home county, Nelson County, immediately to the north of Amherst County. Mrs. Loving was daughter of Captain John L. Snead, a prominent farmer. In 1898 Loving was appointed judge of the county court, and he formed a local law partnership with Judge J. Thompson Brown. Loving's family became part of the governing establishment of the county. He was brother-in-law to both Bland Massie, in 1907 a former state senator, and E. L. Kidd, clerk of the Nelson court. The Kidds in turn were connected by marriage to the Estes family. In 1903 Loving gained a small name in state politics by being one of the impeachment prosecutors of Judge Clarence J. Campbell. In 1904, through a reorganization of judicial offices, Loving lost his judgeship; he then took up the duties of managing Thomas Fortune Ryan's estate at Oak Ridge. Although his personal demeanor would be subject to some dispute, there was little doubt that he was the kind of man who would settle issues through violence. According to the Richmond journalist Evan Chesterman, Loving's brother John (a clerk for the state legislature) was "noted for his gentle, considerate manners, and his extreme conservatism," but William was "the very antipodes of his brother," being "full of fire and dash."[9]

While William Loving was a relative newcomer to the Nelson County elite, Theodore Estes had inherited his status as a member of the county's establishment, for he was the son of the sheriff of Nelson County, Morris K. Estes, who had held this office for over two decades, which testified to his "wide popularity" in the county. Theodore at age twenty-six was "associated in the merchandise business with his aged father." Theodore had more political connections, too. His uncle (and William Loving's brother-in-law), E. L. Kidd, was clerk of the court, and his sister had married John P. Swanson, a merchant and lawyer who was the brother of a prominent politician, Claude Swanson. In 1906 building on his seven terms as a United States congressman, Claude Swanson had become the state's governor. Physically, Theodore Estes was slight, of below-average height and weighing less than 130 pounds. He was characterized as a young man who was "industrious, intelligent, and steady in his habits." One Nelson County resident said that he was "the most innocent boy I ever knew."[10]

Innocence, of course, was prescribed for all young women, so the state press was circumspect in its treatment of twenty-year-old Elizabeth "Lizzie" Loving. Descriptions of her read like snippets from the social pages. Elizabeth was "a graduate of Miss Stuart's school in Staunton, and is universally popular." She was "a beautiful woman of the blond type, and weighs about 145 pounds." "An expert horsewoman," she "has ridden her favorite mount at the Lynchburg fair." Another account quoted Nelson County citizens describing "her ladylike manners and decorous conduct." As a young woman of the upper crust in a rural county, Elizabeth Loving's social schedule included overnight visits with friends and relations. Her stay with Annie Kidd, daughter of E. L. Kidd and cousin of both Theodore and Elizabeth, led to the fatal shooting.[11]

William Loving described what he did this way. "I loaded my shot gun" and took a buggy about four miles "to Lovingston and inquired for" Estes by sending a message into the store. He was told that Estes was at Oak Ridge, unloading fertilizer from a railroad car. Loving drove back to Oak Ridge and "asked Mr. McGinnis if he was there, and he said he was around there somewhere, I left my buggy . . . took my gun and walked down to the car." When he found Estes, Loving recounted that he "said young man I understand you were buggy riding with the young ladies yesterday evening, he mumbled something and turned to run as he did so I shot him and killed him."[12]

Other than the claim that Estes mumbled something and turned to run, the judge's description of the events matched the statements of witnesses. Store-keeper and hotel owner Thomas M. McGinnis confirmed that Loving asked after Estes and that he told him Estes was at the depot. Nick Reid, one of the two black eyewitnesses to the shooting, reported that Loving came to the doorway of the boxcar, "holding the shotgun partially under his coat." Further, he said that Loving waved aside Reid (and his fellow worker, Fayette Foster) and said to Estes, who was "standing in the rear of the car between high sacks of fertilizer: 'So you were out buggy riding with the ladies last night, were you?'" Estes cried, "No, no, my God, no" when Loving drew his gun, "took sight," and fired both barrels. Struck in the side and neck, Estes fell. His "mutilated corpse" lay in the boxcar until his family arranged for it to be removed for preparation for burial.[13]

In the meantime, bystanders — and Judge Loving himself — arranged for the law to be put in motion. Reid summoned McGinnis (who "thinking that nothing was wrong, unless the Negro had been shot, took his time walking to the car"), and McGinnis called to Dr. William M. Tunstall for help. The call for the doctor prompted Loving to say that such aid was useless as he "shot to kill." McGinnis said later that Loving "was as cool as if he had shot a rabbit." Loving then asked McGinnis to accompany him to the nearest magistrate, adding that "I do not like to pass the boy's house, because while I do not care a rap for his death I would not care to see the grief of his relatives." The magistrate, T. B. M. Perkins, informed by phone that Loving was coming, set out for Oak Ridge. When they met on the road, he accepted Loving's surrender and deputized McGinnis to take Loving back to Oak Ridge, where he was kept in McGinnis's hotel under the custody of the local constable, C. A. Wood, pending the investigation of the killing.[14]

That night the coroner's jury met, under Magistrate Perkins's direction, and found that Estes had met his death at the hands of Judge Loving. Constable Wood then arrested Loving, and Perkins held a quick arraignment hearing where Loving apparently made an unsworn statement, which was not made public until the trial. Loving then applied for bail. Complications ensued because the bail commissioner Lewis Brown was a relative and the presiding circuit judge, Bennett T. Gordon, was out of town. Loving telegraphed to Amherst County asking his friend John W. Payne—also a bail commissioner—to come to Nelson to hear his plea. At the same time he retained Lewis Brown and Aubrey E. Strode as counsel. Aubrey Strode was a state senator, an Amherst lawyer, and the son-in-law of William Loving's former law partner. At age thirty-four Strode was a politician on the rise. Like Loving, he had participated in the Campbell impeachment case. He would have a long working relationship with another rising political star, Carter Glass. Also, by employing him Loving improved his chances for bail because Strode, like Commissioner Payne, came from Amherst County.[15]

At the bail hearing on April 23 in McGinnis's hotel, Payne granted Loving bail. At least a dozen men offered to go to bail for the ex-judge, and Payne selected five of them as bondsmen. Apparently a telegraphed offer by his employer, Thomas Fortune Ryan, to post Loving's bail did not reach the principals in time. An "intensely interested" crowd waited outside the hearing site. When "word came out that Judge Loving had been released on bond," the crowd "surged about him," for it contained many acquaintances who wanted to speak with him. Loving quickly left, refusing to make a public statement other than "that he would be ready for trial." He was overheard saying to friends that "he believed that he was right in killing Estes, and that he did not regret the act except for the sake of the boy's parents."[16]

None of these basic facts about the killing and the immediate legal actions afterward were ever in dispute. What was disputed was why William Loving killed Theodore Estes. Many aspects of the chain of events that prompted Loving to empty both barrels of his shotgun into Estes were aired (and contested) in the press within a week after the killing. The first news stories about the killing contained Judge Loving's version of events. In a statement at the bail hearing—and in a conversation with his lawyer Aubrey Strode—Loving claimed that Estes was a sexual predator who had raped Lizzie, motivating him, as her father, to invoke the unwritten law and take Estes's life. Loving's statement to the bail commissioner began oddly for a man who would rely on the insanity defense at trial: "Mr. Commissioner; I am not crazy." Loving quickly backed away from that declaration, by stating, "I will endeavor to make my statement to the best of my present mental condition." He then recounted the events that prompted him to shoot Estes. "On Sunday afternoon my brotherinlaw Mr. Harry Snead took my daughter to Lovingston where she was to spend the night with Mrs. Kidd." On Monday, Snead "told me that about 7:30" that night a "man took my daughter for a drive and when about [a] mile of out town he gave her something to drink after which she lost consciousness, he brought her back about 9 o'clock in an unconscious condition, dishonored, destroyed. It was about two hours after her return before she regained consciousness." Loving portrayed his actions as deliberate: "I did not want to have any trouble, did not want to do anything rash. I sent for my daughter to come home." But she pleaded ill health, so Loving sent his wife to bring her home. "As soon as my daughter reached home, I immediately interviewed her, and when I had the awful story from her dear sweet lips, no power . . . could have prevented my taking that mans life." Loving then told how he hunted Estes and killed him.[17]

Loving told Strode the same story in greater detail, and Strode wrote Ryan an account, capturing much of how Judge Loving related the circumstances of the killing. Strode explained that Harry Snead "was sent for by Mrs. Kidd to consult about the condition of Miss Loving." She "had just returned from a drive with young Estes in a semi-conscious condition." A physician was summoned, who informed Snead "that Miss Loving was suffering from intoxicants and perhaps drugs and possibly other mistreatment." Snead told Judge Loving "what he had seen and heard." Strode also summarized Elizabeth's account to her father.

She had said that "so far as she knew," Estes had taken her driving between six o'clock and sundown and "about a mile from Lovingston . . . produced a small flask ostensibly containing whisky and against her protests finally succeeded in getting her to take some of it. She told her father that after this she knew little or nothing of what took place until she came to herself sometime that night back at Mrs. Kidd's." Judge Loving, after hearing this account, went and killed Estes.[18]

Neither the letter to Ryan nor exactly what the judge said at his bail hearing was readily available when the journalists wrote the first stories on the case. The Ryan letter was private, and the speediness with which the bail hearing was held apparently kept reporters from being there. Moreover, both Judge Loving and his daughter were unavailable to the press. After the shooting they retreated into the family home and refused to make any public statements. Journalists had to construct their first stories from reports of what the witnesses said at the coroner's hearing and the bail hearing, what they were told by friends of Judge Loving, and what Commissioner Payne related in his statement. The early accounts all indicted Estes as a violator of womanhood and saw Loving as a protector of his daughter.

Bail Commissioner Payne's account, reported in two local papers, portrayed Loving as an user of the unwritten law. He began his account with the buggy ride, which he placed at eight o'clock. "No one knew anything that went on during the ride, but the fact remains that Estes brought the girl back to the house late at night drugged and dishonored." Payne said that Estes called a doctor, W. A. Strother, telling him that she was drunk. Payne added that the doctor, after examining Elizabeth, "communicated with her father," and "Judge Loving heard the story from the daughter's lips. Then, and only then did he go seek her traducer and kill him." (A traducer was one who led another astray, who slandered someone, or dishonored a woman; Payne's usage was synonymous with seducer.) Payne added that Loving told him "that neither God nor man could have stopped him when he heard the story from the lips of his loved one." And then, showing how this story appealed to chivalric and honorable notions of the paternal role, Payne concluded that "this was the strongest point for me to admit him to bail."[19]

Various principals supplied information that could be construed to support the seducer or rapist theory. For example, although the doctor refused to confirm to the press what his treatment had revealed, pleading "that it would not be right professionally to tell of the experience which she underwent." the papers stressed that "he communicated the result of his examination" to Loving. Taken together with the belief that Loving waited until he heard the whole tale, even the doctor's equivocal statement supported the idea that Estes was a sexual predator. Thus Payne's statement, buttressed by other material, implied that Estes was a seducer, deserving death at the hands of a male relative of his victim.[20]

Most of the Virginia newspapers first followed this story line. For example, the *Richmond News Leader* in two articles accepted the Loving version of the events. The paper reported rumors that Theodore Estes's return of Elizabeth Loving "in an unconscious condition" and that she "looked as if she had been drugged" sparked the shooting. Its next story, drawing upon Payne's words, reported that while staying with the Kidds, Elizabeth Loving took "a spin along the country roads" with Theodore Estes. The paper asserted that Estes "brought her back drugged, unconscious, and dishonored." Judge Loving "waited until he could get the full story from her own lips . . . before he acted." Finally, following the details laid out in Strode's letter to Ryan (which probably came from one of Loving's friends or lawyers), the paper added that Elizabeth told her father that about a mile from town, Estes "insisted upon her taking a drink . . . and from that time until she found herself in bed at Mrs. E. L. Kidd's in Lovingston, she knew nothing of what happened." The *Charlottesville Daily Progress*'s headline summed it up: "Father Invoked Unwritten Law / Loving Slays Author of Daughter's Ruin."[21]

The early Virginia press coverage of the killing characterized Theodore Estes as a seducer who deserved to die. Evan Chesterman compared Loving's killing to another notable unwritten-law case, the Culpeper County killing by John and Phillip Strother of their sister's seducer. In pointing out the similarities, he wrote that "in both cases, too, the dead have but few to speak in their defense, if their course is capable of any defense." This view of the male seducer of innocent girls was a common one in late nineteenth-century and early twentieth-century America. The common story line was that an innocent young girl was made drunk or drugged by a predatory male and raped. That Theodore Estes "was a small, frail man, who did not weigh over 120 pounds" and that Lizzie Loving "exceeded him both in height and avoirdupois" besides being "an athletic type" was used by the press to explain why the presumed rapist drugged her instead of using force. But whatever the means, it was the common assumption that a woman who lost her virtue lost her essential purity. In popular stories and reform literature, such women usually became prostitutes and died young. Loving used words to define his daughter after he heard her tale that reflected this view: "dishonored, destroyed." And the so-called unwritten law dictated a course of action to protect society from such male predators. Under the unwritten law a father, brother, or other male relative could avenge wrongs against his family's women through violence.[22]

To support the unwritten-law angle, the Virginia press initially portrayed Loving as a man who followed the precepts of honor. One journalist wrote, "Nobody . . . questioned his courage" and "All comment on his daring and his readiness to meet his antagonists in any sort of encounter they might suggest." The papers noted that in the 1880s Judge Loving had proposed a duel. They also recounted Loving's "personal encounter" with Judge Bennett T. Gordon five years before the killing, when Loving was a judge and Gordon was a commonwealth's attorney. To "settle a dispute the two gentlemen" locked themselves in a private office, where "they fought without weapons until neither could stand."[23]

The Loving version of the killing appealed to the constellation of ideas that sanctified the unwritten law, and most of the press proved sympathetic to this appeal. It reported (and implicitly supported the idea) that in Nelson County the killing was seen as proper. One paper reported that "feeling" in the county was "unqualified with Judge Loving." Though Estes "was highly regarded and very popular, the sentiment here appears to be that Judge Loving was entirely justified in his action." Another declared that the killing "has drawn nothing but sympathy for the perpetrator and the bereaved family but not a word of pity is expressed for the dead man." Not every reporter jumped to the conclusion that Theodore Estes was a seducer who deserved death. Chesterman reported that "there is a conservative element" in Nelson County "who cannot reconcile" Estes's "conduct" on the day of his death "with what they fancy would be the attitude of" a guilty man. Although he admitted to drinking too much the night before when he "bought a dose of Bromo-Seltzer," he had worked so hard that day that his body could not have "been thoroughly saturated with the fumes of alcohol." But most reports supported Judge Loving.[24]

Loving's lawyers probably knew that favorable attitudes toward the unwritten law aided his chances of escaping punishment for the killing. They made such views the centerpiece of their defense strategy, which was widely recognized by the press. One paper declared, "The 'unwritten law,' pure and simple will be the plea of ex-Judge W. G. Loving." Although almost all of the early press accounts were sympathetic to Judge Loving, and although his lawyers portrayed his action as reasonable in the circumstances, the county's commonwealth's attorney, Stewart Whitehead, thought otherwise. At the bail hearing Whitehead asked: "Do you think that the simple fact of your daughter being made drunk

justified you in taking this mans life? Don't you think that slapping his jaws or using a cow hide would have been sufficient?" Though Whitehead's question cast
the act within the context of honorable violence, it also asserted that Elizabeth
Loving had not been drugged or violated and that William Loving had over-
reacted. Loving responded, "Mr. Whitehead are you a man are you a man?"
Loving's reply, which did not figure in any of the press coverage of the case,
showed how protection of female virtue was essential to his conception of honorable manhood. Strode also knew that the unwritten law worked in his client's
favor. In his letter to Ryan, Strode wrote that he felt "confident that we shall be
able to secure an acquittal" when Loving went on trial.[25]

As the Virginia newspapers emphasized how honor drove Loving to act,
they also introduced elements that would elevate the human-interest aspects of
the story or make it even more sensational. They used several different methods
to make the killing even more appealing to their readers. First, papers introduced
the idea that the killing might have been avoided. Second, they also raised the
possibility of vengeance killings by the Estes family. And third, one paper in its
invented dialog hinted at a different motive for the killing.

Various papers all related details on how Harry Snead had tried to stop
Loving. Snead, Loving's brother-in-law, "had been apprised of Loving's intention" by a phone call from Mrs. Loving. "Jumping into his buggy," Snead drove
"madly" in a "desperate attempt" to catch the judge. But he missed him, arriving at Oak Ridge, according to one version, "three minutes after" the shooting.
"He immediately telephoned" both Mrs. Loving and Sheriff Estes. The sheriff
"hurried to Oak Ridge and superintended the removal of his boy's body from
the car." In case the moral of Snead's adventure was not clear, the newspapers
drew it: had he not "missed him at the cross roads, the tragedy might have been
averted."[26]

Virginia newspapers also contained two different accounts of potential retaliation by the Estes family. The first detailed how Estes's mother thwarted "another chapter to the tragedy" by stopping one of her sons, Morris, as he ran "out
of the house declaring that he would kill his brother's slayer on first sight." The
pleading by the "stricken woman, tears streaming down her face," prompted
him to give up the attempt. With its intimate details and clichéd language, this
tale has the look of an invented story, and printing it allowed the papers to report a second story of vengeance denied. The papers noted "it was better" that
the killing "was enacted" at Oak Ridge than at Lovingston. If Loving had killed
Estes at the county seat, Sheriff Estes "would have avenged his son's death." On

hearing of Theodore's death, "he vowed to kill Loving," but "the bereaved father was taken to his home . . . and again the mother's wise counsel came into good stead." Thus "all thoughts" of "summary vengeance" had "passed." This story rings little truer than the previous one and was contradicted in the same articles by accounts of the sheriff's supervision of the removal of his son's body. Both stories served a similar purpose in adding a moral point, the value of women's virtuous guidance, to the account.[27]

One afternoon paper created different human-interest appeal in the story. The *Richmond News Leader* sensationalized the killing itself by inventing dialogue. In describing the scene in the boxcar, the *News Leader* reported this exchange. Loving asked, "'Did you drive out with my daughter again last night?' Estes responded, 'I did.' Judge Loving then said, 'Well you will never drive out with her again,' and fired both loads of the gun." The paper's use of the word *again* in Loving's question can be construed to imply that Loving had forbidden his daughter from seeing Estes, thus making the killing the result of the flaunting of a proscribed love affair. This interpretation may have been suggested by a report in another paper that stated, "The attentions of Estes to Loving's daughter are said to have been the cause of the shooting." Apparently other Virginia papers (which are no longer extant) reported that Estes was a beau of Elizabeth Loving, which of course gave the killing a romantic and tragic cast.[28]

Thus within two days of its occurrence, the killing had generated sensationalized press stories that tended to portray Estes as a seducer and Loving as a father driven to wipe out his daughter's dishonor. These stories originated in the local papers but were almost immediately picked up by the state's major papers and by national newspapers. Besides the sensationalism, the state and national press had good reasons to see this homicide as news. What especially peaked the interest of the major newspapers was reflected in the early stories of two newspapers based close to the site of the killing, the *Roanoke Times* and the *Charlottesville Daily Progress*. The *Daily Progress* stressed both the sensational aspect of the killing and the political importance of the families, while the *Times* emphasized the role of Thomas Fortune Ryan. Together the two papers accounts make clear why the case earned statewide coverage, and why this killing in Virginia became national news.

The *Daily Progress* began its initial article with a headline that trumpeted the most sensational aspects of the tale, "Loving Slays Author of Daughter's Ruin." But the article failed to deliver on the headline. Instead the paper stated that the causes which "lead up to the shooting" were not yet "public." The paper also reported that Mrs. Estes had "fainted" when Theodore's body was brought home and that her daughters were "hysterical." These themes would be picked up and embellished in national coverage of the killing. The *Daily Progress* reported that the killer was "one of the most widely known men in the piedmont section" and detailed Loving's professional, political, and family connections. Similarly, it reported that Estes was the son of the sheriff of Nelson County and brother-in-law to John P. Swanson, the governor's brother. Given the nature of Virginia politics, this killing had strong political overtones as a news story.[29]

Like much of the South, Virginia in the early twentieth century had a particular form of politics. Around the turn of the century, white Virginians in the Democratic Party had completed their counterrevolution. In 1902 Democrats pushed through a constitution for the state that effectively disfranchised most blacks. Moreover, the state's poll tax disfranchised the poor, regardless of color. Thus the electorate shrank drastically. For example, between the governor's races in 1901 and 1905, the number of recorded votes dropped by one-third. As a result, the Republican Party virtually ceased to contest elections, save in one congressional district. The state became a one-party state and would remain so until the civil rights revolution.[30]

The main political battles in Virginia were the contests between various Democratic factions, headed by officeholders. The small number of eligible voters elevated the role of officeholders in politics. These officeholders headed small patronage machines comprised of their friends and extended families, and from these power bases they struggled to control the party and the state. Intermarriage was common among the political elites, making political falling-outs particularly personal. Not surprisingly then, factional battles were bitter. The state's newspapers all thought that politics might play a role in the prosecution and trial of Loving and stressed that angle of the story.[31]

The papers pointed out that Loving and Estes belonged to different Democratic factions. Sheriff Estes was a supporter of Thomas S. Martin, the major figure in Virginia Democratic politics from 1893 to his death in 1919. Martin was central in constructing a loosely linked statewide machine that connected business interests with the governing class. Through his machine local officials like Estes, state officials like Claude Swanson, and federal officials like Congressman Henry D. Flood cooperated in setting policy. At all levels they favored small government that did not interfere much with business or people's private lives. Throughout the period the machine was challenged by reform Democrats, who

avidly supported reforms like better schools and prohibition, as well as independent Democrats, who for one reason or another did not affiliate with the machine. Judge Loving supported the reform Democrat Andrew J. Montague
against Martin in the 1907 campaign for the United States Senate. The Estes and
Loving political differences were also local. While Sheriff Estes was "a warm political friend of ex-Senator Bland Massie," Loving "was antagonistic to him."
Indeed, it was said in Nelson County that Loving "encompassed the defeat of
Mr. Massie and was largely instrumental in electing Senator Aubrey E. Strode."
But some Virginia papers emphasized an angle other than politics.[32]

The *Roanoke Times*'s first article on the killing began: "Ex-Judge W. G. Loving, who late yesterday afternoon shot and killed Theodore Estes, at Oak Ridge,
the country estate of Thomas F. Ryan, was today admitted to bail." The paper
probably worked Ryan's name into the opening line of its article because he
was one of the richest men in the nation. A homicide on his Oak Ridge estate,
combined with the sensational nature of the crime, brought the national press
into the story. Moreover, Ryan's past actions and perceived interest in politics prompted Virginia newspapers to add him to the political slant of their
coverage.[33]

Thomas Fortune Ryan, born in Nelson County in 1851, lived a real Horatio
Alger life. Orphaned and penniless at age fourteen, he had by 1907 earned a
space in an exposé of the rich, "The Owners of America." As a boy, Ryan left
Virginia and became a messenger on New York's Wall Street. Like some of Alger's heroes, he married the boss's daughter and soon after became a partner in
his own brokerage firm. As a businessman Ryan had interests in banking, railroads, tobacco manufacturing, and insurance. His role in the New York City's
transportation system made his public reputation. In the 1880s Ryan—a solid
backer of New York's Democratic political machine—used his influence to try to
gain the right to build and run trolleys and street railroads. When an opposing
businessman received the rights to the franchise, Ryan turned to public relations
and politics. He mobilized reformers against the victorious businessman, and
a subsequent investigation led to his loss of the franchise. Ryan picked up the
pieces: in 1886 he organized a company that bought up all the little franchises
and consolidated them. The consolidated company proved a wonderful venue
for financial manipulations, increasing Ryan's fortune. When subways began to
challenge streetcars, Ryan launched an advertising campaign touting the value of
a consolidated transportation system. His competitors agreed to consolidate
their holdings with his, and in 1906 he profitably sold his interest in this new

company. Because of his fame and reputation, the Ryan connection made the Estes and Loving story even more appealing to newspapermen, both in Virginia and across the nation.[34]

For some Virginians, Ryan's presence intensified the political dimensions of the killing. After Ryan bought Oak Ridge from the Snead family in 1901 and began transforming it into an estate worthy of one of the nation's richest individuals, he took an interest in Virginia politics. Ryan's great wealth and the way the machine functioned made it likely that his money could flow into campaign war chests. Ryan's proclivities also led him to favor Martin's organizational politics. The conservative outlook of the machine and its opposition to William Jennings Bryan, and later Woodrow Wilson, pleased Ryan. Some in Virginia political circles feared that Ryan sought a larger role. Two days after the killing, the *Roanoke Times* ran a front-page article entitled: "What Is Ryan after Here? Some Think the New Yorker Wants to Be U. S. Senator or Governor of State." This was not an idle question in view of Ryan's political skills and the Senate's reputation as the millionaire's club. In response, Ryan denied that he had any ambitions for office in Virginia, asserting that he had returned to his native county to enjoy his retirement. A month later another paper amplified Ryan's comments, defending his interest in Virginia affairs by saying he was just being a good citizen. Even so, many of the state's newspapers, because of Ryan's role, would portray the killing as an incident in the state's politics. Such political dimensions of Ryan's role were mostly lost on the national papers that covered the killing and trial of Loving.[35]

For the Hearst, Pulitzer, and other out-of-state papers, Ryan's connection, no matter how remote, made the killing newsworthy. Combined with the lurid details, the circumstance of Estes's death could be inflated into the kind of social melodrama in which the papers specialized. Very soon after the shooting, newspapers from outside of the state picked up the story, and their coverage emphasized both the sensational nature of the killing and the Ryan connection. Although limited in their coverage because none of the papers sent reporters to Nelson County before the meeting of the grand jury, the *New York World*, the *New York Herald*, and the *Baltimore Sun* cast the story in ways that made it more appealing to their audiences. Gruesome (sometimes fictional) details about the killing, the rumors of rape, and Ryan's involvement predominated.[36]

The out-of-state papers emphasized the wronged woman as motive for the killing. The *World* predicted that if Loving stood trial, he would "tell a startling story and plead the unwritten law." The paper portrayed Lizzie Loving as "a great beauty" who was "prominent in the hunting and horse set" and reported her "drugging and dishonoring." Similarly, the *Sun* stressed Elizabeth Loving's attractiveness and the rape; its subhead read: "Victim a Beautiful Blond." Others managed to obliquely focus on the alleged rape by focusing on her current condition. One noted, "Miss Loving is reported to be in a very nervous condition as the result of this affair, being confined to her bed."

If the crime were not sensational enough, the out-of-state papers (either borrowing from the Virginia accounts or inventing stories themselves) dramatized, indeed fictionalized, the shooting. The *World* reported that Loving "rode in a rage to the scene of the shooting." And according to witnesses, when Loving rode up, "after a hot altercation lasting for less than a minute the Judge reached down into his carriage and lifted a double-barreled shotgun. Estes attempted to draw a gun, but Loving" fired first, and the buckshot "almost tore the head from the body. Loving stood unmoved until several minutes later, the young man had breathed his last." The *Sun's* account, although differing in details, shared a similar sensational style. According to the Baltimore paper, Judge Loving appeared to be cool during his search for Estes, and when he reached the car, he accosted and shot him down "like a dog." The *World,* however, went even further in turning the killing into a human-interest story. Believing reports from certain Virginia papers, it raised the specter of vengeance killings by Sheriff Estes or Theodore's brother Morris Jr. In the brother's case only the intervention of "his mother who was almost beside herself with grief" kept him from carrying out his plan.[37]

The papers also gave Ryan a prominent place in their coverage. The *World* referred to Judge Loving as "Thomas F. Ryan's representative in this state" who killed Estes in "Ryan's hometown." It also called Loving the "manager of Ryan's Virginia estate" and noted that Ryan, "who is very fond of Judge Loving," offered by telegraph "to furnish any bail required." Similarly, the *New York Herald* focused on Ryan's role. It reported "that Thomas F. Ryan of New York had made a formal offer of financial assistance to the family of Judge William G. Loving, manager of his Virginia estate and his boyhood friend, in the fight to establish justification for his killing young Theodore Estes."[38]

Although early press reports from the local, state, and national papers made Loving's killing of Estes a sensation, it did not rank as a major event for 1907. That year the national press was packed with thrilling stories about trials. It had covered all the details in the first Harry Thaw trial and was devoting similar attention to the murder trial of William Haywood, which featured Clarence

Darrow for the defense and William Borah for the prosecution. Virginia's papers had given great play to the Strother brothers, who were tried for killing the man who made their sister pregnant and pleaded a combination of insanity and unwritten law. The Strother brothers had won an acquittal, and Thaw's case had ended in a hung jury. With Loving's trial looking to turn on similar legal grounds and being sensationalized like the other trials, the Estes family must have been concerned that the killer of their kin would escape justice. It must have been particularly galling for them to see the press present what was basically Loving's version of events. The Estes family was likely planning action as well as grieving.[39]

Theodore Estes's funeral was held two days after his killing. It was, according to one report, "one of the saddest funerals ever held in Virginia." According to another report, "over the red hills" turned white by apple blossoms "poured scores of stalwart Virginians" to attend the funeral. Over six hundred people, mostly from Nelson County, came "to sympathize with the bereaved." A local minister conducted the ceremony at the family home. Pallbearers from the Lovingston Lodge of the Independent Order of Odd Fellows carried the coffin to the grave site. Not horses but "tender, loving hands bore the casket" to the cemetery. Flowers covered the grave, "sent by friends in Danville, Lynchburg and other points." The "eighteen floral designs" were regarded as remarkable in that "isolated rural section." Estes's funeral stood in stark contrast to that of Stanford White a year earlier; for White, whom the press was widely denouncing as a libertine, a public funeral in New York City was canceled and replaced by a private one on Long Island. Many Virginians, and many in Nelson County, did not think that Theodore was beyond the pale of decent society. The press's close attention to the funeral gave the Estes family an opportunity to begin its attempt to restore Theodore's good name.[40]

"Once the youth was under the sod, the pacific policy observed by his family and friends changed into an aggressive effort to clear" his reputation. The Estes family and friends contested Loving's version of events leading up to the killing and denied some of the more sensational claims of the press. Brother-in-law John P. Swanson told a reporter "that the family wanted the law . . . to take its course" and that there would be no mob violence against Loving. On the day of the funeral, Mrs. Estes indicated that her son's reputation mattered greatly to the family. Papers reported that she said: "I hope Judge Loving is freed if he does not slander my son. If he does we will fight to the bitter end." The Virginia press translated this statement to mean that the family "will spare no effort or cost to show that the charge made against him is without foundation." Mrs. Estes's statement struck at the heart of the judge's position.[41]

Mostly, the nuclear family did not talk to the press publicly. Off the record, the family and friends indicated that they would "show by witnesses to the drive . . . that no violence was offered Miss Loving" and that the drink of whiskey was not Theodore's idea but Lizzie's. The Estes family and supporters alleged that her "condition was due to whisky and that she took it of her own volition" because she was feeling poorly. They admitted that Estes took an occasional drink but denied that he was intemperate and thus liable to be licentious. When pressed by reporters to make a "statement on behalf of his boy," Sheriff Estes thought it would be better "to have all family explanations" be delivered by others: John H. Shipman, a friend of the family, and John P. Swanson, their relation by marriage.[42]

Shipman and Swanson supplied the press with statements protesting and amending the previous press accounts. Shipman said that Estes returned Elizabeth Loving from the drive "just before dark." He declared stories saying Elizabeth was drugged were "without any foundation" and that she "was never maltreated." He asserted that Theodore came by the next morning to convey Elizabeth home, but that she felt too ill to go. Shipman portrayed William Loving as a "cruel, cold-blooded, and heartless" killer, who "shot Estes for giving" his daughter "a drink" and did so "without a word of warning." Also, Shipman denied "the statement of the correspondent that everybody thinks Judge Loving did right." He claimed that only the people's faith "that justice will be meted out" restrained them from mob action. However, none of the Estes family members "have threatened any violence, or made any threats" against Loving.[43]

Similarly, Swanson declared mistaken various press dispatches claiming that "Mr. Estes was a suitor of Miss Loving's" and that various members of the Estes family had sworn vengeance against Loving. Swanson also said that the "statements given out to the press by friends of Judge Loving" perverted "the details leading up to this awful tragedy." He attacked the allegations of rape, asserting that the buggy ride took place in daylight and that the roads the couple traveled were "the main thoroughfares of the county" and were "thickly settled." He declared that "no assault could have been made upon Miss Loving." Moreover, he pointed out that Elizabeth came back merely showing "indications of being under the influence of whisky." He noted that Annie Kidd carried her to her room, undressed her, and put her to bed, implying that Kidd would have seen signs of assault if there had been any. According to Swanson, Theodore Estes was the one who called Dr. Strother, telling him that she "had a little too much whisky." The doctor, after looking at Loving and feeling her pulse, concurred. Swanson read a statement from Strother declaring "that he only prescribed medicine for her indisposition from liquor and that he never thought . . . that there had been any assault." Drawing upon Loving's bail-hearing testimony, Swanson concluded that Elizabeth Loving "has never charged Theodore Estes with an assault." [44]

Swanson's and Shipman's statements showed that the Estes family was determined to restore Theodore's good name and bring his killer to justice. They directly confronted the image that Estes was dissipated, asserting that he was a man with a "high sense of honor" and integrity. He was "courteous and polite and beloved by all that knew him." Swanson said the knowledge that Estes had been charged with "an awful crime" and was unable to refute it because he was dead was "maddening to his kinspeople and friends." Their campaign bore some fruit, as the press made their accounts of seduction less reported fact than contested view. One Virginia paper headline read, "Estes Did Not Drug Girl / Friends of Dead Man Say He Did Not Resort to Stanford White Practice." Even some national papers picked up the nuances; the *World* reported, "Young Estes, It Is Declared, Did Not Wrong the Young Woman Whose Father Killed Him." At the same time Swanson's remarks made it clear that the family was working to help prosecute Loving. It had already "procured" much evidence "in regard to the buggy ride." [45]

Even the unwritten law began to be turned against Loving. Although extolling the unwritten law, some Virginia editorial writers questioned its application in this case. Five days after Loving killed Estes, when the press campaign of the Estes family was well under way, the *Roanoke Times* ran an editorial "invoking the unwritten law." While praising a man who kills to defend "the sanctity of his home . . . against the invasion of the lecherous libertine," the paper wondered if the unwritten law was "being invoked on too slight provocation." Reporting that the Estes family and his friends "are prepared to prove" his innocence and that reports declared him "a model young man who was temperate in all habits," the paper thought he had deserved the opportunity to explain himself before Loving fired. The editorial saw the source of the problem not a defect of society but a failure of law, analogizing the unwritten law to lynching. Like many southerners, the editorial writer blamed lynching on the inadequacy of the law: "If the courts dispense only justice . . . Judge Lynch would adjourn his court forever."

Portraying "the man whose" daughter, sister, or wife had been "disgraced" as "naturally" feeling an injustice that could only be compensated by "the death of the perpetrator" and noting that the law "with its utmost penalty will fall far short of death," the paper argued that taking the law into a man's own hands was an "irresistible impulse." The unwritten law was thus "written in the heart" and "not to be expressed in words and spread upon the pages of our book of statutes."[46]

At the same time some Virginians proposed making the unwritten law part of the state's formal law. In the aftermath of the Strother brothers case, and when it was clear the Loving case was going to turn on unwritten law, State Senator Lewis H. Machen, from Alexandria, advocated passing a law which would allow juries to consider "the provocation of an attack upon the sanctity of the home" in assigning guilt and degree of homicide. Machen thought the legislation would keep killers from invoking the unwritten law "upon mere suspicion or hearsay" to claim justification because now they would have to prove the provocation at their trial.[47]

Others thought the Machen bill "a dangerous proposal." The *Roanoke Times* declared that the bill was the "equivalent to saying that here is a deficiency in our system that can only be met by giving the law over" to private individuals. It quoted the *Washington Herald*'s editorial decrying the proposal as a turn to the "code of private vengeance" which surrendered "every principle upon which civilized society is based." Tradition was added to the arguments against the bill: "We have gotten along these hundreds of years without the necessity of a statute." Another paper denounced the bill as an incitement to homicide: "It is getting to be too common a thing for a man to take the law into his own hands, shoot down his fellow man, and claim immunity from punishment as having acted upon the 'unwritten law.'" This paper, too, favored keeping some latitude between the written law and jury practice. Quoting the judge in the Strother brothers case as admitting juries in the state would always "take into consideration" such provocations as "mitigating" circumstances, the paper asserted, "As long as juries have warm blood in their veins and have sisters and daughters in their homes, they will be slow in punishing a man who avenges the invasion of a home." Juries who acquitted "after hearing all the facts of the case" did not "fall under the censure of public condemnation. But surely the law ought not to openly encourage the taking of human life by writing into the statute book the 'unwritten law.'"[48]

Thus, Judge Loving's lawyers had their work cut out for them. The Estes family's press campaign cost them their early hegemony of the news accounts.

Also, their client had said things that weakened their case. including "I am not crazy" and "I shot to kill." And questions had been raised about the applicability of the unwritten law to their case. The defense also noticed that many papers seemed to emphasize Ryan's role in the case; lines like the one that appeared in the *Richmond Evening Journal*—"His interests are . . . to be backed by the unlimited financial resources of the New York multi-millionaire"—probably worried the lawyers. Strode clipped a *New York Herald* article on the case and marked the passages dealing with Ryan. Because millionaires often were unpopular figures, Ryan's potential prominence could prove to be a problem for the defense. The defense apparently persuaded Ryan stay in the background. After the first wave of stories, he did nothing to generate press coverage. In addition, the defense sequestered Judge Loving and his daughter at their home, thus making sure that they did not talk to the press.[49]

The lawyers overlooked Lizzie's friends, which resulted in another round of statewide press stories unfavorable to the defense. Elizabeth was the subject of much press interest for she was seen as "the all-important witness." On April 25 Lizzie wrote to a friend in Charlottesville, recounting how the family was coping with the crisis. She also said a few things that when leaked to the press and embellished made headlines across the state. Loving wrote, "The different papers have published so many different things that I have to hold my head tight to think what really did happen." She also noted that she was "miserable" and the family's life was "one dark, dark blank." She claimed that she was "trying to bear up, trying to stand it for Father's sake, for you know it will all nearly rest on me." She wrote her friend, "At times I think I *can't* stand it. That it *can't* be true." She mentioned in passing that the family was so glad that her father was "out on bail, and now if we can just get his nerves straightened out." After mentioning that her father had come to see her and comfort her and to tell her "to be brave," Lizzie added, "Isn't it awful?" She ended her letter asking her friend to "think of it, think of it."[50]

According to one news account, the recipient of the letter "'phoned' its contents to a friend, who hanging up the receiver, repeated what" she had heard, "and one of those who heard" that tale, "a woman of the highest standing, repeated it to those who communicated it to the newspapers." The *Daily Progress*, which received this fourth-hand account, conflated its vague and elusive wording. It, and other of the state's newspapers (including the state's leading paper, the *Times-Dispatch*), used this report as evidence of "the extreme unhappiness of the entire family," saying that the whole family was in a "crazed" condition.

The papers also reported that Elizabeth Loving was amazed at her father's act and had "fully exonerated Theodore Estes, adding that he had always treated her with courtesy." She "defends the memory of victim," adding that in Nelson it was an "open secret" that the judge "always has been opposed" to intercourse "between his family" and that of "Sheriff Estes." News of Elizabeth's having a drive with Theodore "excited him greatly." This interpretation made Loving look like a father snuffing out a budding but forbidden romance. The killing became a Romeo and Juliet tale, without the suicide, though that was clearly hinted at as being a possibility in the descriptions of Lizzie Loving's mental state.[51]

Strode soon met with a reporter from a Lynchburg paper to refute the press's recent stories based on Elizabeth Loving's letter. He noted that Elizabeth and William, "in accordance with what they conceived to be the proprieties," chose to remain in seclusion. Strode released the text of Elizabeth's letter, which he had obtained. It contained none of those claims and according to Strode demonstrated "how entirely unfounded were the inferences drawn from it." The defense's action clearly paid off, as the paper that broke the story admitted that the letter was to be discounted because "the party quoting" from it "was in error."[52]

While fighting press skirmishes, the defense was also preparing for the courtroom battle. In the week following the killing, the defense added two more lawyers to its team of Brown and Strode. John L. "Jack" Lee was "more or less acquainted with nearly everybody connected with the case" and was seasoned in trying murders. He and the second lawyer hired, R. Walton Moore of Fairfax, had recently participated in the successful defense of the Strother brothers. In that trial Lee had appealed to the unwritten law in his closing argument while Moore had taken the role of handling the mental experts called in the case. Their addition to Loving's team showed that the defense strategy had not changed.[53]

Before the trial Loving had to be formally indicted by the grand jury. The next convening of the circuit court, with its grand jury hearings, was scheduled for late May. Between the immediate aftermath of the killing and the indictment, press coverage of the affair quieted down. After the letter flap, only a few stories about the killing and the coming trial surfaced in the Virginia papers. Like the story of Lizzie Loving's letter, these reports did not go out over the wire or garner any coverage by the national press. The prosecution took the lead in leaking (and occasionally speaking formally) to the press, and the defense replied with its own leaks.

The Estes family and the prosecution declared that Estes was not a rapist or seducer and stated that they sought a murder conviction. When a Washington correspondent spoke to the sheriff, the elder Estes responded by denying the charge of rape. He asserted (equating himself with the prosecution): "We have positive information that Miss Loving made no charge of assault against Theodore, and that she never said anything about a criminal attack to her father. Dr. Strother says he saw no evidence of an assault and Miss Kidd, who put her to bed after she returned home stupefied from drink, declares nothing was said to her about an assault." Thus, "Judge Loving, in a fit of rage slaughtered my boy without allowing him to deny the charge." If Loving was found guilty, Estes declared, "I want them to deal with him as any cold-blooded murderer should be dealt with." He also claimed that the family "will fight to the last ditch for a verdict of murder in the first degree." And as the defense added to its number, the Estes family joined the race, retaining first John P. Swanson and later Daniel Harmon of Charlottesville to assist the prosecution.[54]

Central to denying the rape was what one journalist called the "alcoholic feature of the case." One newspaper reported "that the very flask . . . will figure in the exhibit of the prosecution and that it will prove that the intoxicant contained no drugs." Later the same paper reported that "startling testimony" would be offered "at trial" concerning the liquor and the drive. It said that Estes did not have the whiskey with him and had to return for it after Loving asked for some. After the drive what remained of the liquor "was given to the stable boy." This young man drank "what remained" without any ill effects. Moreover, the newspaper said, there were witnesses who saw most of the carriage ride and noticed nothing out of the ordinary, other than Lizzie looking ill and Theodore trying to help her. This story that she was not drugged but merely "unexpectedly" drunk put a whole different interpretation on the killing and changed "public sentiment . . . wondrously."[55]

At the same time the defense's policy of reducing the judge and his daughter to a "sphinxlike silence" only served to elevate interest about the pair. Using this interest, the defense may have engineered the leaking of favorable information. For example, the *Daily Progress* ran a story, quoting a Loving friend, that he was a "wreck" and so wrought up he could not sleep. Another story "from a close friend of Judge Loving, who has seen him recently" asserted that "his nerves have been absolutely shattered. Since he killed Estes he has aged rapidly and also has gotten quite gray." Such stories, of course, increased sympathy for the judge and also bolstered his planned insanity defense. Similarly, the defense might have been the source for a rumor that circulated about Nelson County and made it into the press. This tale was that Estes had "been guilty of things well calculated to enrage chivalric Virginians." He supposedly had drugged two other girls with liquor and taken advantage of them. Because this rumor was the perfect counterpunch to the prosecution's campaign to salvage Theodore's reputation, the commonwealth's attorney met it head on. On two occasions he spoke to the press to deny the tale.[56]

In this period two legal questions arose: whether the trial should be held in Nelson County, and whether Judge Gordon should preside. The "difficulty" between Gordon and Loving five years earlier suggested he might be biased, so Gordon asked the governor to appoint a different judge. On May 24 Governor Swanson appointed Judge William R. Barksdale of Halifax County to preside. Apparently he was chosen because his "docket for the next month or so is not crowded." Barksdale took over from Gordon on the third day of the Nelson court's meeting; he presided over the grand jury that indicted Loving and heard arguments concerning bail and concerning change of venue.[57]

William R. Barksdale's courtroom demeanor as the "hurry up judge" overshadowed all else about him. As the *Rockingham Register* put it, "If a lawyer in an argument stops to take too long a breath Judge Barksdale begins making his ruling." The judge spoke "in monosyllables, seldom uttering an unnecessary word." Barksdale lived up to his reputation when he oversaw the indictment, dealt with the issue of bail, and heard all the evidence and arguments concerning the change of venue. After a session that lasted less than an hour, the grand jury indicted William Loving for murder. After an equally quick proceeding, Loving's bail was continued. The session then turned to the question of change of venue.[58]

From the end of April, newspapers had been printing stories about the divisions and passions over the matter in Nelson County. A Lynchburg newspaper admitted that "factional feeling has probably been germinated at Oak Ridge." Because the "elder Estes" had "a large following in the county" and "Judge Loving will likewise present a long line of friends," it was presumed that the number of potential impartial jurors would be low. With the homicide "discussed for miles around," reported another paper, "it will be impossible to draw a jury from Nelson County." Moreover, public opinion had shifted to the Estes camp. An outside correspondent noted that there was "unquestionably a very pronounced sentiment of hostility towards Judge Loving," which was "as patent as the red mud of the Nelson roads."[59]

As a result, the defense made a "tremendous fight for a change of venue" while the prosecution worked to oppose it. The defense's determination underscores that while the press may have seen the killing as an application of the unwritten law, the lawyers feared such a local jury would see the matter differently. The defense through affidavits showed "that not only the sheriff, clerk of the court and some of the minor officials were related to Estes family, but that the proprietor of the two hotels in which the jurors must be confined were related" also to the Estes. The defense also asserted that Commonwealth's Attorney Stewart Whitehead held too many interviews of citizens in the county in seeking affidavits because he was attempting to use those interviews to mold public opinion against Loving. In turn, the prosecution produced over twenty witnesses to say that it was possible to hold a fair trial in Lovingston. Judge Barksdale agreed to change the venue, picking Halifax County—his home county—and June 24, 1907, as the time and the place for the trial. The county seat was a tiny town in the Southside; now known as Halifax, it bore the name of Houston from 1890 to 1920 in the vain hope of enticing a benefactor by that name to bring it some manufacturing. Changes of venue were not common in early twentieth-century Virginia, and the press quickly pointed out that the change would make the proceedings much more expensive. Moving the trial would require that prosecution and defense witnesses be transported, at state expense, to the new location.[60]

Moving the trial did not change the nature of the press attention; Virginia and national papers continued to focus on William Loving and his daughter. The reports were aimed at both setting the scene and heightening the drama. Thus some Virginia papers described Loving in court as "a little paler than yesterday," while others noted Loving "did not indicate in countenance or manner that he was suffering mentally or physically." Because the press was denied access to Elizabeth Loving (she reportedly traveled to Lovingston heavily veiled and was sequestered in a side room), they focused on what they considered her plight. The *Roanoke Times* reported: "Miss Loving seems to be the object of special sympathy because of the fearful predicament in which she will be placed on the witness stand. The case is turning strongly on what she told her father and mother that led to the shooting."[61]

The coming trial was guaranteed to get the full treatment from the sensation-loving papers of Pulitzer and Hearst. The *New York American*'s reporter in Lovingston wrote a long account of the preliminary hearings, confusedly reporting them as the trial and attributing prosecution positions to the defense. Factual errors aside, the story and accompanying illustrations characterized the yellow press's treatment of the case. Under the bold headline "Scenes and Principals in Virginia's Great Murder Trial," the paper ran four photos and one line drawing. The captions under them captured the tone of the coverage: "Photograph of main street in Lovingston, Va"; "Photographs of the courthouse at Lovingston, taken when Judge Loving had his preliminary hearing"; "Judge W. G. Loving, whose fate depends on daughter's evidence"; "Theodore Estes, who was shot down by Judge Loving." The sketch showed Loving, dressed in a black frock coat and a black hat, standing before Estes and leveling his gun at him; Estes stands (dressed in a suit) with his hands raised in surrender. The article—while covering the background, the setting, and the hearings—focused on Elizabeth Loving, declaring that "her position is one of the hardest that ever a young girl had to face." When she testified, "she will be called upon to choose between besmirching the character of a dead man or helping to place the felon's stripes on the back of her own father, or mayhap, a rope around his neck." The report elaborated: "If Estes was innocent of the crime alleged, her position will be doubly hard, for then it will be directly her duty to save her father. If she tells the truth, in that event, her father will go to prison. If she saves her father, she will condemn herself for all time in her own consciousness."[62]

In part, because they did not have to deal with Virginia proprieties in their coverage, the national papers could focus more fully on the human-interest aspects of the case. Lack of local connections allowed these papers to be freer in their speculations and reporting. Thus the sympathy for Lizzie's plight in the Virginia papers was merely that, sympathy. For a Virginia paper in its news reports to suggest that a respectable woman would commit perjury would violate the canons of acceptable press behavior. But the *American* could imply that in testifying that she might lie. No doubt its skepticism was fueled by the common view that Evelyn Nesbit Thaw had lied in Harry Thaw's case earlier that year. And the national press could work the rumors of Estes's attacks on other women, reporting, "It is understood that at least one of these young women will be placed on the stand to testify for Judge Loving." In doing so, the paper promised future sensations.[63]

Moving and delaying the trial also allowed one final spasm of press speculations fueled by leaks. In early June "a prominent citizen of Nelson County" talked with reporters in Richmond, hinting at surprises in defense strategy. This unnamed source also denied the stories that Loving had broken down physically or was a nervous wreck; although it was of some advantage for the public to think of William Loving as mentally not stable, too much emphasis on his ill health harmed his chances. Juries were reluctant to free raving lunatics on an insanity plea, and declining physical or mental health could be interpreted as signs of a guilty conscience. On the other hand, both Virginia and national papers reported after the indictment "that at the time of his death," Estes "was engaged" to "the young daughter of the Hon. Bland Massie, a beautiful girl, now attending a woman's college at Lynchburg." This fact, of course, helped to rehabilitate Estes's reputation. Also, the *Roanoke Times,* disclosing that the state intended to call seventy-five witnesses, wondered why. "To the outside layman it is hard to see how more than the six or eight persons who were immediately concerned in the tragedy can be used as witnesses for the state."[64]

Changing the location of the trial did bring about some adjustments in what one paper called the "array of counsel," while merely transferring the social divisions in Nelson County to a new venue. The move to Halifax County required that its commonwealth's attorney, Wood Bouldin, prosecute the case. Daniel Harmon, the lawyer hired earlier by the Estes family, assisted Bouldin. In addition, Stewart Whitehead, though not counsel of record, sat at the prosecution table and offered his aid. To balance Bouldin, the defense retained a local lawyer, W. Peter Barksdale. While he was well known (he was the former state senator, as well as a very distant relation to Judge Barksdale), W. Peter Barksdale was elderly and ill, and his role in the trial was minimal. All examinations of witnesses and cross-examinations were performed by Strode, Lee, and Moore, with the father-and-son team of J. Thompson and Lewis Brown assisting. These changes in the "corps of lawyers" did not mean that the basic nature of the case or the sides had changed. Indeed, during the rail journey each side, apparently so they would not be forced to mingle, reserved a "private car" for their use. In Houston they continued their mutual segregation. Each side stayed at one of the town's two hotels, and "no one from one" visited the other. In these clearly defined groups, each side faced the press gathered in Houston.[65]

The press was well represented in Halifax County's seat. Correspondents from all the major Virginia newspapers covered the trial, including Allen Potts of the *Richmond Times-Dispatch* and Evan Chesterman of the *Richmond Evening Journal.* Former judge Clarence J. Campbell was "engaged in covering the case for his newspaper at Amherst Courthouse" and also, as one paper noted, taking "the opportunity to 'even up'" against Loving for having been one of the prosecutors in his impeachment. Beyond the Virginia press, reporters from the *New York Herald, New York World, New York American, Baltimore Herald, Baltimore*

Sun, Washington Post, Washington Herald, and the Associated Press attended the proceedings. It was easy for the press to convey every aspect of the trial to the state and nation. The clerk of the court "provided facilities, the like of which never before were seen by newspaper men," and Western Union Telegraph Company established a special office "in the basement of the court-house for the quick handling of business."[66]

The trial was held in the county's recently renovated "large and well-planned" courthouse. In 1904 the county built an extension on the original brick courthouse that emphasized its imposing pediment and Ionic columns. The new courtroom was "large and well arranged" with "tiers of seats" that could accommodate 250 people. Nevertheless, one press account asserted that the courtroom would "not hold one-fourth of those who will endeavor to enter." The trial moved at a pace that showed that Judge Barksdale more than lived up to his nickname. On the trial's first day—Monday, June 24, 1907—a jury was impaneled, the prosecution presented its case, and the defense opened its case.[67]

The jury was chosen from a venire of sixty-four Halifax citizens. In less than two hours, the lawyers questioned twenty-six of the venire. Six were excused for admitting to having fixed opinions, three fell to legal technicalities, and another was disqualified when he said he would not follow the law "but that he would have to follow out his idea of what the law should be in such cases." The defense, after a twenty-minute conference among the lawyers, struck off four of the men. Of the remaining twelve, eleven were farmers, and one was a merchant. Nine of them were married, and all but two were between forty and sixty years of age. Some indication of their temper can be gauged by their electing as foreman the merchant, who was probably the most wealthy among them.[68]

Once the jury was sworn and seated, the indictment was read, and "then, with hardly ten minutes' delay, the examination of witnesses began." The prosecution waived giving an opening statement and immediately began calling witnesses. The defense asked few questions in cross-examination, and the prosecution's case took less than two hours to present. Brevity made its case one that pointed to all the hallmarks of murder: homicide, malice, and premeditation.[69]

The prosecution's witnesses proved the homicide. Three eyewitnesses testified to Loving's coming to the boxcar, confronting Estes with his question about buggy riding, and shooting Estes before he could respond. Fayette Foster added a previously undisclosed fact: that Nick Reid had said to him while working in the boxcar that Judge Loving was approaching and that Estes "showed no uneasiness whatsoever, and went along working." Although this fact was somewhat undercut by the defense's cross-examination questions which raised the possibility that Estes may not have heard the exchange, it seemed to point to Estes's having no reason to fear the arrival of Loving. Three witnesses (Postmaster L. W. Wood, undertaker J. Oscar Loving, and family friend John Shipman) who prepared the body for burial described Estes's wounds. One displayed Estes's bloodstained clothing to the court.[70]

A number of witnesses testified to facts designed to show Loving's premeditation and malice. Shipman described Loving, whom he saw at the Estes family's store before the shooting, as appearing angry. Wood testified to the distance from Loving's home to the site of the killing, underscoring that Loving had time for reflection. Julia Hubbard told of Loving's sending her into the store in Lovingston to inquire for Theodore; when she came back and asked if "old man Estes would do," Loving "responded with an emphatic, 'no.'" W. N. Dawson testified that he saw Loving along the route from Lovingston to Oak Ridge. And William Powers, who was at McGinnis's stable on the day of the killing, told the court that when Loving arrived he gave his reins to Powers to hold, took the shotgun from the buggy, went to the boxcar, and returned after a few minutes.[71]

The prosecution attached malice to Loving's homicide of Estes through the testimony of two officials, Magistrate T. B. M. Perkins and Constable C. A. Wood, who relayed what Loving said in his statement at the preliminary hearing. Their versions differed only by a few words, even though no stenographic record was made of the statement. According to Perkins, Loving said, "One near and dear to me was driven in a buggy" and "was brought back drugged and unconscious at a late hour. I sent for her, and when I got it from her own lips my blood boiled and every nerve and fibre in my body was aroused and I deliberately sought his life." Wood testified that "he took possession" of Loving's gun as well as "four loaded shells and two empty shells." The gun, "a twelve bore hammerless, double-barrel shot gun," and the shells loaded with buckshot were shown to the jury. The gun, whose effects any farmer would be familiar with, and the witnesses' testimony as to what Loving said strengthened the prosecution's case. Loving's brief statement admitted both premeditation and malice. To take the sting out of this damaging evidence, Jack Lee in cross-examination of Wood turned to the issue of rape and (over the prosecution's objection) asked Wood whether he got the impression from Loving "that his daughter had been ruined." Wood answered yes, but on redirect admitted that Loving had said nothing in his statement about an assault or an attempted assault. After Wood "stepped down Commonwealth's Attorney Bouldin said the prosecution" rested.[72]

Despite its clarity the prosecution's case seemed weak to some observers, and its brevity provoked some speculation in the press. The *Times-Dispatch* declared "that practically every witness introduced by the Commonwealth seemed to lean toward the defense." The prosecution also left unanswered a major question: if a handful of witnesses were all that were needed to prove the crime, why were sixty-four summoned from Nelson County? But the defense left little time for spectators or reporters to ponder the effect of the prosecution's case or the purpose of the remaining witnesses, as it quickly began its presentation. Because Loving's defense team had given few hints as to their plans, the opening of the defense's case took the spectators and reporters by surprise. "Almost before anyone realized what had happened," Judge Loving was called as the first witness. When Loving was called, the *Baltimore Sun* reported that "from the expression on the faces of those outside the railing one would have thought a bomb had exploded."[73]

The defense started by turning to the heart of its case. Under the direct examination of Moore, Loving began his testimony by recounting his biography. After this brief account the questioning and Loving's answers turned to Elizabeth Loving and her visit to Harry Snead's home on April 21. Loving began recounting how "on the following morning Harry came to me just after breakfast and, after a good deal of hesitation told me—" Commonwealth's Attorney Bouldin interrupted Loving, objecting to the testimony as "irrelevant." With the jury removed, the two sides began a half-hour legal "wrangle" over the admissibility of the news of Lizzie returning incapacitated from the buggy ride. The defense contended that it should be allowed to introduce evidence "that Judge Loving had been told such a story as would cause him to think Estes had ruined his daughter." The defense first asserted that such information would be necessary to show "the condition of" the defendant's "mind." But the defense was not content only to rely on an insanity defense; the defense lawyers said that such testimony could be used in mitigation to "reduce the crime from murder to manslaughter."[74]

The defense sought to get the full story of why Loving invoked the unwritten law into the trial by two different routes, insanity and mitigation, while the prosecution sought to block both paths. Both sides were prepared with authorities and precedents to support their positions. The prosecution focused almost exclusively on the issue of mitigation, arguing the long-established doctrine that mere words or information was insufficient to reduce murder to manslaughter. The prosecution added that although "instant provocation" could reduce the degree of crime, "when the blood had time to cool it became murder." Harmon, making a preemptive strike at the unwritten law, said that "if a man merely acted on information he took the law into his own hands and made himself judge, jury, and executioner." The defense, in turn, focused on the issue of cooling time, contending that the amount of time it took for the blood to cool was a matter for the jury to decide and therefore the evidence should be presented. On the insanity issue the prosecution fell back on the idea of hearsay to limit what Loving could say. In reply, the defense asserted that it must be allowed to admit evidence that showed the defendant's state of mind when he killed Estes. Strode declared, "If this man is not allowed to tell his provocation . . . it would be a mockery of justice." Judge Barksdale ruled that Loving was "entitled to all the evidence tending to prove the state of his mind at the time" of his act and that Loving could testify to what others told him.[75]

Back on the stand, William Loving repeated, with some new details, the account of how he learned of the buggy ride and Elizabeth's stupor, his interviewing her about it, what she said to him, and his seeking and killing Estes. Recounting what Harry Snead had told him, Loving detailed the story of Elizabeth's returning from the buggy ride incapacitated, the summoning of the doctor, and a flurry of activity by Mrs. Kidd, Snead, and another relative, W. B. Lea, concerning Elizabeth's state. Lea told Snead that Estes had told Dr. Strother that Elizabeth was drunk, and Snead passed this information on to Loving. Loving also recounted how he summoned his daughter (admitting "I did not want to go after her . . . I had control of myself, and did not want to go where I could meet Estes") and questioned her about the events. According to Loving, after the family had lunched together, he had a private interview with Elizabeth. She "got down on her knees and began to sob" and told him about the drive. Estes had offered her a drink from a flask, and she had "a very small portion of the liquor." Soon after she felt faint and asked to be returned to Lovingston. When asked if Estes had attempted to assault her, Elizabeth "told me that Estes had forced himself upon her" and that she resisted and then blacked out. Loving recounted his feelings upon hearing this tale: "My daughter was my pride. . . . I admired her purity." Learning that she had been "defiled rended my heart strings and there was no power that could have restrained my hand." Much of "the rest of Judge

Loving's direct testimony was corroborative of evidence already adduced," detailing how he had searched for and shot Theodore Estes.[76]

Loving also testified to his mental condition and invoked the unwritten law. Loving concluded his direct testimony by recounting his own long struggle with drink. According to Loving, from 1887 to 1895 he was a drunkard. In this period, when he suffered the delirium tremens, his wife left him, and he lost all his property. But then he took the Keeley cure (often known as the gold cure) at one of the many branch Keeley institutions. Except for occasional binges, the last one occurring in February 1907, he was now drink free. This frank confession "was a part of the program of his lawyers" to lay the basis of his mental instability. Also, much of Loving's testimony appealed to traditions of honorable vengeance. Loving "laid an awful crime at the doors of Estes," one which justified violence as a corrective. Loving's only loss of "emotional equipoise" came when he described the "alleged defilement of his daughter." The emotional appeal apparently touched many. Loving's own attorneys "showed moist eyes," a "lawyer of the opposition looked desperately uncomfortable," and some reported that "two or three of the jurors were inclined to grow lachrymose." Seeing the effect of the Loving's testimony, "a reporter for one of the New York papers wrote the prophetic word 'Acquittal'" and showed it to other reporters.[77]

Loving's cross-examination was brief. The prosecution wisely left alone the issue of what Harry Snead and Elizabeth Loving had told him and focused on Loving's premeditation and his mental condition. The prosecution forced Loving to reiterate that he had deliberately chosen buckshot before setting out. It also asked him if he remembered saying at an earlier hearing that he was not crazy, which Loving did not deny. After less than an hour on the stand over two days, Loving stepped down. The defense followed his testimony by calling in sequence the two people who had shaped William Loving's view of the carriage ride: Harry Snead and Elizabeth Loving. Harry Snead spent much time on the stand, telling in great detail how and what "he had told Judge Loving." Snead did not hold up well under cross-examination, refusing to specify at what time Estes returned Elizabeth from the buggy ride and retreating into vagaries on what he told William Loving about Elizabeth's condition. He was followed on the witness stand by Elizabeth Loving.[78]

Lizzie, between frequent sobs—in a courtroom cleared of spectators—testified as to what she told her father about the buggy ride. She related how Annie Kidd persuaded her to go driving with Theodore Estes. She told how they, after going toward Oak Ridge, returned to Lovingston where Estes went into his house for a few moments. Then they continued in the opposite direction toward a nearby gap in the hills. Theodore offered her whiskey, and she took "a swallow of it." Elizabeth told her father that the liquor "must have been drugged because immediately she began to get dizzy" and "could not see things; everything commenced to dance before me." She asked to be taken home, but Theodore took the road into the mountains, not the one to Lovingston. "So father then asked me if he attempted to assault me. I told him that he had forced himself upon me." Lizzie reported that she lost consciousness and remembered nothing until waking in bed late at night in the Kidds' house. She concluded by telling the effect of her story on her father. "When I told him . . . he got so white and unnatural-looking that it scared me. . . . I believed I had killed my father." According to the *New York Times,* "Her story was exactly the one which Judge Loving had previously testified she had told him." Elizabeth's story left it open as to whether the rape had been attempted or completed. But in general her testimony went a long way to finishing the construction of a defense based on the unwritten law.[79]

Cross-examination of Elizabeth Loving focused on the veracity of her story. Of course, the prosecution's lawyers were limited in the tactics they could use. The attorneys could not verbally browbeat Loving with contradictions in her story. Such a direct assault would probably backfire by turning chivalric Virginians against them. So Bouldin (with the assistance of Harmon) used an indirect approach. He asked, "in a fatherly, deferential fashion," a great number of questions about the route, timing, and occurrences on the buggy ride. Mostly Elizabeth replied to these questions by pleading loss of memory, although she did add the detail that when she screamed, Theodore smothered her cries with a hand over her mouth. These questions were designed to set up an array of prosecution witnesses who would rebut the story of an attack on the buggy ride. To downplay the possibility of rape having occurred, the prosecution forced out of Elizabeth the admission that her underclothes showed no evidence of having been interfered with or treated roughly. Moreover, in an attempt to undercut her assertion that from one swallow she became dazed, Bouldin asked Elizabeth if before she left to go on the buggy ride, she took "a drink of liquor at Estes's store," to which she replied, "Yes." But his attempt to ask more questions about her drinking habits to suggest that "Miss Loving was addicted to drink" were withdrawn after defense objections.[80]

In a series of questions, the prosecution raised the possibility that Elizabeth Loving's activities on the day after the shooting were hardly those of a victim of a sexual attack. It forced her to admit "that she had not mentioned a single word of her experience on the evening prior" to the people she met the day of the shooting. In the morning she met with a dressmaker and was fitted for a gown; she lunched with the Kidds and "talked pleasantly with" Theodore's mother when she called. After she returned home and had spoken with her father, and he had left "to hunt up young Estes and take his life," Elizabeth did not act abnormally. She and her mother met a visitor coming by train at the private railroad siding on the estate and entertained an unexpected gentleman caller. The whole time William Loving was away, Elizabeth was surrounded by various relations and friends participating in "casual conversation" with "no reference to what was happening."[81]

In the cross-examination of Elizabeth Loving, the prosecution revealed how it intended to meet the defense's use of the unwritten law. With the cross-examination concluded, it was clear that the prosecution planned to impeach her testimony further "by other witnesses." Indeed, the lion's share of its witnesses from Nelson County were brought to testify as to "all that occurred on" the buggy drive. Asked directly by Judge Barksdale whether the prosecution would "endeavor to prove that Mr. Estes offered Miss Loving no indignities on the drive," Bouldin replied. "We will." But before the prosecution could call rebuttal witnesses, the defense had to finish its case.[82]

The last witnesses for Loving (a friend of long standing, an insurance agent, two doctors who knew him, and a mental expert) put the final touches on the insanity defense by showing that Loving's mind was "a wreck." Sheriff John P. Beard of Amherst County and Beverley D. Harrison, an insurance agent (and former state legislator), testified "as to Loving's excessive drinking" and "the change it had brought on him." Dr. William Tunstall testified that Loving looked deranged when he saw him soon after the shooting, while Dr. H. B. Melvin testified about the deleterious effects of excessive drinking on mental health. Finally, Dr. Charles Emmons (formerly of the Hammond Hospital in New York City but now working at a sanatorium in Washington, D.C.) gave expert testimony that his examination of Loving showed "that dissipation had left its deadly mark on" his "mental apparatus." His reply to the ponderous hypothetical question posed by the defense (that recapitulated Loving's history and the defense narrative of events leading to the shooting) was that "the act of Judge Loving" in shooting Estes "was the result of a diseased mind." At the conclusion of his testimony, the defense rested, and after a brief break the rebuttal began.[83]

The prosecution sought to rebut the defense's witnesses as to Loving's mental condition and what happened on the buggy ride. When the prosecution called Annie Kidd to the stand, as the first of over forty witnesses to tell of the events of the evening, the defense objected. Harmon explained their goals in court and then in a subsequent statement read to the press. In order to undercut the idea that Loving had provocation which mitigated the killing to manslaughter, they wanted to show that Elizabeth Loving was "merely intoxicated; not unconscious; not drugged," and that during the period Loving had claimed she was unconscious, she saw and talked sensibly to a number of people. Among those she talked to was Annie Kidd, who would testify that Elizabeth admitted that her condition was a result of too much drink and asked that it be hidden from "Mrs. Kidd and a visitor in the house," most likely Lea. Most of the witnesses were scheduled to show that the buggy ride took place in daylight, "and at every point there were three witnesses in whose full view she was before" along the ride. Others would say that there was a buggy behind them with a "man and woman who saw the trip out and where they turned back." The prosecution had a witness ready to testify that he consumed what was left of the flask of liquor with no ill effects. Moreover, Harmon argued, Judge Loving "acted in haste in shooting young Estes, as he could have gotten all the facts and information about the buggy ride" in Lovingston "without going out of his way." In a rhetorical question he appealed to the general idea of fairness, "Is human life so cheap that you or I may be shot down on the mere statement of one individual?"[84]

The defense was ready for this line of argument. Strode had prepared a legal argument to exclude this rebuttal evidence, and if the judge ruled the evidence admissible, he had prepared to attack the credibility of each of the witnesses, alleging that they had been swayed by the influence of the powerful Estes family. Strode, "in a lengthy speech, flanked by a number of cases," objected to admission of this evidence on the grounds that what happened on the buggy ride and what Elizabeth did later at the Kidds' home did not bear on "the question at issue": the defendant's state of mind at the time of the killing. Discarding the claim that Elizabeth's and Snead's stories should work toward mitigation of the crime, Strode argued that their evidence had been admitted by Judge Barksdale solely to show how it affected William's mind. Thus "the truth or falsity of the accusation made by Miss Loving was collateral." The only question relevant to rebuttal was, what did Elizabeth Loving tell her father? Moore supported this position by citing a number of precedents to show that such evidence had been excluded, including the ruling of the judge in the first trial of Harry Thaw in New York. This line of argument prompted one out-of-state reporter to remark, "We were now treated to the old Thaw argument as to the cogency of exciting information on the mind of the hearer, whether the same be true or false."[85]

The next day Judge Barksdale delivered a "decisive blow" to the prosecution's plans to rebut Elizabeth Loving's testimony on the buggy ride. Ignoring William T. Jerome, the prosecuting attorney in the Thaw case, who telegraphed a number of citations from other states that had ruled such evidence admissible, Barksdale ruled inadmissible the prosecution's proposed evidence. Citing precedents from other jurisdictions that were "strongly persuasive," Barksdale ruled that Elizabeth Loving's testimony concerning "the ride and her return to Lovingston" were "collateral and cannot be contradicted." Moreover, the judge discounted as "unnatural and unreasonable" Bouldin's argument that Loving failed to ascertain the truth of his daughter's statements and found no reason to introduce the rebuttal testimony. He declared "neither the character of Miss Loving nor of the unfortunate young man" were "in issue in this trial," which was solely to determine William Loving's guilt or innocence. With Barksdale sustaining the defense objection, over forty witnesses for the prosecution were dismissed and sent home; the prosecution used most of its remaining witnesses to rebut the claims of Loving's insanity.[86]

The prosecution's last witnesses, six laymen and one expert, all spoke to Loving's physical and mental condition. The lay testimony added up to avowals of the lack of insanity in the Loving family, declarations of Loving's fine physical health, denials that he appeared mad, and assertions that he was a sober citizen, though "high tempered." The defense undermined these lay witnesses' credibility either by showing their marriage or social relations to the Estes family or by demonstrating that they did not know Loving well. The defense had more trouble weakening the testimony of the prosecution's mental expert, Dr. Joseph S. DeJarnette, superintendent of the Western State Hospital at Staunton. A strong believer in hereditary causes of mental weakness and insanity, DeJarnette's predilections led him away from perceiving Loving as insane. After establishing his status as an expert, the prosecution presented DeJarnette with a "long, tedious," hypothetical question. It closely resembled the defense's question in setting out Loving's history of drinking and the hearing of the news of his daughter's alleged attack. When asked what effect such experiences "would have on the mind of this man," DeJarnette replied, "He was very angry because he thought his daughter had been ruined by this young man, but not insane." On cross-examination DeJarnette "tenaciously clung" to his opinion that Loving was sane when he killed Estes. And on that note, testimony in the trial ended.[87]

The closing statements (four for the defense and two for the prosecution) followed the trial strategies of each side. In summation, Harmon and Bouldin both underscored the time for reflection that Loving had before he acted. They argued that his selection of buckshot showed premeditation and his admission that he did the killing deliberately showed malice. They sought to invoke sympathy for the Estes family with its "broken-hearted mother" and its "stricken old father." They denied that Loving was insane, pointing to his words, "I am not crazy," said to Commissioner Perkins. The prosecution insisted that Loving knew right from wrong because he quickly turned himself in to authorities. Harmon emphasized that if the jury acquitted Loving by reason of insanity, following Virginia law "it shall so specify in its verdict," while Bouldin suggested that Loving's madness was manufactured for the trial, saying that "there was no suspicion in the mind of any one" about his mental condition "until this unfortunate affair." In short, the prosecution wanted the jury to brand Loving either a murderer or a madman.[88]

In their closing arguments defense attorneys Barksdale, Lee, Strode, and Moore argued the unwritten law, although they "reinforced" their appeals with "legal arguments" on insanity. Barksdale, who "was too feeble to speak long," did not invoke the unwritten law directly, "but he dwelt much on the sanctity of the home and womanly purity." Moore, after claiming "we stand by the written law," went on to tell the jury to send a message about the "preservation of the sanctity of Virginia homes." A conviction, he asserted, "would not raise the moral standard or elevate the womanhood of Virginia." He urged the jury not to "put the felon's stripes on a Virginia gentleman." Lee asserted that liquor was "the most prolific cause of the downfall of young women." The homes of Virginians, "nurseries of God, from which spring noble men and chaste women," were under assault from men with "ulterior" motives who tempted women with liquor. Such men were beyond the pale of society. He compared Virginia to the North where women "were looked upon as . . . legitimate prey." Such invasions of the home could not be borne by Virginia gentlemen. Similarly, Strode extolled Virginian values, declaring that "the people of Halifax and Nelson counties cherish the same traditions and the same sentiments. The heritage of Virginians is common to us all." Those sentiments included honor and the unwritten law. "The commonwealth demands the life of the defendant, and for what? I do not undervalue life, but there is something sweeter to all Virginians—the purity of our women." He continued, "We have written in our laws that if a man attempts to attack one of our daughters he has forfeited his life."[89]

If Strode was saying that the unwritten law was part of Virginia statute law, he was mistaken, and if he was talking of the penalty for attempted rape, he was being remarkably vague. His vagueness implied that the unwritten law was part of the state's law. That it was not, prompted a long wrangle between defense and prosecution over the instruction on the topic given to the jury. The two sides met to devise mutually agreeable instructions; when this effort failed, each side presented a set of instructions to the judge while objecting to certain of the other side's instructions. As the closing arguments were proceeding, Judge Barksdale reviewed these instructions, devising a compromise on the points in dispute. Initially, the judge decided that a prosecution instruction saying that the unwritten law was not part of Virginia law was "superfluous." Then, perhaps moved the defense's general reliance on the unwritten law, he reversed himself, sending to the jury an instruction that declared the so-called unwritten law should not figure into the jury's deliberations. The remaining thirty-two instructions covered distinguishing murder from manslaughter and the application of the insanity plea.[90]

The jury retired for less than an hour and returned with a verdict of not guilty. The jurors, whom Chesterman had characterized during the testimony phase of the trial as "absolutely inscrutable," who had only shown "any semblance of interest in anything . . . when they were allowed to inspect a newspaper picture of themselves," made up their minds quickly. The hour was consumed in having the instructions read to them. On the first ballot, by a show of hands, they unanimously voted for acquittal. When later asked by reporters what their verdict was based on, foreman B. S. McGraw, claiming to speak for other members of the jury, replied, "Insanity." But McGraw may have been merely hiding the jury's belief in the unwritten law. According to the *Baltimore Sun,* "Several of the jurymen were cornered by the newspapermen, and they all declared that Judge Loving only did what any father would do." If so, the jurors seemed to think that insanity should be a blanket rule in these circumstances; according to these jurors, after hearing such a story from his daughter, a father could not be held responsible for his acts because his reason would be dethroned. Another juror told a Virginia paper's reporter "that the verdict was based on the 'unwritten law,' and that there was no doubt in the minds of any juror but that Judge Loving had acted properly."[91]

Another action by the jury showed that it believed in the value of female virtue that animated the unwritten law. "Within a half an hour after the rendition of the verdict," to quote Strode, "two of the jury," saying they were "a committee representing the entire jury," delivered a message "to Judge Loving, his wife and daughter." They said the jury believed that "Miss Loving's statement on the witness stand of what she had told her father was a true account of what she communicated to him, yet not for a moment did the jury entertain the opinion that an actual assault had been committed by the deceased upon the young lady, . . . but that there had been an attempted assault." This statement was an effort to restore Elizabeth's virtue, asserting that her bodily purity remained intact.[92]

Strode, who released this information to the press, added his own qualifying statements, which ironically raised the issue that Elizabeth lied by omission on the stand. In saying that the jury's position on the rape was "absolutely correct," Strode added that the defense "had learned before the trial that Miss Loving had not been actually assaulted and we had fully expected that the prosecution upon cross-examination would bring out the fact from the lips of the young lady." If the prosecution had cross-examined her "on this as they did about other incidents of the drive, . . . they would have learned from Miss Loving that no actual assault had taken place." Strode's statement directly contradicted what Elizabeth testified to in court: swooning under attack and remembering nothing until waking at the Kidds' home. Perhaps aware of the discrepancy, Strode asserted that she testified in court as to what she had told her father (which prompted him to believe that the "assault had been both attempted and consummated") but later she "learned after inquiry that the assault had not been actually consummated and was prepared so to testify." (Strode was being deceptive; if Lizzie learned that the rape had not taken place through other persons, she could not testify to that effect as it would have been hearsay.) Strode justified the defense's obfuscation of whether the rape had been completed by saying that legal issue of the trial was what "communication Miss Loving made to her father." To bring it up would throw "down the bars to the introduction of a great deal of matter which . . . would have been immaterial," confusing to the jury, and resulting "in bitter and conflicting statements" of what happened on the ride. This last statement pointed to the brilliance of the defense's strategy of keeping all evidence as to what happened on the ride, except what Elizabeth Loving said about it afterwards, from the jury. It preserved Elizabeth as an idealized woman whose virtue needed guarding by precluding assertions by others that she was lying about what happened on the buggy ride. In light of the jury's verdict and statements, the value of this strategy is plain. Strode's statement, however, underscored that Loving killed Estes under a false impression, undercutting the honorableness of his act. But the immediate courtroom and public reaction to the verdict portrayed William Loving differently.[93]

The majority of press reports in the aftermath of the verdict indicated that Loving's friends and family were moved to joyful tears. One claimed that "Judge Loving and his wife were surrounded by hundreds of happy-faced men, many of whom cried as they shook" his hand; another reported that "tears streamed from the eyes of both the defendant and his wife." The judge thanked each member of the jury, some of whom were crying. Another paper asserted that Loving "was showered with congratulations as he walked from the court room." In the crowd outside the Lovings "had to pause many times" as they descended the stairs at the front of the courthouse leading to the green. They walked between "rows of people" on the way to the hotel where Elizabeth had remained. "The girl was weeping with joy as her father and mother walked up the steps and in an instant she was in her father's arms." Loving made a statement thanking the people of Halifax for their "fairness and justice" and the press for their "fair and considerate reports." The Lovings' return to Nelson County by train was a triumphant procession, with crowds lining the stations for glimpses of the family. One unsympathetic observer complained that William Loving was treated as if he were "some hero, who had performed some meritorious and noble deed." On the trip William at each stop would circulate among the crowds while Elizabeth waved her handkerchief from the train. The interest of the crowds in William and Elizabeth Loving reflected how the press had featured them in its coverage of the trial.[94]

At the opening day of the trial, the *World*'s headline "Daughter Weeps As Judge Loving Is Tried for Life" captured the essence of the story as told by the sensation-mongering papers. Given their roles in the trial, it was natural that the press would focus on William and Elizabeth Loving. But the *World*'s headline also underscored the human-interest aspects of the story. Emphasizing their roles as father and daughter universalized their situation, making it more appealing to a mass audience. It invited the readership to identify with the Lovings as they faced various turns of fortune in the trial. To this basic formula were added various "spices," such as Elizabeth's beauty or William's emotional breakdown. Other headlines, including "Mind a Wreck," "Estes' Acts," "Miss Loving Tells of Estes's Insults on Lonely Drive," and "Loving in Tears" boosted the lurid and sensational aspects of the trial.[95]

The sensation-loving press portrayed William Loving as a man trapped by fate. Descriptions of him read like romantic fiction. "He is tall, slender and straight, and has piercing black eyes, which are set off by the blackest of eyebrows." Another account described Loving during his testimony as showing "a determination to exonerate himself . . . and escape the meshes of the law." Depending on the paper or the particular event in the trial, he was either being crushed by the experience or bearing up well. "He appears keen, erect and alert as a falcon," not the "nervous wreck" that his friends said he was. On the other hand, according to another account, William wept when the indictment was read. Later in the trial the same paper reported that he "looked sad and careworn," but it attributed his condition to "the awful strain he underwent yesterday, when he took the stand in his own behalf" and heard his daughter testify how Estes "had offered her an indignity." Also, the reporters sympathetically chronicled his recounting of the interview with Elizabeth on the day following the buggy ride. Chesterman declared that Loving asked the court to excuse him and "bowed his head for a minute and wept." Allen Potts, in the *Times-Dispatch,* wrote that the judge's testimony "was not less pitiful than his daughter's, and more than once he broke down in the narrative. . . . He described brokenly his grief and anguish, as he listened to the story of ruin." The press was sure "that the father's testimony must have burned itself into the minds of the twelve men" of the jury. Elizabeth, as befitting her role in the trial—and her gender—was given a slightly different and more intense treatment.[96]

Out-of-state papers ran stories with similar foci, features, and headlines that revealed the basic sensational-story treatment of Elizabeth Loving. For example, the *World* carried photographs of William, Elizabeth, and Theodore under the banner "Girl Whose Story Caused Father to Kill, the Father and the Slain Youth." Its opening-day article detailed Elizabeth Loving's physical manifestations of her emotional distress, mentioning that "her eyes" were "swollen and red from weeping," that "several times" she "appeared on the verge of collapse," and that her one smile on opening day appeared "hysterical." The story speculated that she was thinking of "the hour of her own ordeal on the witness-stand." If a paper did not run a photograph of Elizabeth Loving, it would describe her and her apparel in detail. According to one paper she was a "pretty young woman" who was a "decided blonde" possessing a "pretty figure." Virginia papers joined in; for example, the *Evening Journal* ran a headline, "Miss Loving in Tears," and went on to describe her attire. "She wore a black skirt and white linen waist, jaunty sailor hat, and white veil. Miss Loving is unmistakably pretty and attractive." Whether out-of-state or Virginian, the papers' sensationalism reached its peak with her time on the witness stand.[97]

What the *American* called the "daughter's sacrifice" proved the dramatic centerpiece of the press's coverage. The *World* illustrated its story of Elizabeth's testimony with a line drawing of her crying on the stand, with her father in an inset, weeping as she told her story. The *Richmond Times-Dispatch* described "the spectacle of a young and beautiful girl, refined and well born, sacrificing all that a woman holds sacred upon the altar of her affection for her father" as the "most pathetic and touching scene ever witnessed in a court of law in this Commonwealth." This treatment of Loving combined idealized portrayals of women's role and nature with the inherent drama of the situation: "If her story is true she has been horribly handled by fate." In a rare Virginia press admission that she might be lying, the paper continued, "If the story is not true and she is sacrificing her life and good name to save her father's life, her martyrdom is no less cruel." Invoking the similarity to the Harry Thaw trial, the *Roanoke Times* declared in a headline that "Miss Loving's Story Rivals Evelyn Thaw's." Its story (like many other papers) fell into the traditions of sob-sister journalism by sympathizing with the narrator of the seduction tale. The papers focused on the melodrama of the tale told and sentimentalized the story. This approach predisposed the press, and its readers, to see Elizabeth Loving as an innocent victim, not as a witnesses who might be lying. This tendency was expressed particularly in the coverage of her cross-examination, which the press portrayed as an "ordeal" for the witness and for her family: "How Miss Loving ever managed to survive the terrible experience without fainting . . . is more than this writer can understand, for she was asked questions which must have harrowed her very soul."[98]

Although the press coverage centered on Elizabeth and William Loving, other stories increased the air of sensationalism during the trial. A rumor of Thomas Fortune Ryan's presumed role and an anonymous note threatening to blow up Houston offered interesting sidebars to the main story. Just before the trial opened, the Associated Press ran a story claiming that Loving was "backed by the millions of Thomas F. Ryan." But because Ryan was not in the courtroom and Loving's supporters quickly denied that Ryan was "backing Loving," saying that he "was taking absolutely no part in the trial," the Ryan story quickly faded. Similarly, only a few papers made much of a "Black Hand" letter sent to Judge Barksdale threatening vengeance on Houston if Loving was acquitted. Barksdale treated the letter with contempt, and thus even the Hearst press could do little with the threatening epistle.[99]

The press also generated its share of minor human-interest stories—most notably making black witnesses the butt of jokes and stories praising Houston and its inhabitants—that functioned as interludes highlighting the drama of the ordeals of Judge Loving and his daughter. Chesterman had a sharp eye for racist description of blacks. He described Julia Hubbard, who testified about William Loving looking for Estes at the store, as "an old negro woman, dressed most jauntily in her Sunday bravery and wearing a coquettish black-beaded hat." No white woman was treated so cavalierly by Chesterman or any other journalist. Similarly, Fayette Foster's eyewitness testimony was played for humor. Chesterman reported that Foster replied to a question asking whether he knew Estes's first name by saying, "Naw, sir; all I knows is that they called him Mr. Theodore Estes." His was the only voice rendered in dialect.[100]

While the treatment of black witnesses by Chesterman (and some other southern journalists) was cruel and condescending, his handling of the town of Houston and its white residents bordered on hagiography. He dismissed its blacks by noting that "the Halifax darkey is keen for 'backsheesh'" and at any opportune moment would smile "their most benignest, give-me-a-quarter smiles." But according to Chesterman, Houston's homes were "the loveliest to be found in Virginia, and the yards most beautiful." At times he sounded as if he was writing real estate copy: "Boxwood hedges and giant oaks are a feature of the town," and at twilight "the whippoorwills commence their melancholy love messages in the gardens and hedges, and as soon as they cease the mocking birds begin supplying nocturnes." He praised the inhabitants, reporting that "their hospitality has been lavish." He concluded that "every hen in Halifax is doing her part to meet the demands of the cuisine, and the cows are constituting themselves into a Niagara of milk. Spring chickens also are cheerfully giving up their lives to help things along." Of course, by presenting pastoral images Chesterman offered a contrast to the dark and dramatic tales of William and Elizabeth Loving that were the center of his, and almost all the papers', coverage.[101]

Even the Estes family was overshadowed during the course of the trial by the press's focus on the Lovings. Perhaps because the family did not speak to reporters, the press did little more than keep track of which members attended the proceedings. Near the end of the trial, the Estes family became part of the press's sensationalized stories. On June 29 the *New York World* reported (based on rumors that had been around for several days) that the Estes family, fearing Loving's acquittal, was "planning other means of clearing" Theodore's name. Declaring that the sheriff "was greatly disappointed" at Barksdale's ruling disallowing testimony from eyewitnesses to the buggy ride, the paper declared that the family was preparing a civil suit against William Loving. Swanson denied the story and asserted that the family members "have never entertained or contemplated a suit against Judge Loving." The next day the story emerged in a new form when reports surfaced that the family planned to employ Julian Hawthorn, who covered the trial for the *New York American,* to write an article "clearing" the name of Theodore Estes. Using his "graphic style," Hawthorn "will present the side of the case disclosing the evidence which was held to be 'collateral and irrelevant.'" This too proved to be a rumor, probably fueled by the family's taking a "number of affidavits from their witnesses . . . in order to form the nucleus of a statement showing what the family had proposed proving before the exclusion of their evidence" and by Sheriff Estes's comment that "all I want to do is clear the good name of my boy." Estes's statement implied that Virginia's legal system had not done justice to Theodore's reputation, a key component of honor.[102]

The newspapers also revealed that the opinion shapers in Virginia were uncomfortable about applying ideas of honor and redeeming violence to the Loving case. The very facts of the case, the lack of outsiders playing a key role in the case, the convergence of sensational coverage by papers from out of state and within Virginia, and the nature of rare criticism of the case from out-of-state journalists influenced Virginians' reaction to the use of the unwritten law in the Loving case. Virginians did not rally round the decision as an example of the merits of southern justice. Rather, many of them condemned it and sought ways to overcome the difficulties they saw in it. This lack of a defensive posture toward the operation of their system of justice should not be read to mean that Virginians had fully abandoned honor—though some who rejected honor criticized the case—but that they had their doubts about its application in this case. On the other hand, when discussing the role and treatment of women during and after the trial, Virginia newspapers consciously compared honorable southern society to degenerate northern society.

It is instructive to compare the Loving case to the Leo Frank case of 1913-15. That Georgia case of violated womanhood was dominated by southerners' fear of "foreign threats" often linked to the changing economy. Virginians shared similar concerns about the loss of their social values to the new values of the age. For example, the speech that won the prize oration contest at Richmond College in 1907 was "The Threat of Commercialism." But circumstances in the Loving case (among them that the alleged rapist was a white Virginian and that the symbol of eastern economic power, Thomas Fortune Ryan, was kept off the front pages) seem to have kept Virginia from exploding into xenophobic rages as

Georgia did. Indeed, as W. Fitzhugh Brundage has shown in his study of lynching, there was a significant difference between how Georgia and Virginia reacted to the stresses of the early twentieth century.

The treatment of the Loving case by Virginia (and southern) papers and by northern (or national) papers as an unwritten law case was remarkably similar; in addition, there was a noticeable lack of outsiders—like Thomas Fortune Ryan or even non-Virginia journalists—featured in the trial coverage. The sensationalism that pervaded the coverage was born in the Virginia papers. Every northern urban paper's article with images of Lizzie crying was matched by a Virginia paper's story displaying her photograph. And Loving's connection with Ryan, which initially made his killing Theodore Estes national news, petered out soon after the story broke. There were no long articles detailing how a rich millionaire was thwarting Virginia justice to inflame public opinion. The stillborn Ryan connection, the coming new trial of the Thaw case, and the pyrotechnics of Darrow's efforts in the Haywood case combined to keep the Loving case off the editorial pages of northern papers.[103]

The rare editorial commentary that appeared in the northern press came bundled with other examples that kept Virginians from becoming defensive about the trial. For example, the *Nation,* the leading journal of liberal opinion, portrayed Elizabeth Loving in a harsh light when it compared her to a Belgian woman's unwritten law case. It wrote, "As in the recent Loving case in Virginia, the evidence did not show that the injured person was wholly fitted to teach in a Sunday-school." It also cited the use of the unwritten law by black and women defendants to show that the unwritten law was attempting to "become an established part of our system of jurisprudence." The *Baltimore Sun* expressed the same point in an editorial calling for outlawing the practice: "The 'unwritten law' has its champions in every one of the 45 States of this Union." Using the Thaw case and the Loving case as examples, it said "the man who invokes the 'unwritten law' is no more southern than he is northern or western." The paper also mentioned European examples of legally sanctified private vengeance. The *Times-Dispatch* used the same case from Belgium to assert that "Belgium is one country which cannot afford to sneer at America or Virginia or to rebuke us in connection with the 'unwritten law.'" And reflecting how broad it thought the phenomenon was, the *Times-Dispatch* consulted experts on the unwritten law in North Carolina and New York. Reading such articles, Virginians did not see the few attacks on the unwritten law as attacks on the South. Indeed, some out-of-state editorials (one in the *Sun* and another, titled "Murder Made Easy," by the prominent editor of the *Louisville Courier-Journal,* Henry Watterson) were quoted favorably by Virginia editors in their own commentary on the course and outcome of the Loving trial.[104]

For Virginia papers, which had already expressed doubts at the applicability of the unwritten law to Loving's case, Judge Barksdale's ruling to exclude the rebuttal witnesses and the jury's verdict prompted a reassessment of the issue of the unwritten law. The judge's ruling was printed verbatim in newspapers across the state (in one paper under the headline "Judge Barksdale's Talked about Ruling") along with editorials denouncing it. Most newspapers thought that the statutes and laws should not make such a decision possible. One small-town paper editorialized that if Barksdale's ruling was allowed to stand, then the laws of Virginia "are out of harmony with decency, fairness and justice." Another called Barksdale's decision "a strange and unreasonable ruling." The jury fared no better. A Newport News newspaper declared it was "to the shame of Virginia that a jury has been found within its limits which . . . has freed a man without even a reprimand who killed . . . in the most deliberate manner." In a perhaps oblique reference to the trial, another paper, while discussing the likelihood of Japan's adopting the jury system, admitted that "the jury system does not always" provide "justice." Thus, according to the *Roanoke Times,* the press was "a unit in condemnation of the farcical trial."[105]

Letters to the editor showed discomfort with the course and outcome of the Loving trial. A letter in the *News Leader* from "a machinist" covered a range of targets in declaring the case a "miscarriage of justice." The writer attacked Judge Barksdale's application of the law by saying that "it would not surprise me if some judges would declare that the ten commandments were unconstitutional." He cited two of those commandments, "Thou shalt not kill" and "Thou shalt not bear false witness against thy neighbor," implying that William was a killer and Elizabeth a liar. As for her character, he hinted that she might not be the innocent young woman that society presumed her to be. "I think in selecting a jury for such trials there ought to be six old men and six young men, because the young ones could tell older men things that did not exist in their young days and this is a fast age now." Further, the letter writer implied that lawyers coached their clients by asking, "I wonder what the testimony in such case would be if counsel were not allowed to see their client until the trial?" He concluded by suggesting that a victory banquet be held with "Mr. Abe Hummel," a New York lawyer noted for his flagrantly illegal tactics and questionable clients, "as toastmaster."[106]

The convergence of the unwritten law and the insanity defense explains much about these negative reactions to the case. According to the *Times-Dispatch*, the "unwritten law had no place in the criminal jurisprudence of Virginia," and the "brainstorm is the enabling clause of the unwritten law." An insanity defense allowed the evidence of provocation to be brought in to show the state of mind of the defendant and precluded (as in the Thaw and Loving cases) any attempt to show that the provocation was false because it was collateral. The implications of this combination of the insanity defense and the unwritten law bothered a number of newspapers, which explored them in variants on the theme "Murder Made Easy." The *News Leader*'s editorial typified them. "Suppose some man in Virginia with a murderous heart had a grudge against Judge Barksdale?" Under the current law that "man could walk into the court-room at Houston empty two loads of buckshot into Judge Barksdale's body and when arrested could have one of his woman relatives to swear that she told him that she had been grossly insulted or wronged by the judge." In the resulting trial "it would make no difference that" Barksdale's "whole life and character contradicted the possibility of his committing such an offense." And though there might be "evidence to show that he was a thousand miles away when the alleged wrong was done," it could not be admitted. "The case would go to the jury as that of injured relative protecting the honor and avenging the wrongs of a woman of his family." The dead man "would lie in his grave with the records standing against his name convicting him of an act which his own character and the conditions alike made impossible."[107]

Because the Estes family never had an opportunity to clear Theodore's name, some Virginia papers hinted that Elizabeth Loving was lying, making the trial a mockery. "The evidence in this case showed that a young man of high standing . . . while in the peaceful pursuit of his daily avocations was shot down in cold blood without mercy, without an opportunity to defend himself, without an instance given him to explain." Some found it hard to believe Elizabeth's story. One paper remarked that it was surprising "that an unsophisticated, shy, country boy, unacquainted with the high-handed ways of the world, . . . could be so morally depraved as to devise a scheme" to ruin "a playmate of his childhood days." Another asserted the trial allowed a witness "to deliberately swear away the character of the innocent dead."[108]

Although the Virginia editorials pictured Theodore Estes as possibly innocent, they saw Judge William Loving as anything but. The *Scottsville Courier* called him "a self-confessed, debauched murderer." Another paper contended that the judge's drinking was no reason to excuse him from responsibility for the crime. Two wrongs (drinking until becoming an inebriate, thus losing "self restraint," and killing) did not make a right. Loving's action of killing without first ascertaining whether the provocation was true was deemed unacceptable. Evan Chesterman presented this view in a way particularly appealing to Virginians: "The trial, outside of lawyers' fees, cost $1,064.40. In other words, Virginia must pay this sum because Theodore Estes was killed without a minute's opportunity to explain his alleged misdeeds." The *Charlottesville Daily Progress,* summing up the press's opinions, asserted "that Judge Loving should have been punished at least to some extent, for his hasty action." [109]

In response to the jury verdict, newspapers and individuals across the state endorsed the Machen proposal to make the unwritten law a written law or suggested other remedial action. One Roanoke paper said, "If the unwritten law is to have such a strong place" in the law, "it is high time the rights claimed under it be specifically defined." A Richmond newspaper wanted a Machen-like law "with the many conditions which shall justify an appeal to" the now written law "clearly set forth." It said the public should demand that "our statutes should require that a man who undertakes the responsibility of taking human life shall . . . be abundantly sure of his provocation." Similarly, another characterized the Loving verdict to be "a menace to human life" and urged that "public sentiment must be aroused and crystallized, and there must be a radical revision of the criminal law by the next Legislature." But that body never enacted such legislation. [110]

Others, with no more success, sought different changes to reach the same end. Stewart B. Whitehead, perhaps still smarting from the defeat, sought to change the law to preclude future cases from turning on the same combination of the insanity defense and unwritten law. He suggested that the legislature should declare "that only things 'seen' should be allowed in evidence to reduce the grade of offense." If this proposal had been law at the time of the Loving trial, William's testimony about what Snead and Elizabeth told him and Elizabeth's testimony as to what she told her father would have been excluded from the trial. If that were not enough, Whitehead urged that "whenever insanity is relied on as a defense, upon acquittal of the accused, when the homicide is proved," "the court ought to be required to commit the accused to a criminal insane asylum, to be kept for life, regardless of whether he recovers or not." Whitehead justified this point on the grounds that society needed to be protected, for "if a man has a brain storm and kills one man, he is likely to have another brain storm and kill

another man." If it had been in effect during the trial, Whitehead's second suggestion would have confined Loving to life in an asylum upon his acquittal. The
legislature enacted neither of Whitehead's proposals.[111]

Other Virginians questioned the unwritten law directly. The system of values that formed the unwritten law was attacked on the grounds that it failed to
live up to God's law and was a remnant of barbarism. A reader named Theodore
Low wrote the *Roanoke Times* that the solution to the problems of the Loving
trial was to put "the people in remembrance of the 'old-time religion.'" Virginians needed to rededicate themselves to religion, swear off "Satan's strongest
ally—whisky," and "fear God and keep his commandments." Similarly, a semi-
narian, Robert K. Massie, attacked the unwritten law, lynch law, and mob violence as symptoms of "this age of organization." He urged that "every man who
transgresses law must be disciplined as a responsible being. It is the law of God."
The law should be purged of "sentimentality and technicality" so it could better
render God's justice.[112]

In a more secular manner, three letter writers and one editorial called for
the preeminence of law over vengeance. A front- page letter to the *Daily Progress*
from "H. W. M." saw the Loving trial as "worse than an outrage upon law and
order." The writer denounced the unwritten law prevailing over law that has
been "carefully complied by legislatures, the representatives of the people themselves, and which crystallizes the experience and wisdom of many generations."
If the unwritten law could be invoked by a "man in his passion, the community
is in danger of relapse to primitive conditions." J. D. Ayers thought that findings
like the Loving case weakened the people's respect for law and increased "their
contempt for courts," threatening the political order. Similarly, Robert C. Jackson, a Wytheville judge, asserted personal vengeance was contrary to modern
civilization. "Men must be taught that self control and obedience to law."
The public's "peace" and its "safety" were "far more important than private revenge." Further, the *Lynchburg News* also asserted that law should prevail over
vengeance. "We lay down the broad proposition that if by virtue of a crime a man
deserves to die, then the law would inflict the penalty," not "the citizen who is
outraged by the crime." It dismissed the Machen proposal as tending "to legal-
ize or at least to justify by law the dictates of private vengeance." Along the same
lines Plemmer F. Jones argued that no man should be allowed to take the law into
his own hands. If he did, innocent people could be killed because a man could
easily kill without considering "the facts necessary to determine the simplest of

extenuating circumstances." Also, "no law, written or unwritten, should allow a man to ruin his own life by making a murderer out of himself."[113]

Significantly, these Virginians' criticisms of the outcome of the Loving trial make it clear that honor as a functioning system was in decline. The very terms used by Virginians against the unwritten law ("private vengeance," "primitive conditions") applied equally to honor. Indeed, because the lawyers chose to use the unwritten law through the insanity defense, they raised questions about character of the defendant. Because the unwritten law shared many of the components of honor, the trial also raised questions about honor. Most damning were variations on these: could a man whose mind had been weakened by alcohol abuse have a legitimate claim to honor? If so, what meaning did honor then have?

In attacking the unwritten law, some writers questioned whether it achieved its goal of protecting womanhood. Jones, although recognizing Virginia as "the home of chivalry, and the one place upon the western continent where woman occupies the highest place in the thoughts of men" and proclaiming his descent from "many generations of Virginians," argued that the killer's womenfolk suffered from publicity because the "bullets of . . . avengers" serve "as stupendous advertisement." To spare their shame and distress, he asserted it was better to trust the law. The *Lynchburg News* took on the analogy that justified the unwritten law. "It is a mistake to say that in killing a betrayer a man is defending his home." It was not as if he killed a burglar in his home, when he "slays to prevent a capital crime—to secure himself and his household from peril." Rather, "the wrong has been done and his act of killing spells revenge—personal revenge, pure and simple." Such an act was wrong as "after consummation of a crime the law should be the only recognized source to impose and execute a penalty." These attempts to turn the protection of women against the unwritten law showed the strength of the womanly ideal in Virginia society.[114]

Similarly, the press's comparisons of the action and treatment of women in the North and in Virginia, both during the trial and afterward, underscored Virginians' belief in the womanly ideal. During the trial, in describing the questioning of Elizabeth Loving, the Virginia papers pointed out that the lawyers were never "brutal, undignified or disrespectful." These descriptions of the gentility of southern lawyers were a subtle jab at New York lawyer William T. Jerome, widely criticized in the press for his "inquisition" of Evelyn Nesbit Thaw during the first Thaw trial.[115]

Along the same lines, as the trial was winding down, the *Times-Dispatch* published an editorial entitled "Virginia Women" that pointed out the differences between northern and southern society. "Remembering the mad rush of New York women to secure cards admitting them" to the Thaw trial, "northern newspapers have already directed attention to the fact—which seems remarkable to them—that not a single woman entered the courtroom at Houston." The paper declared that "there would be surprise and mortification if the women of Virginia showed the least desire to be present when a terrible story was being unfolded on the witness stand. Their very nature rebels against the thought." They possessed "sympathy and compassion . . . for one of their sex who has been placed in a position more trying than death itself, and they prefer to show it by remaining away." The paper concluded that Virginia women "thank God are not depraved. Their modesty and sense of decency make them shudder at the thought of piling into a foul courtroom." Their behavior was "so thoroughly typical of all that is true of the Old Dominion that we might eliminate all reference to it, except to remind the newspapers of the North that there is no justification for the delightful feeling of surprise."[116]

The issue was more complicated than the *Times-Dispatch* indicated. First, no woman was in the courtroom during Elizabeth Loving's testimony because the judge had cleared the court of spectators. Second, according to Chesterman, who sat through the whole trial, at least one member "of the fair sex" beyond "those connected with the" families appeared "among the spectators" for a brief period during the trial. Third, Chesterman thought that the rural nature of Halifax County explained the lack of vulgar curiosity among both women and men. Although praising the citizens of Houston for sparing Elizabeth Loving the "embarrassment, so far as being subjected to the gaze of the inquisitive," he asserted that she would not be treated "with such gracious consideration" in any Virginia city. He cited the large Lynchburg crowd at the station filled with the "rubbering contingent," struggling to get a glimpse of the principals in the case. It is likely that the crowd in Lynchburg was similar to the crowd of men and women captured by photographers in Richmond when the Lovings returned home. The *Times-Dispatch* discounted the "backwoods" explanation, asserting that "if the Loving trial had been sent to Richmond instead of Houston, the conditions would have been the same": no women would have been present.[117]

Commending southern womanhood was a common response to the Loving trial. For example, the *Rockingham Register* noted that "several Virginia newspapers" saw the "absence of women spectators" from the trial "as gratifying."

Some of these same papers saw the presence of women from the Loving and Estes families at the trial in an equally favorable light. For example, one paper described Mrs. Loving as "the very embodiment of womanly grace, dignity and sweetness." It praised her for being "happy-hearted and courageous at all times. Not once did she whimper when the jury was out." Her every movement reflected her "good taste and good breeding." Best of all, "her loyalty shone with striking lustre." Looking at the behavior of the women at the trial, the *Rockingham Register* asserted that it was "typical of Virginia standards—and indeed of the standards throughout the South." The paper rhapsodized that even though the Old South had passed away, "we have not departed from the old customs." Virginia, and the South, was still the "land of chivalrous men; and of women pure in heart." Such women were "eager always to avoid rather than confront that which brings notoriety, or to listen to that which is not attuned for woman's ear to hear." Southern women's "inborn gentility of character"—their "exalted conception of the true sphere of womanhood"—kept them from "attending sensational criminal trials," except to support their men.[118]

The mere existence of sensational trials involving women as participants worried some Virginians and prompted calls for restoring the old standards. An editorial in one Roanoke paper, prompted by Elizabeth Loving's testimony of drinking with Estes, proclaimed that there was "a great lesson here" for girls. Although neither "young Estes" nor "the father" were "without blame," the editorial writer stressed that the "very fact that she accepted a bottle and drank whisky was the first cause of all the trouble." Men would "take liberties" if they were "indirectly invited" by "wildness." In short, "it is the first and last duty of a girl or woman to be a lady." Along the same lines, a Richmond paper's editorial entitled "Old and New Virginia" lamented the "recent instances of Virginia women figuring" in sensational murder trials and scandalous divorce cases. It worried that "something must be wrong . . . with our social conditions. These things did not used to happen in Virginia, or if they did happen the participants had sufficient regard for the proprieties to keep them quiet." The paper sought a revival of standards: "Hadn't we better take a grip on ourselves and our families in time and restore the old ways, no matter how much labor, care and contention it may cost us?"[119]

If the old ways included community justice, then perhaps Virginians in Nelson County did retain the old ways. The later lives of William and Elizabeth Loving and the final resting places of William Loving and Theodore Estes reveal how Nelson County society saw them. The friends of Theodore Estes and the

Estes family turned to the social realm when law failed them in their quest to restore Theodore's good name. They built a memorial to Theodore, paid for with
public subscriptions, with an inscription declaring that it was "erected to his
memory by the friends who knew and loved him and by those in many states,
who not knowing him, asked to pay their tribute also, to his innocence and
worth." The historian of Oak Ridge, Lee Marmon, noted in 1992 that "the resulting obelisk . . . still dominates the Lovingston community cemetery."[120]

Moreover, others in the community apparently made it clear that they
thought William Loving and his daughter to be beyond the pale. A year after the
trial, perhaps succumbing to the community's views, Ryan removed William as
his estate manager, and Loving left the county. Lizzie apparently left at the same
time and probably moved directly to Atlanta, Georgia. William (perhaps with
Ryan's help) secured a job in Florida as a lawyer with Seaboard Railroad but gave
it up to practice law in Atlanta. He died in 1919 and was buried privately in the
Snead family cemetery on the Oak Ridge estate. Today, the cemetery is so over-
grown that Loving's grave is unreachable in the summer months.[121]

Elizabeth Loving started over in Atlanta, that epitome of a New South city,
where she married and had at least one son. She died in 1970. Whatever her life
was like in Georgia, her reputation in Nelson County was sullied beyond repair.
In the area's folklore the rebuttal witnesses who never took the stand turned into
a potential parade of people who would testify that Lizzie was hard drinking and
unchaste, that she was not a lady deserving of protection through the unwritten
law. As one newspaper editorialized about the outcome of the Loving's trial,
"There are some victories as bad as defeat. His daughter is disgraced by her own
testimony and the brand of Cain is upon him. We don't know but what the fate
of Estes is preferable to that of either of the survivors."[122]

Nearly forty years after H. Rives Pollard's death, a crime was committed in Oak
Ridge, where he was buried. This homicide shared some characteristics of the
earlier Pollard and Moffett killings. The Estes homicide also shows, for the Virginia papers, that the political dimensions continued to be an important part
of the story. Similar to the earlier cases, the interest of outsiders—in this case
the national yellow press—prompted the state's newspapers into assertions
of southern distinctiveness. But those assertions were rather muted, in part because of the sectional rapprochement in the Progressive period and in part because to the national sensational press the Loving case did not look different. For

honor, which had been so vital in the Grant trial and a part of the Clark case, was in this case reduced to the limited but related notion of the unwritten law. Even the unwritten-law defense was unconnected to the social moorings of Nelson County society. The community showed strong support for the victim, and it was unlikely that the appeal to the unwritten law would have worked with a local jury. Also, in the Loving case the role of outsiders, including the sensational and national newspapers, was less participatory and more limited than in the earlier cases. In part, this probably came about from the shrewd work of Loving's lawyers, who apparently kept Thomas Fortune Ryan's role hidden from the press's scrutiny. The financial resources of the Loving family (whether or not aided directly by Ryan) allowed them to keep both the Virginia and the national press at a distance. Twenty-eight years later another Virginia family caught up in a murder trial would not have such means. As a result, the press, and outsiders, would figure far more prominently in the case. And like the Loving case, that case too would raise questions about the role of women in Virginia society.

Four

"EDITH AND HER PAPPY"

IN THE EARLY MORNING of July 21, 1935, H. T. "Trigg" Maxwell of Pound
died in his home. His wife, Anne, and his daughter Edith were soon arrested for
his murder. Edith, a twenty-one-year-old schoolteacher, was tried twice for the
crime in the Wise County courthouse (the second time after a successful appeal
to Virginia's highest court); each time she was convicted. The national press and
outside groups took a great interest in this case from a remote Appalachian
county. Their actions and words prompted Virginians, including Virginia newspapermen, to rebut what they considered inaccurate reporting and to defend the
reputation of Virginia justice.[1]

When this case occurred, daily newspapers had an established hegemony on
news, but they were being threatened by new media. News reels and radio offered alternative means of disseminating news. News reels were restricted to a
special venue and were, compared to papers, relatively expensive. Radio had the
great advantage of being able to reach people at home and at work, but papers
hampered radio's ability to function as a news provider. Papers bought up stations and limited their news broadcasts by restricting access to the wire services
and forbidding them from reading newspaper stories without compensation.

Newspapers also forced a deal which limited how much time the early radio networks could devote to news. In addition, radio's news value was undercut by network rules against broadcasting recorded material and by technical limitations. Until radio allowed taped broadcasts (after the 1937 Hindenburg disaster), its coverage was limited to stories in areas easily connected to broadcasting equipment. Thus papers kept their dominance over the audience. Press chains and cooperative news-sharing—which linked the majority of the nation's newspapers—supplied a steady stream of stories for the ever-growing number of readers. Those readers were again exposed to the papers' accounts because weekly news magazine routinely retooled the news stories of the daily press. Moreover, the partisan press had almost disappeared, and the most sensational aspects of the yellow press had moved into a new format, the tabloid. And the idea of objective reporting, asserted originally by the independent press against the partisan press, was now being applied to the sensational press. As the sensational press toned down its luridness, daily newspapers from the independent tradition adopted many of the former hallmarks of yellow press: simpler words, numerous illustrations, and sensational stories. At the same time various groups—like feminists—continued to present their views of events through their advocacy newspapers, offering a counterpoint to the main developments in American mainstream journalism. And by the 1930s the leading southern newspapers, edited by men following the path of H. L. Mencken at the *Baltimore Sun,* made their papers, in style and substance, resemble the rest of the nation's newspapers.[2]

The Maxwell case became a national story because it was a sensational case. Building on the statement of a witness, the press widely reported that Edith Maxwell admitted to striking Trigg Maxwell with a high-heeled shoe—in 1930s parlance, a slipper—and she was quickly dubbed "the slipper slayer." Beyond the lurid aspect, the national press interjected into the Maxwell story reams of local color and human-interest angles. It portrayed the trial as a clash between old-fashioned Appalachian culture and modern society over the role of women. In addition, the press reports portrayed this part of Virginia as being an economic and social backwater, out of step with the nation's progress. Also, the big city and national syndicates became directly involved in the case. Some papers raised defense funds for Maxwell, hired attorneys for her, and paid for experts to testify on her behalf. Moreover, the press reports brought the case to the attention of women's organizations.

Indeed, in many ways Maxwell's case was a woman's-issue case. In the wake of the press reports of her first conviction, several women's organizations took up Maxwell's cause. Several out-of-state organizations raised money for her appeal. One organization, the National Woman's Party, went further and supplied lawyers to Maxwell. Working alongside Maxwell's other lawyers, the lawyers from the party sought an appeal on the grounds that all male juries—required by Virginia law—were unconstitutional.

Thus outsiders were deeply involved in the Maxwell trial, often criticizing Virginia society or its legal system. The press's treatment of the story and the organized groups' actions prompted Virginians to defend their state. On the social front they denied the allegations of economic and social backwardness. Time and time again they said that southwest Virginia was as good as any other part of the nation. On the legal front Virginians replied to their critics by emphasizing the propriety of their legal procedures. Significantly, in their defenses of their region, Virginians did not use the idea of honor.

Honor had little to do with this case, for two reasons. First and most importantly, honor suffered a significant decline as a functioning social system in the twentieth century. As Edward L. Ayers has pointed out, even at the end of the previous century "the men who steered the South into 'progress' tended to have little use for old fashioned honor." It was not just the hierarchical system of honor that declined but the more democratic postwar system also. Before disfranchisement, a democratic honor system had been a necessary component in the construction of white male cohesiveness. But after blacks lost virtually all their voting power and after segregation became entrenched, honor lost much of its functionality. Similarly, the changing status of women contributed to its decline. As women—by joining reform organizations, entering professions, and after 1920 participating in politics—eroded away the barriers that separated male and female spheres, honor was again weakened as a social system. Women no longer needed the social protection of honorable men, and this fact called into question the very gender distinctions that defined manly honor. In short, honor—though not dead—had lost its centrality with the social and economic changes of the twentieth century.[3]

Second, the circumstances of the case also worked against the emergence of honor as an issue in the trial or in the press coverage. Even if honor had been viable, it would have been hard for the prosecution or the defense to invoke it. Edith Maxwell was a woman and thus under the precepts of the system could have no claim to honor. Trigg Maxwell, despite his gender, was also a weak

Edith Maxwell.
(AP/Wide World Photos)

Edith Maxwell's reaction to verdict in second trial. (AP/Wide World Photos)

candidate for honor. His record of drunkenness and his failure to exercise patriarchal control over his family would have undercut any casting of him as an honorable man. Moreover, it was in the prosecution's interest to portray him as a victim. Despite the lack of debate over honor, the pattern of interaction between region and nation remained the same; the case of Edith Maxwell shows how Virginians rebutted the images disseminated in the national press about their region and their legal system.

Wise County, formed in the 1850s, was named after Governor Henry A. Wise, who testified in the Grant trial of 1869. Located in the Cumberland mountains of far southwestern Virginia and bordering Kentucky, Wise County was transformed (like much of Appalachia) into one of many "outposts of heavy industry" in the two decades surrounding the turn of the twentieth century. Following the expansion of the extractive industries of mining and timbering, the railroads came to the county. Wise became Virginia's center of coal and coke production. The result was tremendous population growth, increasing the county's population almost fivefold in thirty years. By the late 1930s and early 1940s, when the virgin timber was gone and the depression had dropped demand for coal and coke, the population stabilized. Wise County was overwhelmingly rural; only one in seven of its people lived in its mill towns.[4]

Wise County responded to this growth by building public buildings, roads, and schools. In 1896 the county built an imposing Renaissance Revival courthouse of yellow brick with stone trim. Also, beginning around the turn of the century, various jurisdictions within the county began to build modern roads, and by the 1930s it had a substantial road network connected to the state and national highway system. A federal highway—Route 23—ran through the county's main towns of Big Stone Gap, Appalachia, Norton, and Wise (and through the unincorporated town of Pound) north to Jenkins, Kentucky. In a state that spent per capita about half the national average on schools, Wise and the other Virginia Appalachian counties spent relatively lavishly. The school year was shorter than the state's average, and a higher number than the state's average of students attended one-room schoolhouses, but there were community high schools—like Pound's Christopher Gist High School—with state-accredited teachers. These high schools graduated students who met state standards and thus could—and did—attend Virginia's teachers colleges.[5]

These economic, demographic, and social transformations did not change how the rest of America perceived the people of Wise and other "mountaineers" living in Appalachia. Appalachians had become the subject of popular interest around the turn of the century. As industry and people pressed into the southern mountains, the lifelong inhabitants were seen as possessing sharply different folk cultures than average Americans. These different folkways became the subject of much attention, a good deal of it sensationalistic and romanticized. In particular, Americans created full-scale myths of mountain violence by building on images developed in the 1870s when the federal government attempted to enforce the liquor excise tax in the southern mountains and popularized by Christian missionaries to the backcountry. It is important to remember that the national media—and many northerners—conflated Appalachia with the South, even if it was, to borrow Virginius Dabney's phrase, a "South that never was." Emblematic of these southern myths, Americans were introduced to the Hatfield and McCoy feud.[6]

Wise County did its bit to contribute to this Appalachian mythology. From the 1890s until his death in 1919, John Fox wrote novels and stories set in Appalachia. Fox's *The Trail of the Lonesome Pine* was set in Wise County and was one of the first books in America to sell more than a million copies. Fox, born in Kentucky and educated at Harvard, came to the county as a mine manager and a land speculator. He gained fame and wealth through writing stories and books, eventually becoming as famous as his friend Thomas Nelson Page. Using a technique that stretched back as far as Sir Walter Scott, Fox took real people from the area, changed their names, expanded on their exploits, and put them into his stories and novels. His books were filled with attempts to re-create the mountaineers' speech patterns. According to the *Louisville Courier*, "His rendering of the mountain dialect is simple and unaffected and rings as true as Mr. [Thomas Nelson] Page's negro talk." The mountaineers in Fox's work emerged as sharp-eyed, quick-tempered, ignorant barbarians who made moonshine, drank too much, and were prone to violence. In short, they were hillbillies. In Fox's plots they were inevitably brought into contact with people from the modern world so the novelist could explore the conflict between traditional and modern life. Fox's was not an accurate picture, but it became the standard image of Appalachians.[7]

By the 1930s the hillbilly caricature had spread throughout American culture. The term was first used in a New York newspaper in 1900 to define a free white citizen of Alabama "who lives in the hills, has no means to speak of, dresses as he can, talks as he pleases, drinks whiskey when he gets it, and fires off his revolver as the fancy takes him." Save for the place of residency, this definition accurately reflected the major components of the stereotype of hillbilly as it moved into the popular culture. By the 1930s the hillbilly image was well established across a broad spectrum of American media. In film a version of *The Trail of the Lonesome Pine* released in 1923 reached a broader audience than Fox's words. And in 1934 the introduction of two comic-strip figures, "L'il Abner" and "Snuffy Smith," made the hillbilly stereotype a household image of southern whites. Both characters, like Fox's mountaineers, were out of step with modern civilization. This component of the hillbilly stereotype became a staple of the press coverage in the Maxwell case.[8]

The Maxwell family was a real Appalachian family from a real Appalachian community. The Maxwells lived in the oldest (unincorporated) town in the county, Pound, also known as "the Pound," sited along the bottom of the valley of the Pound River where it bends. The main street of the town (Route 23) followed the course of the river, and a majority of the town's buildings stretched for almost a mile along this road. Despite its singular geography, Pound resembled many American 1930s rural towns, with gas stations, small restaurants, a third-class post office, a Piggly-Wiggly chain store, and many smaller establishments that sold everything from hardware to alcohol. In the 1930s the town was electrified through the efforts of local resident Chant Branham Kelly, and it had a water system built by the Works Progress Administration. Trigg Maxwell and his wife, Anne Dotson Maxwell, were from established Wise County families. The Maxwell family's roots extended back to the first eighteenth-century white settlers of the region. The Dotsons came later, but they were more prominent. Anne's father, Marcus De Lafayette Dotson, owner and operator of grist and saw mills, also served as Pound postmaster and magistrate. Trigg was a miner who worked in the mines of Jenkins, Kentucky. He also had worked as a farmer and a blacksmith. Part of the building in which Trigg and his family lived since 1927 was rented out. Aged fifty-two, he was a member of the United Mine Workers and the International Order of Odd Fellows. He and Anne had six children. Two of their adult children had moved away from the region: the only son, Earl, to New York City and Alma to Detroit. Another married daughter, Gladys (Mrs. H. C. Robinson, also spelled Roberson), lived in Pound. At the time of Trigg's death, he, his wife, Anne, and their daughters Mary Katherine, Anna Ruth, and Edith lived in the family home.[9]

Edith Maxwell had just begun a career when she was arrested for killing her father. She spent her childhood in rural Wise County, the mill town of Jenkins, Kentucky, and the roadside town of Pound. Edith attended Christopher Gist

High School, graduating with honors. In 1932, with money borrowed from her aunt and supplemented by a college loan, she entered East Radford State Teachers College, an all-female institution in a small town about 150 miles from Wise County in Virginia's Blue Ridge Mountains. In the 1930s the Radford campus was a small and intimate place with six buildings roughly arranged around a pentagon-shaped common. There Edith belonged to the Athletic Association, the Ingles Literary Society, and the YWCA. She roomed with her cousin Ruth Baker, also from Pound. Earning her teaching diploma in 1934, Edith returned to Pound and took a teaching job.[10]

While teaching for two terms at a nearby one-room school on Mill Creek, Edith lived in her family's home. From the night of Trigg's death through Edith's last legal proceeding, the Maxwell family and others would comment about the relations among Trigg, Anne, and Edith. All these statements—whether delivered in the formal setting of the courthouse, whispered at community gatherings, or told to reporters—carried the partisan messages of Edith's defenders or prosecutors. What life was like in the Maxwell family home became a key contested issue in each of Edith's trials and in the subsequent public debate over the proceedings. Depending on the source, Trigg was a drunken tyrant, or Edith and Anne abused a mild-mannered man. From these biased and contradictory sources, it is impossible to divine the reality of the Maxwells' home; but whatever that life was like, it ended the night of Trigg's death.[11]

Around two A.M., twelve-year-old Mary Katherine called neighbors Chant Branham Kelly, Dr. E. L. Sykes, and Lovell Sowards to the Maxwell home, saying her father was dying. The Maxwell home was a converted garage, squeezed between Route 23 in front and the Pound River behind. Its wood-siding facade offered a door and window to the street, while its back ended about two feet from the river. The family lived in four rooms, one which served as kitchen and dining room; the other three served as sitting and bed rooms. Edith slept on a couch in one room, Trigg slept in one room, while Anne and the two younger girls shared a room. In addition, a screened porch opened off the kitchen and stretched between the river and road. The other half of the building contained a gift store and the post office run by Kelly. Next to the post office, four feet away, were Kelly's drugstore and living quarters. On the other side of the Maxwell home, separated only by the porch, were the offices and residence of Dr. Sykes. Kelly was first on the scene and found Trigg Maxwell—dressed only in long underwear and socks—on his back, directly in front of the kitchen door, convulsing in his "death struggle." According to an early press account, Maxwell "had been injured about the head." The Maxwell family contended that Trigg "had fallen and had hit his head against a meat block which was found near where the body was found." The neighbors did not believe this account and looked for evidence of foul play.[12]

In part, the neighbors' suspicions fell on the adults, Anne and Edith, because of what Kelly had heard earlier in the night. He reported hearing Edith being dropped off by a car "shortly after midnight Sunday" and the quick commencement of "arguments in the Maxwell home, which finally were followed by the pleading and groaning of the father." He then "rushed out of his home to the Maxwell home, but had been told by Edith Maxwell that there was no fire, and that it was none of his affair." After failing to gain admittance, he returned home, only to be summoned by Mary Katherine less than half an hour later. While they were attempting to revive Trigg and then laying out his corpse (and as more neighbors and family gathered), the neighbors also searched the Maxwell home. Kelly and Sowards noted the lack of blood on Maxwell's head and the absence of blood and hair on the meat block. They also noticed several areas of the kitchen floor that showed signs of having recently been cleaned. Their investigations, combined with rumors of hostility between Trigg and Anne as well as Trigg and Edith, brought Trigg's death to the law's attention.[13]

Sheriff J. Preston Adams and Commonwealth's Attorney Fred B. Greear investigated Maxwell's death as a homicide. Doctors G. T. Foust and T. J. Tudor performed a private autopsy on the body and found that Maxwell had died from brain trauma, suffered more than one blow to the head, and had bruises on his arms. Moreover, a search of the household turned up "an electric iron and bed sheet both having blood-like stains on them." Moving quickly, the authorities arrested both Edith and Anne Maxwell on Sunday afternoon. The grand jury was in session, and on Monday, July 22, it indicted them both for the murder of Trigg Maxwell. Trial was set for August 20. Anne was released on bond, but Edith was kept in jail, under the custody of her uncle C. J. Dotson.[14]

The next day, Greear subjected Edith Maxwell to "a two hour grilling" and Edith confessed to killing her father. That day, Greear announced to the press, that Edith claimed her mother had "nothing to do with the case." Further he declared, that Edith "admitted striking her father with the latter's heavy shoe, after he had scolded her" and "threatened to whip her." The source of quarrel according to Greear was Edith's "alleged attention to a certain man and for her late hours." Within two days, Anne Maxwell confirmed Edith's story saying that "the weapon was an ordinary work shoe with a solid rubber heel." Mary Katherine, "an eyewitness, said a woman's slipper was used." Both Anne and her youngest daughter apparently spoke to reporters around the time of Trigg's funeral.[15]

Maxwell's funeral exposed a number of crosscurrents within the Maxwell family. The funeral was held in the home of Trigg's daughter Gladys Robinson and was attended by most of the family. "Evidence of strong resentment by relatives" at the site prompted the sheriff and the commonwealth's attorney to "deny" Edith "attendance" at the funeral. The previous day Edith had viewed her father's body, showing—according to various newspaper reports—"no emotion." Maxwell had a funeral befitting "a prominent citizen of southwest Virginia," showing that he was well regarded in the community. The service was presided over by three ministers and was marked by "a special chorus" singing hymns. Members of the Jenkins local of the United Mine Workers bore the coffin to the graveyard, where another service was held by the Odd Fellows. Large crowds, "including many notables of Wise and Dickenson County" and reporters, showed up on both days. The notables came because they were related to the family; for example, Anne Maxwell was a sister of the former commonwealth's attorney of the county, W. W. G. Dotson, and Trigg Maxwell was brother-in-law to the former Wise County sheriff B. Lee Skeen, currently a federal deputy marshal. The reporters attended because the Maxwell case had become news.[16]

Edith's confession, as reported by Greear, provoked the sensation-loving press to dramatize her crime. A generation after the Loving trial, the number of sensationalist newspapers—including tabloids—had grown significantly. Moreover, these papers' demands for dramatic copy had made the wire services into scouts for material suitable for their melodramatic style. Some wire services, like Hearst's Universal Service, specialized in providing thrilling tales and human-interest stories. Crime was particularly attractive to newspapers because it would guarantee repeat business, as the investigation and trial followed the event. On July 25, 1935, Hearst's Universal Service produced its first story on the Maxwell case. Headlines over this story revealed their recasting of the crime: "Mountain Beauty Killed Father to Keep Love Tryst / Teacher Sobs Confession to Clear Mother / Blue Ridge Tragedy Is Laid to Whipping Threat by Parent." The story, bylined to Norton in Wise County, opened, "Here, close by the trail of the lonesome pine, a new story of Blue Ridge Mountain love was blazed as the hill folks buried Trigg Maxwell and charged his 21-year old pretty daughter, Edith, with murder." Although mostly reporting what other papers already had said about the case, the article contained probably fictional details. It alleged that Edith's beauty "was the talk of Big Notch Gap." Further, it reported, using Edith's voice in the first person, that she struck her father after he "threatened to lay a hand on me for staying out late with my boy friend." The article repeatedly characterized the Maxwell home as a "cabin." This article with stereotyped mountain setting, thwarted love story, and the first-person quotes presaged future press coverage of the story.[17]

The Hearst service sent reporter Fulton Lewis to Wise County, and he soon produced a series of stories, based mostly on interviews with Edith and her supporters, which shaped how the Maxwell story would be told to the nation. The *Washington Herald,* a Hearst paper, published four of his signed articles beginning on July 29, and other stories were available through the Universal Service and appeared in venues like the *New York Evening Journal* and the *San Francisco Examiner.* Lewis's stories focused on Edith. Her beauty was highlighted with photos of her in a bathing suit and another supposedly of her sitting "with a 'boy friend.'" The stories also played up Edith's use of "her frail highheeled" slipper in hitting her father. They contained extensive passages in her own words. Edith became the way for Lewis to portray Trigg Maxwell's killing as a "dramatic struggle between the archaic family codes of the mountains and the encroaching freedom of modern youth." Lewis asserted that a curfew existed in Wise County requiring that "all unmarried girls to be off the streets at sundown" and that the youth of the county rallied behind Edith, as their "Joan of Arc." He claimed her father wanted to beat her either for coming home late or for talking to a married man. His articles were filled with stereotypical references to Appalachian life. The men were pictured as "grizzled mountaineers," while the women were seen as burdened with overwork and male tyranny. Edith was marked out as different because of her "school larnin'" and her "storeboughten clothes." Such colorful coverage portended the press's treatment of the first trial.[18]

Edith's family dominated the defense preparations for her first trial. Three members of Edith's immediate family—her mother, her brother, and her sister Mary Katherine—were central to those efforts. In addition, her uncle the jailer gave her preferential treatment and made it easy for reporters to see her. Another uncle, William Washington Gernade Dotson (a former commonwealth's attorney for the county and two-time independent Democratic state representative), agreed to represent her at trial. Nearing seventy years old, Dotson had been associated with trials resulting from crimes fictionalized by Fox. Edith's brother, thirty-year-old Earl, a wholesale salesman for a candy company in New York, coordinated her defense. He apparently persuaded Alfred A. Skeen, younger than Dotson and a former circuit judge and commonwealth's attorney from neighboring Dickenson County, to join the defense team. Apparently also through Earl's actions, the defense was further strengthened by the addition of Democratic state senator R. P. Bruce from Wise, known as a "silver tongued orator," who had been admitted to the bar almost fifty years before the Maxwell trial and, like Dotson, had participated in the county's more notorious cases. Bruce and Skeen would do all of the questioning of witnesses for the defense.[19]

The Maxwell family also played a role in the prosecution. The commonwealth's attorney, Fred B. Greear, led the prosecution team. Thirty-six-year-old Greear, active in Democratic politics, was just completing his first term in office and would be reelected to the position in 1935 with the highest vote count of any Democrat in the county. Oscar M. Vicars and Lewis McCormick, both of Wise, were "employed by some relatives of Mr. Maxwell" to assist Greear. Vicars was judged "one of the outstanding criminal lawyers" in the state. It is probable that Trigg Maxwell's sister Chlora, married to United States marshal B. Lee Skeen, retained these lawyers. Greear and Vicars would almost evenly split the questioning for the prosecution.[20]

Completing the family connections, the case was scheduled to be tried before seventy-six-year-old circuit judge Henry Alexander Wise Skeen. Skeen's judicial baptism had come in the 1892 trial of "Talt Hall, a 'Trail of the Lonesome Pine' character," and he was related to Trigg Maxwell's brother-in-law B. Lee Skeen and to defense lawyer Alfred A. Skeen. At the original trial date, the defense sought a continuance, a separation of the cases of Edith and Anne, and a change of venue. Judge Skeen denied the change of venue petition but granted the continuance and the separation of the cases. The prosecution moved that Edith's trial be scheduled first; the judge granted that motion, and her trial was set for November 1935.[21]

From start to finish Edith Maxwell's first trial lasted just two days, November 18 and 19, 1935. Jury selection was completed in about thirty minutes. From a venire of thirty, three men were excluded because they were distantly related to the defendant, and another was excused because he took a ride with the prosecutor when hitchhiking to court. The lawyers' opening and closing statements extended for four hours, but no newspaper reported their words. (By the 1930s newspaper accounts of trials were relatively brief compared to trial coverage from earlier periods, in part because the predominance of pictures and special-topics sections reduced the amount of space that had previously been used for trial reports.) The jury deliberated for thirty minutes. About two-thirds of the remaining time was devoted to direct examination of witnesses. The prosecution attempted to prove that Edith was guilty of first degree, while the defense sought to show that Edith had struck her father in self-defense, and at most, her crime was manslaughter.[22]

The prosecution mounted a credible but not a strong case. The prosecution was denied the use of Edith's confession to Greear when Judge Skeen ruled it inadmissible because it had been coerced from her by inducements. The prosecutors also weakened their own case by failing to fix upon a single item as a weapon for the crime. The prosecution balanced these deficiencies. First, it announced it would not seek the death penalty. Historically, American juries have proved reluctant to convict when it might lead to a woman being sentenced to death. In 1934, the year before the Maxwell trial, only 1.5 percent of prisoners sentenced to death and held in state and federal prisons across the nation were women. Moreover, from 1908 to 1942 in Virginia, 180 people were put to death, 156 black men, 25 white men, 1 black woman, and no white women. So by seeking only imprisonment, the prosecution improved its odds. Second, it used a wide array of witnesses, mustering five different types: the neighbors, who were observers of the events of the night Trigg Maxwell died; the doctors, who could testify as to the cause of death; law enforcement officials, who could testify to their investigation; various people who could testify about strife between Edith and Trigg; and rebuttal witnesses to various parts of the defense's case. The strength of its case lay in the many correlations among the testimony of its witnesses.[23]

Chant Kelly testified about the events of the night Maxwell died. Kelly testified to hearing "a racket" at the Maxwells', raised voices both male and female, and "shuffling" followed by Trigg's voice at a "holler" saying, "Oh, Lordy." When Kelly went to investigate, Edith refused him entrance at the door to the porch, and the moaning stopped. Kelly testified that the Maxwells' radio began playing loudly and, soon after it began, he heard Edith telling her younger sister to get her clothes because she was leaving. Kelly said that a half hour later, Mary Katherine called him over for her father was dying. He testified that Anne, Edith, and Mary Katherine all said Trigg had fallen and hit his head against the meat block on the porch. He reported that he saw no blood on Maxwell or the porch but he noticed wet areas in the kitchen and a miner's hatchet on the porch where Trigg died.[24]

Supporting Kelly's statements, Martha Strange, Verna Hubbard, Clarence Groeschen, and J. L. Sowards all testified about what they saw and heard at the

Maxwell house on the night of July 20-21. Groeschen added that the argument, in which he recognized Edith's and Trigg's voices, began after she was dropped off by a car. Hubbard and Strange both testified to hearing the "fuss" and noises. Hubbard and Groeschen testified to Trigg's calling out, "Oh Lordy," for around ten minutes. Hubbard, Strange, and Groeschen all confirmed that the radio at the Maxwells' was turned on loudly after the argument. Hubbard buttressed Kelly's account of a conversation between Edith and Mary Katherine when she testified that Mary Katherine said, "Edith come back in the house. Daddy's got blood all over hisself," and Edith replied by telling her to fetch her a dress and shoes because she was leaving. Two witnesses supported Kelly's testimony that the Maxwell women had attributed Trigg's death to a fall: Strange asserted that Anne, in Edith's presence, said Trigg had fallen and hit his head, while Sowards testified that Edith said Trigg was drunk and fell on the meat block. Sowards said that after being "tipped off," he examined what he could see of the Maxwell house, noticing that the kitchen floor had been scrubbed with water.[25]

Sheriff J. Preston Adams, Deputy Sheriff R. S. Hubbard, county policeman Ed Delong, and county policeman Paris Mullins testified to what they found at the Maxwell home and about the Maxwell women's assertions that Trigg had met his death by falling against the meat block. Hubbard, Mullins, and Delong testified to finding a pillow, pillowcase, and sheet, wet and stained with what looked like blood, under other items in a laundry basket on the porch. Delong testified about seeing the hatchet and iron. Hubbard and Adams testified that when Edith was arrested she said that her father was drunk and had died as a result of a fall on the porch. Edith's and Anne's assertions, according to the testimony of prosecution witnesses, that Trigg had died from a fall were undercut by the testimony of the physicians.[26]

Doctors Foust and Tudor, who had performed the autopsy on Trigg Maxwell (after his body had been embalmed), testified that he had died of brain injury. They said that Maxwell had suffered three blows to the front of his head, one which cut through his scalp into the skull. They testified also that Trigg had a bruise on the bridge of his nose and a black eye, an area of small bruises about three or four inches long on his left forearm, and a small cut on the back of one of the fingers on his right hand. The implication of this testimony was that Trigg had been in a fight of some sort. The doctors asserted that the wounds on the head were made by something with a sharp surface. Their description of the weapon encompassed the items that press accounts and trial testimony linked to Trigg's death: an iron, a miner's hatchet, or a shoe.[27]

To make the case against Edith Maxwell one of murder, the prosecution called a number of witnesses who testified to animosity or difficulties between Maxwell and her father, implying premeditation on Edith's part. J. L. Sowards, G. C. Branham, Munsey Ellison, and Herman Ellison testified concerning an incident between Edith and Trigg earlier in the day. According to their collective testimony, Edith had spoken in public to a local truck driver while standing close to him—according to Greear, "belly to belly." This scene provoked Trigg apparently to rebuke Edith, and she was heard (by three witnesses) to reply, "If you don't like it, what are you going to do about it?" The prosecution asserted that this encounter was the topic of Edith's and Trigg's argument and prompted her to strike him.[28]

The testimonies of Edith's neighbor Chant Kelly; her college roommate, Ruth Baker; her fellow teachers Alta Cantrell and Conrad Bolling; and her friend Everett Holyfield were suggestive of malice. Kelly testified to another "racket" between the pair in which Edith threatened to "bust his brains out." Baker testified that Edith, while at college, said many times that she would kill her father. (Cross-examination showed that Baker had never warned her uncle Trigg or her mother—his sister—of these threats, indicating that she may not have taken them seriously.) Cantrell testified that Edith many times expressed dislike for her father, but he could recall no exact words. Holyfield testified that a year before Edith had said to him that she hated her father and that she "couldn't keep from laughing if she seen him laid out dead." Bolling's testimony tied these vague statements of hatred to threat of action. He told the court that a year before, he, Edith, and others were driving in a car and were seen by Trigg. Holyfield teased her about being whipped by her father, and he testified, "She said, 'I would just like for him to try it,'" and that she would kill him. When Holyfield said she should be "ashamed of herself," she replied there was no need, it was the truth.[29]

To show that Edith and Anne (and to a lesser extent Mary Katherine) were not telling the truth, the prosecution relied on a number of witnesses. Some offered rebuttal testimony as to what the Maxwells said at the trial concerning a number of issues, like the bloody bedclothing. Others offered evidence to contradict Edith's and Anne's assertions—made first in the press and later at trial—that Trigg Maxwell was drunk that night. Verna Hubbard testified that she saw Trigg in the street within an hour of the argument in the Maxwell house and saw no indications that he was intoxicated. J. L. Sowards said that Maxwell bought three beers in the course of the day at his restaurant but seemed sober. Ned Deaton testified that late that night when he saw Maxwell, he "was perfectly sober as far as I could tell." Dr. Sykes, who Edith testified had gotten drunk that night with her father, denied it, asserting that he and Maxwell each had two bottles of beer at the Lonesome Pine Restaurant, one in the afternoon and one at night. County police officer Paris Mullins asserted, in contradiction to the defense's claims that Trigg for months had been getting drunk on Saturdays, that since Trigg had " 'fessed for hope" some months back, he had not seen him "under the influence of whisky." In all, using over two dozen witnesses, the prosecution built its case for murder and attempted to rebut the defense's positions.[30]

In contrast to the prosecution's plethora of witnesses, the defense called only three principal witnesses: Anne, Mary Katherine, and Edith. As the defense summoned no character witnesses, these main witnesses bore the burden of proving the claim of self-defense. The strength of the defense's case rested on the mutually consistent tales told by Anne, Mary Katherine, and Edith. These witnesses had the added advantage that only they knew what had happened inside the home the night Trigg died. The weakness of the defense was that it all depended on the credibility of the Maxwell women, a credibility that was tested in the cross-examination.[31]

Anne, Mary Katherine, and Edith all testified about their family life and what happened the day and night of July 20 and 21. All asserted that Trigg was addicted to drink. Anne said he drank all his adult life, save for a period of ten months following a religious conversion, and that for six months before his death, Trigg drank "nearly every Saturday." Edith and Anne recounted that Trigg was quarrelsome when drunk. Anne, Mary Katherine, and Edith asserted that he had been drinking through the course of the day and was drunk that night. Mary Katherine reported that by dark her father seemed "pretty high if anyone knowed him." Anne and Mary Katherine told the court that Trigg had come into their bedroom around 10:30 P.M. and argued with Anne over her "primping" before going berry picking; further, he threatened to give her thirty minutes to leave in the morning, and when he discovered that Edith was not home, he got angry. According to Mary Katherine, he announced, "A man ought to break her God damned neck." Then he left the house, returning near 12:30 and going into his own room about ten minutes before Edith came home.[32]

Edith testified that she and her first cousin had gotten a lift to Wise to socialize. Around 11:00 P.M. she, along with five other adults and a baby, got a ride out of Wise with Raymond Meade. After the others were dropped off, she and Raymond drove through Pound to a roadhouse, the Little Ritz; while Edith nibbled potato chips and drank ginger ale, Raymond drank some liquor. She testified that she urged him to take her home early, but Raymond spent much time chatting with various people; he brought her home around 12:30. All testified that when she came home, Anne and Mary Katherine told Edith, who needed to fetch her covers from her father's room, that he was drunk and had threatened to "run off" her mother. As Edith undressed and prepared for bed, she and Trigg began to argue, ending up in the kitchen. Anne and Mary Katherine said they went to the kitchen when they heard Edith say, "Poppy don't stab me."[33]

Edith, Anne, and Mary Katherine testified that Edith and Trigg struggled first in the kitchen and then in Anne's bedroom, which opened onto the kitchen. Mary Katherine said that when they came in, a knife was on the floor and she picked it up and hid it. Edith said that at first her father had threatened her with a chair, put that down, then picked up a butcher knife but put that down also, and after that they were locked in struggle. Anne and Mary Katherine said that in the struggle the two knocked down some pans and tipped over a bucket of water. Edith said that Trigg was pulling her by the hair, but she got loose; even while Anne begged them to stop fighting, he grabbed Edith by both the neck and the strap of her slip, shaking and pushing her into the bedroom, where they fell over a chair.[34]

Only Edith testified to her striking her father for Anne and Mary Katherine both said that they did not see Edith strike any blows because the fight ended quickly in the bedroom. Mary Katherine explained that she was cleaning the kitchen when the two were in the bedroom. Anne, who admitted to following them into the bedroom, said she saw no blows. Edith's testimony filled in this gap. She told of falling on the floor with a hard object beneath her back. Her father was choking her. In fear for her life, she reached for the hard object under her, which she later determined to be a shoe, and "struck at him." She added: "I don't know how many licks I struck coming up. I don't know whether I struck him even." She reported that she wrenched herself free, threw the shoe down, and ran away. According to Anne and Mary Katherine, when Edith fled outside her father remained in the house, saying, "Look what she's done to me." Anne and Mary Katherine both testified that when he wiped his brow, blood got on his shirt and the floor.[35]

After the fight Anne and Mary Katherine testified to calming Trigg. In his room, they said, he continued to rant and curse, kicking over a mason jar filled with carbide, a fuel for miners' lamps. They said they managed to get Trigg into bed, where he ripped off his torn, blood-stained shirt and demanded a new one.

Anne said she supplied him one and washed his face with water and alcohol rub. She cleaned up the carbide and put it with the torn, bloody shirt in the cold kitchen stove, where they were burned the next day when the stove was lit. She denied that there was much blood on his head, and Mary Katherine asserted that there was little blood spattered about the house. According to Edith and Mary Katherine's testimony, Edith had left the house and was outside the lattice door on the steps leading to a crawl space beneath the porch. When Kelly came over, she retreated behind the lattice door and told him to go home, there was no fire. Edith claimed that since the disastrous fire that destroyed his home and crippled his wife, Kelly got "up at all times of the night . . . and goes out and goes from one house to the other looking for a fire." All three Maxwells said that Edith planned to leave, but after her mother's pleas she stayed, spoke briefly to her father in his room, turned the radio on and then off, and settled down to go to sleep.[36]

Within fifteen to thirty minutes from the end of the fight, the Maxwell women said they heard Trigg stir from his bed. Edith testified that Mary Katherine offered to fetch him water, but he refused, saying he wanted to spit. According to all three, he went to the porch, and then they heard a crash. Anne testified that she reached him first, finding his head against the meat block. She recalled telling Edith that he must have fainted and hit his head against it. Anne, Edith, and Mary Katherine all testified to moving him to try to administer to him; water was dashed on his face, and both Mary Katherine and Edith ran for help. By the time Dr. Sykes (who did not stay very long) and the neighbors arrived, Trigg's life was fading. A suggestion for heat to be applied to his body led to Trigg being covered with blankets and the electric iron plugged into a socket, though it is unclear if the heat was applied to his body before he died. On the whole, the testimony of Anne, Mary Katherine, and Edith made a good case for the claim of self-defense on Edith's part.[37]

Contradictions between their testimony and what others had said and especially Edith's and Anne's responses to cross-examination undermined their veracity, weakening the defense. All three denied that the radio was on loudly or for more than a minute or so after it warmed up. They also denied that Trigg was hollering "Oh Lordy" for a long period of time. Each admitted that he took the Lord's name in vain over his struggle with Edith and kicking over the carbide. Edith and Mary Katherine denied saying to the neighbors that their father's fall against the meat block had caused his death. Similarly, Mary Katherine could not remember whether Edith asked for clothes when she was outside, while Edith asserted that she did not call for them. Most damning was Edith's denial in cross-examination of saying to her father, "If you don't like it, what are you going to do about it?" when he allegedly rebuked her for speaking to the man in the street. When three rebuttal witnesses testified to hearing that exact language, it made Edith look like a liar.[38]

The prosecution's cross-examination was aimed at making especially Anne and Edith appear to have been lying in their testimony and trying to cover up a crime. For example, Vicars questioned Anne as to why, after she had summoned Dr. Sykes, she failed to tell him that Trigg had been drinking, had fought with Edith, and had blood running down his face. No matter what her answers, these questions pointed out that she had lied by withholding information from Sykes and thus might have hindered Sykes's treatment of Trigg. Anne testified that the first person she told about the fight was her son, Earl, after he arrived from New York, tacitly admitting that she had lied by omission when the family gathered after Trigg's death. Asked if she told the officers who arrested her about the fight, she pleaded loss of memory; pressed further with the question, "Why didn't you tell them about the trouble?" she replied, "I didn't think it was anything only a little family racket." Similarly, when asked why she had not told the doctor that she had struck her father, Edith said, "I didn't think of it." Further, Edith, when questioned by Greear as to why she did not show to the arresting officers the bruises and scratches she said she had gotten in the struggle with her father, replied, "I didn't think it was any honor to tell them we had been in a family racket."[39]

Beyond showing the Maxwells to be liars, the prosecution used cross-examination, especially Greear's questioning of Edith, to suggest a different picture of life inside the Maxwell home, alternate scenarios of the causes of the struggle to which they had testified, and other means by which Trigg could have met his death. The prosecution's strategy was to make Edith's answers matter less than Greear's questions. Concerning life in the household, his questions suggested that Anne and the children were always "picking on" Trigg, that there had been long-standing friction between Anne and Trigg, and that Edith and her mother had previously blackened his eyes. Further, his questions asserted that Edith started the fight by telling Trigg to shut up or that the fight was prompted by the "belly to belly" incident. Similarly, Greear's questions suggested different courses for the fight and its aftermath, such as that Anne or Mary Katherine had come to Edith's aid when Trigg had her by the hair by hitting him with a hatchet or hammer, that Edith had continued striking her father after he had freed her, and that they had turned on the radio to drown out Trigg's moaning. Thus the prosecution expended much effort in trying to weaken the defense's strong case before the jury.[40]

The jury, guided by a simple set of instructions, deliberated briefly and found Edith Maxwell guilty of first-degree murder. The prosecution's instructions declared that first-degree murder was the "willful, deliberate and premeditated killing with malice aforethought." They stipulated that malice was presumed from the killing and the defense bore the burden of disproving malice. A willful, premeditated killing without malice was second-degree murder. The defense instructions asserted the presumption of innocence and detailed the law of allowing the use of force, even deadly force, to repel an attack. The jury was thus presented with the poles of conviction of murder (in the first or second degree) and acquittal, but it was not told of the law of manslaughter. This omission did not seem to matter, because the jury found Maxwell guilty of first-degree murder. It sentenced her to twenty-five years in the state penitentiary, five years over the minimum required legal penalty for first-degree murder. The jury apparently believed the prosecution's case and discounted the defense's claim to self-defense. Maxwell's lawyers quickly began to plan Edith's appeal, while her jailer, her uncle C. J. Dotson, kept most newspapermen from speaking to her.[41]

As the Maxwell trial was a media event, the press was well represented in Wise. The clerk of the county court, Charles Johnson, later described how the journalists "assembled in large numbers" at the trial. They used messengers to deliver bulletins to the Western Union office at Norton to be sent "to the outside world" at the rate of up to 10,000 words daily. The major wire services—Associated Press, United Press, and International News Service—sent writers, some with photographers. Some of the reporters specialized in sensational stories of violence; for example, the United Press writer Harry Ferguson had covered the Hauptmann trial, the Huey Long assassination, and the union-management wars of Harlan County, Kentucky. Although the AP stories downplayed the "lonesome pine" aspects of the story (the service, though carrying on the traditions of human-interest stories, reported that the courthouse was an impressive building three stories high and made of stone and that the spectators at the trial were "hard-working miners, goodhearted and courteous"), the UP and Hearst's International News Service gave free rein to their "yellow journalism." They produced "copy that the wires would carry," writing passages that rested on a "few facts" but were coated "with such color that can only come from an imagination that is reeking of the required shade of paint."[42]

In addition to emphasizing the human-interest aspects of the trial, the press portrayed it as a conflict between mountain ways and modern civilization. By lavishing attention on Edith's dress, appearance, and reaction to the verdict—she was reported to have declared upon conviction, "For God's sake take care of my mother I don't care about myself"—the press utilized a standard human-interest trope. Some reporters, especially those writing for the UP and International News Service went further; their articles were sprinkled with phrases written in dialect and highlighting the local color of the "land of lonesome pine," proclaiming that the case captured a struggle between modern and old-fashioned civilizations, between freedom for youth and women and the old order.[43]

Building on Fulton Lewis's earlier accounts, the major urban press, linked to the Universal Press, reported the existence of an 8:00 P.M. curfew (marked by a siren) for young folk in Wise County, thus leading some journals to call it the curfew case. The opening UP story captured the essence of the more lurid coverage: "A curfew siren sent hoarse noises up the trail of the lonesome pine tonight, and the hill people boarded up their cabins because tomorrow everybody will be up early to start for 'Gov'ment court,' where pretty Edith Maxwell goes on trial for killing her father with a frivolous sharpheeled shoe that he thought was a sin to wear." The curfew was just one manifestation of a "mountain code" of conduct. Patriarchy, according to these reports, dominated life in the hills. "Hereabouts most of the mountain women still walk a respectful two feet behind their menfolk." And physical punishment of the children and wives to maintain this order was common. The UP story quoted a spectator as saying, "Many is the time my 'pappy' whipped me and I never lifted a hand to strike back." Thus the law that kept women off the jury in Virginia was cast in some papers as required by local custom; the jury "consisted entirely of men, because women are still considered not quite equal to men here."[44]

These same papers interpreted Edith's crime as modern youth challenging this age-old morality of the hills. She "had left the hills to go to" college "in the outside world and had come back with new-fangled notions" like female assertiveness. "It was such ideas as rouge, curled hair, smart clothes and suede shoes that brought her into conflict with her father, who thought the outside world taught women things that were disgraceful." Edith Maxwell became a symbol of the new womanhood and of the "right of youth everywhere to go its own way." And when her father sought to impose "upon her an ancient code of morals in this day and time when youth makes its own rules," she grabbed "a high heeled slipper—an emblem of the civilization he despised" to defend herself. Neither the twelve men on the jury nor the "mountain elders" were "interested in points of law" about self-defense; to them there was "no plea" she could "make against the unwritten law of the trail of the lonesome pine." [45]

In their stories of Maxwell's trial, the three national news weekly magazines distilled what one called "the sociological significance of the case." *Literary Digest* described Edith as "a mountain-born girl with a modern education" and said she struggled with her father in his "rude cabin in the Blue Ridge Mountains" while her mother "cowered in a corner." Quoting the Universal Service, it announced that the case "pitted the youth of these mountains . . . against the outworn mode of life in" the "back woods." Seeing the case as a struggle between traditional ways and a "modern young woman of twenty-one," the magazine declared that the case "had become a symbol of modern youth's stand against the ancient, flinty laws of the hills, which say that a father shall rule his family and that unmarried women shall be indoors by sundown. . . . Last week a jury of twelve men reared to think as her father thought convicted her." *News-Week* was more colorful but equally pointed in its coverage. Its article set the scene: "Mountain people came down from hills" to see a trial before a judge who opened a window to spit out his tobacco juice. It asserted that "neighbors from the Pound . . . swore she often violated the unwritten law that no unmarried woman may stay out after 8 P.M." It recounted only the defense's view of the evidence. On the other hand, *Time* covered both the prosecution's and the defense's cases as well as quoting some testimony from the trial. But it also called Edith Maxwell a "school marm" and characterized the spectators, who "slouched back to their mountain homes" after the verdict, as "satisfied with the 'Gov'ment' court's attitude toward disobedient daughters who keep late hours." Epitomizing the thrust of their treatment, all three magazines quoted a spectator agreeing with the verdict: "It's a lesson in what's sinful all right." [46]

From the end of the first trial, on November 20, through September 11, 1936, when the Virginia Court of Appeals took the case under consideration, the Edith Maxwell case became the number-one state news story for 1936 in the estimation of the Richmond bureau chief of the Associated Press. A cascade of actions, reactions, and interactions kept the story on the front page of the state's papers. As Edith and her defenders sought a new trial, press interest escalated. In particular, the Hearst interests and the *Washington Post* intensified their coverage of the plight of Edith Maxwell. Almost uniformly, the resulting flood of articles portrayed the Maxwell case as a miscarriage of justice. Learning of the case from the newspapers, various women's groups (some representing national organizations) took action to aid Maxwell. Similarly, many Virginians saw the Maxwell verdict as unjust; the state's press decried it. The expanded press coverage prompted residents of the area to denounce the stereotypical images of their region. And the interest of outside groups in the case caused some Virginians to worry.[47]

Soon after the verdict Maxwell sold the exclusive interview and photographic rights of her "story" to the Hearst publishing interests. A Hearst syndicated columnist, Marguerite Moores Marshall, flew from New York to Bristol and then traveled to Wise County with a photographer. Soon Hearst papers across the nation began carrying her sob-sister stories on Edith, the community, the injustice of the trial, the barbarity of the conditions in the jail, and the plans for further legal action. Typical of Marshall's treatment were appeals for action: "Is the rest of the country, the rest of their own splendid State, with its traditions of gallant men and worshipped women, going to let" the hillbillies "get away with it?" Accompanying these stories were photographs of Edith in jail. Under the headline of "25 Years of This," the *New York Daily Mirror*, a Hearst tabloid, ran a large front-page photograph of Edith grasping the bars of her cell. By December, Maxwell's story of the night her father died had been retold in the Sunday magazine the "American Weekly," carried across the Hearst chain. Following the accounts by Marshall and other writers from Hearst's stable, King Features— Hearst's syndication service—began serializing Edith Maxwell's "My Own Life Story." Supplemented with many photographs of Edith in jail and scenes from Wise County and ostensibly written by Edith herself, the life story appeared widely in Hearst papers. It was repackaged later for special Sunday features and eventually became a twenty-three installment series (under the byline of Arthur Mefford) for the *Daily Mirror*.[48]

Among the Hearst papers that ran the various Maxwell features was the *Washington Herald*, and its coverage sparked the rival *Washington Post*'s interest in the story. Since 1930, the *Washington Herald* had been edited by the flamboyant Eleanor M. "Cissy" Patterson. Born to a newspaper family (her grandfather founded the *Chicago Tribune*, her cousin Robert McCormick published it, and her brother was the founder and editor of the *New York Daily News*), Patterson was also a Washington insider. Her aggressive scandalmongering and local reporting dramatically boosted the paper's circulation and sparked intensive competition with other city papers. When the *Herald* began devoting much space to the Maxwell story and started a defense fund, the *Washington Post* quickly followed suit. Beginning on November 26, 1935, the *Post* assigned Virginia Lee Warren to the Maxwell story. She traveled to Wise and stayed in the county until the following January, sending a steady stream of stories on the case to Washington. Unable to have access to Edith, Warren featured the rest of the immediate Maxwell family. The *Washington Post* published stories about Anne and Mary Katherine preparing a Thanksgiving dinner for Edith in jail, strategies of Earl and her lawyers as they prepared a motion for new trial, and the behavior of people in the community toward Earl, Anne, and Edith. The *Post* also contracted with Earl Maxwell for him to tell the story of his life in the Maxwell family, the trial, and the aftermath. The first installment ran on Christmas Day.[49]

The *Washington Post* (and other papers), determined to make Edith a martyr to the patriarchal code of the hills, compared her to another Wise County patricide. On November 29 sixteen-year-old Haugemen "Abram" Falin killed his father after a fight over the breakdown of the family car. He claimed he shot in self-defense because his father had beaten him with a pistol and threatened to shoot him. The press portrayed young Falin's story of what happened as "almost a repetition of the 21-year old school teacher's defense in her trial." When Falin was put on probation following the trial in juvenile court, the discrepancy in the treatment of the two cases seemed evident to many. But there were significant differences in the two cases, including the defendants' age, the elder Falin's bad reputation in the community, the testimony of wounds on Abram Falin's head, and the testimony of ten witnesses on his behalf. Nevertheless, *Post* readers were presented with Falin's case as proof of the injustice of Maxwell's treatment. Thus almost every story filed by Warren, every story printed under Earl Maxwell's byline, and nearly every story on Falin came accompanied a coupon for the *Washington Post* defense fund for Edith Maxwell, "the mountain girl, who faces 25 years in prison." By mid-January the fund stood at over $800.[50]

The *Post*'s readers were not the only ones interested in Edith Maxwell and Wise County. In December 1935 *Washington Daily News* traveling columnist (and former managing editor) Ernie Pyle traveled to Wise County to report on the Maxwell case. The titles of his two articles, "Ernie Finds Neither Curfew Nor Child-Beating in Pound, VA" and "'Furriner' Finds Wise, Va., Is Just like Other Small Towns," captured his impressions of the county and stood in contrast to most journalistic coverage of the case. Pyle found the people belied the stereotypes about mountaineers. Although admitting there were "people in Wise County like those in the cartoons," Pyle noted that the county also had sophisticated people with "polish and city personalities." But he found the "great majority" to be "just folks" who were "good-hearted" and "not very backward." They were poor, and he argued that "some of the reporters have confused rural poverty with quaintness." Indeed, Pyle concluded that Wise was very much like the rest of rural America and declared, "If I didn't already know, I couldn't tell you from look whether Wise was in Vermont or Iowa." Pyle had not yet gained his reputation as a great journalist, and his views did not change the thrust of the daily papers' coverage of the case that portrayed Wise County as backward and Edith Maxwell as a victim.[51]

The message that Maxwell suffered "at the hands of bigoted mountain justice" and needed assistance worked its way into other venues besides daily papers. In April 1936 the Macfadden magazine *Voice of Experience* published a long article on Maxwell's case presenting only the defense's view of the trial and portraying it as a struggle between ignorance and enlightenment. It urged its readers to take action and "help free Edith Maxwell." The magazine "set aside a page to be used as a petition" and asked its readers to "tear it out" and "acquaint your friends" with Maxwell's "plight." Over two hundred such petitions made their way to the office of the governor of Virginia.[52]

Readers of the daily press and the *Voice of Experience* were not the only ones aroused by what they read to take action to aid Edith Maxwell. Women's organizations, moved by coverage of the case and prompted by the press's calls to action, mobilized to assist Maxwell in winning a new trial. A day after the verdict, *New York World-Herald* columnist Dorothy Dunbar Bromley asserted that Maxwell's trial was a "clear case" of "sex discrimination." Pointing to the all-male jury, she argued that Maxwell had not been judged by a jury of her peers, and she called for groups like the American Civil Liberties Union and the National Woman's Party "to go to bat for a fair trial for Edith Maxwell." The first group to get involved was the Knoxville, Tennessee, chapter of the Business and Professional Women's Clubs of America. Women's clubs had emerged in the 1920s and were predicated on the belief that women had the right to participate in public affairs and business, and they sought to guarantee such access by networking and lobbying. Within a week after the verdict, the Knoxville club began to raise a defense fund.[53]

The club's motives for coming to Maxwell's aid were mixed. Mr. and Mrs. L. C. Stair of Knoxville prompted the club's action, believing that Maxwell's conviction was "a rank injustice" because she "seemed guilty only of having an education and of acting to save her life from a drunken father." They also argued that the defense of the South necessitated action. "Unless we in the South do something . . . this case will be spread in papers throughout the country as an example of southern backwardness." The Knoxville club joined forces with the local newspaper to set up a defense fund for Maxwell and quickly raised over two hundred dollars. Its action inspired the president of the national organization of Business and Professional Women's Clubs to endorse the defense effort and to call Judge Skeen and ask him "to consider favorably" Maxwell's motion for a new trial. The club appointed a delegation to visit Maxwell in the Wise County jail, 150 miles from Knoxville. There they ran into a rude surprise. Because Maxwell had sold the rights to her story, the clubwomen were not permitted to speak with her beyond simple greetings. They announced that they had been duped by "sensationalized and untrue newspaper accounts" and were now sure that Maxwell had been "accorded a fair trial, before an intelligent jury, and judge whose decisions have seldom been reversed." The clubwomen dropped the plans for Edith's defense fund. Their public statements, their letter to the governor of Virginia, and their return of the money already raised prompted other clubs to withdraw their support of Maxwell.[54]

Another women's group, the National Woman's Party, was not deterred from supporting a "woman who commercialized on a murder conviction." The National Woman's Party, the leading feminist organization of the 1920s and 1930s, saw Maxwell as a victim of male justice whose case would fit into their already existing campaign to secure jury service rights for women. Born in 1913, when Alice Paul led her supporters out of an earlier organization, the National Woman's Party embraced the militant tactics of the British suffragettes in seeking a national woman's suffrage amendment. Following the victory of the Nineteenth Amendment, the National Woman's Party turned its attention to bringing about full equal rights for women through an equal rights amendment. As a nonpartisan lobbying group, the party was organized into state branches that were autonomous in theory and a national branch that in actuality tried to run the whole organization from top to bottom. The party's unadulterated feminist and equalitarian rights ideology, its strong leadership under Alice Paul, and its mastery of generating press interest were put to use in its campaign for an equal rights amendment.

The party thought that a constitutional amendment would ensure women the right to serve on juries across the nation, but when it made little headway in Congress, they turned to other means, working to pass state laws. Yet at the opening of the depression decade, only about half the states allowed women to serve on juries. After a decade of trying to get legislation passed, the National Woman's Party undertook a litigation campaign to make jury service a federal right. In 1931-32 the party litigated a Massachusetts jury service case; after losing in the state's highest court, the party appealed to the United States Supreme Court, only to have it refuse to take the case. Thus in 1935, when the Maxwell case emerged as a national issue, the party saw it as a way to revive its efforts to secure jury service for women and to generate publicity for its ideas.[55]

The National Woman's Party supplied Maxwell with lawyers, started a defense fund on her behalf, and used her as a poster girl for their campaigns for a state jury service law and for the equal rights amendment. In a December 15, 1935, letter, the state branch president, Elsie M. Graff, offered Maxwell legal assistance. By late December, Maxwell accepted, and the party hired Richmond attorney M. J. Fulton to work on her appeal. Fulton was assisted by Gail Laughlin, a prominent member of the party from Maine, who was an expert on women and juries. She had drafted the California jury service law and had participated in drafting the brief in the case the party had taken to the United States Supreme Court. Moreover, the National Women's Party used Maxwell's case to stir up publicity about the issue of women on juries, including Edith's story in its convention resolutions of that year; in many articles in its Baltimore weekly, *Equal Rights;* and in its appeals across the nation. These efforts portrayed the injustice of the verdict as a reason for a Supreme Court decision requiring jury service for women, as an argument for passage of various state jury service laws, and as an example of why the nation needed to adopt the equal rights amendment. Beyond this, in a campaign to raise funds for the appeal, the party started a "dime-fund campaign" for Maxwell. It issued small metal boxes labeled "Give a Dime for Justice" and literature on the case to its campaign workers and sent them out to canvass money for Maxwell. It utilized International News Service photographs of Maxwell (including the one of her inside her cell looking out through the bars) to attempt to arouse sympathy for her.[56]

The National Woman's Party was joined by another women's organization, the Women's Moderation Union, in raising money for Maxwell's defense. This was a "small, meagerly financed New York group" dominated by M. Louise Gross, a philosophical liberal of the John Stuart Mill stripe with connections to New York's Democratic political machine, Tammany Hall. The Women's Moderation Union had grown out of the Molly Pitcher Clubs of the Association against the Prohibition Amendment and had little connection with larger and more influential antiprohibition women's organizations. Following repeal (and before Gross turned her attention to the cause of legalizing gambling), this organization kept going by attempting to ameliorate the effects of alcohol abuse to prevent a backlash against the nation's change of liquor policy. The common view of the press that Edith was defending herself from a drunken Trigg made her case a good cause for them. In February 1936 the organization hosted a public appeal in the Majestic Theater on West 4th Street in New York City. Between 500 and 800 people attended to see Earl, Anna Ruth, and Mary Katherine Maxwell. According to James Thurber, who wrote an article about this evening and the case for the *New Yorker*, Gross asserted that Edith was "known to all of us . . . as the Trail of the Lonesome Pine girl"; Thurber suggested that she should have also called her "'the Curfew Girl.' It depends on whether you read the *Daily Mirror* or the *American*." His account detailed the rehearsed exchanges between Gross and Mary Katherine, poetry reading, dancing, and singing of popular songs, including "The Trail of the Lonesome Pine." Earl spoke for twenty minutes, impressing the audience with his "quiet and straightforward account . . . of the night his father died, a night on which occurred what has been variously described as 'just another sordid murder' and 'one of the worst miscarriages of justice in the proud history of Virginia.'"[57]

Indeed, editorial writers and letter writers from outside Virginia denounced the verdict as unjust and called for efforts to bring about its reversal in the higher courts. A Minnesota man wrote a letter calling Maxwell's "severe sentence" a crime "being committed under the law." To him she had "merely" been fighting "off a man himself engaged in a crime—that of illegally spanking a grown-up girl." Worried that Maxwell would not have good representation because "Edith . . . cannot command the funds of the Loebs and the Leopolds," he asserted that the case was one for champions of the downtrodden like Clarence Darrow or Robin Hood. He called for a higher court to "set aside this harsh and inhuman sentence." Along the same lines a New York daily editorialized that the sentence seemed "a monstrous stupidity against which vigorous protest should prove effective." Dotting its editorials with phrases about the clash of modern America and "squirrel rifle country," the paper declared: "Hope lies in appeal to the higher courts of Virginia and possibly in a pardon by the Governor. This appeal is not to a set of hill-billies, but to men no more benighted than any other Americans." Certainly "outside help will be needed" to press the effort to secure "enlightened mercy" for Maxwell.[58]

Many Virginians agreed that the verdict in the first Maxwell trial was a miscarriage of justice. An eighty-two-year-old woman from Lyells, Virginia, wrote that only a jury of men "deeply imbued by the cave-man's belief in a father's absolute right over his children" could have rendered such an "impossible" verdict. Similarly, another Virginian included a letter to the *Washington Post* with her dollar donation to the *Post*'s Maxwell defense fund, urging some Washington lawyers to volunteer to help her. She avowed, "I am almost ashamed to admit being a resident of the great state of Virginia, if such injustice is to be permitted within her courts; especially if I thought . . . that it represented the State's attitudes a whole." This writer fixed the cause of the "unjust verdict" on the people of Wise County and was sure a change of venue for a new trial would bring about real justice. Along the same lines Thomas Lomax Hunter, in his *Richmond Times-Dispatch* column "As It Appears to the Cavalier," fixed the blame on the "tribal viewpoints" of the mountaineers. Believing that the "hillman of Wise" held "the patriarchal notion of fatherhood" common to "all primitive peoples," Hunter claimed that the verdict represented the community's conceptions of "the right of parental discipline." As "few Richmond men claim the right to beat their adult daughters," Hunter asserted that "had Miss Maxwell been tried in Richmond . . . she would have been acquitted." And one letter writer, a Virginian living in Troy, New York, who felt "keenly the stigma that is being ascribed to a 'Virginia court'" over the case, wrote to say that this miscarriage of justice could not have occurred in Virginia and that the Wise referred to in press accounts must be in West Virginia. If it proved that Wise was in Virginia, the letter writer contended, "I shall be ashamed to continue to acknowledge my native-state."[59]

For some Virginians, ideas about liquor dominated how they thought about the case. When Mrs. Clara Manley from Montross wrote to the one Richmond daily approving of the verdict because Edith lived under her father's roof and should have abided by his discipline, she provoked at least one impassioned letter in reaction. Courtney Overcash of Richmond responded that Manley must have "never been attacked by a drunken man, and if you were I am sure you would resent an attempt to restrain you from protecting yourself." Characterizing Trigg as a "drunkard" and Edith as "a young lady" of "fine character," Overcash claimed that Maxwell deserved "the praise of society and should not be required to comply with the narrow and silly demands of a drunken father." Although the verdict "proved the bias of the mountain locality," the "reaction of public opinion" in the state "proves that society still believes in justice." Another letter writer shifted all the blame of the crime and verdict to Trigg, by declaring, "If the father had not been drinking, his daughter would not be where she is to pay the penalty of his weakness." Similarly, another correspondent, lamenting the turmoil created in homes by whiskey, pictured both Edith and Anne as victims of a "roaring drunkard." This writer called "to the manhood of our state, to our honorable Governor, to the sons of those fathers who followed Robert E. Lee . . . to help this little mountain girl and her stricken mother."[60]

Virginians' outrage against the verdict was tempered by their resentment of the press's stereotyping of southwestern Virginia. The reaction began in Wise. Mrs. Carter Tiller defended Pound from the newspaper accounts that made it "a notorious little spot on the map inhabited by crude country codgers, and whose speech is identical to the brogue spoke by our ancient mountaineer ancestors." She pointed out that the town had an accredited high school, modern department stores, and "about all of the conveniences of any small town." Luther Addington, Wise's high school principal and sometime reporter, wrote an article for the weekly *Big Stone Gap Post* explaining how "the wheels of tabloid reporting go around." On the evening before the trial, he had been visited by some of these reporters ("fellows of great imaginations") and "learned that they had already" filed their stories about Pound without doing any research. When he asked if they had been to the town, one answered, "We passed through . . . stopping long enough to mail a post card." Taking the papers to task for misconstruing Wise County and the trial, Addington produced a series of examples of their preposterous practice of giving "a story in the hills the color of the 90's" when the "90's passed from the hills at the same time they passed from every place." Similarly, the editor of the *Norton Coalfield Progress*, Pres T. Atkins, declared that "the entire community was slandered" in order to add color to the sensational press's "fiction of the struggle between the modern and the out-of-date."[61]

Letter writers expressed similar sentiments about stereotyping and defended the trial. J. C. Horton, writing from Swords Creek, Virginia, claimed that "the newspapers ballyhooing" the Maxwell case were "getting most of their material from John Fox's novels instead of the court sessions." He claimed that the "tabloid" reporters coined expressions like "Gov'ment Court" or "swiped" them "from some good old mountain folk-ballad written by a 'Tin Pan Alley Mountaineer.'" Similarly, J. Willard Horne wrote that once the New York journalists learned there "was hardly any difference between" the inhabitants of Wise and themselves, they "drew upon their memories of the stories they had heard of the 90's" and "added some of the brilliant yellow their journalistic offices always keep on hand" to produce their articles. Another writer complained that the press "let their pre-conceived ideas run riot." Lawyers in particular took umbrage at the writing up of the trial "as a conflict between 'book-larnin' and a 'snuff-dippin' hill-billy pappy.'" Some like J. P. Buchanan and Fred Newland praised the judge and the jury and claimed that Maxwell received a fair trial.[62]

Soon similar comments about the press coverage worked their way into the state's daily papers. A staff writer for the *Richmond Times-Dispatch* managed to get the community's reaction on the front page of the state's major paper. There he quoted Addington saying that earlier press accounts were "absurd and downright fallacious" when they reported that the community did not want its children to go to college. The article also quoted one of Edith's lawyers, Robert P. Bruce, who said, "They referred to our court building as 'the little log cabin courtroom on the ridge,' as he pointed to "the three story brick and stone" courthouse. Another resident, who remained anonymous so it would not "come out in the paper that I'm just a tobacco-chewing hillbilly come to town," asserted that there was no such thing as the curfew siren. Cynthia A. Boatwright, a vice-president of the Wise County Federation of Women's Clubs, wrote a letter to the press defending the verdict and her county against the "outrage" of the "wrong impressions" of the county and its people created by the Hearst and other newspapers.[63]

It was not just the image of Wise County that disturbed Virginians, but that such press coverage was prompting misinformed outside groups to enter the case. The editor of the *Big Stone Gap Post* said it was "unfortunate that women's organizations in certain cities, ministers and lawyers have been moved by the imagination of irresponsible news reporters." Similarly, Boatwright asserted that groups everywhere were "letting their emotional sympathy 'runaway' with them," clouding the real issues in the case. She said that "if the true facts" had been known, no "honorable, upright citizen would" have "intruded" into the Maxwell case. Her statement implied that the withdrawal of the Knoxville club from the case at the end of November showed that "a thorough investigation" revealed that no injustice had been done. Other letter writers agreed that the jury had done a good job. Even those worried about America's rising crime rate and "the new freedom of women" defended the verdict. But disgust with lurid press stories and the involvement of outsider groups did not always translate into satisfaction with the jury's verdict.[64]

Virginius Dabney, the leading editorial voice in the state, denounced the stereotyping of Wise County, worried about the introduction of out-of-state interests into the case, and argued that the verdict was unjustified. The day after the Knoxville women's club withdrew from the Maxwell case, Dabney, editor of the *Richmond Times-Dispatch* from 1936 to 1969, wrote his first editorial on the Maxwell case. He agreed with the club's statement that the case had "been grossly exploited and distorted by sensational newspapers." But he "respectfully" disagreed with the implication of their statement that the "verdict was a proper one." Dabney asserted that from a review of the evidence it was hard to see premeditation of the killing. Although sympathizing "with the people of Wise" over their portrayal as "primitive, uncouth hill-billies," Dabney thought the sentence was too harsh. Moreover, he worried about an "ominous" development, "the entry of the Hearst interests into the case." Dabney regretted that Maxwell's attorneys allowed the "Hearst papers and syndicates to exploit this girl's misfortunes." Reviewing the entry of the International Labor Defense into the Scottsboro and Angelo Herndon cases, Dabney asserted that such outsiders drove away "a large segment of opinion which otherwise would have been strongly favorable" to the defendants. He worried that a similar fate would befall Maxwell, "for if anything can alienate local opinion from her, it will be the Hearstian tactics." He hoped that the complications arising from the press coverage would not interfere with the "orderly processes of justice," which he hoped would grant Maxwell "a new trial."[65]

Dabney reached for a national audience for his views of the case. In a *New Republic* article, published after the trial judge had denied a new trial and while the appeal was pending before the Virginia Supreme Court of Appeals, Dabney asserted that "few cases have ever been buried under a thicker coating of journalistic horse-feathers, baloney and banana oil." Quoting the editor of a Wise County weekly, Dabney declared that "most of the news stories on the Maxwell case have been written in hotel rooms with a bottle of 'corn' in one hand and 'The Trail of the Lonesome Pine' in the other." Dabney blamed primarily the "sob-sisters and trained seals" of Hearst press (but he also indicted others) for the press's creation of "a wholly incorrect understanding of the case throughout America." He sought to debunk the one-sided coverage of the trial by discussing the evidence offered by both the prosecution and the defense. Similarly, he attempted to counter the image of Wise County being "inhabited by bobcats, turkey-buzzards, quick-triggered feudists and hill-billies drowned in moonshine and tobacco juice" by boasting of the county's nine high schools, one hundred school buildings, and four hundred "young men and women off at college." And he clung to the same position he had asserted two months earlier: that Maxwell deserved a new trial.[66]

Within sixty days of the verdict, Maxwell's lawyers filed eleven motions, in two separate batches, for arrest of judgment (commonly called a motion for a new trial) before Judge Skeen. The first set of motions were drafted by Maxwell's original lawyers, Bruce, Skeen, and Dotson; the second set of motions came from

Maxwell's new lawyers. In addition to the two lawyers provided by the National Woman's Party—M. J. Fulton and Gail Laughlin—Maxwell acquired the services of Charles Henry Smith. Supplied to Maxwell courtesy of the *Washington Post* and probably the *Washington Herald* (which according to editor Cissy Patterson "kept completely in the background"), this Alexandria lawyer specialized in criminal defense law. They sought arrest of judgment on several grounds. First, the defense argued that there was insufficient evidence to support a verdict of first-degree murder because the intent to kill was not proved. Second, they contended that the judge had erred in not instructing the jury on the law of manslaughter and in admitting certain testimony in the trial. Third, they presented new evidence: buttressing their motion with affidavits from coroners from Richmond, New York City, and Washington, D.C., who had read the autopsy report, the defense contended that Trigg Maxwell had not died as a result of his wounds. Fourth, and finally, the defense brought up the constitutional issue that Maxwell was denied a jury of her peers because women could not serve on Virginia juries. Judge Skeen denied all the motions.[67]

Upon failing to win a new trial, Edith's lawyers asked for a stay as they sought a writ of error to have her case reviewed in the Virginia Supreme Court of Appeals. On March 2 A. J. Skeen, with Fulton and Smith in attendance, petitioned the court to overturn the conviction, merely repackaging the motions they had filed as motions for arrest of judgment. On March 18, 1936, the justices granted the petition and took the case under consideration. In May the state's attorney general filed a brief contending that Maxwell had received a fair trial. While the justices deliberated, Edith Maxwell remained in the Wise County jail, and the issues raised by her case reverberated around the state.[68]

As Maxwell's case worked its way through the legal system, public officials hardened their stands against outside interference. Since July 1935 Virginians had expressed dismay at the sensational press's coverage of the story and suspicion of the interest of women's groups in the case. When the National Woman's Party joined Maxwell's defense, it was added to the list of outside influences despite its Virginia branch. Virginia newspapers' coverage of Gail Laughlin's role in the motions for new trial and appeal stressed that she was a Yankee critic of Virginia justice. During a visit to Richmond in early January, she denounced the case as a "gross miscarriage of justice," and the *Roanoke Times* declared, "Maine Woman Lawyer Raps Virginia Justice." Prosecutor Greear was the first Virginia official to go on record defending the court's verdict. In a talk with reporters, he claimed the nation's press coverage was "pure bunk" and defended the judge and jury from criticism. In a late December 1935 letter in *Time*'s publication *To Letters—A Magazine,* Greear again attacked the press's misrepresentation of the case and maintained that the jury "was made up of intelligent, honest, and upright men." Similarly, in reply to the perceived onslaught of attacks on the legal system, Governor George C. Peery defended it. Peery, who had once been Vicars's law partner, praised Judge Skeen as a fair and "just judge." Further, he declared that he agreed with the Knoxville women's club "that the kindest thing that can be done is to leave the matter to the orderly processes of the courts without outside interference."[69]

Editorial writers followed the officials' lead. In late December the *Roanoke Times* praised Governor Peery's statement about the case, lauding him for not "usurping the powers of the courts." The paper expressed faith that the Court of Appeals would decide fairly whether Maxwell deserved a new trial. Similarly, Dabney in two different editorials defended the state's legal process and criticized outside interference. In a late December editorial, he asserted that it was likely that the "outside activity will do more good than harm" in the case because "those who have interested themselves in Miss Maxwell have done so under serious misapprehensions concerning the reasons for her conviction" created by the "hands of sensational newspapers." Dabney backed away from his earlier editorial saying the sentence was too harsh, but he maintained his belief that Maxwell should "have every opportunity to prove her innocence." Thus he supported a new trial and expected that Judge Skeen, "the capable jurist who tried the case," would grant one. In January, when Skeen ended all hopes of an arrest of judgment, Dabney supported Maxwell's appeals and commented on her options on appeal. He thought it unlikely that the United States Supreme Court would take up the jury question; on the other hand, the Virginia Supreme Court of Appeals might well find that the urban coroners' affidavits constituted new evidence to justify another trial. Dabney was "confident that if" the high court "feels another trial to be necessary, it will not hesitate to order one."[70]

On September 11, 1936, the Court of Appeals overturned Maxwell's conviction, finding that "the evidence was insufficient to sustain a verdict of murder in the first degree." Over a strong dissent which asserted that the trial "was no backwoods inquisition," a majority of five justices thought the state had failed to show that Edith murdered Trigg in a deliberate, planned manner required to constitute first-degree murder. In such a situation the most serious crime the jury could have convicted Maxwell of was second-degree murder; thus the trial judge erred in not setting aside the verdict. Edith's new trial was scheduled for the next meeting of the circuit court in Wise County.[71]

Before Maxwell's second trial she was released from jail, she changed her counsel, and the first trial judge was replaced by another jurist. Alfred Skeen and Robert Bruce withdrew from her defense. Maxwell's new defense team consisted of five lawyers: her uncle W. W. G. Dotson (the only remaining lawyer from her first trial), her first cousin Richmond lawyer A. T. Dotson, the National Woman's Party's lawyers Laughlin and Fulton, and the *Washington Post*'s Smith. Press reports claimed that Smith would "conduct" the defense. In mid-September 1936 Maxwell was released on bond. Her presence in Wise County induced gawking crowds to form, so Maxwell went to live with relatives on a farm outside Richmond. In early November, Judge Skeen learned from a defense motion that he was "distantly related to Miss Maxwell's paternal grandmother" and removed himself from the case "because of the possible influence of the kinship on the public mind." A hearing on change of venue was delayed until the new judge was on board. Governor Peery soon appointed Judge Ezra T. Carter from neighboring Lee County to hear Maxwell's case.[72]

In late November 1936 Judge Carter convened a hearing for the request for a change of venue. The defense had filed sixty-nine virtually identical affidavits and called seven witnesses who claimed that Maxwell could not get a fair trial in Wise County. Summarizing the witnesses' views, Smith contended a fair trial was impossible because the case had been widely discussed by the people of the county and the "great majority of them" had formed opinions as to Maxwell's guilt or innocence. Further, he pointed to a "general resentment" against Maxwell stemming from the "outside reports on people of the county during the first trial" and an "unfriendly atmosphere" toward Maxwell in Wise County. Greear, for the commonwealth, called fifteen witnesses who declared that a fair trial was possible. He also contended that the resentment "aroused" by news reports "was directed at writers of articles rather than Miss Maxwell." Carter agreed with the prosecution's view that "news accounts had very little effect on the people of Wise County." He ruled that the defense failed to show sufficient hostility toward Maxwell to justify removal of the trial to another county and set the second trial to begin on December 9, 1936.[73]

The second trial of Edith Maxwell—"whose name," according to the *Richmond Times-Dispatch*, "is almost as familiar to Americans as hill-billy music"—lasted eight days. Jury selection took less than a day, as did opening and closing arguments combined. The remaining time was devoted to hearing witnesses. Smith, Fulton, Laughlin, and A. T. Dotson sat at Maxwell's side while three lawyers sat at the prosecution's table. For this trial Trigg's relatives hired two lawyers to aid Greear, Oscar Vicars (who had assisted in the first trial) and Lewis R. McCormick. Smith dominated the defense, apparently shaping the trial strategy and questioning far more witnesses than either Fulton or Dotson. Laughlin only spoke during jury selection, where she laid the foundation for an appeal on the grounds that women were excluded from the jury. On the other side, Vicars handled the most sensitive parts of the prosecution's case, while Greear did most of the work.[74]

The prosecution followed "the plan of the first trial with much additional emphasis laid on the argument that Maxwell's family had him [Trigg] figuratively speaking 'in the dog house' for many, many years." Through "witness after witness," including "friends, relatives," and "her room-mate in college," the prosecution showed that Edith had previously threatened her father. Her attitude toward her father, according to these witnesses, was one of "hatred, mingled with scorn and contempt." The prosecution's witnesses alleged that both Edith and Anne abused Trigg, striking him with a poker on one occasion. Having drawn a picture of a "bedeviled middle-aged man" defeated and dejected by his wife's and daughter's treatment, the prosecution called the many witnesses to the events of the day and night of July 20 and July 21, 1936. They repeated the earlier stories of an altercation between Edith and Trigg in the street, confirmed that Trigg did not appear intoxicated on the night of his death, related hearing arguments and noises from the home, told of the summoning of neighbors, recalled the first stories told by the Maxwell women, and detailed the investigation and arrest of Edith and Anne. The prosecution was able to introduce evidence (which was subsequently ruled inadmissible) that an ax that the Maxwells often borrowed from neighbors, which should have been in the house, had disappeared on the day of Trigg's death. Showing the jury a similar ax bought at a local store, the prosecution contended that such an ax might have been the murder weapon. The prosecution ended its case by having the local doctors and undertaker who embalmed Maxwell describe his wounds and testify that blows to the head had killed him.[75]

The defense presented a three-part strategy. First, it laid extensive groundwork for appeal. Second, the defense attacked the medical evidence, contending that Trigg had not died from a blow to the head but from a heart attack or apoplexy. And third, it reused the defense from the first trial, claiming that Edith struck her father in self-defense. These various parts of the defense's program did not fit well together. Moreover, their case was weakened by their decision not to place either Anne or Edith on the witness stand because they thought the women had been poor witnesses in the first trial. That decision did not stop the defense from being undercut by cross-examination and by errors on the part of their witnesses that permitted the prosecution, in rebuttal, to introduce damaging testimony.

During jury selection Fulton raised questions about the legal process used to summon the venire, and Laughlin challenged the jury law as unconstitutional. Thus even before the first witnesses took the stand, the defense had laid the foundation for an appeal. It continued to broaden that foundation by objecting to much of the evidence offered by the prosecution, including the doctors' autopsy reports and testimony about Edith's hatred of Trigg and about the ax. The defense did not just rely on the "hope of reversible errors" and constitutional appeal; the burden of its effort was focused on the self-defense claim and the assertion that Trigg had not died from blows to the head.[76]

According to Smith, "Trigg died a perfectly natural death." The defense contended that two Wise County doctors never discovered the cause of death, and to prove this point it called two of the three coroners who had submitted affidavits for the motions of retrial and appeal. Their testimony "was a dreary affair to jury and spectators." As experts, Dr. J. H. Scherer, coroner of Richmond, and Dr. A. Magruder McDonald, coroner of Washington, D.C., testified that Maxwell had not died from a blow to the head. To buttress these witnesses from outside the county (one of whom admitted being retained by the *Washington Post*), the defense also called Wise's County's coroner, Dr. Nicholas Hicks. Hicks testified that he did not believe that the hemorrhages described in the autopsy report could have "caused death so quickly." Unfortunately for the defense, this local expert fared very badly under Greear's cross-examination, replying to a battery of questions about the functions of various parts of the brain with variants of the answer, "I'm just a little rusty on that." The doctors' testimony gained collateral support from the testimony of an insurance agent who claimed that Maxwell refused to obtain a policy because he said he would not pass the physical.[77]

The defense also used witnesses who testified about the night of Trigg's death. Mary Katherine's "frail shoulders" carried "the family burden" of testifying to what happened that night. In her direct testimony she repeated the story that she told at the first trial, recounting that she had seen her father drinking earlier in the evening and, like the daughter in *Ten Nights in a Bar-Room,* had urged him to come home. She testified that when he returned he quarreled with Anne, saying he was going to throw her out of the house in the morning, and threatened Edith's life. She continued that when Edith returned later, she and their father struggled in the kitchen and their mother's room. She recounted Edith's flight, the arrival and departure of Chant Kelly, and Edith's return to the home. She ended by testifying about Trigg rising from his bed and falling and the summoning of help.[78]

Vicars's cross-examination of Mary Katherine Maxwell was aimed at showing inconsistencies in her story and introducing the prosecution's own evidence. Maxwell usually flatly denied any inconsistency that Vicars identified, and so he caught her in only one minor inconsistency. The prosecution also used cross-examination of Mary Katherine to introduce Trigg's bloody sheet and pillowcase to the jury; they could have done this during the presentation of their case but probably held back for a better psychological moment, after Mary Katherine had testified that her father did not bleed much. Beyond undermining her story, Vicars's questions cast the night of Trigg's death in a different light, "one of hurried whispered plotting and swift, purposeful action. It was a scene as sinister and fearful as any in Macbeth." His cross-examination strongly put "the state's theory of the murder before the jury."[79]

Rebuttal witnesses called by the defense often served the prosecution as well. For example, Edith's brother-in-law Clay Robinson testified that relations within the Maxwell household were not as described by prosecution witnesses, but on cross-examination he admitted that he "took part in the search for the missing" ax believed by neighbors to have been used to kill Trigg. Similarly, Catherine Jessie, who was called to rebut prosecution witnesses' statements about Maxwell threatening her father, also said on the stand that she never heard Maxwell confess to hitting her father. Her testimony allowed the prosecution in rebuttal to call "three trim, well-dressed young women, all of Norton." They told the jury that Jessie, who had visited Maxwell in jail, "repeated to them a confession" made by Maxwell that she hit her father with an iron. Although this evidence was hedged with the judge's warning that it should only be considered as rebuttal evidence against Jessie, it went to the jury. It was clear to one paper that "the last day for taking evidence was a black one for the defense."[80]

The summations and instructions followed the strategies laid out by each side in the opening statements. The jury was sent to deliberate with what Greear called "stock instructions" from the prosecution and with instructions from the defense that stressed both self-defense and the possibility that no homicide had been committed. The jury deliberated for about an hour and a half and returned to declare Edith Maxwell guilty of second-degree murder. It fixed her sentence at the maximum, twenty years of prison. Unofficial reports from the jury "said there was little disagreement among" them. "They were unanimous" in believing her guilty and only debated the prison time. Two of the twelve favored shorter terms but were "won over." Edith and her brother, Earl, who had sat beside her through the trial both wept. Earl was reported to say, "Well they have won one round of this fight, but we aren't through." And the *Washington Post* headline declared, "She Lost but The Fight Goes On."[81]

Readers across the nation learned of Edith's reaction to the verdict because the press was well represented at the second trial. The *Coalfield Progress* reported that thirteen "news men and women, including photographers," covered the trial. Area newspapers like the *Roanoke Times,* major state papers like the *Richmond Times-Dispatch,* Washington dailies like the *Washington Post,* and the press syndicates like the Associated Press sent reporters to Wise. And because Judge Carter did not impose the restrictions on taking pictures that Judge Skeen had, the trial was "a field day" for the photographers. Outside the courtroom the press contingent made an impression, "staying at the most expensive hotel in Norton." The reporters proved devoted to the story. At "press row," set up in their hotel, "the boys and girls . . . never dropped the case." Their discussions were "enlightening" as they "analyzed every bit of testimony and every move by the commonwealth and defense." As the trial neared its end, "they became an informal unorganized and unofficial jury, a cross section of their views being a quite accurate reflection of the jury's verdict." Despite their understanding of legal proceedings, the reporters displayed a reliance on the existing Appalachian stereotypes to color their work.[82]

By the time of the second trial and its aftermath, it was clear that Wise County could not escape its association with John Fox's fictional world or its related stereotypes; in fact, in some ways the inhabitants of the county had accepted these images. Demonstrating the ubiquity of Fox's images, during July 1936 the Bolling Theatre in Norton showed Walter Wagner's technicolor remake of *The Trail of the Lonesome Pine* starring Henry Fonda and Sylvia Sidney. Also, by late 1936 Warner Brothers began producing a film with parts that were loosely based on the sensational press's construction of Maxwell's case, and news of this production was available in Wise County. *Mountain Justice* was directed by Michael Curtiz and starred Josephine Hutchinson. A pivotal scene in the film was the struggle between the character played by Hutchinson and her father. He beats her with a mule whip, prompting her to strike him and kill him. A reviewer who found the movie "just tol'able" described it as a "hill-billy anthology, covering most of the recent headline material—the Maxwell case, child marriage, mountain health clinics, even a lynching."[83]

The locals also adopted the trappings of Fox's work. One of the major weekly papers, the *Big Stone Gap Post,* carried on its masthead the banner "Published in the Land of the Lonesome Pine." By 1938 the other major county paper, the *Norton Coalfield Progress,* had a column by James Hare called "Lonesome Pinings." Wise's Colonial Hotel offered for sale picture postcards siting it "on the trail of the lonesome pine." Restaurants, like the one Trigg Maxwell visited the day of his death, also used the "lonesome pine" in their names. But although some of the people of Wise County had adopted some of the phrases used by Fox in portraying their community in his fiction, it did not mean that they (or other Virginians) agreed with the more sensational works that used Fox's fiction as a starting point for lurid reporting about their community or their legal system.[84]

Virginians proved unwilling to give the press much latitude in its handling of the trial. Even before the trial opened, both local newspapers warned reporters from the yellow press to behave themselves. Quoting an article filed by an International News Service reporter which opened, "Sentiment is distinctly hostile to the girl, who violated the code of the hill country," an editorial in the *Big Stone Gap Post* told the "news boys from flatlands" to "stick to the facts" and to "give the county a break." Similarly, in his regular column in the *Coalfield Progress,* editor Pres T. Atkins declared that his paper was "more than willing to leave the case with the courts, confident in a fair trial." He said he would trust the lawyers, the judge, the Wise County jury, and the processes of law. He hoped that other "newspapers let the court conduct the trial."[85]

Such preemptive warnings did not come only from local papers. The *Richmond Times-Dispatch*'s reporter LaMotte Blakely wrote a scathing sidebar article on press coverage for the trial's opening day. Blakely expressed his surprise that as a reporter driving a car with a newspaper's name on it, he did not get a rock thrown through his windshield or get "shot at for a 'revenuer.'" He filled his article with sarcastic renderings of the yellow press's treatment of the people of Pound: the men were "hairy-faced hill dwellers," and the students playing at the "modern school building" were "blithely oblivious of their primitive origins and the coming struggle with stone age pappies." Although he asserted that small-town knowledge and gossip probably contributed to Edith Maxwell's first conviction, he mocked the press claim that the trial was filled with "profound social" implications such as "a struggle between medievalism, surviving as stern, paternal discipline, and modernism, represented by a courageous young woman who had left the hills, got 'book larnin' and come back to fight for her rights and her self respect." He attributed such reports to what he called "Jeep" journalism. "Readers of the Popeye will remember that the Jeep hears sounds not audible to the human ear and sees things not visible to mortal eye."[86]

The pleas and warnings seemed to have some effect. Even Virginius Dabney admitted that second trial's press coverage "was far more accurate than at the first trial." The "tone of the dispatches" was more refined than the previous trial, and "references" to the "mountain code" and similar terms were "much less in evidence." Yet some reporters covered the second trial much as their predecessors had covered the first. Hearst's *New York Evening Journal*'s coverage contained a rich mix of human-interest and mountain stereotypes. It described Edith as "pale and nervous as her second ordeal opened," and its picture caption called her a "Mountain Schoolmarm." Because the Dotson family rallied around Edith Maxwell while most of the Maxwells supported the prosecution, another *Journal* article claimed to see a "feud in the making." This article revived "the patriarchal code of 'mountain justice'" to explain the verdict. It was illustrated with a picture of a smiling Maxwell with the caption, "Hopeful Smile Vanishes."[87]

But the Maxwell story was pushed off the front pages of papers by one of the biggest media events of the 1930s, the abdication of England's King Edward VIII. As a result, only one national news magazine carried a story on the second trial. This article was more fair-handed than the 1935 news magazines had been in covering both the defense's and prosecution's cases. It leavened its evenhandedness with a dollop of mountaineer stereotypes. Implying that the people of Wise were provincial, the article attached the adjective *foreign* to Maxwell's defense council and to many of the doctors brought in to testify for her. Drawing upon the *Washington Post*'s coverage of the case, it declared the trial was a holiday for the locals and claimed that "a blind musician strummed hillbilly tunes" outside the courthouse for the crowd.[88]

The *Washington Post* was the only big-city paper that went all out in covering Maxwell's second trial, and its treatment favored Maxwell and was filled with hillbilly stereotyping. Reporter Edward T. Folliard filed daily front-page stories from Wise. Because the paper paid for one of Maxwell's lawyers and one of her medical experts, such an effort was to be expected, as was the *Post*'s tendency to favor the defense. Thus, Folliard wrote about Mary Katherine's testimony, quoting the defense attorneys, that "nobody could doubt" that this "little 12 year old" was "telling the truth." When the jury found Maxwell guilty, the *Post* declared in an editorial that it was "no more" impressed with this decision than with the first one. "The conduct of the trial and the swift decision of the jury" suggested "that the people of Wise County have convinced themselves that she ought to be punished, regardless of the actual evidence in the case." The paper portrayed the people of Wise as hillbillies and the county as a backwater. On opening day Folliard wrote that "the courtroom fairly bulged with mountaineers . . . men, women, and babies from all over in the Lonesome Pine country, many of who must have got up before dawn to come down the trails and find seats." He claimed that when Laughlin addressed the court with pretrial motions, the crowd gawked. "They never had seen such a spectacle down in the Lonesome Pine country—a 'lady lawyer,' a Portia who came into the courtroom and stood up there and argued with the men folk about the equal rights of women."[89]

Folliard's reports prompted Virginius Dabney to write an editorial about press coverage in the second Maxwell trial. Worried about "another flood of journalistic phantasmagoria," Dabney appealed to journalistic standards to preclude "More Maxwell Fairy-Tales." Naming Folliard in his piece, Dabney told him "to stop repeating fairy-tales about the Maxwell case." Dabney pointed out two statements Folliard had included in his background article on the first trial: that the prosecution said Edith struck Trigg with a slipper and that Trigg was in a drunken rage during their struggle. Dabney pointed out that the prosecution never claimed the slipper was used against Trigg and that whether or not Trigg was drunk was a contested fact in the first trial. Such reporting, Dabney insisted, "badly distorted" the "issues involved" in the trial. The editorial beseeched "newspaper correspondents who are writing about the case" to "refrain from making . . . . assertions which are contrary to the record." He lectured the profession to restrain its impulses toward "further imaginative excursions" and instructed other journalists on the importance of not commenting editorially on the evidence until the trial was over. He assured his readers that Maxwell "will be given a fair and impartial hearing."[90]

With the verdict in the second trial, some Virginians believed that Maxwell had gotten such a hearing. One of them, reporter LaMotte Blakely, attributed Maxwell's conviction to her failure to testify in her own behalf and "the very multiplicity of" defense "stratagems," which "antagonized" the jury. Similarly, the

Roanoke Times reviewed the whole affair in an editorial after the second conviction. It decried the sensational press coverage that had created the "impression
that Edith had not received a fair hearing and that the punishment passed out to
her was unduly harsh" and brought about a "hue and cry" on her behalf. "The
northern press created a great deal of interest in" Maxwell's case, but the paper
doubted that "it did her cause any real good." It was happy she had gotten a new
trial, not because it believed the overwrought claims of the northern press
but because if there "was the least scintilla of doubt about her guilt . . . that
doubt should be resolved" in her favor. So it praised the decision by the Court
of Appeals to grant Maxwell the chance "to establish her innocence to the satisfaction of a Virginia jury." Now that a second jury had convicted her, the *Times*
trusted the appeals process again. "Her case rests with the Virginia courts . . .
and not with the newspapers of Washington, Chicago, New York and other
northern cities."[91]

Others shared the belief that Maxwell had gotten a fair trial, but at the same
time they asserted that Maxwell might not have killed her father. In two editorials published on December 18 and 19, Dabney adopted this position, decrying
the *Washington Post*'s position that Maxwell's second trial was not fair: "We see
no reason to criticize either Judge Carter . . . or the jury . . . or the people of the
community." According to Dabney, all seemed "to have conducted themselves
well," and the jury "reached its verdict after an impartial review of the evidence."
But he was "disturbed over the possibility that Maxwell died a natural death."
Dabney found the testimony of the expert witnesses for the defense compelling,
and he trusted their expert judgment on the cause of death over that of the general practitioners relied upon by the prosecution. Dabney did not fault the jury
for not understanding that a pathologist could "be absolutely positive" on death
from a blow because it "naturally had in mind . . . that medical experts in other
fields sometimes contradict one another." In his view the jury doubtlessly "concluded that the experts in this case were like the others." Dabney declared that
the twenty-year sentence was "too severe" and questioned whether the "verdict
[should] be permitted to stand."[92]

Ideas like these prompted some Virginians to go further than Dabney in denouncing the verdict. They shared the sentiment with observers from outside
the state like the president of the District of Columbia Federation of Women's
Clubs, who thought the second verdict "the grossest miscarriage of justice" and
criticized the jury for their "one-track minds" and for disregarding Mary Katherine's testimony. Writing to the governor, a Methodist minister in Middleburg,

Virginia, declared that the state was "on trial. The two trials Miss Maxwell has had have been a disgrace of the state." Like Dabney he weighted the expert coroners' evidence more heavily than that of the regular doctors, finding it unbelievable that the jury could have convicted her. The "honor and integrity of the state of Virginia" were "at stake." Such sentiments expressed to Governor Peery usually were followed by the suggestion that he pardon Maxwell. But Peery adhered to the line laid out by the editorials in the state's newspapers, saying that he could not "consider any appeal for pardon until the courts have disposed finally of the matter."[93]

From December 1936 to November 1937, while Maxwell's appeals were pending, many changes occurred in her situation and her defense team. Her bail was extended, and for a while she took a job as a hostess in a Richmond restaurant and lived with relatives on a farm in Chesterfield County just outside the city. Maxwell's legal representation decreased dramatically after her conviction. Her cousin A. T. Dotson immediately decided not to give any active assistance to her quest for a new trial. In mid-February, Maxwell asked the National Woman's Party to stop representing her. Why she jettisoned the party remains a mystery. Perhaps the various sets of counsel had disagreed over trial strategy and could no longer work together, or perhaps Maxwell was convinced that as radical "outsiders" the party hindered her chance of receiving consideration for a pardon from Governor Peery. The party's departure also removed the main chance that Maxwell's case would be appealed to the United States Supreme Court on the jury service issue because it was the only group associated with Maxwell that could raise the money or had the expertise to carry a case into the federal courts. Maxwell's own contribution to her efforts to overturn the verdict was to engage in a magazine debate with Greear over her trials. This action kept her case alive in the national court of public opinion, even though Maxwell's legal chances were limited to the Virginia courts.[94]

Smith, Maxwell's remaining counsel, sought to reverse her conviction, first by a motion for a new trial and then by another appeal to the Supreme Court of Appeals. In March, Smith pleaded for a new trial, focusing especially on the claim that the medical facts did not support the contention that Trigg Maxwell had died from a blow to the head and thus the verdict was counter to the evidence. Judge Carter denied his pleas, and Smith immediately filed an appeal to the state's highest court. In August the Supreme Court of Appeals accepted the case; in September, Smith argued basically the same points before it. On November 12, 1937, Justice Edward W. Hudgins, for an unanimous court, denied

Maxwell a new trial, finding no reversible error. Having exhausted recourses available to her in the courts, Maxwell surrendered herself to the state prison on December 2, 1937, and announced that she would seek a pardon from the governor. Maxwell said she was sure that "when the governor hears the facts away from all the excitement that attended the case, he probably will free me."[95]

Maxwell's prediction of an early pardon ignored that editorial opinion across the state had hardened against her. When she filed for a new trial, the papers predicted that Maxwell would get justice from the courts. When Judge Carter denied the motion, papers assured their readers that the higher court would "give her every consideration." These papers declared that "people at a distance will do well to understand that the state of Virginia will never send a young woman to prison for twenty years for a crime of which she is innocent." But Virginia newspapers asserted that Maxwell had "failed" so far "to establish her innocence." The *Roanoke Times* decried the statement by the *Washington Post* that Maxwell could not get a fair trial in Wise as "inexcusable slander deserving naught but contempt." As she was seeking an appeal, Dabney continued his campaign against exploitation of the case by the sensational press. In an article distributed by the Southern Newspaper Syndicate which appeared during April 1937 in the *Roanoke Times,* he again turned his ire toward the *Washington Post* and the Hearst interests for burying the real facts of the case under "maudlin sentimentality and depressing nonsense."[96]

When the Court of Appeals denied her petition, editorial attitudes solidified behind the idea the state had been maligned by out-of-state papers and that the legal system had worked well in her case. Dabney wrote that his paper had "concluded after long and serious thought" that Maxwell "was given a fair trial" and that the "uproar over her case . . . was unjustified." He concluded that "further lachrymose jeremiads . . . about the poor mountain gal . . . who merely socked her drunken pappy with a slipper in self-defense, aren't apt to help her much now." Similarly the *Roanoke Times* said that "as far as the courts" were concerned, Maxwell's case was closed. Quoting an anonymous letter sent earlier to the *Washington Post,* it warned the "meddling reporters and reformers" to leave the case alone. Maxwell was "judged by her own kind and class" and was not a victim of "intolerance and injustice." Pres T. Atkins, after the appeal had failed, argued that Maxwell was "an unfortunate Wise County girl" who was "the miserable victim of the most vicious and misguided publicity that ever gathered around a criminal case in southwest Virginia." He also blamed her for her predicament for she lied in her original statements about what happened that night and then was "caught up in the publicity and believed in 'an unreal defense' [natural death] that resulted in the maximum penalty."[97]

According to the many, Maxwell's only hope lay in seeking a pardon from the governor. Papers predicted she would not serve her full sentence for "she is not without friends and they will keep up the fight to restore her to" freedom. They claimed that "governors of Virginia" were merciful and said that "when the time is ripe a petition for her pardon will doubtless receive careful executive consideration." But Governor Peery pointed out that Maxwell had "gone through two trials represented by able counsel and her case has twice been reviewed by the supreme court," implying that justice had been done in her case. Under Governor Peery, time was never ripe for Maxwell's pardon. Perhaps because of his political connections with Greear and B. Lee Skeen, his belief that she had received justice, his roots in southwest Virginia, or perhaps some combination of these reasons, Peery refused to pardon Maxwell, despite the pleas of her supporters.[98]

Maxwell's champions included Virginians and people from outside the state. In May 1938 five prominent Leesburg women (including the widow of a state senator), claiming to be acting independently of any organization, gathered more than 2,200 signatures on a petition calling for Maxwell's pardon. The women induced Loudoun County "businessmen, doctors, lawyers, preachers," and even county officials to sign their petition. They mobilized what they characterized as "the leading citizens of the county" behind the idea that "the injustice of" Maxwell's "sentence" was "manifest" and that she should be granted a pardon. Beyond such Virginia support for Maxwell, the publisher of the *Washington Herald* remained interested in her case. At the time of Maxwell's conviction, Cissy Patterson apparently contacted Virginians to discuss the feasibility of Maxwell's being pardoned. She recounted later that "we were told to wait— maybe two years, maybe three—and that then, after the passions of these primitive mountain people had at least partially cooled, and the outside world had partially forgotten the girl stood a good chance for pardon." Following that time frame, Patterson sought the assistance of Eleanor Roosevelt in 1941. She sent the first lady a report on the Maxwell case, which Roosevelt forwarded on to the governor of Virginia with her own letter declaring that "the sentence has been unduly severe and there are certain extenuating circumstances."[99]

Maxwell's chances of being pardoned had increased when James Price became governor in January 1938. Price ran as an independent in the 1937 election. Indeed, a poem sent to him indicated that placating the machine and punishing independents like Edith's uncle W. W. G. Dotson were part of the reason for Maxwell's prosecution. Price supported the Roosevelt administration at a time when the machine was breaking with the national administration. His term as governor was marked by a battle between his faction and the machine for the federal patronage, and in 1940 the machine punished Price by defeating all of his major legislative proposals. At the end of his term, Price had no reason to placate machine supporters like Greear who had been instrumental in prosecuting Maxwell. In addition, Price's inclinations toward leniency in pardoning prisoners can be seen in his record on commutations of sentences. Of the governors of Virginia in the 1920s and 1930s, Price granted the greatest numbers of commutations of sentences while Harry Byrd gave the fewest. Even so, in 1940 when Smith sounded him out about a pardon for Maxwell, Price said that it was probably too early yet. But by 1941 when Eleanor Roosevelt wrote him, Price responded that "confidentially" he intended to "take some action" soon. "The girl has been dreadfully exploited by newspapers and other agencies. What she really needs is an opportunity to get away from so much publicity and to have a free and fair opportunity to start life over again." [100]

On December 19, 1941, just before he left office, Price granted Maxwell a conditional pardon, dependent "on her good behavior in civilian life." If ever again convicted of crime in Virginia, Maxwell would "have to serve the remainder" of her original sentence. She apparently was relocated out of the state and into the hands of a charitable organization which had promised to secure her employment as an office worker. After her pardon Maxwell dropped from the historical record, though oral tradition in Wise County contends that she moved to Florida, married, and returned to schoolteaching. [101]

By pardoning Maxwell, Price did not restore Virginia's reputation for justice in the eyes of some. News of the pardon prompted individuals to write letters to the governor praising his action but condemning Virginia's legal system. A chairman of the Democratic Executive Committee of Fairfax County wrote to Price expressing his gratitude. He added, "I have always felt that the young lady was persecuted and it was a dark blot on our Virginia Government." An Ohio woman wrote to thank him for exercising "the courage of your convictions and" pardoning Maxwell, although she asserted that she and "many others have always felt she had been punished wrongly." A man from Nebraska declared, "I never could see any JUSTICE in the sentence of this girl." A New Yorker summarized the case by writing, "Justice hauls via ox cart speed in Virginia." Adding that "Virginia has need to be ashamed of the way she handled the Maxwell case," this correspondent thought that women jurors would improve the state's system of justice. A Seattle letter writer classified Price's pardon as "better late than never" and indicted the officials of the state for having been "asleep at the switch." A Pennsylvanian whose "people were all Virginians" wrote to praise Price for undoing "what many believe was not justice to this girl." The letter writer concluded sadly, "I used to be so proud of Virginia, believing that her laws were just." [102]

Nearly seventy years after the death of Rives Pollard, the dynamic of Virginia relations with the national media and outsiders had not changed, even if the issues raised by the critics and Virginians' responses had. Although tropes of honor did not appear in the outsiders' critiques of the state, Virginia was still portrayed as different. When Maxwell turned to "outsiders"—the Hearst press, the Women's Moderation Union, and the National Woman's Party—her case became a national cause. The state's system of justice, which kept women out of the jury box, and the stereotypical images of backward Wise County prompted many across the nation to believe that Virginia did not give Maxwell a fair trial. In the national court of public opinion, Virginia justice stood indicted as hypocritical, and Virginia was portrayed as a backwater. Virginians—especially editors like Dabney—responded to these criticisms by asserting that its society, even in the remote mountains, was as advanced as any other part of the nation and that its justice system could be counted on to deliver justice just like the courts of the other states.

CONCLUSION

THE FOUR CRIMES and trials in this book were explored more for what they could tell us about the press's view of southern exceptionalism than to recount the lives of people caught up in the machinery of the law. The specific personal details of the crimes—what Mary Grant's and Horace Ford's relations were, whether John Clark lay in wait for John Moffett, whether Theodore Estes drugged Elizabeth Loving, and what happened inside the Maxwell home late one night—matter here far less than how the press covered the crimes and trials. The statements of reporters and other observers (both Virginian and outsiders) about these crimes tell us much about how they viewed the state's legal system and the society of the South. In the press's coverage important themes of southern exceptionalism were expressed and reinforced. Because these cases involved outsiders to one degree or another, the enunciation of those themes was particularly clear in the press. The pattern showed a wide variety of emphasis. Themes of southern exceptionalism were expressed in all the trials, but with changing constellations of emphasis. Yet taken together these cases show that long before the civil rights era made the phrase *southern justice* synonymous with racial injustice, themes of southern exceptionalism dominated the press coverage of criminal trials in the region. And although there were continuities in some of the ideas of southern exceptionalism expressed over time, more significant are the changes in the way people perceived the South through these criminal trials.

When discussing southern exceptionalism, it is important to remember that the distinctions were not mere discourse. From Reconstruction through the New Deal, the South (even the uppermost southern state of Virginia) was different. It was different in its economics, its demographics, its politics, and its culture. In economics, agriculture predominated in the South even after it was replaced by industry as the driving force in the rest of the nation's economy. For much of this period, the South lagged behind other regions of the nation in terms of wealth. Its population remained more rural than that of other regions. There was no massive influx of immigrants from abroad into the southern states. Nor did the out-migration of large numbers of African Americans in the twentieth century change the reality that the largest concentrations of African Americans were found in the South through the New Deal, a demographic fact that shaped much of the region's politics. After the bitter divisions of the Reconstruction era, the emergence of segregation and disfranchisement transformed the region's politics into the system of one-party, white-man rule. And culturally, the culture of honor as a functioning social system—which helped define gender relations— had a far longer and stronger career in the South than in the rest of the Union. Also, the South had suffered defeat in war, which put a stamp of difference on the region's culture, ranging from its heroes and symbols to its place-names. Honor and the Lost Cause remade southern culture into an culture that was oppositional to the culture of the North. But perceptions of what constituted southern exceptionalism varied from these concrete differences. Newspapers, which were important shapers of public opinion in the South and in the nation, did not print long stories about culture, economics, race, and demographics. They did publish stories about crimes and trials and almost inadvertently highlighted differences, helping to define southern exceptionalism.

Press coverage of all four of these crimes and the resulting trials showcases the unique political culture that help define southern distinctiveness. Grant's case highlighted the tensions between those seeking to restore the old political order in which elite white men ruled and those seeking to revolutionize the state through black voting rights. The revolution was stillborn, as blacks kept their voting rights for only a generation. In the 1880s and 1890s an insecure white-supremacist Democratic Party demanded white solidarity in politics. Thus the Democratic press in its coverage of Moffett's death and the trial of Clark attempted to deny the political aspects of the case while the Prohibition

Party press pointed to the fraud and violence necessary to maintain Democratic rule. With the emergence of the one-party South, the political landscape solidified into a pattern distinct from much of the rest of the nation. Virginia's politics was marked by seemingly endless factional struggles and the predominance of political machines. These political realities influenced the coverage of the Virginia press in the Loving trial by highlighting the factional differences between the Loving and Estes families, a theme ignored by the national papers. Similarly, factional politics surfaced in the press with the campaigns for Edith Maxwell's pardon because the machine Democrats were presumed to be unfriendly to Maxwell. The strong continuity in the political distinctiveness of the state, as revealed by these cases, was matched in its views of gender relations.

Throughout all the cases Virginians expressed the idea that their society was defined by its chivalrous treatment of white women. In the Grant case the special status of women—as innocent domestic beings requiring the protection of male family members—was key to the origins of the killing and to how Virginians saw the crime. Although not central, these ideas were still quite vital during the Clark trial, as shown by Aylett's tribute to womanhood in his closing argument. Indeed, because Aylett's tribute had nothing to do with the case, it is even more revealing of the nature of Virginia culture that he made it and that the press thought it worthy of coverage. During Loving's trial, again, the notion that every Virginia gentleman valued the purity of Virginia womanhood appeared as motivating factors in the killing, in the lawyers' comments in court, and in the press's explanations of the crime and the verdict. The few dissenting voices— who saw that women might not be innocent, that they could lie, drink, and be "wild"—were overwhelmed by the assertions that the state was home to pure women who avoided the courtroom when Elizabeth Loving testified because of their modesty and decency. Even in the Maxwell trial, after women had gained the suffrage and a toehold in the professions, Virginians continued to appeal to the special nature of women in the commentary on the case. Again and again, supporters of Edith Maxwell sought to inspire the men of the state to come to the protection of the little mountain girl. That they used such appeals tells us the speakers thought that those would motivate Virginians. Despite the changes in women's status, Virginians clung to their old rhetoric. Thus reverence for womanhood remained, at least rhetorically, a chief attribute of the way Virginians, in the press, defined their society.

But over time, some of that distinctiveness did fade, and the press's portrait of the region changed. The cases points to the slow erosion of the economic distinctiveness—based on cash-crop agriculture—of Virginia and the South. In the late 1860s mainstream southern newspapers railed against the commercialism of Yankee civilization and praised their region's agricultural economy. James Grant's family obtained its wealth from the oldest of Virginia's crops, tobacco, symbolic of the state's strongly rooted agricultural economy. A generation later John Moffett's ministry in a booming textile town and William Loving's position as the estate manager of a wealthy financier indicated that Virginia had become part of the system of America's industrial capitalism. And a generation after that Trigg Maxwell's mining career showed how the forces of market capitalism had reached to the farthest borders of the state.

Social and economic change would result in an erosion of the culture of honor. Its place in the society was undermined by the expansion of the community, by economic change, and by the changing status of women. By the third decade of the twentieth century, although honor was not fully dead, it was no longer the vital system it once had been, either before the Civil War or even in its more democratic postwar form. The press's reporting of these cases reflects the slow fading of the prevalence of honor while at the same time highlighting some of the greatest differences between national and Virginia press treatment of the cases in framing southern distinctiveness. In 1868 and 1869 ideas of honor—of a man's duty to uphold his family's and therefore his own reputation even if it called for violence—precipitated the killing of Pollard and was successfully invoked as a defense by Grant's counsel. The national press condemned honor, while the Virginia press mostly avoided such condemnations, emphasizing the region's difference from the rest of the nation. In 1892 and 1893 the values of honor infused the Moffett and Clark affair, even if the appeal to honor by Clark's lawyers failed before the jury. Significantly, the regular Democratic papers saw the killing as a personal difficulty, as an affair of honor, while the national prohibition paper asserted that the killing was political. By 1907 honor as the key social factor had been displaced by the related idea of the unwritten law. In contrast to the Grant case, the unwritten law alone could not save Loving from a conviction; it had to be linked to the insanity defense. Moreover, the national and local press converged in their coverage and in their editorial condemnation of the outcome of the trial, showing the decline of honor in Virginia. By the time of the Maxwell trial, honor had diminished even further as a functioning social system. Honor did not enter into the trial or the press coverage, and it was no longer even a central part of idea of southern exceptionalism.

But the idea that the South was economically and socially backward, a common (if pejorative) exceptionalist idea, cropped up in the beginning and end cases. Most importantly, Virginians offered strikingly different responses to charges of backwardness in the 1860s and 1930s. Much of the thrust of editorial writers in the North in discussing Grant's killing of Pollard highlighted the social backwardness of the South by pointing out that the region still relied on private vengeance. In the 1860s much of Virginia press defended its social system of honor. Because the circumstances of Pollard's death made a direct defense difficult, the papers resorted to different means, treating the Grant family sympathetically or pointing to deficiencies in northern society. These stances reinforced the idea that the South was distinct and different. In the 1930s, when the national media portrayed Wise County as socially and economically primitive, with a legal system to match, the Virginia press responded, with some vacillation among certain papers, by asserting similarity, not difference. According to Virginia papers, the county had schools, roads, and chain stores, just like the rest of the nation. And they reiterated that the state's legal system was as procedurally regular and fair as that of any other state. In short, Virginians asserted that they were not different.

No matter how the picture of the society changed or remained stable, each of the sensational trials underscored the importance of Virginians' reaction to outside interference in their legal affairs. In the Grant trial the outsiders were part of the legal process, and Grant's lawyers and the press constantly lamented the foreign interference in the state's legal system. In Clark's trial the defense equated, perhaps successfully, Moffett with the meddlesome, out-of-state Prohibition Party. Loving's trial cast an interesting light on this facet of Virginia's culture. The judge's lawyers, worried about early press attempts to link Loving to Wall Street financier Thomas Fortune Ryan, apparently took (very successful) steps to keep Ryan out of the story. And Maxwell's support by the press syndicates and by organized groups from outside the state worried many Virginians, concerned with the image of their state. In each case Virginia saw itself as a distinctive society, defining itself in opposition to forces from outside the state, in effect defining itself by what it was not. This trait survived even as Virginia as a distinctive society died.[1]

During World War II this self-definition of Virginia society in reaction to outsider criticism of its legal system remained intact, although the scale of intervention from outside the state, focusing especially on the issues of race, increased dramatically. From 1940 to 1942 the case of Odell Waller revealed the escalation of interest in Virginia justice from outside the state's borders. In Pittsylvania

County, Waller, a black sharecropper, shot and killed Oscar Davis, his white landlord. Waller's case attracted the attention of numerous organizations, including the National Association for the Advancement of Colored People, the Brotherhood of Sleeping Car Porters, the American Civil Liberties Union, the Worker's Defense League, the International Labor Defense, and the Revolutionary Workers League. After he was convicted of first-degree murder and was sentenced to death, Waller's supporters spent a year and a half seeking to have his sentence overturned. In state and federal courts they argued for a new trial on the grounds that he was denied a fair trial because his jury had been composed only of poll-tax payers. When those efforts failed, they sought to have his death sentence commuted to a lesser penalty.[2]

In their efforts on behalf of Waller, his supporters engaged in tactics previously employed by critics of Virginia justice (though at unprecedented levels), making Waller front-page news in the state. Like earlier organizations—most notably the Women's Moderation Union and the National Woman's Party in the Maxwell case—Waller's supporters organized speaking tours (Waller's mother toured the nation speaking about his case), media campaigns, and petition and letter writing campaigns on his behalf. All these relied on the tried and tested tropes of the human-interest story and stood in stark contrast to Virginia papers' treatment of black criminal defendants. People were asked to identify with the black man facing the death penalty, and the Virginia papers (with the exception of Dabney's *Richmond Times-Dispatch*) found these appeals disturbing. While the leading liberal magazines espoused his cause, and the state government was flooded with mail concerning Waller, most of the Virginia press continued to call for his execution.

Waller's supporters also used means far beyond those utilized by previous critics of Virginia justice. They organized mass demonstrations and behind-the-scenes persuasion to try and save his life. At a huge June 16, 1942, rally at New York City's Madison Square Garden called by A. Philip Randolph, Waller's cause was linked to more general protests against segregation. Waller's supporters, including Eleanor Roosevelt, prompted President Franklin Roosevelt to write privately to the governor of Virginia urging him to commute Waller's sentence. The governor declined to commute the sentence, a move popular with the state's white population and in the Virginia press, and Waller was executed in July 1942.[3]

The political and social foundations that made the governor's action popular crumbled in the aftermath of World War II and during the civil rights revolution. The war began the process by reconstructing the demography of the state. In 1940, when the Waller case began, Pittsylvania County was the most populous county in the state. By the end of the war boom, it would lose this predominance to the suburban counties near Washington. With the growth of an "urban corridor" stretching from Washington to the counties surrounding the military bases and industry at Norfolk and Newport News, Virginia went from a primarily rural state to one with significant urban population. The shift of population weakened the political machine that had rooted itself in the rural counties. The machine's disastrous gamble on massive resistance destroyed its image of moderation and competence. Federal civil rights action completed the transformation, erasing the very mechanisms by which the machine had maintained power. By the mid-1960s the Twenty-fourth Amendment had abolished the poll tax as a qualification for voting in federal elections, and federal courts had declared the poll tax a violation of the Fourteenth Amendment in state elections. In addition, the Voting Rights Act of 1965 empowered federal officials to scrutinize the actions of Virginia officials in running elections. Moreover, federal courts mandated reapportionment in the state to favor the urban counties. Just as dramatically, change came to the social bases that had sustained several generations of Virginia's legal culture. The ending of legally mandated segregation, growth of the Washington suburbs, massive migration into the state, and decline of farming altered Virginia's social system. In the face of new realities, ideas of Virginia distinctiveness could no longer command the allegiance that they had during the trials of Grant, Clark, Loving, and Maxwell.[4]

Today, nearly seventy years after Maxwell's case, the old dynamic—of outside media criticizing some aspect of the society or legal system in Virginia and Virginians responding in defense of their own—has disappeared. Sensationalism certainly has not faded from the coverage of crime and resulting trials; regular papers, news magazines, tabloids, radio, and television thrive on such crime stories. And Virginia has recently generated cases—like the Bobbit affair—that have caught the attention of all the media. But such cases are not portrayed as representing a distinct Virginian or southern society. The established pattern of national critique and criticism of Virginian justice is gone. Indeed, thanks to the homogenizing forces of the media and social, political, and economic changes, Virginia is far less distinct from the rest of the nation than it once was.

The transformation of Virginia from the time of these trials to the present day can be seen by anyone who visits Wise County, site of the last case studied in this book. A modern visitor will have a hard time imagining the Wise of the 1930s. Driving from Norton past Wise to Pound—as Edith Maxwell did the night of her father's death—a visitor will see a landscape transformed from that of the 1930s. Strip mining has changed the very contours of the land. Highway 23 has been remade as a bypass, and it is now a four-lane divided highway that skirts the towns along its route instead of going through them. Along the highway just north of Norton looms a Wal-Mart, a clear example of how franchises have stripped uniqueness from the landscape. Business Route 23 might carry a visitor closer to the Wise County of Edith Maxwell's day. It is a narrower, two-lane road that winds and twists, following the lay of land far more than a modern highway. Old buildings, some stretching back to the 1930s, and mature trees line its route. But the area has many more mature trees now than it did in the 1930s after almost forty years of timbering. The few roadhouses that remain are outnumbered by video stores. The radio stations may tend toward country and Christian music, but rap, oldies, and talk radio share the spectrum.

On the other hand, the area strives to keep part of its past. In Big Stone Gap there is an annual outdoor play production of the *Trail of the Lonesome Pine*. It has been designated as an "official state drama" by the governor and has been recently celebrated in a native daughter's first novel, *Big Stone Gap*. The town of Wise is home to the Lonesome Pine Regional Library. A visitor can eat at the Lonesome Pine Restaurant in the Norton Holiday Inn. The local phone book shows the Lonesome Pine label affixed to at least a dozen different businesses, including a cellular phone company. For the tourist trade the whole region is called the Lonesome Pine area, marked on maps and interstate road signs. In an attempt to retain some distinctiveness in a landscape becoming more homogenized, Wise County has adopted wholesale the trappings Fox's fictional world. And this franchising of a mythological past places another barrier between the present and the past.[5]

Yet the historical records of these four cases let us look through such barriers into the past. Hence these homicide stories, in the words of Lawrence Friedman, tell us "of social changes, character changes, personality changes, changes in culture; changes in the structure of society; and ultimately changes in the economic, technological and social orders." The controversies that emerged when outsiders, including representatives of the national press, became part of the stories in these crimes and trials prompted Virginians to explain in the press the ideas that underlay their legal system. Therefore, these cases give an idea of some of the working principles that observers of the time thought formed the social basis of Virginia's legal system from Reconstruction through the New Deal.[6]

Notes

ABBREVIATIONS

AEJ	*Albany Evening Journal*
Aylett Scrapbook	William Roane Aylett, Scrapbook, 1890–93, in Aylett Family Papers, VHS
BN	*Bristol News*
BS	*Baltimore Sun*
BSGP	*Big Stone Gap Post*
CC	*Charlottesville Chronicle*
CDP	*Charlottesville Daily Progress*
Chesterman	Evan R. Chesterman Scrapbook, vol. 13, Trials in the *Richmond Evening Journal,* VHS. Note: undated items are cited by headline.
CTT	Clark trial transcript: *Was Rev. J. R. Moffett Murdered? Clark vs. Commonwealth* (Richmond, n.d.), copy in VBHS
DR	*Danville Register*
ERP	Eleanor Roosevelt Papers, FDRL, Hyde Park, N.Y.
FDRL	Franklin D. Roosevelt Library, Hyde Park, N.Y.
LDV	*Lynchburg Daily Virginian*
LN	*Lynchburg News*
LVA	Library of Virginia, Richmond
Moffett Correspondence	"Correspondence between W. W. Moffett and *Richmond Times-Dispatch* concerning Reverend John R. Moffett," bound typescript, VBHS
Moffett Diary	John R. Moffett Diary, manuscript and typescript copies, VBHS

MTT	Maxwell Trial Transcript, first trial transcript, Slemp Collection, University of Virginia's College at Wise Library, Wise, Va.
NCP	*Norton Coalfield Progress*
NV	*Norfolk Virginian*
NWPP	National Woman's Party Papers, microfilm ed. Library of Congress, Washington, D.C.
NYA	*New York American*
NYDT	*New York Daily Tribune*
NYEJ	*New York Evening Journal*
NYT	*New York Times*
NYW	*New York World*
RD	*Richmond Dispatch*
RDD	*Richmond Daily Dispatch*
RNL	*Richmond News Leader*
RoT	*Roanoke Times*
RR	*Rockingham Register*
RT	*Richmond Times*
RTD	*Richmond Times-Dispatch*
RW	*Richmond Whig*
Slemp	Evelyn Slemp Collection, University of Virginia's College at Wise Library, Wise, Va.
SO	*Southern Opinion*
Strode Papers	Aubrey Strode Papers, UVA
UVA	The Albert and Shirley Small Special Collections Library, University of Virginia Library, Charlottesville
VBHS	Virginia Baptist Historical Society, University of Richmond, Richmond
VHS	Virginia Historical Society, Richmond
WH	*Washington Herald*
WP	*Washington Post*
WTI	*Warrenton True Index*

INTRODUCTION

1. This work follows in the long tradition of using crimes and trials to explore southern society. Through legal cases scholars have examined some of the central themes of southern history: slavery, race relations, modernization, hostility toward immigrants, and fear of radicals; see McLaurin, *Celia;* Merril, *Jefferson's Nephews;* Carter, *Scottsboro;* Goodman, *Stories of Scottsboro;* Martin, *Herndon Case and Southern Justice;* Cortner, *A Mob Intent on Death;* McGovern, *Anatomy of a Lynching;* Barnes, *Who Killed John Clayton?;* Dinnerstein, *Leo Frank Case;* Baiamonte, *Spirit of Vengeance.* Virginia has received its fair share of attention from historians who use legal cases to study society; see Sherman, *Case of Odell Waller;* Rise, *Martinsville Seven;* Best, *Witch Hunt in Wise County;* Hatfield, "Mountain Girl Who Went Modern."

2. For other works that deal with the press and trials using more than one case, see Tucher, *Froth and Scum;* Hartog, "Lawyering, Husbands' Rights, and 'the Unwritten Law'"; Hixon, *Murder, Culture, and Injustice;* Chiasson, *Press on Trial;* Benedict, *Virgin or Vamp.*

3. For the basic formulation of the Anglo-American law of homicide, see Blackstone, *Commentaries on the Law of England* 4:176–204; on degrees of homicide, see Friedman, *History of American Law,* 248–49, 280–81; Green, "Jury and the English Law of Homicide"; for the way Americans liberalized concepts of self-defense, see Brown, *No Duty to Retreat.*

4. Darrow, *Story of My Life,* 350; Friedman and Percival, *Roots of Justice,* 259; Friedman, *Crime and Punishment,* 250–55, quote at 254; Lule, *Daily News, Eternal Stories,* 3, 17, 18, 21. For an echo of Darrow's point, see Hartog, "Lawyering, Husbands' Rights, and 'the Unwritten Law,'" 69–70 n. 4. For media spectacle trials as both "soap operas" and serious political discourse, see Gordon, *Great Arizona Orphan Abduction,* 275.

5. In functioning as outsiders the press in these cases fulfills some of the same roles that the French priest fulfills in Gordon, *Great Arizona Orphan Abduction,* 80.

6. On the goal of high circulation and the ubiquity of newspapers in this period, see Leonard, *News for All,* 33–61, 150–201, esp. chart on 178. Journalism history has been mostly an exercise in what Herbert Butterfield categorized as Whig history, the examination of the past for the explanation of the creation of current trends. It has focused on the rise of the penny press as the first mass form of newspaper, on the changing ownership patterns culminating in corporate control, and on the emergence of the standard of objectivity. Thus important historical trends have tended to be downplayed, most notably the strong persistence of ideological journalism into the twentieth century. See chap. 2. For the development of American press, see Mott, *American Journalism;* Schudson, *Discovering the News;* Demers, *Menace of the Corporate Newspaper.*

7. Emery, *Press in America,* 534; Mott, *American Journalism,* 646, 711, 818; Schwarzlose, *Nation's Newsbrokers,* 219, 229–31; Lukas, *Big Trouble,* 632–86; Czitrom, *Media and the American Mind,* 21–29; Demers, *Menace of the Corporate Newspaper,* 45–47.

8. On the look of papers, which captures these changes in a snapshot, see Barnhurst and Nerone, *Form of News,* 195.

9. On the development of the southern press, see Summers, *Press Gang,* 205, 208–12; Osthaus, *Partisans of the Southern Press,* 118–97, 211–12; Dinnerstein, *Leo Frank Case,* 11–19; Kneebone, *Southern Liberal Journalists;* Clark, *Southern Country Editor,* 51–65; Clark, *Rural Press and the New South;* Carter, *Their Words Were Bullets;* Williams, *Baltimore Sun;* Willey, *Country Newspaper,* 6.

10. For press coverage of crime, see Hughes, *News and the Human Interest Story;* Darnton, *Kiss of Lamourette,* 60–93; Tucher, *Froth and Scum.* For trials as theater, see MacDougall, *Interpretive Reporting,* 421; Grossberg, *Judgment for Solomon,* 89–90, 92, 171.

11. Hughes, *News and the Human Interest Story,* vii, 212–13, 255.

12. Smythe, "The Reporter, 1880–1900," 2, 3, 5–6, 7; Darnton, *Kiss of Lamourette,* 86–90. For an example of how the professionalizers thought crime should be covered, see Bush, *Newspaper Reporting of Public Affairs,* 16–116, 150–78, 260–94.

13. Osthaus, *Partisans of the Southern Press,* 131, 190. For the southern editors' failure to construct a proslavery defense by culling stories from the northern press before the Civil War, see Leonard, *News for All,* 77.

14. Escott and Goldfield, *Major Problems in the History of the American South,* v; Grantham, *South in Modern America.*

15. Woodward, *Origins of the New South;* Tindall, *Emergence of the New South;* Wilson and Ferris, *Encyclopedia of Southern Culture;* Ayers, *Promise of the New South;* Goldfield, *Cotton Fields and Skyscrapers;* Hobson, *Tell about the South;* Larry J. Griffin, "Why Was the South a Problem to America?" 10–32, and David L. Carlton, "How American Is the American South?" 33–56, in Griffin and Doyle, *South as an American Problem;* Louis D. Rubin Jr., "The American South: The Continuity of Self-Definition," in Rubin, *American South,* 3–23.

16. Ayers, *Vengeance and Justice,* 33, 273. The first wave of honor studies tended to focus on the Old South. Bertram Wyatt-Brown's stress on the deep, archaic traditions of honor—which emphasized the continuities with the past—dominated the treatment of the topic. According to Wyatt-Brown, honor emerged from the ancient "Indo-European tribes" and was passed down from generation to generation in the South. The work of Grady McWhiney and Perry D. Jamieson by emphasizing the strength of the Celtic tradition in the South and that of David Hackett Fischer by detailing the survival of European folkways in the South reinforced the idea of honor as a long cultural tradition. These accounts dovetailed with Ayers's treatment of honor's course during the later nineteenth century. Modernization suppressed honor. In the course of the nineteenth century, honor "increasingly came under attack from within and without the South" and withered. But forms of honor were kept alive right to modern times in places that resisted modernization. Thus in black urban communities and mountain communities, people lived in worlds integrated into the nation's state and economy but "took many of their val-

ues and actions" from cultures with honor traditions rather than "from the mass society" (Wyatt-Brown, *Southern Honor,* xi, 17, 33, 36, 441, 463; McWhiney and Jamieson, *Attack and Die,* 171–74; Fischer, *Albion's Seed;* Gispen, *What Made the South Different?* 40–48; Wyatt-Brown, *Shaping of Southern Culture,* 255–93).

17. See Wyatt-Brown, *Shaping of Southern Culture,* 293.

18. Tyler-McGraw, *At the Falls,* 184–89, 208–10; Blight, *Race and Reunion,* 267–70; Kinney, "'If Vanquished I Am Still Victorious'"; on politics, see Kousser, *Shaping of Southern Politics.*

19. For southern exceptionalism, see Woodward, *Burden of Southern History;* Taylor, *Cavalier and Yankee;* Vandiver, *Idea of the South;* Osterweis, *Myth of the Lost Cause;* Wilson, *Baptized in Blood;* Foster, *Ghosts of the Confederacy;* O'Brien, *Idea of the American South;* Kirby, *Media-Made Dixie;* Gaston, *New South Creed;* Grantham, *South in Modern America;* Degler, "Thesis, Antithesis, Synthesis"; Blight, *Race and Reunion.* For northern views of the South, see Current, *Northernizing the South;* Mitchell, *Civil War Soldiers,* 90–147; Silber, *Romance of Reunion.*

20. *RoT,* extra, June 14, 1907, 1; the quoted headline was the largest headline of the year. While strongest in the South, this tendency was found in other parts of the nation. Robert Darnton related how, as a novice reporter for the *Newark Star Ledger* in the 1950s, he uncovered a "spectacular" story of "murder, rape, and incest" while scrutinizing the daily police bulletins. When he attempted to pursue the story, he was told, "Can't you see that it's 'black,' kid? That's no story." (Darnton, *Kiss of Lamourette,* 85). For the price Republican newspapermen paid for seeking a black readership, see Nerone, *Violence against the Press,* 130–38. For using the techniques of the human-interest story to support racist interpretations of events, see Gordon, *Great Arizona Orphan Abduction,* 277–78.

21. Unlike in the realm of the press, after Reconstruction there was little direct federal intervention in the process of criminal justice in the states. It was not until the twentieth century, building on the doctrinal foundations of *Moore v. Dempsey,* 261 *United States Reports* 86 (1923), that the United States Supreme Court actively oversaw the states' due process procedures in criminal trials. *Moore* and the cases that followed until the civil rights revolution of the 1950s and 1960s were mostly high law, far more observed in the breach than observance; see Eric J. Sundquist, "Blues for Atticus Finch: Scottsboro, Brown, and Harper Lee," in Griffin and Doyle, *South as an American Problem,* 181–209.

1. "A GOOD AND EFFICIENT REMEDY FOR LIBEL"

1. Christian, *Richmond,* 301–32. This chapter's title is from *Nation,* Dec. 10, 1868, 477.

2. On the partisan and other press traditions, see Mott, *American Journalism;* Schudson, *Discovering the News;* Schudson, "Preparing the Minds of the People";

Schudson, *Origins of the Ideal of Objectivity;* Leonard, *News for All;* Summers, *Press Gang;* Ritchie, *Press Gallery;* Kaplan, "American Press and Political Community"; Crouthamel, *Bennett's New York Herald;* Dary, *Red Blood and Black Ink;* McGerr, *Decline of Popular Politics,* 14–21, 107–8, 135; North, *History of the Newspaper,* 111.

3. Summers, *Press Gang,* 205, 208–12; Osthaus, *Partisans of the Southern Press,* 118–97, 211–12.

4. Tyler-McGraw, *At the Falls,* 104–5, 113, 123–25, 170–71; Chesson, *Richmond after the War,* 135–36.

5. Chesson, *Richmond after the War,* 92, 104–5; Tyler-McGraw, *At the Falls,* 149, 166; Maddex, *Virginia Conservatives,* 46–67; Lowe, *Republicans and Reconstruction in Virginia,* 25–163; Moger, *Virginia,* 1–13.

6. Tyler-McGraw, *At the Falls,* 176.

7. For a good chronology of the Davis case, see Christian, *Richmond,* 282–88; for the aborted trial, see Strode, *Jefferson Davis,* 258–301, and McElroy, *Jefferson Davis* 2:524–611; for typical Virginia press coverage, see *RW,* Dec. 8, 1868, 1, 4; *CC,* Feb. 13, 1869; *RDD,* Dec. 1, 1868, 1.

8. *RW,* Nov. 20, 1868, 1; *CC,* Dec. 15, 1868, 2; *NV,* Dec. 1, 1868, [1], Nov. 27, 1868, [2].

9. *RW,* Dec. 8, 1868, 2, Dec. 18, 1868, [1], [4]; *NV,* Dec. 4, 1868, 3; see also *WTI,* Nov. 28, 1868, 2; *RDD,* Dec. 4, 1868, 3.

10. *RDD,* Dec. 3, 1868, 1; *NV,* Nov. 30, 1868, 1; *RW,* Nov. 20, 1868, [2], Dec. 18, 1868, [1], Dec. 22, 1868, [3].

11. *RDD,* Dec. 12, 1868, 1, 2, Dec. 25, 1868, 1, Dec. 26, 1868, 1, Dec. 30, 1868, 1, Dec. 31, 1868, 1; *RW,* Jan. 1, 1869, [1], *CC,* Dec. 17, 1868, 2; Schwarz, *Twice Condemned,* 13, 210–14, 297–99.

12. Franklin, *Militant South;* Wyatt-Brown, *Southern Honor;* Wyatt-Brown, *Shaping of Southern Culture,* 31–80; Ayers, *Vengeance and Justice;* Ireland, "Acquitted yet Scorned"; Wilson, *Honor's Voice,* 276–83; Ethington, *Public City,* 81, 83; Freeman, *Affairs of Honor;* Schmeller, "Liberty of the Cudgel." A limited form of honor seems to have been alive across most of the United States throughout the whole nineteenth century; see Hartog, "Lawyering, Husbands' Rights, and 'the Unwritten Law,'" 67–96; Ireland, "Insanity and the Unwritten Law."

13. Wyatt-Brown, *Southern Honor,* xvi–xix, 46, 53, 57, 233, 234; Ayers, *Vengeance and Justice,* 29; Fischer, *Albion's Seed,* 207–418, 605–782, and esp. 217, 225, 256, 279, 643–50, 668, 682, 687, 754–60, 770–76; Isaac, *Transformation of Virginia,* 95–98, 161–77; Shearer Davis Bowman, "Honor and Martialism in the U.S. South and Prussian East Elbia during the Mid-Nineteenth Century," in Gispen, *What Made the South Different?* 19–40. For the slaves' own honor system, see Wyatt-Brown, *Shaping of Southern Culture,* 3–30; for the role of honor in gender relations in the South, see Clinton, *Half Sisters of History;* Clinton and Silber, *Divided Houses.* But perhaps scholars have overextended the view that honor was only for men. For examples of female honor, see Fox, *Trials of Intimacy,* 155; Grossberg, *Judgment for Solomon,* 10.

14. Wyatt-Brown, *Southern Honor,* 61, 88, 350, 355; Ayers, *Vengeance and Justice,* 16; Bowman, "Honor and Martialism," 38–40.

15. Wyatt-Brown, *Southern Honor,* xiii, 88, 365, 63; Boorstin, *Americans,* 209.

16. Wyatt-Brown, *Southern Honor,* 9–10, 14, 15, 42, 43, 45, 53–54; Ayers, *Vengeance and Justice,* 13. For southern honor and violence, see Gorn, " 'Gouge and Bite, Pull Hair and Scratch' "; Williams, *Dueling in the Old South;* Ireland, "Homicide in Nineteenth Century Kentucky"; Lane, *Murder in America,* 84–213; Courtwright, *Violent Land,* 28–30; Bellesiles, *Arming America,* 367–79, 433–35, 437–41.

17. For honor's relationship to slavery, see Greenberg, *Masters and Statesmen;* Greenberg, *Honor and Slavery;* Stowe, *Intimacy and Power.* On the Sumner incident, see Bowman, "Honor and Martialism," in Gispen, *What Made the South Different?* 23; Williams, *Anson Burlingame,* 11–12; Wyatt-Brown, *Shaping of Southern Culture,* 196–98. For the same linkage of honor needing fair play made in California after an 1859 duel, see Ethington, *Public City,* 177–79; for a similar view that the South falsely claimed to be honorable, see Dinnerstein, *Leo Frank Case,* 133.

18. For example, the "Feejee Mermaid" episode, a dispute over a scientific exhibit, in 1843 Charleston was instigated by newspaper articles; much of it was carried on in the press; if it had come three decades later, no doubt it would have been a wire story that would have traveled across the nation (Greenberg, *Honor and Slavery,* 4–5).

19. Stewart, *Honor,* 75–87; Bowman, "Honor and Martialism," in Gispen, *What Made the South Different?* 34.

20. *National Cyclopaedia of American Biography* 9:339; Herringshaw, *Herringshaw's Encyclopedia of American Biography,* 750. On Edward Pollard, see Maddex, *Reconstruction of Edward A. Pollard;* Blight, *Race and Reunion,* 260–61; *RDD,* Nov. 25, 1868, 1; on the Pollards' roles during the war, see Andrews, *South Reports the Civil War,* 30–32; on operation of the *Examiner,* see Osthaus, *Partisans of the Southern Press,* 94–177.

21. Osthaus, *Partisans of the Southern Press,* 117, 105, 155; Pollard, *To the People of the South,* broadside, 1865, and *The Southern Opinion,* broadside, Nov. 20, 1866, VHS; *American and Commercial Advertiser,* Nov. 25, 1868, [4]; Summers, *Press Gang,* 50–52; *Harper's Weekly,* Dec. 12, 1868, 788; *CC,* Mar. 2, 1869, 2. Former Confederate general Daniel H. Hill founded the magazine *The Land We Love* in 1866 for the same reason Pollard founded his paper; by 1869 it had become the *Southern Magazine,* a leading developer and disseminator of the Lost Cause ideology (Blight, *Race and Reunion,* 78).

22. *SO,* Dec. 5, 1868, 1; H. Rives Pollard, *Lecture: The Chivalry of the South,* broadside, May 2, 1867, VHS; *RDD,* Nov. 25, 1868, 1.

23. *RDD,* Nov. 25, 1868, 1; Dabney, *Pistols and Pointed Pens,* 57–60; Williams, *Dueling in the Old South; BS,* Nov. 26, 1868, 1; *American and Commercial Advertiser,* Nov. 25, 1868, [4].

24. *NYT,* Nov. 26, 1868, 1; Dabney, *Pistols and Pointed Pens,* xiii, 57–60; Boorstin, *Americans,* 216–17; *RDD,* Mar. 2, 1869, 2. A similar pattern of violence against editors

and editors going armed existed in the West; see Dary, *Red Blood and Black Ink,* 105–26; see also Schmeller, "Liberty of the Cudgel."

25. Quoted in *NYT,* Nov. 26, 1868, 1; *SO,* Dec. 5, 1868, 1.

26. Willis, "Ghosts of 1008 East Clay Street," 33; Miss Claiborne, "Clover Nook" (1860), VHS; *RDD,* Nov. 25, 1868, 1; Tyler-McGraw, *At the Falls,* 110.

27. *SO* rept. in the *NYT,* Nov. 26, 1868, 1; *NV,* Nov. 25, 1868, 1; *RDD,* Nov. 25, 1868, 1.

28. A series of letters by Horace Ford to his Richmond friend Lewis T. Gwathmey, from Texas, supports the supposition that something took place between him and Mary Grant. For instance, Ford described a near shipwreck on the way to New Orleans, a fact which also appeared in the *Southern Opinion*'s article. Showing his interest in courtship, he complained of the quality of the young women in Texas and inquired after ladies in Richmond. Most tellingly, he wrote that although he wanted to go back to Virginia, he would have to go "in cog" (Horace Ford to Lewis Temple Gwathmey, Apr. 19, Aug. 22, October 26, 1871, July 22, 1872, Apr. 14, 1873, Gwathmey Family Papers, VHS).

29. *Harper's Weekly,* Dec. 12, 1868, 788; *NYT,* Nov. 26, 1868, 1.

30. *RDD,* Nov. 25, 1868, 1; *NYT,* Nov. 26, 1868, 1. Three accounts of the killing published within a day of the event, appearing in *NYT, RDD,* and the *Richmond State Journal* (reprinted in the *BS*), have been used to construct this narrative of the killing and immediate aftermath.

31. *BS,* Nov. 26, 1868, 1, 2; *NYT,* Nov. 26, 1868, 1; *RDD,* Nov. 25, 1868, 1, Nov. 26, 1868, 1, Mar. 2, 1869, 2; Pollard, *Memoir of the Assassination,* 7.

32. *NYT,* Nov. 26, 1868, 1; *RDD,* Nov. 25, 1868, 1, Nov. 26, 1868, 1; *State Journal* quoted in *BS,* Nov. 26, 1868, 1; *Richmond Evening Journal* quoted in *BS,* Nov. 28, 1868, 4.

33. *RDD,* Nov. 25, 1868, 1, Nov. 26, 1868, 1, Mar. 4, 1869, 1.

34. Ibid., Nov. 25, 1868, 1, Nov. 26, 1868, 1. Jury questions were not recorded, but occasionally the press noted when testimony was directed to a juryman or the foreman of the panel.

35. *Petersburg Index* quoted in *NV,* Nov. 30, 1868, 3; *BS,* Nov. 28, 1868, 4.

36. For example, the *Chicago Tribune* picked up its story from its Washington correspondent and then supplemented this account with the work of its New York correspondent, who utilized the dispatches sent to New York by Kappa. The *Tribune* story then became the basis for the news articles of a small-town, downstate Illinois paper, the *Oquawaka Spectator,* on the case. Thus the basic facts of the story were readily available for editorial writers of the nation to use as they saw fit (*Chicago Tribune,* Nov. 25, 1868, 1, Nov. 26, 1868, 1; *Oquawaka Spectator,* Dec. 3, 1868, [2]). As the Associated Press tended to present the southern, white side of most issues, it is somewhat surprising that such detailed stories were sent nationwide. Perhaps, as Edward Pollard repeatedly said, the personal spite of Richmond reporters facilitated the dissemination of the tale. See Summers, *Press Gang,* 191–234, esp. 218–20.

37. *NYT,* Nov. 25, 1868, 1, Nov. 26, 1868, 1, Dec. 9, 1868, 11, Jan. 29, 1869, 2, 4; *New York Herald,* Nov. 26, 1868, 4.

38. Letter to the *Tribune* printed in *AEJ*, Nov. 27, 1868, 2, and reprinted in *RDD*, Nov. 28, 1868, 1.

39. *RDD*, Nov. 25, 1868, 1; *State Journal* quoted in *BS*, Nov. 26, 1868, 1; *NV*, Nov. 25, 1868, 2; *BN*, Nov. 24, 1868, [2]; *WTI*, Nov. 28, 1868, [2].

40. *RDD*, Nov. 27, 1868, 1; *NV*, Nov. 27, 1868, 1; *CC*, Nov. 28, 1868, 3.

41. *RDD*, Dec. 21, 1868, 1; Chesson, *Richmond after the War*, 105.

42. *RDD*, Nov. 26, 1868, 1, Nov. 27, 1868, 1; *CC*, Dec. 5, 1868, 4; *RW*, Dec. 29, 1868, [3]; *WTI*, Dec. 5, 1868, [2]. On Wise's career, see Sutherland, *Confederate Carpetbaggers*, and Davis, "Very Well-Rounded Republican."

43. *NV*, Nov. 30, 1868, 3; *RDD*, Nov. 28, 1868, 1; *BS*, Nov. 11, 1868, 1; *LDV*, Nov. 30, 1868, [3]; Chesson, *Richmond after the War*, 80.

44. *LDV*, Nov. 30, 1868, [3]; *NYT*, Nov. 30, 1868, 4; *BS*, Nov. 30, 1868, 1. For example, the *Richmond Examiner*'s version reprinted in the *BS* used "female."

45. *RDD*, Nov. 28, 1868, 1, Nov. 30, 1868, 1; *RW*, Nov. 28, 1868, quoted in *NYT*, Nov. 30, 1868, 4; *LDV*, Nov. 30, 1868, [3].

46. *LDV*, Dec. 3, 1868, [3]; *CC*, Dec. 1, 1868, 3; *RDD*, Dec. 7, 1868, 1.

47. *SO*, Dec. 5, 1868; see also *BN*, Dec. 11, 1868, [3]; *LDV*, Dec. 9, 1868, [3]; *RDD*, Dec. 7, 1868, 1; *NYT*, Jan. 4, 1869, 5.

48. *SO*, Dec. 5, 1868; Pollard, *Memoir of the Assassination*, 3.

49. *SO*, Dec. 5, 1868, also rept. *NYT*, Jan. 4, 1869, 5; a slightly different version appears in Pollard, *Memoir of the Assassination*, 3.

50. *BN*, Dec. 18, 1868, [2]; *NYT*, Jan. 7, 1869, 4; Summers, *Press Gang*, 109–22. One publisher who specialized in blackmail, beginning in the 1890s, was William D'Alton Mann, who used his weekly paper *Town Topics* to extort money from some of New York City's richest individuals by threatening to publish embarrassing stories (O'Connor, *Courtroom Warrior*, 157–68).

51. *RDD*, Feb. 17, 1869, 1, Feb. 18, 1869, 1, Feb. 19, 1869, 1; Christian, *Richmond*, 290; Peters and Peters, *Virginia Historic Courthouses*, 113, 125–26, 157–59.

52. *RDD*, Feb. 17, 1869, 1, Feb. 18, 1869, 1, Feb. 19, 1869, 1, Mar. 8, 1869, 1; United States Army, 1st Military District, Richmond, *Special Orders* (Richmond, 1867–70), 6; Boyd, *Directory of Richmond City*, 59; Bundy, *Early Days in the Chippewa Valley*. See letter from C. S. Bundy on "Military and Naval Claim Agency" letterhead that advertises "officers's accounts settled with despatch" (www.sbauctioneers.com/mar02/228.html). C. S. Bundy Esquire of Washington, D.C., married Mattie P. Emery of Chenango County, N.Y., in December 1867 (www.rootsweb.com/~patioga/newspaper/tag1867/a.htm). For the cases cited, see Brandt, *Congressman Who Got Away with Murder*, 156–57, 169–70, 177–81, 187–88; Schuma, *Dead Certainties*, 73–318.

53. *RW*, Feb. 23, 1869, [3], Feb. 26, 1869, 1; *RDD*, Feb. 23, 1869, 1, Feb. 24, 1869, 1, Feb. 25, 1869, 1, Feb. 26, 1869, 1.

54. *RDD*, Feb. 23, 1869, 1, Feb. 24, 1869, 1, Feb. 25, 1869, 1, Feb. 26, 1869, 1; *RW*, Feb. 26, 1869, 1; *NYT*, Mar. 1, 1869, 4.

55. *Abingdon Virginian,* Mar. 5, 1869, [2]; *RW,* Feb. 23, 1869, [3], Feb. 25, 1869 [2]. The accounts in the *Dispatch* are much toned down; see *RDD,* Feb. 23, 1869, 1, Feb. 25, 1869, 1.

56. *RDD,* Mar. 1, 1869, 1.

57. Ibid., Mar. 2, 1869, 2, Mar. 3, 1869, 1, Mar. 4, 1869, 1; *RW,* Mar. 2, 1869, [3], Mar. 3, 1869, [3]; *NV,* Mar. 6, 1869, 3.

58. *RDD,* Mar. 2, 1869, 2, Mar. 3, 1869, 1, Mar. 4, 1869, 1; *RW,* Mar. 2, 1869, [3], Mar. 3, 1869, [3]; *NV,* Mar. 6, 1869, 3.

59. *RDD,* Mar. 4, 1869, 1; *NV,* Mar. 6, 1869, 3. Wise was proponent of the code of honor; before the war he had been involved in a number of duels (Greenberg, *Honor and Slavery,* 90, 159 n. 17).

60. *RDD,* Mar. 4, 1869, 1.

61. Ibid., Mar. 4, 1869, 1, Mar. 5, 1869, 2; *RW,* Mar. 5, 1869, [3].

62. *RDD,* Mar. 4, 1869, 1, Mar. 5, 1869, 1, 2.

63. Ibid., Mar. 5, 1869, 2.

64. Ibid., 1.

65. Ibid., Mar. 6, 1869, 1.

66. Pollard, *Memoir of the Assassination,* 9; *RDD,* Mar. 6, 1869, 1, Mar. 8, 1869, 1.

67. Pollard, *Memoir of the Assassination,* 10–11, 15, 21–22, 25; *RDD,* Mar. 8, 1869, 1.

68. *RDD,* Mar. 6, 1869, 1, Mar. 8, 1869, 1; Pollard, *Memoir of the Assassination,* 26–29.

69. *RDD,* Mar. 8, 1869, 1; Pollard, *Memoir of the Assassination,* 26–29.

70. *RDD,* Mar. 8, 1869, 1; *RW,* Mar. 9, 1896, [1]; see also *BS,* Mar. 8, 1869, 1; *NV,* Mar. 8, 1869, 4.

71. *RW,* Mar. 9, 1896, [1].

72. *NYT,* Nov. 26, 1868, 1, Nov. 27, 1868, 1, Mar. 1, 1869, 4.

73. *Oquawaka Spectator,* Dec. 3, 1868, 2, 3, Mar. 18, 1869, 2. It is also possible that the Pollard affair contributed to Mark Twain's classic short story that constructed an image of postwar southern journalism and society as being a juxtaposition of raw violence and elevated manners and language, "Journalism in Tennessee" (Clemens, *Complete Short Stories of Mark Twain*).

74. *NYDT,* Nov. 25, 1868, 4, Nov. 28, 1868, 4; Summers, *Press Gang,* 14. The characterization of journalism as "a noble profession" typified the conception of the role of the press that Greeley had championed nearly a generation earlier; see Tucher, *Froth and Scum.*

75. *NYDT,* Dec. 1, 1868, 4. The *Tribune's* position was consistent with earlier northern attacks on chivalry; see Silber, *Romance of Reunion,* 18–26.

76. *NYDT,* Nov. 27, 1868, 1, Dec. 1, 1868, 4.

77. *Harrisonburg Patriot* quoted in *SO,* Dec. 5, 1868, 2.

78. *New York Herald,* Nov. 26, 1868, 4, Mar. 8, 1869, 6.

79. *AEJ,* Nov. 26, 1868, [2], Nov. 27, 1868, [2].

80. Ibid. Even though it had coverage of Virginia political affairs, the *Evening*

Journal, like the *New York Tribune,* had nothing on the trial (see Mar. 10, 1869, [2]). On later southern violent outbreaks against radical papers, see Summers, *Press Gang,* 217. On the other hand, the *Times* editorialized that Pollard had not been "shot for asserting the freedom of the press but rather for his misuse of his press power." Although labeling Grant's act murder and calling him "a cowardly assassin," the *Times* objected "to any attempt to justify or extenuate" Pollard's "exceedingly base" conduct "under pretended regard for the freedom of the press" (*NYT,* Nov. 26, 1868, 1, Nov. 27, 1868, 1, Jan. 7, 1869, 4).

81. *Nation,* Dec. 3, 1868, 455; Mitchison, *History of Scotland,* 133; Fry and Fry, *History of Scotland,* 154–55; Lee, *James Stewart, Earl of Moray.*

82. *Nation,* Dec. 10, 1868, 476–77. Honor was directly related to character, and character was more easily attacked thanks to the proliferation of the press. Thus in a few years all main parties in the Beecher-Tilton affair would complain of attacks on their character by the press, and a generation later, after the decline of honorable violence in response to press criticism, E. L. Godkin would try to set ground rules in the treatment of private character by the press, asserting that a citizen had a right "to his own reputation" (Fox, *Trials of Intimacy,* 33, 50; Godkin, "Rights of the Citizen").

83. *Nation,* Dec. 10, 1868, 476–77.

84. *NV,* Nov. 28, 1868, 2.

85. *RDD,* Dec. 3, 1868, 2. The murder of the beautiful cigar girl refers to the killing of Mary Rogers; see Strebnick, *Mysterious Death of Mary Rogers;* Tucher, *Froth and Scum.* The infanticide case was that of Hester Vaughn, a cause célèbre among American feminists; their agitation eventually resulted in her pardon (see Goldsmith, *Other Powers,* 172–76).

86. *RDD,* Dec. 4, 1868, 3. Apparently the *Dispatch's* approach was novel; see Leonard, *News for All,* 77.

87. *RDD,* Dec. 3, 1868, 2.

88. *Virginia Gazette,* Mar. 11, 1869, [2]. This paper was published in Williamsburg by Robert A. Lively and edited by E. H. Lively.

89. Willis, "Ghosts of 1008 East Clay Street," 34; Maddex, *Reconstruction of Edward A. Pollard;* Davis, "Very Well-Rounded Republican."

90. Tyler-McGraw, *At the Falls,* 177–78. On the end of Reconstruction in Virginia, see Pulley, *Old Virginia Restored,* 1–16; Lowe, *Republicans and Reconstruction in Virginia,* 164–82.

91. Osthaus, *Partisans of the Southern Press,* 148.

2. "A DANVILLE DIFFICULTY"

1. For other accounts, see Pearson and Hendricks, *Liquor and Anti-Liquor in Virginia, 1619–1919,* 217–18; Mantiply, *History of Moffett Memorial Baptist Church,* 4–12. This chapter's title is from *RD,* Nov. 12, 1892, 1.

2. Mott, *American Journalism;* Schudson, *Discovering the News;* Schudson, "Preparing the Minds of the People"; Schudson, *Origins of the Ideal of Objectivity;* Leonard, *News for All;* Schiller, *Objectivity and the News;* Emery, *Press in America;* Baldasty, "Nineteenth Century Origins"; Baldasty, *Commercialization of News;* McGerr, *Decline of Popular Politics;* Smythe, "The Reporter"; Kluger, *Paper;* North, *History of the Newspaper,* app. A, table 1, 170-71; Mott, *History of American Magazines* 3:4-5, 6-12, 4:2, 11, 199-200.

3. Clark, *Southern Country Editor;* Clark, *Rural Press and the New South;* Carter, *Their Words Were Bullets;* Williams, *Baltimore Sun;* Osthaus, *Partisans of the Southern Press,* 118-97, 211-12; Silber, *Romance of Reunion;* Blight, *Race and Reunion,* 171-299, 338-98.

4. On ideas about honor, see Wyatt-Brown, *Southern Honor;* Ayers, *Vengeance and Justice,* 266-72; Moore, "The Death of the Duel," 259-76, esp. 275-76; Greenberg, *Honor and Slavery,* 15; Nisbett and Cohen, *Culture of Honor,* 25-55, 57-71, 87-89, 92-94. For the perpetuation of honor-based violence (and its interaction with other forces) to the modern era, see Butterfield, *All God's Children;* Becky L. Glass, "Women and Violence: the Intersection of Two Components of Southern Ideology," in Dillman, *Southern Women,* 191-201; Courtwright, *Violent Land,* 60-61, 225-69.

5. Stewart, *Honor,* 21, 41, 54-55, 64-70, 130-31, 141-46; Parker, "Law, Honor, and Impunity in Spanish America"; Bellesiles, *Arming America,* 433-35, 437-41.

6. Shearer Davis Bowman, "Honor and Martialism in the U.S. South and Prussian East Elbia during the Mid-Nineteenth Century," and Edward L. Ayers, "Commentary [on "Bowman's Honor and Martialism]," in Gispen, *What Made the South Different?* 19-48, quote at 45-46.

7. Ireland, "Suicide of Judge Richard Reid," 127, 144-45; Ayers, *Vengeance and Justice,* 271. In South Carolina one of the last formal duels in the South took place in 1880 and was widely denounced in the state's press. Even as the dueling code, "with its aristocratic pretensions," was fading in the South, "the language of honor persisted," and significantly the surviving duelist was found not guilty by reason of self-defense (Wyatt-Brown, *Shaping of Southern Culture,* 270-81).

8. *Account of the Curtis Homicide,* 4-5, 41-44, 52-54. For the vitality of honor in the 1870s courts of Kentucky, see Ireland, "Buford-Elliott Tragedy," 418. On honor's survival in the public sphere, see Dailey, "Deference and Violence in the Postbellum Urban South"; Ireland, "Homicide in Nineteenth Century Kentucky," 142-44, 148-55.

9. Kousser, *Shaping of Southern Politics,* 171. For the Readjusters, see Moore, *Two Paths to the New South;* Pearson, *Readjuster Movement in Virginia;* Degler, *Other South,* 269-315, esp. 279 for their many electoral victories; Pulley, *Old Virginia Restored,* 24-47; Dailey, *Before Jim Crow.*

10. John W. Daniel quoted in Calhoun, "Danville Riot and Its Repercussions," 35; *Richmond State,* Nov. 7, 1883, quoted in Woodward, *Origins of the New South,* 105 (see also 93-98); Dailey, "Deference and Violence in the Postbellum Urban South," 562.

11. *RD* quoted in Wynes, *Race Relations in Virginia,* 40; Moger, *Virginia,* 56; Kousser, *Shaping of Southern Politics,* 171–72; Pulley, *Old Virginia Restored,* 48–65; Perman, *Struggle for Mastery,* 5–6.

12. Pearson and Hendricks, *Liquor and Anti-Liquor in Virginia,* 170–80, 205–16; Cherrington, *Standard Encyclopedia of the Alcohol Problem* 6:2772.

13. Tilly, *Bright-Tobacco Industry, 1860–1929;* Siegel, *Roots of Southern Distinctiveness;* Pollock, *Illustrated Sketch Book of Danville,* 196–97; Hairston, *Brief History of Danville, Virginia,* 32, 102; Pearson and Hendricks, *Liquor and Anti-Liquor in Virginia,* 208; Thompson, *Life of John R. Moffett,* 145.

14. Wynes, *Race Relations in Virginia,* 53–54; 1880 figures from Calhoun, "Danville Riot and Its Repercussions," 34, while the later percentage is from Kousser, *Shaping of Southern Politics,* 175.

15. Dailey, ""Deference and Violence in the Postbellum Urban South," 563–84; Calhoun, "Danville Riot and Its Repercussions," 34–43, 49; *Report of Committee of Forty;* Pollock, *Illustrated Sketch Book of Danville,* 83–99.

16. Simpson, *Men, Places, and Things,* 266–74; *CTT,* 171, 177. For a hotel serving as similar function in the Southwest, see Gordon, *Great Arizona Orphan Abduction,* 92.

17. Thompson, *Life of John R. Moffett,* 113–14.

18. Ibid., 1–13; Moffett Diary, 6 (typescript).

19. Moffett Diary, 2, 5, 13, 41 (typescript); Thompson, *Life of John R. Moffett,* 19–22, 26–29, 37, 71–73.

20. Moffett Diary, 8–17 (typescript); Thompson, *Life of John R. Moffett,* 38–69, 74–79, quote at 44.

21. Moffett Diary, 26, 27, 30–31, 35, 38, 44, 46, 53, 56, 65, 99, 116, 119, 129, 137, 139, 143, 159 (typescript); Thompson, *Life of John R. Moffett,* 80–94; Pearson and Hendricks, *Liquor and Anti-Liquor in Virginia,* 217. For the Prohibition Party and the Templars, see Colvin, *Prohibition in the United States,* 61–62, 119; Fahey, *Temperance and Racism.*

22. *DV* and *Danville Times* clippings pasted in Moffett Diary, 149–51, 172–73 (typescript), Page comment, 63 (manuscript); *Cyclopaedia of Temperance and Prohibition,* 451; Moore, "Negro and Prohibition in Atlanta," 53; Herd, "Prohibition, Racism, and Class Politics," 78, 80–83. On Thomas Nelson Page, see Friedman, *White Savage,* 67–74, 151, 167–68; Silber, *Romance of Reunion,* 113, 117, 186; Pulley, *Old Virginia Restored,* 60–61; Blight, *Race and Reunion,* 222–27; Anne E. Rowe, "Page, Thomas Nelson," in Wilson and Ferris, *Encyclopedia of Southern Culture,* 891. On Page's public speaking, see Pond, *Eccentricities of Genius,* 521–22.

23. *DV* and *Danville Times* clippings pasted in Moffett Diary, with his reactions, 149–51, 153 (manuscript), 170–73 (typescript); Moger, *Virginia,* 66–67.

24. Moffett Diary, 149, 174, 153, 172, 175 (typescript).

25. *Danville Times* clipping, ibid., 153, 155 (manuscript), 179 (typescript).

26. Ibid., 187, 201 (typescript); Pearson and Hendricks, *Liquor and Anti-Liquor in Virginia*, 217–18; *CTT*, 193–94.

27. Simpson, *Men, Places, and Things*, 301; *RT*, Feb. 10, 1893, 2; Moffett Diary, 183 (manuscript), 190, 227 (typescript); Thompson, *Life of John R. Moffett*, 101–13, quotes at 112; *CTT*, 170–80; Pearson and Hendricks, *Liquor and Anti-Liquor in Virginia*, 78.

28. Thompson, *Life of John R. Moffett*, 253–66, quotes at 261–62; Dickinson quoted in Pearson and Hendricks, *Liquor and Anti-Liquor in Virginia*, 216.

29. Thompson, *Life of John R. Moffett*, 113–16, W. W. Moffett quoted at 114; *RoT*, Nov. 4, 1892, 1. In this position Moffett typified what scholars have called the "Third Party Tradition in American Politics"; enunciating a vision of governance larger than that of the party organizations—ironically like most such reformers in the party period—Moffett could best broadcast this idea by joining a "third party" (see Voss-Hubbard, "'Third Party Tradition' Reconsidered").

30. Thompson, *Life of John R. Moffett*, 113–16, W. W. Moffett quoted at 114; *RoT*, Nov. 4, 1892, 1; *RD*, Nov. 9, 1892, 1.

31. *CTT*, 184; *RD*, Feb. 11, 1893, 1; *CTT*, 59–61; Moffett quoted in Thompson, *Life of John R. Moffett*, 121–23; *RD*, Nov. 9, 1892, 1; Moffett Correspondence, 9, 29.

32. *CTT*, 178, 179.

33. Ibid., 170–72, 180–81.

34. Thompson, *Life of John R. Moffett*, 125–26; *RD*, Nov. 12, 1892, 1.

35. Moffett to Copeland, May 15, 1903, Moffett Correspondence, 29–30.

36. Moffett to Copeland, May 15, 1903, Copeland to Moffett, Apr. 22, 1903, ibid., 16–18, 29–30; *CTT*, 28–35, 43–51.

37. Thompson, *Life of John R. Moffett*, 126–30; *CTT*, 26, 28–35; Moffett to Copeland, May 15, 1903, Moffett Correspondence, 29–30.

38. *Voice*, Nov. 17, 1892, 2. The article was written by W. E. Nichols; see Thompson, *Life of John R. Moffett*, 103.

39. *Voice*, Nov. 24, 1892, 1, 2, 4.

40. Ibid., Dec. 8, 1892, 2, letter of J. Manning Dunway, 5, Dec. 15, 1892, 2, Dec. 29, 1892, 1.

41. Thompson, *Life of John R. Moffett*, 132, 141–44, 190; *Religious Herald*, Nov. 24, 1892, 2; *Organizer*, Dec. 1, 1892; *Minutes of 104th Annual Session of Roanoke Baptist Association*, 21–23; *Minutes of 69th Annual Session of Baptist General Association of Virginia*, 48–49; *Register* editorial quoted in Moffett to Copeland, May 15, 1903, Moffett Correspondence.

42. *DV*, Feb. 8, 1893, in Aylett Scrapbook; Pollock, *Illustrated Sketch Book of Danville*, 115; Simpson, *Men, Places, and Things*, 385–87; Barnes, *Who Killed John Clayton?* 4.

43. *DV*, Feb. 8, 1893, in Aylett Scrapbook; *DV*, "Taking of Evidence on Both Sides Closed, Saturday," clipping in Scrapbook of Charles Vivian Meredith, Meredith Family

Papers, VHS. For Moffett's friendship with the Aylett family, see Moffett Diary, 124 (typescript); *CTT*, 193; Ferrell, *Claude A. Swanson of Virginia*, 26.

44. Thompson, *Life of John R. Moffett*, 166; *DV*, Feb. 8, 1893, in Aylett Scrapbook; *RT*, Feb. 7, 1893, 2. Ross probably contributed to the dispatches about the trial that appeared in the *Voice* and apparently came away from the trial convinced of the validity of the conspiracy theory.

45. Thompson, *Life of John R. Moffett*, 166; *DV*, Feb. 8, 1893, in Aylett Scrapbook; *RT*, Feb. 7, 1893, 2.

46. *CTT*, 14–15; *DV*, Feb. 8, 9, 1893, in Aylett Scrapbook; *RT*, Feb. 7, 1893, 2, Feb. 8, 1893, 2, Feb. 9, 1893, 2.

47. *CTT*, 29–35, 43–45, 51–55, 62–63, 69–70, 72–74, 79–82, 84–87, 109–14; *DV*, Feb. 10, 11, 1893, in Aylett Scrapbook; *RT*, Feb. 10, 1893, 2.

48. *CTT*, 90–93, 94–97, 99–100, 102–3, 105–7, 114–16; *RT*, Feb. 10, 1893, 2; *RD*, Feb. 10, 1893, 1; Simpson, *Men, Places, and Things*, 266, 286–87; *DV*, Feb. 11, 1893, in Aylett Scrapbook.

49. *CTT*, 117–34; *DV*, Feb. 11, 1893, in Aylett Scrapbook.

50. Thompson, *Life of John R. Moffett*, 154–59.

51. *CTT*, 37, 134–45, 170–90, quote at 174; see also *LDV*, Feb. 11, 1893, 1; *RT*, Feb. 11, 1893, 2; *RD*, Feb. 11, 1893, 1.

52. *CTT*, 37, 177–80, 183; *RD*, Feb. 15, 1893, 1.

53. *DV*, Feb. 10, 1893, and clipping "The Great Trial," Aylett Scrapbook; *CTT*, 45–51, 145–53, 164–67; *LDV*, Feb. 11, 1893, 1.

54. "Argument in the Great Case to End Today," *DV*, "Nearing the End" *DV*, Aylett Scrapbook; see also *RD*, Feb. 15, 1893, 1.

55. *Lynchburg Daily Virginian*, Feb. 15, 1893, 1, Feb. 16, 1893, 1; *RD*, Feb. 14, 1893, 1, Feb. 16, 1893, 3, Feb. 17, 1893, 1; "Argument in the Great Case to End Today," Aylett Scrapbook.

56. *LDV*, Feb. 17, 1893, 1; *RD*, Feb. 15, 1893, 1.

57. *CTT*, 23–25; see also *Clark v. Commonwealth*, 90 *Virginia Reports* 360, 363–65 (1893).

58. *Voice*, Feb. 16, 1893, 1.

59. *RD*, Feb. 14, 1893, 1, Feb. 15, 1893, 1; *RT*, Feb. 15, 1893, 2, Feb. 18, 1893, 2; *LDV*, Feb. 15, 1893, 1; *DV*, "The Clark Trial: Interest in the Great Murder Trial Unabated," Aylett Scrapbook.

60. *RT*, Feb. 14, 1893, 1, Feb. 16, 1893, 2, Feb. 18, 1893, 2; *Daily Virginian*, Feb. 15, 1893, 1; *DV*, "The Clark Trial: Interest in the Great Murder Trial Unabated," Aylett Scrapbook.

61. *DV*, "The Clark Trial: Interest in the Great Murder Trial Unabated," Aylett Scrapbook; *RT*, Feb. 14, 1893, 2; *RD*, Feb. 14, 1893, 1.

62. *RT*, Feb. 18, 1893, 2.

63. *CTT,* 177, 189–90.

64. Ibid., 170, 171, 174, 175, 180, 181, 182, 190; Moffett to Copeland, May 15, 1903, Moffett Correspondence, 41.

65. *CTT,* 170, 171, 174, 175, 180, 181, 182, 190.

66. Ibid., 176–77, 180, 183–84, 185.

67. *Roanoke Baptist Union Report;* see also *Minutes of 104th Annual Session of Roanoke Baptist Association; Voice,* Feb. 23, 1893, 1; *Clark v. Commonwealth,* 90 *Virginia Reports* 360.

68. *RT,* Feb. 18, 1893, 2; *RD,* Feb. 18, 1893, 2.

69. Grantham, *Southern Progressivism,* 160–77; Rabinowitz, *Race Relations in the Urban South,* 314–15.

70. Pearson and Hendricks, *Liquor and Anti-Liquor in Virginia,* 232, 237. Herd, "Prohibition, Racism, and Class Politics," shows that the prohibitionist successes came with the price of increased racism within the movement.

71. Kousser, *Shaping of Southern Politics,* 173–75; Wynes, *Race Relations in Virginia,* 52–53; Ferrell, *Claude A. Swanson of Virginia,* 24; Perman, *Struggle for Mastery,* 195–223. In 1893 the Populists (a fusion of the Republicans, Prohibitionists, and Populists) garnered 41 percent of the vote.

72. Pearson and Hendricks, *Liquor and Anti-Liquor in Virginia,* 232, 237, 244.

73. *RTD,* Apr. 17, 1903, 4, May 20, 1903, 4; *American Issue,* Dec. 28, 1900, 5. The level of knowledge concerning the crime and trial makes it likely that Copeland was the author of the commentary.

74. Moffett to Copeland, May 15, 1903, Moffett Correspondence, 27, 29, 33; E. J. Jordan Jr., Guide, Walter Scott Copeland Papers, UVA.

75. Thompson, *Life of John R. Moffett,* 141–44; *RTD,* May 26, 1903, 4; Gordon, *Great Arizona Orphan Abduction,* 209–10.

3. "GIRL WHOSE STORY CAUSED FATHER TO KILL"

1. The basic story is well presented in Estes, "The Loving/Estes Murder Case." This chapter's title is from *NYW,* June 25, 1907, 1.

2. Mott, *American Journalism;* Schudson, *Discovering the News;* Schudson, "Preparing the Minds of the People"; Schudson, *Origins of the Ideal of Objectivity;* Emery, *Press in America;* Leonard, *News for All;* Dicken-Garcia, *Journalistic Standards;* Schudson, "Question Authority"; Kluger, *Paper;* Abramson, *Sob Sister Journalism;* Gramling, *AP;* Schwarzlose, *Nation's Newsbrokers;* Czitrom, *Media and the American Mind;* Lukas, *Big Trouble,* 423–24, 467.

3. Osthaus, *Partisans of the Southern Press,* 149–97, 211–13; Dinnerstein, *Leo Frank Case,* 11–19.

4. Vandiver, *Idea of the South;* Osterweis, *Myth of the Lost Cause;* Wilson, *Baptized in Blood;* Foster, *Ghosts of the Confederacy;* Gaston, *New South Creed;* Grantham, *South in Modern America;* Current, *Northernizing the South;* Degler, "Thesis, Antithesis, Synthesis"; Blight, *Race and Reunion,* 171–299, 338–39; Silber, *Romance of Reunion;* Wyatt-Brown, *Southern Honor,* xvii; Chesterman Scrapbooks, VHS.

5. Ireland, "Libertine Must Die," 27; Hartog, "Lawyering, Husbands' Rights, and 'the Unwritten Law'"; Umphrey, "Dialogics of Legal Meaning"; Ireland, "Insanity and the Unwritten Law"; Ireland, "Thompson-Davis Case and the Unwritten Law."

6. Friedman, *History of American Law,* 590–92, Sayre, "Mens Rea," 974–1026; Friedman, *Crime and Punishment,* 143–47, 401–2. For the insanity plea in notable trials, see Rosenberg, *Trial of the Assassin Guiteau;* Brandt, *Congressman Who Got Away with Murder.*

7. Collins, *Glamorous Sinners;* O'Connor, *Courtroom Warrior,* 171–242; Mooney, *Evelyn Nesbit and Stanford White;* Baker, *Stanny;* Abramson, *Sob Sister Journalism;* Sherwin, *When Law Goes Pop,* 76, 93–105. Some notion of the national reaction to the Thaw case can be gleaned from Kernan, "Jurisprudence of Lawlessness."

8. Chesterman, Apr. 24, 1907; Moger, *Virginia,* map opposite 112.

9. Chesterman, "Tragedy Will Divide County" and June 25, 1907; *CDP,* Apr. 23, 1907, 1; *RoT,* Apr. 24, 1907, 1. On the Campbell impeachment, see Lombardo, "Eugenic Sterilization in Virginia," 42–57; on the judicial reorganization, see Perman, *Struggle for Mastery,* 203.

10. *RoT,* Apr. 26, 1907, 1, May 29, 1907, 1: *RNL,* Apr. 24, 1907, 1; Chesterman, Apr. 24, 1907, July (misdated June) 1907; Ferrell, *Claude A. Swanson,* 37.

11. *CDP,* June 25, 1907, 5; *RNL,* Apr. 24, 1907, 1; Chesterman, Apr. 24, 1907.

12. Typescript, undated, Loving statement attached to A. J. Hanger to Strode, May 23, 1907, Strode Papers, box 109; *LN,* Apr. 24, 1907, 1; *CDP,* Apr. 24, 1907, 1.

13. *LN,* Apr. 24, 1907, 1; Chesterman, Apr. 24, 1907, and "Such Story of Nelson Affair;" *CDP,* Apr. 23, 1907, 1; *RTD,* Apr. 23, 1907, 1.

14. Chesterman, Apr. 24, 1907; *LN,* Apr. 24, 1907, 1.

15. *RTD,* Apr. 23, 1907, 1, June, 25, 1907, 2; *CDP* Apr. 23, 1907, 1, Apr. 24, 1907, 1; *LN,* Apr. 24, 1907, Apr. 26, 1907, 1; Chesterman, dateline Apr. 23; Lombardo, "Eugenic Sterilization in Virginia," 35–67.

16. *RNL,* Apr. 24, 1907, 1; *NYW,* Apr. 24, 1907, 1, 2 ; *LN,* Apr. 24, 1907, 1; *CDP,* Apr. 24, 1907, 1; Chesterman, Apr. 24, 1907.

17. Loving statement, Strode Papers, box 109.

18. Strode to Ryan, Apr. 24, 1907, Strode Papers, box 66.

19. *CDP,* Apr. 24, 1907, 1; *LN,* Apr. 24, 1907, 1.

20. *CDP* Apr. 24, 1907, 1; *LN,* Apr. 24, 1907, 1; *RoT,* Apr. 24, 1907, 1.

21. *RNL,* Apr. 23, 1907, 1, Apr. 24, 1907; *RTD,* Apr. 23, 1907, 1; *RoT,* Apr. 24, 1907, 1, *CDP,* Apr. 23, 1907, 1.

22. Chesterman, Apr. 24, 1907. On purity ideas, see: Hobson, *Uneasy Virtue;* Rosen, *Lost Sisterhood;* Connelly, *Response to Prostitution;* Pivar, *Purity Crusade.*

23. Chesterman, "Tragedy Will Divide County" and Apr. 25, 1907; *CDP,* Apr. 26, 1907, 1.

24. *CDP,* Apr. 24, 1907, 1; *LN,* Apr. 24, 1907, 1; Chesterman, Apr. 24, 1907.

25. *LN,* Apr. 24, 1907, 1; *CDP,* Apr. 24, 1907, 1, Apr. 25, 1907, 1; Strode to Ryan, Apr. 24, 1907, Strode Papers, box 66; Loving Statement, ibid., box 109.

26. *LN,* Apr. 24, 1907, 1; *RoT,* Apr. 24, 1907, *CDP,* Apr. 24, 1907, 1.

27. *LN,* Apr. 24, 1907, 1; *CDP,* Apr. 24, 1907, 1.

28. *RNL,* Apr. 23, 1907, 1; Chesterman, "Such Story of Nelson Affair."

29. *CDP,* Apr. 23, 1907, 1, Apr. 24, 1907, 1.

30. Moger, *Virginia,* 166–202, 214; Pulley, *Old Virginia Restored,* 48–171; Kirby, *Westmoreland Davis,* 46–60.

31. Moger, *Virginia,* 166–202.

32. Chesterman, Apr. 25, 1907, and "Fierce Fight"; *CDP,* Apr. 26, 1907, 1; Moger, *Virginia,* 203–64; Kirby, *Westmoreland Davis,* 43–60; Pearson and Hendricks, *Liquor and Anti-liquor in Virginia,* 249–51; Wilkinson, *Harry Byrd and Virginia Politics.*

33. *RoT,* Apr. 24, 1907, 1.

34. *Dictionary of American Biography,* s.v. "Ryan, Thomas Fortune"; Lewis, "Owners of America II."

35. *BS,* Apr. 23, 1907, 2; Moger, *Virginia,* 268–73; *RoT,* Apr. 25, 1907, 1, May 9, 1907, 4, May 14, 1907, 1; *CDP,* May 28, 1907, 4; see also Ferrell, *Claude A. Swanson,* 63, 88–89; Larsen, *Montague of Virginia,* 208–12.

36. *NYW,* Apr. 23, 1907, 2.

37. Ibid., Apr. 23, 1907, 2, Apr. 24, 1907, 1, 2; *BS,* Apr. 25, 1907, 2; *WH,* Apr. 24, 1907, 1.

38. *NYW,* Apr. 23, 1907, 2, Apr. 24, 1907, 1, 2; *New York Herald,* undated clipping after Apr. 25, 1907, Strode Papers, box 26.

39. For Haywood and associated matters, see Lukas, *Big Trouble.*

40. *LN,* Apr. 24, 1907, 1; *CDP,* Apr. 24, 1907, 1; Chesterman, Apr. 24, 1907, and "Fierce Fight"; *RTD,* Apr. 25, 1907, 1; Mooney, *Evelyn Nesbit and Stanford White,* 232–33.

41. Chesterman, "Fierce Fight" and Apr. 24, 1907.

42. Chesterman, "Fierce Fight"; *RTD,* Apr. 24, 1907, 1, 4.

43. *CDP,* Apr. 24, 1907, 1; *RTD,* Apr. 24, 1907, 4; *RoT,* Apr. 25, 1907, 1; Chesterman, Apr. 25, 1907.

44. Chesterman, "Fierce Fight" and Apr. 25, 1907; *RoT,* Apr. 26, 1907, 1; *LN,* Apr. 26, 1907, 1; *CDP,* Apr. 26, 1907, 1.

45. *CDP,* Apr. 27, 107, 1; *RoT,* Apr. 25, 1907, 1; *NYW,* Apr. 26, 1907, 2; Chesterman, Apr. 25, 1907, 1.

46. *RoT,* Apr. 27, 1907, 4; Ayers, *Vengeance and Justice,* 246–47; Brundage, *Lynching in the New South,* 98–102.

47. Chesterman, Apr. 24, 1907; *RoT*, May 9, 1907, 4. Machen's proposal was in line with what Thomas J. Kernan suggested for such cases; see Kernan, "Jurisprudence of Lawlessness," 451–53, 458–63. Martha Merrill Umphrey argues that trials like Thaw's (and by implication Loving's) helped to remake the criminal law; see Umphrey, "Dialogics of Legal Meaning," 409–11.

48. *RoT*, May 9, 1907, 4; *CDP*, Apr. 25, 1907, 4.

49. Chesterman, Apr. 25, 1907; *New York Herald*, Apr. 25, 1907, clipping, Strode Papers, box 109.

50. Chesterman, Apr. 24, 1907; Elizabeth Loving to Louise, [Apr. 25, 1907], Strode Papers, box 109; see also *LN*, May 3, 1907, 1.

51. *CDP*, Apr. 29, 1907, 1; *RTD*, Apr. 30, 1907, 1; *WP*, May 4, 1907, clipping, Strode Papers, box 109.

52. Strode, draft of statement, Strode Papers, box 109; *LN*, May 3, 1907, 1; *CDP*, May 2, 1907, 2.

53. *RTD*, Apr. 29, 1907, 1; *CDP*, May 6, 1907, 1, May 11, 1907, 1; on Strother case, see Chesterman, "Brothers Not Responsible" and "Seeks to Save the Strothers from Terms in the Penitentiary."

54. *CDP*, May 1, 1907, 1, May 11, 1907, May 13, 1907, 1.

55. Chesterman, "Fierce Fight"; *CDP*, Apr. 27, 1907, 1, May 2, 1907, 2, May, 14, 1907, 1.

56. Chesterman, June 22, 1907, and "Review of Case"; *CDP*, May 2, 1907, 2, May 11, 1907, 1, May 14, 1907, 1, May 15, 1907, 1, May 28, 1907, 1.

57. *LN*, Apr. 26, 1907, 1; Chesterman, Apr. 25, 1907; *CDP*, May 11, 1907, 1, May 25, 1907, 1, May 29, 1907, 1.

58. *RR*, May 31, 1907, 1; *NYW*, May 29, 1907, 7; *CDP*, May 25, 1907, 1, May 28, 1907, 1; *RoT*, May 29, 1907, 1.

59. *LN*, Apr. 26, 1907, 1; Chesterman, Apr. 25, 1907; *CDP*, May 15, 1907, 1, May 28, 1907, 1.

60. *CDP*, May 11, 1907, 1, May 15, 1907, 1, May 28, 1907, 1; *NYW*, May 29, 1907, 7; *RoT*, May 29, 1907, 1, May 30, 1907 1.

61. *NYW*, May 29, 1907, 7; *CDP* May 28, 1907, 1; *RoT*, May 29, 1907, 1, May 30, 1907, 1; *NYA*, June 2, 1907, 3L.

62. *NYA*, June 2, 1907, 3L.

63. Ibid.; *BS*, June 24, 1907, 1.

64. *CDP*, June 12, 1907, 1; *RoT*, May 30, 1907, 1, June 25, 1907, 1; *NYA*, June 2, 1907, 3L; Chesterman, "Fierce Fight."

65. *BS*, June 24, 1907, 1; Moger, *Virginia*, 205; *RTD*, June 24, 1907, 1, June 26, 1907, 1; *RNL*, June 24, 1907, 8. John P. Swanson, though present in the court, did not participate in the courtroom activities of the prosecution.

66. *RNL*, June 24, 1907, 1, June 25, 1907, 1L; *RTD*, June 25, 1907, 2; Chesterman, June 28, 1907. Even though women journalists had been quite notable in their

"sob-sister" coverage of the Thaw trial that year for the Hearst press, apparently no female reporters covered the Loving trial; see Abramson, *Sob Sister Journalism.*

67. Peters and Peters, *Virginia Historic Courthouses,* 83–84; *RTD,* June 24, 1907, 1, June 25, 1907, 1; Chesterman, June 25, 1907.

68. Chesterman, June 24, 25, 1907; *BS,* June 25, 1907, 1; *RTD,* June 25, 1907, 1; *RNL,* June 24, 1907, 1; *CDP,* June 25, 1907, 1; *RoT,* June 30, 1907, 1.

69. Chesterman, June 25, 1907 (misdated 1905); *RTD,* June 25, 1907, 1, 2; *RNL,* June 24, 1905, 1, 8, June 25, 1907, 1, 8; *BS,* June 25, 1907, 1; *CDP,* June 25, 1907, 1, 5; *RoT,* June 25, 1907, 1, 5.

70. Chesterman, June 25, 1907 (misdated 1905); *BS,* June 25, 1907, 1.

71. *RTD,* June 25, 1907, 2; Chesterman, June 25, 1907; *BS,* June 25, 1907, 1.

72. *RTD,* June 25, 1907, 2; Chesterman, June 25, 1905; *RNL,* June 24, 1905, 1, 8, June 25, 1907, 1, 8; *BS,* June 25, 1907, 1; *CDP,* June 25, 1907, 1, 5; *RoT,* June 25, 1907, 1, 5.

73. *RTD,* June 25, 1907, 1; Chesterman, June 25, 1907; *BS,* June 25, 1907, 1.

74. *RNL,* June 25, 1907, 8; *BS,* June 25, 1907, 1, 12; *RTD,* June 25, 1907, 1, 2; *RoT,* June 25, 1907, 1; *CDP,* June 25, 1907, 5; Chesterman, June 25, 1907.

75. Chesterman, June 25, 1907; *RTD,* June 26, 1907, 1, 2; *BS,* June 25, 1907, 1, 12; *CDP,* June 25, 1907, 5; *RoT,* June 26, 1907, 1.

76. *RTD,* June 26, 1907, 1, 2, 3; Chesterman, June 25, 26, 1907; *RR,* June 28, 1907, 1; *RNL,* June 25, 1907, 1, 8; *RoT,* June 26, 1907, 1, 5.

77. *RTD,* June 26, 1907, 1, 2, 3; Chesterman, June 25, 26, 1907; *RR,* June 28, 1907, 1; *RNL,* June 25, 1907, 1, 8; *RoT,* June 26, 1907, 1, 5. For Dr. Leslie Keeley's cure for alcoholism and drug addiction, see Lender and Martin, *Drinking in America,* 122–24; Barclay, "The Keeley League."

78. *NYT,* June 26, 1907, 2; *RTD,* June 26, 1907, 1, 2, 3; Chesterman, June 25, 26, 1907.

79. *NYT,* June 26, 1907, 2; *RTD,* June 26, 1907, 2; *RoT,* June 26, 1907, 5; *BS,* June 26, 1907, 8; *CDP,* June 26, 1907, 1.

80. Chesterman, June 26, 1907; *RTD,* June 26, 1907, 3.

81. *RTD,* June 26, 1907, 3; *RoT,* June 26, 1907, 5; *BS,* June 26, 1907, 8; *CDP,* June 26, 1907, 1; Chesterman, Apr. 24, June 26, 1907.

82. *RTD,* June 26, 1907, 2.

83. Chesterman, June 26, 1907 (misdated July); *RNL,* June 26, 1907, 1, 5; *NYT,* June 27, 1907, 5; *RoT,* June 27, 1907, 1; *CDP,* June 27, 1907, 1; *RTD,* June 26, 1907, 5; *CDP,* June 26, 1907, 4; *BS,* June 26, 1907, 8; *NYW,* June 26, 1907, 3.

84. *NYT,* June 27, 1907, 5; *RoT,* June 27, 1907, 1; *CDP,* June 27, 1907, 1, 4; Julian Hawthorne, "Judge Loving's Act," *NYA,* clipping, Strode Papers, box 26.

85. *RoT,* June 27, 1907, 1; *CDP,* June 27, 1907, 1, 4; Julian Hawthorne, "Judge Loving's Act," *NYA,* clipping, Strode Papers, box 26; *NYT,* June 27, 1907, 5; Chesterman, June 27, 1907 (misdated July); *RNL,* June 28, 1907, 5. On Strode's preparations, see list

of witnesses and map of route, Strode Papers, box 109. The defense was prepared to go so far in plans to impeach Annie Kidd as to call witnesses to accuse her of "misbehaving with Theodore Estes earlier in the day of the buggy ride; see *BS*, June 30, 1907, 1.

86. Chesterman, June 27 (misdated July), June 28, 1907; "Jerome Wires Legal Opinions," *NYW*, clipping, Strode Papers, box 26; *CDP*, June 28, 1907, 1, 4; *RNL*, June 27, 1907, 1, 4; *Roanoke News*, June 29, 1907, 1.

87. Testimony of E. L. Kidd, William Dawson, John Loving, L. J. Sheffield, John T. Fitzpatrick, and John Horsley, *CDP*, June 28, 1907, 1, 4; *RNL*, June 27, 1907, 1, June 28, 1907, 5; *RoT*, June 28, 1907, 1; Chesterman, June 28, 1907, and "Decisive Blow to Prosecution"; *NYT*, June 28, 1907, 1; *NYW*, June 28, 1907, 3. On DeJarnette's career, see Lombardo, "Involuntary Sterilization in Virginia."

88. *LN*, June 29, 1907, 1; Chesterman, June 29, 1907; *RoT*, June 30, 1907, 1; *CDP*, June 29, 1907, 1; *RTD*, June 30, 1907, 2; *RNL*, June 29, 1907, 1, 4; *BS*, June 30, 1907, 11; *NYW*, June 29, 1907, 2; *NYT*, June 29, 1907, 1, 2, June 30, 1907, 1; "Court Warned by Black Hand," "Judge Refuses to Bar," "Loving Not Guilty," *NYA*, clippings, Strode Papers, box 26.

89. *LN*, June 29, 1907, 1; Chesterman, June 29, 1907; *RoT*, June 29, 1907, 1, June 30, 1907, 1; *BS*, June 30, 1907, 11; *RTD*, June 30, 1907, 1, 2; *RNL*, June 28, 1907, 1, 5, June 29, 1907, 1; *CDP*, June 29, 1907, 1; Strode's notes, Strode Papers, box 26.

90. Chesterman, June 29, 1907; *LN*, June 29, 1907, 1; *RNL*, June 29, 1907, 4; "Court Warned by Black Hand," "Judge Refuses to Bar," *NYA*, clippings, Strode Papers, box 26. The defense's instructions were "almost identical with those of the defense in the Strother case"; see *RNL*, June 28, 1907, 1.

91. *BS*, June 30, 1907, 1; *RTD*, July 1, 1907, 1; *RoT*, June 30, 1907, 1; *NYT*, June 30, 1907, 1.

92. Typescript note about jury, Strode Papers, box 109; *RoT*, June 30, 1907, 1; *NYT*, June 30, 1907, 1; *RR*, July 2, 1907, 3; *CDP*, July 7, 1907, 1; *RTD*, July 1, 1907, 1; Chesterman, July 1, 1907.

93. Typescript note about jury, Strode Papers, box 109; *RTD*, July 1, 1907, 1, 2.

94. *RoT*, June 30, 1907, 1; *NYT*, June 30, 1907, 1; *BS*, June 30, 1907, 1; undated *NYA* clipping, Strode Papers, box 26; Chesterman, July 1, 1907; *RTD*, June 30, 1907, 1, July 1, 1907, 1, 2, July 2, 1907, 1; letter from H. W. M., *CDP*, July 1, 1907, 1, July 9, 1907, 1.

95. *NYW*, June 25, 1907, 1; Chesterman, June 25, 1907 (misdated 1905), June 26, 1907; *RTD*, June 26, 1907, 1; *BS*, June 26, 1907, 8.

96. Chesterman, June 25, 1907 (misdated 1905), June 26, 1907; *RNL*, June 24, 1907, 1, 8, June 26, 1907, 1; *RTD*, June 26, 1907, 1.

97. *NYW*, June 25, 1907, 1; *BS*, June 24, 1907, 1; Chesterman, June 24, 1907, 1.

98. "Judge Refuses," *NYA*, clipping, Strode Papers, box 26; *NYW*, June 26, 1907, 2; *RTD*, June 26, 1907, 1; *RoT*, June 26, 1907, 1, 5; Chesterman, June 26, 1907.

99. *RNL*, June 24, 1907, 8, June 25, 1907, 8; *NYA*, clipping, Strode Papers, box 26; Chesterman, June 28, 1907; *RoT*, June 30, 1907, 4.

100. Chesterman, June 25, 1907. On the other hand, neither the *News Leader* nor the *Times-Dispatch* played Foster's testimony for humor, though the *Times-Dispatch* admitted that he "dropped his hat on the floor in old-fashioned style." Similarly, the *Times-Dispatch* merely described Hubbard as "an old colored woman" while the *News Leader* called her "a dignified negro woman." The *Baltimore Sun* reported Foster's statement's verbatim but called Julia Hubbard "an old 'mammy' " and claimed she nursed Theodore Estes and was known widely as "Aunt Julia" (*RTD,* June 25, 1907, 2; *RNL,* June 25, 1907, 8; *BS,* June 25, 1907, 1).

101. Chesterman, June 28, July 1, 1907.

102. *CDP,* July 1, 1907, 1, July 2, 1907, 1; *BS,* June 30, 1907, 1; *NYW,* June 29, 1907, 2; *NYT,* July 6, 1907, 4; *RR,* July 2, 1907, 3; Chesterman, July 1, 1907.

103. *RoT,* May 5, 1907, 13; Dinnerstein, *Leo Frank Case;* Brundage, *Lynching in the New South.*

104. *Nation,* July 25, 1907, 70–71; *BS,* July 1, 1907, 4; *RNL,* July 6, 1907, 4; *RTD,* July 1, 1907, 2.

105. Chesterman, June 28, 1907; *CDP,* June 28, 1907, 4, July 3, 1907, 1; *RoT,* July 5, 1907, 4, July 6, 1907, 4.

106. *RNL,* July 9, 1907, 4, l. The "fast age" letter writer may have had in mind conversations like the one quoted in Ullman, *Sex Seen,* 1. Hummel was one of the partners in the infamous firm of Howe and Hummel; in March 1907, stripped of his law license, he started to serve a year's imprisonment for conspiracy to obstruct justice (O'Connor, *Courtroom Warrior,* 114–45; Rovere, *Howe and Hummel,* 160–63).

107. *RNL,* July 1, 1907; 4, *RoT,* quoting Henry Watterson from the *Louisville Courier Journal,* July 5, 1907, 4; *CDP,* June 28, 1907, 4, July 2, 1907, 4; *RTD,* June 30, 1907, D4, July 2, 1907, 6. For Harry Thaw's reaction, see ibid., July 1, 1907, 2.

108. *Richmond Evening Journal* quoted in *RoT,* July 3, 1907, 4; *RoT,* June 27, 1907, 4; *Scottsville Courier* quoted in *RoT,* July 3, 1907, 4.

109. *Bristol Herald* and *Richmond Evening News* quoted in *CDP,* July 3, 1907, 1; Chesterman, July 1, 1907.

110. *Roanoke World* quoted in *CDP,* July 3, 1907, 1; *RNL,* July 1, 1907, 4; *RTD,* June 30, 1907, D4; see also letter by Machen in *RTD,* July 13, 1907, 6.

111. *LN,* July 5, 1907, 2, clipping, Strode Papers, box 26.

112. *RoT,* July 2, 1907, 4; *RTD,* July 14, 1907, D4.

113. *CDP,* July 9, 1907, 1; *RoT,* July 7, 1907, 4; *RTD,* July 4, 1907, 6; *LN,* undated editorial, Strode Papers, box 26; *RNL,* July 13, 1907, 4.

114. *RNL,* July 13, 1907, 4; *LN,* undated editorial, Strode Papers, box 26.

115. Chesterman, June 26, 1907; *RTD,* June 26, 1907, 1; O'Connor, *Courtroom Warrior,* 217–30; Abramson, *Sob Sister Journalism,* 49–88.

116. *RTD,* June 28, 1907, 5.

117. Chesterman, June 25, July 1, 1907; *RNL,* June 28, 1907, 5, July 2, 1907, 1.

118. Chesterman, July 1, 1907; *RR,* July 2, 1907, 2. The gentility of southern women

was part of the definition of southern exceptionalism; since Reconstruction southern papers had lamented women's invasion of the male preserve in northern courtrooms. For example, see the *Mobile Register* quoted in Fox, *Trials,* 94.

119. *RoT,* June 27, 1907, 4; *RNL,* July 10, 1907, 4. On the other hand, it should be noted that the *News Leader* covered extensively the very cases it decried.

120. *RTD,* July 10, 1907, clipping, Strode Papers, box 26; Marmon, *Measure and Mirror of Men,* 76; conversation with Leland Estes Jr., Aug. 3, 2000; photograph of memorial supplied by Leland Estes Jr.

121. *CDP,* May 2, 1919, 6; phone conversation with Lee Marmon, July 18, 2000. On Atlanta in this period, see Doyle, *New Men, New Cities,* 87–100, 136–58, 189–225; Brownell, *Urban Ethos in the South,* 10–13. On Ryan's role in the Seaboard line, see Thomas, *Lawyering for the Railroad,* 165.

122. Clipping from *Atlanta Journal,* Jan. 7, 1970, in fax, Leland Estes Jr. to author, Nov. 14, 2000; *CDP,* May 2, 1919, 6; Read, *Loving Family in America,* 76; Fox, *Trials of Intimacy,* 16; conversation with William Obrachta, Aug. 8, 1991; newspaper editorial quoted in Marmon, *Measure and Mirror of Men,* 76. Some idea of how long Elizabeth Loving's reputation remained sullied might be inferred from the fact that her name was not mentioned in her father's 1919 obituary, but it did surface in her mother's 1948 obituary. Moreover, the Loving family genealogy does not show that Elizabeth married or had children. Certainly shame attached to the whole incident among the Estes family. Not until he was seventy-five years old did Leland Estes Jr. learn from his Aunt Josephine that "Judge Loving, Aunt Lela's husband, shot and killed" her uncle Theodore Estes (Estes, "The Loving/Estes Murder Case," introduction; fax, Leland Estes Jr. to author, Nov. 7, 2000).

4. "EDITH AND HER PAPPY"

1. Other treatments of this case are Best, *Witch Hunt in Wise County;* Hatfield, "Mountain Girl Who Went Modern"; and speech by John Farmer at the Pound High School, Mar. 13, 1990, typescript in Slemp. This chapter's title is from Dabney, "Edith and Her Pappy," 69.

2. Bliss, *Now the News,* 37–38; Czitrom, *Media and the American Mind,* 84–88, 130; Marquis, "Written on the Wind," 393, 401–6, 412; Lewis, *Empire of the Air,* 229–33; Morton, *Off the Record,* 48–73. Radio did cover some sensational trials (near major radio studios). There was extensive coverage of the 1934 Bruno Hauptmann trial for the kidnapping of the Lindbergh baby. Radio's coverage consisted of live daily reports from the scene about the testimony and live daily analysis—like that given of future Supreme Court justice Earl Warren in California—broadcast over local stations in the evening. This pattern of coverage revealed the limitations and potential of radio as a challenger to newspapers (Cray, *Chief Justice,* 71–72). For press developments, see Mott, *American*

Journalism; Schudson, *Discovering the News;* Schudson, "Preparing the Minds of the People"; Schudson, *Origins of the Ideal of Objectivity;* Schiller, *Objectivity and the News;* Emery, *Press in America;* Leonard, *News for All;* Kluger, *Paper;* Demers, *Menace of the Corporate Newspaper,* 31–57; Kneebone, *Southern Liberal Journalists.*

3. Ayers, *Vengeance and Justice,* 273.

4. Ayers and Willis, *Edge of the South,* 7; J. I. Burton, "Geography," in Addington, *Story of Wise County,* 116; Wolfe, "Aliens in Southern Appalachia"; Robert Weise, "Big Stone Gap and the New South, 1880–1900," in Ayers and Willis, *Edge of the South,* 173–93; Bolling, "Wise County's Other Industry"; Shifflett, *Coal Towns,* 18–19, 30–32, 218–19; *Virginia,* 257; Martin-Perdue and Perdue, *Talk about Trouble,* 60–105 (on women's lives in the depression), 329–35 (on the coal country during the depression), 45–48 (on Wise County before the depression).

5. Peters and Peters, *Virginia Historic Courthouses,* 175–76; Link, *Hard and Lonely Place,* 129, 196, 201, 209, 211; "Reminiscences of J. J. Kelly"; Addington, *Story of Wise County,* 141–50.

6. Miller, *Revenuers and Moonshiners;* Shapiro, *Appalachia on Our Mind;* Waller, *Feud;* Stanley, "Apology for a Race"; Silber, *Romance of Reunion,* 143–52; Dabney, "The South That Never Was," in *Below the Potomac,* 18–21. For the many myths that surround feuding, see Kathleen M. Blee and Dwight B. Billings, "Where 'Bloodshed Is a Pastime': Mountain Feuds and Appalachian Stereotyping," in Billings, Norman, and Ledford, *Confronting Appalachian Stereotypes,* 119–37. Southwest Virginia led the state in lynching (Brundage, *Lynching in the New South,* 143–49). On the day Trigg Maxwell died, another man was also killed in a domestic dispute in the county (*NCP,* July 25, 1935, 1, 8). For the use of the term *hillbillies* to describe all poor white southern migrants to Chicago, see Killian, *White Southerners,* 100–101.

7. Fox, *Trail of the Lonesome Pine;* Williams, "Southern Mountaineer," 211–22; Kirby, *Media-Made Dixie,* 39–43; Darlene Wilson, "A Judicious Combination of Incident and Psychology: John Fox Jr. and the Southern Mountaineer Motif," in Billings, Norman, and Ledford, *Confronting Appalachian Stereotypes,* 98–118, *Louisville Courier* quoted at 110

8. Schuster and McCrumb, "Appalachian Film List," 376; Arnold, "Al, Abner, and Appalachia"; M. Thomas Inge, "Comic Strips," at 914–15, and hillbilly definition quoted in W. K. McNeil, "'Hillbilly' Image," at 504–5, in Wilson and Ferris, *Encyclopedia of Southern Culture;* Williamson, *Hillbillyland,* 1–20, 33–44.

9. Hatfield, "Mountain Girl Who Went Modern," 6–11; Addington, *Story,* 198; Robertson and Brown, *History,* 187; Best, *Witch Hunt in Wise County,* 29; *NCP,* July 25, 1935, 1, 8.

10. Hatfield, "Mountain Girl Who Went Modern," 13–17; MTT, 205. The Radford College yearbook suspended publication from the crash through 1937. Basic facts of Maxwell's attendance and organizations she joined were supplied by Office of the Reg-

istrar, Radford University; Hines, *Radford State Teachers College Handbook,* 35, 39; Lewis-Smith, *Radford College,* 60.

11. MTT, 205.

12. Ibid., 76, 80; *RoT,* July 23, 1935; *NCP,* July 25, 1935, 1. The *Roanoke Times* items used in this chapter are clippings in the Slemp Collection so references to that paper appear without page citations.

13. *NCP,* July 25, 1935, 1; *RoT,* July 22, 1935; *WP,* July 23, 1935, 7; MTT, 76, 78–80, 105–6.

14. *NCP,* July 25, 1935, 1; *RoT,* July 22, 23, 24, 1935; *Knoxville News-Sentinel,* July 22, 1935, quoted in Hatfield, "Mountain Girl Who Went Modern," 20; *WP,* July 23, 1935, 7.

15. *RoT,* July 24, 1935; *NCP,* July 25, 1935, 1, 8; *RTD,* July 24, 1935, 1, July 25, 1935, 2; *WP,* July 24, 1935, 7; *Knoxville News-Sentinel,* July 24, 1935, 4, quoted in Hatfield, "Mountain Girl Who Went Modern," 21.

16. *WP,* July 23, 1935, 7, July 24, 1935, 7; Hatfield, "Mountain Girl Who Went Modern," 19; *RTD,* July 25, 1935, 3; *NCP,* July 25, 1935, 1, 8.

17. *NYEJ,* July 25, 1935, 2.

18. Ibid., July 30, 1935, 3; Best, *Witch Hunt in Wise County,* 40; Hatfield, "Mountain Girl Who Went Modern," 62–65; *WH,* July 28, 1935, 4, July 31, 1935, 6, Aug. 1, 1935, 5; Dabney, "Edith and Her Pappy," 69.

19. Hatfield, "Mountain Girl Who Went Modern," 21–22, 25; Johnson, *Narrative History of Wise County,* 202–12, 215–17, 248–49; *RoT,* Aug. 2, 16, 21, 1935.

20. *RoT,* Aug. 16, Nov. 11, 1935; Hatfield, "Mountain Girl Who Went Modern," 22–23; Johnson, *Narrative History of Wise County,* 248–49.

21. *RoT,* Aug. 21, Nov. 18, 1935; Hatfield, "Mountain Girl Who Went Modern," 23–24; *NCP,* Aug. 22, 1935, 1, 6.

22. Hatfield, "Mountain Girl Who Went Modern," 27–35; Best, *Witch Hunt in Wise County,* 47–75; for AP stories, see *RTD,* Nov. 18, 1935, 2, Nov. 20, 1935, 1, 4; for UP stories, see *WP,* Nov. 19, 1, 4, Nov. 20, 1935, 1, 4.

23. MTT, 142–45, 171–73. The sex ratios of death penalty prisoners are derived from Cahalan, *Historical Corrections Statistics in the United States,* 18; figures on the death penalty in Virginia come from Sherman, *Case of Odell Waller,* 165.

24. MTT, 68–89.

25. Ibid., 90–108.

26. Ibid., 135–40, 252–57.

27. Ibid., 124–34.

28. Ibid., 260–64.

29. Ibid., 81–83, 116–24.

30. Ibid., 94, 104, 109–11, 253–55, 259–60.

31. For their testimony and cross examinations, see ibid.: Anne: 46–59, 159–71, 174–80, 245; Mary Katherine: 180–205; Edith: 205–45; Baker: 246–48, 267.

32. Ibid., 146–49, 156, 182–83, 190–91, 210, 216, 218.

33. Ibid., 205–8.

34. Ibid., 149, 184, 187, 193, 195–96.

35. Ibid., 149–53, 170, 184–85, 193–97, 209.

36. Ibid., 150–52, 158–59, 162, 184–86, 197–99, 210, 239.

37. Ibid., 151–55, 185, 203, 211.

38. Ibid., 155, 158, 168, 169, 186, 187, 203, 204, 211, 217–18, 236, 237, 244.

39. Ibid., 164–66, 170, 233, 243. Beyond the lies about the fight, the prosecution tried to show that the Maxwells lied about many smaller points (ibid., 161–64, 169, 174–76, 204, 236, 238, 256–57).

40. Ibid., 216, 218, 222–23, 226, 230, 236–37, 241.

41. Ibid., 268–74.

42. Johnson, *Narrative History of Wise County*, 248, also quoted in Hatfield, "Mountain Girl Who Went Modern," 27; *NCP*, Nov. 14, 1935, 1, Nov. 21, 1935, 1; *BSGP*, Dec. 11, 1935, 6. For AP stories, see *RTD*, Nov. 18, 1935, 2, Nov. 19, 1935, 1, 14, Nov. 20, 1935, 1, 4, Nov. 21, 1935, 1, 6. Hatfield has subjected some of the coverage of the Maxwell trial to content analysis; see Hatfield, "Mountain Girl Who Went Modern," 68–87, esp. chart on 75.

43. *WP*, Nov. 20, 1935, 4.

44. *NYEJ*, Nov. 19, 1935, 1, 5; *WP*, Nov. 18, 1935, 1, Nov. 19, 1935, 1, 4.

45. *WH*, Nov. 15, 1935, 1, Nov. 17, 1935, B-9, Nov. 18, 1935, 3, Nov. 19, 1935, 1, 4, Nov. 20, 1935, 1, 4; *WP*, Nov. 18, 1935, 2; *NYEJ*, Nov. 18, 1935, 3, Nov. 19, 1935, 1, 5, Nov. 20, 1935, 3.

46. *Literary Digest*, Nov. 30, 1935, 26; *News-Week*, Nov. 30, 1935, 39; *Time*, Dec. 2, 1935, 12–13.

47. *RoT*, Jan. 1, 1937.

48. *NYA*, Nov. 23, 1935, 3, 4; *RoT*, Nov. 26, 1935; *New York Daily Mirror*, Nov. 27, 1935, 1; *American Weekly*, Dec. 12, 1935, 6, in *WH*; Hatfield, "Mountain Girl Who Went Modern," 37, 67; Dabney, "Edith and Her Pappy," 70. In December 1935 the *San Francisco Examiner* ran "My Own Life Story" in sixteen installments, and the *WH* ran it in eighteen. Best, *Witch Hunt in Wise County*, 89–109, summarizes and captures the flavor of Edith's King Features life story. He used the sixteen-part version published in the *San Francisco Examiner*, Dec. 15–31, 1935.

49. Martin, *Cissy*, 266, 277; Healy, *Cissy*, 4, 15; *WP*, Nov. 11, 1935, 1, 4, Nov. 26–29, Dec. 3–31, 1935, Jan. 1, 1936, 5, Jan. 2, 1936, 5, Jan. 5, 1936, X-6, Jan. 15, 1936, 7, Jan. 16, 1936, 1, 7, Jan. 17, 1936, 13, Jan. 18, 1936, 5.

50. *WP*, Dec. 1, 1935, 1, 6, Dec. 2, 1935, 1, 6, Dec. 5, 1935, 1; *WH*, Dec. 1, 1936, 1, Dec. 10, 1935, 5; *RTD*, Dec. 1, 1935, 1, 2, Dec. 7, 1935, 1, 2, Dec. 27, 1935, 1; *RoT*, Dec. 10, 1935, Jan. 9, 1936; *NCP*, Dec. 12, 1935, 4, Jan. 2, 1936, 3.

51. Pyle quoted in Hatfield, "Mountain Girl Who Went Modern," 12–13; see also Nichols, *Ernie's America*.

52. H. M. Sherman, "Mountain Justice," *Voice of Experience*, Apr. 1936, 20–23, 89–90, in Slemp; Best, *Witch Hunt in Wise County*, 118–19. Bernarr Macfadden pioneered "confession magazines" like *True Confessions;* his *Voice of Experience* was compiled from similar stories that had originally been broadcast on radio (Hughes, *News and the Human Interest Story*, 181).

53. Bromley quoted in Best, *Witch Hunt in Wise County*, 78. On professional women, see Cott, *Grounding of Modern Feminism*, 215–39.

54. *WH*, Nov. 23, 1935, 3; *Knoxville News-Sentinel*, Nov. 20, 1935, 1, quoted in Hatfield, "Mountain Girl Who Went Modern," 36; *New York Herald Tribune*, Nov. 23, 1935, 2; *RoT*, Nov. 23, 26, 28, 29, 30, 1935; *RTD*, Nov. 29, 1935, 1, Nov. 30, 1935, 1, Dec. 2, 1935, 4; Hatfield, "Mountain Girl Who Went Modern," 36–42, Best, *Witch Hunt in Wise County*, 81–82.

55. Lunardini, *From Equal Suffrage to Equal Rights;* Becker, *Origins of the Equal Rights Amendment;* Kraditor, *Ideas of the Woman Suffrage Movement*, 219–48; Ford, *Iron-Jawed Angels;* Zimmerman, "Jurisprudence of Equality"; Bredbenner, *Nationality of Her Own;* Cott, *Grounding of Modern Feminism*, 53–81; *Commonwealth v. Welosky*, 276 *Mass* 398 (1931), and 284 *United States* 684 (1931).

56. Hatfield, "Mountain Girl Who Went Modern," 43–45; *Equal Rights*, Jan. 4, 1936, 347. On publicity for the earlier appeal, see Alma Lutz to Burnitta Matthews, Sept. 12, 1931, [Anna Wiley] to Alma Lutz, Sept. 22, 1931, Edith Hooker to Muna Lee, Oct. 17, 1931, Jane Norma Smith to Muna Lee, Nov. 11, [1931], NWPP, ser. 1, reel 46. On how Maxwell was used, see *Equal Rights*, Dec. 7, 1935, 317, Feb. 2, 1936, 380–81, Mar. 21, 1936, 1, Mar. 28, 1936, cover, Dec. 26, 1936, cover; clippings from *Red Bank Register* (New Jersey), Feb. 20, 1936, Feb. 27, 1936, NWPP, ser. 1, reel 57.

57. Kyvig, *Repealing National Prohibition*, 48, 122; Rose, *American Women and Repeal*, 67–70, 74, 77–79, 82, 129, 132–34; *NYT*, June 29, 1934, 9, Feb. 16, 1936, 18, Dec. 6, 1936, 24; Hatfield, "Mountain Girl Who Went Modern," 46–47; Best, *Witch Hunt in Wise County*, 125–26; Thurber, "Crime in the Cumberlands"; *RTD*, Feb. 17, 1936, 2.

58. Minnesota man quoted in Sturgill, "Maxwell Case," 18; *New York World-Telegram* quoted in *RTD*, Nov. 28, 1935, 8; see also letters of "Justice" and "A Subscriber," *WP*, Nov. 24, 1935, 8; letter of Julian Fahy, ibid., Dec. 6, 1935, 8; letter of "A Subscriber," ibid., Dec. 19, 1935, 8. For more examples of the letters that streamed into various officials in Wise, see *NCP*, Nov. 28, 1935, 2.

59. Letter of Evelyn D. Ward, *WP*, Nov. 24, 1935, 8; letter of L. Turner, ibid., Nov. 28, 1935, 8; *RTD*, Nov. 29, 1935, 12; letter of Mrs. E. C. Lindsay, ibid., Nov. 28, 1935, 8; see also letter of Mrs. J. A. Carter, ibid., Dec. 1, 1935, sec. 4, 2; letters of John Caldwell and William Leigh, ibid., Nov. 28, 1935, 8.

60. *RTD*, Nov. 28, 1935, 8, Dec. 2, 1935, 8, Dec. 10, 1935, 2; letter of Mrs. E. D. Battie, ibid., Dec. 7, 1935, 18; letter of R. P. Waring, ibid., Nov. 30, 1935, 8.

61. Letter of Mrs. Carter Tiller, *NCP*, Aug. 15, 1935, 8; *BSGP*, Dec. 12, 1935, 6; *NCP*, Nov. 28, 1935, 2; see also Sturgill, "Maxwell Case," 19–20. Addington became the histo-

rian of the county; see his *Story of Wise County* and short sketch of him in Shackelford and Weinberg, *Our Appalachia,* 44.

62. Quoted in Sturgill, "Maxwell Case," 20–24. The reaction against this type of reporting was not limited to Virginia; in Knoxville, readers protested the *Sentinel's* carrying of UP stories and prompted a change in coverage (see Hatfield, "Mountain Girl Who Went Modern," 26, 78).

63. *RTD,* Nov. 29, 1935, 1, 2, Dec. 3, 1935, 10; see also *NCP,* Dec. 5, 1935, 4, Dec. 12, 1935, 5.

64. *BSGP,* Dec. 12, 1935, 4; *RTD,* Dec. 3, 1935, 10; letter of Samuel B. Woods, *WP,* Dec. 5, 1935; letter of W. J. G., *WP,* Nov. 28, 1935, 8. Not all criticism of the entry of outside groups was limited to Virginia papers; the *Greensboro Daily News* decried some of the methods used by women's groups in the Maxwell case (quoted in *RTD,* Dec. 1, 1935, sec. 4, 2).

65. *RTD,* Nov. 30, 1935, 8. For Dabney's career and influence, see Kneebone, *Southern Liberal Journalists;* Virginius Dabney, "Richmond Times-Dispatch," at 971, and John T. Kneebone, "Dabney, Virginius," at 951–52, in Wilson and Ferris, *Encyclopedia of Southern Culture.* On the Scottsboro case, see Carter, *Scottsboro;* Goodman, *Stories of Scottsboro;* on the Herndon case, see Martin, *Herndon Case and Southern Justice.*

66. Dabney, "Edith and Her Pappy," 69–70. Dabney also wrote articles for the *New York Times* on the case; for commentary on his *Times* articles, see Thurber, "Crime in the Cumberlands," 42–43. Dabney distilled his views on the Maxwell case in a chapter entitled "The South That Never Was" in *Below the Potomac,* 18–21, and in *Across the Years,* 141–42.

67. MTT, 280–92; *WP,* Nov. 26, 1935, 1, 7, Dec. 2, 1935, 1, 6, Dec. 11–20, 1935, Dec. 27, 1935, 5, Dec. 29–31, 1935, Jan. 1–3, 1936, Jan. 5, 1936, X-6, Jan. 15–17, 1936; *NCP,* Jan. 2, 1936, 1, 6, Jan. 16, 1936, 1, 4, Dec. 10, 1936, 1; Hatfield, "Mountain Girl Who Went Modern," 42–46; Best, *Witch Hunt in Wise County,* 121–32; *RoT,* Dec. 12, 13, 21, 24, 25, 26–31, 1935, Jan. 1, 9, 12, 15, 16, 1936; *RTD,* Jan. 16–18, 1936. The affidavits by the coroners had been obtained by Earl Maxwell, and his attempts to find evidence to show that his father had died of natural causes were chronicled (and criticized) in the press; see *WP,* Dec. 15, 1935, 1, Dec. 16, 1935, 4, Dec. 18, 1935, 13, Dec. 19, 1935, 16, Dec. 20, 1935, 1; Dabney, "Edith and Her Pappy," 70. On Smith also being hired by the *Herald,* a fact that never made it into the public record, see Eleanor Patterson to Eleanor Roosevelt, Oct. 14, 1941, ERP, ser. 100, FDRL.

68. *RoT,* Jan. 18, Mar. 3, 10, 19, May 24, 31, 1936.

69. Ibid., Dec. 17, 1935, Jan. 9, 1936; *NCP,* Dec. 10, 1936, 1; *RTD,* Dec. 7, 1935, 1, 2, Dec. 9, 1936, 5; Sturgill, "Maxwell Case," 16–17; on Peery, see Heinemann, *Depression and New Deal in Virginia,* 83–85, 129. Greear also wrote a letter to a New York lawyer defending the verdict; see Best, *Witch Hunt in Wise County,* 86–87.

70. *RoT,* Dec. 18, 1935; *RTD,* Dec. 28, 1935, 10, Jan. 17, 1936, 16.

71. *Maxwell v. Commonwealth of Virginia,* 167 *Virginia* 490 (1936), esp. 497–500, quote at 510.

72. *RoT,* Sept. 15, 18, 20, 21, Nov. 5, 8, 10, 11, 12, 22, 1936; *NCP,* Sept. 24, 1936, 1, Nov. 12, 1936, 1, 2, Dec. 10, 1936, 1, 2; *BSGP,* Nov. 12, 1936, 2.

73. *BSGP,* Nov. 26, 1936, 1, 6; *RoT,* Nov. 8, 23, 24, 1936; *NCP,* Nov. 26, 1936, 1, 8; *RTD,* Nov. 24, 1936, 1; Hatfield, "Mountain Girl Who Went Modern," 50–51. For the local papers' denial of the defense claim of a deep resentment in Wise County against Maxwell, see *BSGP,* Nov. 12, 1936, 2; *NCP,* Nov. 12, 1936, 2. See *WP,* Jan. 5, 1936, 6-x, for Smith's assertion upon taking the case that mountain communities thought "anyone from outside their own community is inclined to look down on them. That isn't true of course but it's always hard to convince the mountaineers it isn't."

74. *RTD,* Dec. 9, 1936, 1; *NCP,* Dec. 17, 1936, 1, 5; *RoT,* Dec. 8, 12, 1936; for other accounts of second trial, see Hatfield, "Mountain Girl Who Went Modern," 52–53; Best, *Witch Hunt in Wise County,* 139–52.

75. *RTD,* Dec. 10, 1935, 1, 3, Dec. 11, 1936, 1, 12, Dec. 12, 1936, 1, 6, Dec. 13, 1936, 1, 20, Dec. 15, 1936, 1, 2; *RoT,* Dec. 10, 11, 1936; *WP,* Dec. 10, 1936, 1, 3.

76. *RTD,* Dec. 10, 1936, 1, 3, Dec. 11, 1936, 1, 12; *RoT,* Dec. 13, 1926; *WP,* Dec. 10, 1936, 1, 3; *NYEJ,* Dec. 9, 1936, 3.

77. *RTD,* Dec. 11, 1936, 1, 12, Dec. 13, 1936, 1, 20, Dec. 15, 1936, 2; *RoT,* Dec. 13, 1936; *WP,* Dec. 11, 1936, 1, 4, Dec. 14, 1936, 1, 8.

78. *RTD,* Dec. 15, 1936, 1, 2, Dec. 16, 1936, 5, Dec. 18, 1936, 9; *RoT,* Dec. 15, 1936; *WP,* Dec. 15, 1936, 1, 13.

79. *RTD,* Dec. 15, 1936, 1, 2, Dec. 16, 1936, 5, Dec. 18, 1936, 9; *RoT,* Dec. 15, 1936; *WP,* Dec. 15, 1936, 1, 13.

80. *RTD,* Dec. 15, 1936, 2, Dec. 16, 1936, 1; *RoT,* Dec. 16, 1936. The witnesses were Louise Bolling, Pauline Hutchinson, and Lucile Blevins.

81. *RTD,* Dec. 16, 1936, 5, Dec. 17, 1936, 1, 12, Dec. 18, 1936, 1; *RoT,* Dec. 17, 18, 1936; *NCP,* Dec. 17, 1936, 1; *WP,* Dec. 18, 1936, 1, 8; *New York Journal,* Dec. 17, 1936, 1.

82. *NCP,* Dec. 17, 1936, 1, 5; *BSGP,* Dec. 17, 1936, 1.

83. Frank S. Nugent, "Mountain Justice," *New York Times Film Reviews,* May 13, 1937, 31, quoted in Hatfield, "Mountain Girl Who Went Modern," 54–55, 125; Best, *Witch Hunt in Wise County,* 157; untitled 1936 King Features story, Slemp.

84. *BSGP,* July 9, 1936, 2; Hatfield, "Mountain Girl Who Went Modern," 54–55, 125; Best, *Witch Hunt in Wise County,* 157; untitled 1936 King Features story, Slemp; *NCP,* July 14, 1938, 8; MTT, 259–60.

85. *BSGP,* Dec. 10, 1936, 4; *NCP,* Dec. 10, 1936, 1, 5.

86. *RTD,* Dec. 9, 1936, 5.

87. Ibid., Dec. 19, 1936, 10; *NYEJ,* Dec. 9, 1936, 3, Dec. 11, 1936, 19, Dec. 17, 1936, 1, 3.

88. *News-Week,* Dec. 26, 1936, 31–32; see *WP,* Dec. 10, 1936, 1, 3.

89. Quotes from *WP,* Dec. 10, 1936, 1, Dec. 14, 1936, 1, 8, Dec. 18, 1936, 10. For *WP* coverage, see Dec. 10, 1936, 1, Dec. 11, 1936, 1, Dec. 14, 1936, 1, 8, Dec. 15, 1936, 1, 13, Dec. 16, 1936, 1, 4, Dec. 17, 1936, 1, 4, Dec. 18, 1936, 1, 8. There were women lawyers in Virginia in this period; see Wallenstein, "These New and Strange Beings."

90. *RTD,* Dec. 10, 1936, 10.

91. Ibid., Dec. 18, 1936, 1, 5; *RoT,* Dec. 18, 1936.

92. *RTD,* Dec. 18, 1936, 14, Dec. 19, 1936, 10; for letters in response to Dabney's editorials, see *RTD,* Dec. 22, 1936, 10, Dec. 23, 1936, 14.

93. Club president and minister quoted in Best, *Witch Hunt in Wise County,* 153–55; *RoT,* Jan. 14, 1937.

94. *RTD,* Dec. 18, 1936, 1, 9, Dec. 19, 1936, 1, 4, Dec. 20, 1936, 2, Feb. 24, 1937, 1, 2; *RoT,* Dec. 19, 20, 21, 1936, Jan. 2, 1937; Elsie M. Graff to Helen West, Feb. 23, 1937, NWPP, ser. 1, reel 58; the Maxwell/Greear articles, in Nov. and Dec. 1937 and Jan. 1938 issues of *Actual Detective* magazine, reprinted in Robertson and Brown, *History of the Pound,* 108–63.

95. *Maxwell v. Commonwealth,* 169 *Virginia* 886 (1937); *RoT,* Feb. 28, Mar. 3, 9, 10, 1937, May 23, 1937, June 16, 1937, Aug. 14, 1937, Sept. 15, 1937, Nov. 12, 16, 1937, Dec. 3, 1937; *RTD,* Mar. 10, 1937, 1, 2, Nov. 12, 1937, 1; *NCP,* Mar. 11, 1937, Nov. 11, 1937, 1, 8.

96. *RoT,* Mar. 11, 1937, Apr. 18, 1937.

97. *RTD,* Dec. 12, 1937, 14; *RoT,* Nov. 25, Dec. 11, 1937 (also printed in *NCP,* Dec. 16, 1937, 2); *NCP,* Nov. 25, 1937, 1.

98. *RoT,* Nov. [no day], 1937; *NCP,* Nov. 25, 1937, 2; Best, *Witch Hunt in Wise County,* 84–85, 158–59.

99. *RTD,* May 4, 1938, 2; *RoT,* Dec. 14, 1937, May 4, 1938; Eleanor Patterson to Eleanor Roosevelt, Oct. 6, 1941, Roosevelt to Patterson, Oct. 8, 1941, to James H. Price, Oct. 8, 1941, Patterson to Roosevelt, Oct. 14, 1941, ERP, ser. 100, FDRL. See also Charles S. McNulty to James H. Price, May 5, 1938, Executive Papers, Governor James H. Price, box 155, LVA. Some sign of attempted group mobilization for Maxwell can be inferred from an unsigned plea to circulate a petition for pardon for Maxwell sent in December 1937 to the "President of the Community League" from the county next to Loudoun to the county next to Wise (*RTD,* May 4, 1938, 2)

100. Sherman, *Case of Odell Waller,* 138; Best, *Witch Hunt in Wise County,* 32–34, 159–69; Price to Eleanor Roosevelt, Oct. 28, 1941, ERP, ser. 100, FDRL; Jackson memo in Maxwell folder, June 6, 22, July 3, 1940, Executive Papers, Governor James H. Price, box 155, LVA. On Price's career and administration, see Syrett, "Politics of Preservation"; Syrett, "Ambiguous Politics"; Heinemann, *Depression and New Deal in Virginia,* 148–64.

101. Price to Roosevelt, Oct. 28, 1941, ERP, ser. 100, FDRL; Best, *Witch Hunt in Wise County,* 162–69; Jackson memo in Maxwell folder, June 6, 22, July 3, 1940, Executive Papers, Governor James H. Price, box 155, LVA.

102. P. J. Summer to Price, Dec. 21, 1941, R. R. Bucklery to Price, Dec. 21, 1941, Vivien H. McIntire to Price [n.d., but by reply late Dec. 1941; see Price to McIntire, Jan. 2, 1942], Clyde M. Moore to Price, Dec. 20, 1941, J. S. Bushneed to Price, Dec. 21, 1941, J. G. McGeary to Price, Dec. 23, 1941, Executive Papers, Governor James H. Price, box 155, LVA.

CONCLUSION

1. Woodward, *Burden of Southern History;* Vandiver, *Idea of the South;* O'Brien, *Idea of the American South;* Kirby, *Media-Made Dixie;* Current, *Northernizing the South;* Bass and DeVries, *Transformation of Southern Politics,* 339–68. On the transformation in the southern economy and society, see Grantham, *South in Modern America,* 259–80; McMillen, *Remaking Dixie.* On the change in the traits that make up the South's regional identity, see Grantham, *South in Modern America,* 311–31. On direct federal intervention to curb white racial violence, see Belknap, *Federal Law and Southern Order.*

2. Sherman, *Case of Odell Waller;* Pauli Murray, *Autobiography of a Black Activist,* 150–76.

3. Sherman, *Case of Odell Waller,* 33–73, 109, 130–32; Black, *Casting Her Own Shadow,* 93–95; Goodwin, *No Ordinary Time,* 351–54; Morgan, *FDR: A Biography,* 174–75; Franklin Roosevelt to Colgate Darden, June 15, 1942, President's Secretary's File, General "D," Franklin D. Roosevelt Papers, FDRL.

4. Sherman, *Case of Odell Waller,* 2, 189; Wilkinson, *Harry Byrd and Virginia Politics,* 89–198; *Colgate Darden,* 83–88; Lechner, "Massive Resistance."

5. Darlene Wilson, "A Judicious Combination of Incident and Psychology: John Fox Jr. and the Southern Mountaineer Motif," in Billings, Norman, and Ledford, *Confronting Appalachian Stereotypes,* 98–118, quote at 102; Trigiani, *Big Stone Gap.*

6. Friedman, *Crime and Punishment,* 11.

Selected Bibliography

MANUSCRIPTS

Library of Congress, Washington, D.C.
National Woman's Party Papers. Microfilm edition.

Library of Virginia, Richmond
Governor James H. Price Executive Papers

Nelson County Historical Society, Lovingston, Va.
Leland Estes Jr., comp. "The Loving/Estes Murder Case," transcriptions from the
    Lynchburg News.

Franklin D. Roosevelt Library, Hyde Park, N.Y.
Eleanor Roosevelt Papers
Franklin D. Roosevelt Papers

*The Albert and Shirley Small Special Collections Library, University of Virginia
    Library, Charlottesville*
Walter Scott Copeland Papers
Aubrey Strode Papers

University of Virginia's College at Wise Library, Wise, Va.
Evelyn Slemp Collection

Virginia Baptist Historical Society, University of Richmond, Richmond
John R. Moffett Diary. Manuscript and typescript copies.
W. W. Moffett. "Correspondence between W. W. Moffett and *Richmond Times-
    Dispatch* concerning Reverend John R. Moffett." Bound typescript.

Virginia Historical Society, Richmond
Aylett Family Papers
Evan R. Chesterman Scrapbook, vol. 13: Trials in the *Richmond Evening Journal*

Gwathmey Family Papers
Meredith Family Papers
Pollard, H. Rives. Lecture: *The Chivalry of the South,* Broadside, May 2, 1867.
——. *The Southern Opinion.* Broadside, Nov. 20, 1866.
——. *To the People of the South.* Broadside, Richmond, 1865.

ALL OTHER SOURCES

Abramson, Phyllis Leslie. *Sob Sister Journalism.* New York, 1990.
An Account of the Curtis Homicide and the Trial of John E. Poindexter. Richmond,
    1879.
Addington, Luther F. *The Story of Wise County.* Wise, Va., 1956.
Andrews, J. Cutler. *The South Reports the Civil War.* Princeton, N.J., 1970.
Arnold, Edward T. "Al, Abner, and Appalachia," *Appalachian Journal* 17 (1990):
    262–75.
Ayers, Edward L., and John C. Willis, eds. *The Edge of the South: Life in Nineteenth-
    Century Virginia.* Charlottesville, Va., 1991.
Ayers, Edward L. *The Promise of the New South: Life after Reconstruction.* New York,
    1992.
——. *Vengeance and Justice: Crime and Punishment in the Nineteenth-Century
    American South.* New York, 1984.
Baiamonte, John V., Jr. *Spirit of Vengeance: Nativism and Louisiana Justice, 1921–1924.*
    Baton Rouge, La., 1986.
Baker, Paul R. *Stanny: The Gilded Life of Stanford White.* New York, 1989.
Baldasty, Gerald J. *The Commercialization of News in the Nineteenth Century.* Madison,
    Wis., 1992.
——. "The Nineteenth Century Origins of Modern American Journalism," *Proceedings
    of the American Antiquarian Society* 100, pt. 2 (1990): 407–19.
Barclay, G. A. "The Keeley League," *Journal of the Illinois State Historical Society* 57
    (1964): 341–65.
Barnes, Kenneth C. *Who Killed John Clayton? Political Violence and the Emergence of
    the New South, 1861–1893.* Durham, N.C., 1998.
Barnhurst, Kevin G., and John Nerone. *The Form of News: A History.* New York, 2001.
Bass, Jack, and Walter DeVries. *The Transformation of Southern Politics: Social Change
    and Political Consequence since 1945.* New York, 1976.
Becker, Susan D. *The Origins of the Equal Rights Amendment: American Feminism
    between the Wars.* Westport, Conn., 1981.
Belknap, Michal R. *Federal Law and Southern Order: Racial Violence and
    Constitutional Conflict in the Post-"Brown" South.* Athens, Ga., 1987.
Bellesiles, Michael A. *Arming America: The Origins of a National Gun Culture.* New
    York, 2000.

Benedict, Helen. *Virgin or Vamp: How the Press Covers Sex Crimes*. New York, 1992.

Best, Gary Dean. *Witch Hunt in Wise County: The Persecution of Edith Maxwell*. Westport, Conn., 1994.

Billings, Dwight B., Gurney Norman, and Katherine Ledford, eds. *Confronting Appalachian Stereotypes: Back Talk from an American Region*. Lexington, Ky., 1999.

Black, Allida M. *Casting Her Own Shadow: Eleanor Roosevelt and the Shaping of Postwar Liberalism*. New York, 1996.

Blackstone, William. *Commentaries on the Law of England: A Facsimile of the First Edition of 1765–1769*. Chicago, 1979.

Blight, David W. *Race and Reunion: The Civil War in American Memory*. Cambridge, Mass., 2001.

Bliss, Edward. *Now the News: The Story of Broadcast Journalism*. New York, 1991.

Bolling, Jim. "Wise County's Other Industry," *Historical Sketches of Southwest Virginia*, no. 10 (1976).

Boorstin, Daniel J. *The Americans: The National Experience*. New York, 1965.

Boyd, William H., comp. *Directory of Richmond City*. Richmond, 1869.

Brandt, Nat. *The Congressman Who Got Away with Murder*. Syracuse, N.Y., 1991.

Bredbenner, Candice Lewis. *A Nationality of Her Own: Women, Marriage, and the Law of Citizenship*. Berkeley, Calif., 1998.

Brown, Richard Maxwell. *No Duty to Retreat: Violence and Values in American History and Society*. New York, 1991.

Brownell, Blaine A. *The Urban Ethos in the South, 1920–1930*. Baton Rouge, La., 1975.

Brundage, W. Fitzhugh. *Lynching in the New South: Georgia and Virginia, 1880–1930*. Urbana, Ill., 1993.

Bundy, Charles Smith. *Early Days in the Chippewa Valley*. Menomonie, Wis., 1916.

Bush, Chilton. *Newspaper Reporting of Public Affairs: An Advanced Course in Newspaper Reporting and a Manual for Professional Newspaper Men*. New and enlarged ed. New York, 1940.

Butterfield, Fox. *All God's Children: The Bosket Family and the American Tradition of Violence*. New York, 1995.

Cahalan, Margaret Werner, with the assistance of Lee Anne Parsons. *Historical Corrections Statistics in the United States, 1850–1984*. Rockville, Md., 1986.

Calhoun, Walter T. "The Danville Riot and Its Repercussions on the Virginia Election of 1883," *Studies in the History of the South, 1875–1922* 3 (1966): 25–51.

Carter, Dan T. *Scottsboro: A Tragedy of the American South*. 1969; rev. ed. Baton Rouge, La., 1979.

Carter, Hodding. *Their Words Were Bullets: The Southern Press in War, Reconstruction, and Peace*. Athens, Ga., 1969.

Cherrington, Ernest, ed. *Standard Encyclopedia of the Alcohol Problem*. Westerville, Ohio, 1925–30.

Chesson, Michael. *Richmond after the War, 1865–1890.* Richmond, 1981.

Chiasson, Lloyd, Jr., ed. *The Press on Trial: Crimes and Trials as Media Events.* Westport, Conn., 1997.

Christian, W. Asbury. *Richmond: Her Past and Present.* Richmond, 1912.

Clark, Thomas D. *The Rural Press and the New South.* New York, 1948.

———. *The Southern Country Editor.* Gloucester, Mass., 1964.

Clemens, Samuel L., *The Complete Short Stories of Mark Twain.* Garden City, N.J., 1957.

Clinton, Catherine, ed. *Half Sisters of History: Southern Women and the American Past.* Durham, N.C., 1994.

Clinton, Catherine, and Nina Silber, eds. *Divided Houses: Gender and the Civil War.* New York, 1992.

Cohen, Patricia Cline. *The Murder of Helen Jewett: The Life and Death of a Prostitute in Nineteenth-Century New York.* New York, 1998.

Colgate Darden: Conversations with Guy Friddell. Charlottesville, Va., 1978.

Collins, Frederick L. *Glamorous Sinners.* New York, 1932.

Colvin, David Leigh. *Prohibition in the United States.* New York, 1926.

Connelly, Mark T. *The Response to Prostitution in the Progressive Era.* Chapel Hill, N.C., 1980.

Cortner, Richard C. *A Mob Intent on Death: The NAACP and the Arkansas Riot Cases.* Middletown, Conn., 1988.

Cott, Nancy F. *The Grounding of Modern Feminism.* New Haven, 1987.

Courtwright, David. *Violent Land: Single Men and Social Disorder from the Frontier to the Inner City.* Cambridge, Mass., 1996.

Cray, Ed. *Chief Justice: A Biography of Earl Warren.* New York, 1997.

Crouthamel, James L. *Bennett's* New York Herald *and the Rise of the Popular Press.* Syracuse, N.Y., 1989.

Current, Richard N. *Northernizing the South.* Athens, Ga., 1983.

Cyclopaedia of Temperance and Prohibition. New York, 1891.

Czitrom, Daniel J. *Media and the American Mind from Morse to McLuhan.* Chapel Hill, N.C., 1982.

Dabney, Virginius. *Across the Years: Memories of a Virginian.* Garden City, N.Y., 1978.

———. *Below the Potomac: A Book about the New South.* New York, 1942.

———. "Edith and Her Pappy," *New Republic,* Feb. 26, 1936, 69–70.

———. *Pistols and Pointed Pens: Dueling Editors of Old Virginia.* Chapel Hill, N.C., 1987.

Dailey, Jane. *Before Jim Crow: The Politics of Race in Postemancipation Virginia.* Chapel Hill, N.C., 2000.

———. "Deference and Violence in the Postbellum Urban South: Manners and Massacres in Danville, Virginia," *Journal of Southern History* 63 (1997): 531–90.

Darnton, Robert. *The Kiss of Lamourette: Reflections in Cultural History.* New York, 1990.

Darrow, Clarence. *The Story of My Life.* New York, 1932.

Dary, David. *Red Blood and Black Ink: Journalism in the Old West.* New York, 1998.

Davis, Curtis Carroll. "Very Well-Rounded Republican: The Several Lives of John S. Wise," *Virginia Magazine of History and Biography* 81 (1963): 461–87.

Degler, Carl N. *The Other South: Southern Dissenters in the Nineteenth Century.* New York, 1974.

——. "Thesis, Antithesis, Synthesis: The South, the North, and the Nation," *Journal of Southern History* 53 (1987): 1–18.

Demers, David Pearce. *The Menace of the Corporate Newspaper: Fact or Fiction.* Ames, Iowa, 1996.

Dicken-Garcia, Hazel. *Journalistic Standards in Nineteenth-Century America.* Madison, Wis., 1989.

Dillman, Caroline Matheny, editor. *Southern Women.* New York, 1988.

Dinnerstein, Leonard. *The Leo Frank Case.* 1966; rept. Athens, Ga., , 1987.

Doyle, Don H. *New Men, New Cities, New South: Atlanta, Nashville, Charleston, Mobile, 1860–1910.* Chapel Hill, N.C., 1980.

Emery, Edwin. *The Press in America: An Interpretative History of Mass Media.* 2d ed. Englewood Cliffs, N.J., 1972.

Escott, Paul D., and David R. Goldfield, eds. *Major Problems in the History of the American South,* vol. 2, *The New South.* Lexington, Mass., 1990.

Ethington, Philip J. *The Public City: The Political Construction of Urban Life in San Francisco, 1850–1950.* New York, 1994.

Fahey, David. *Temperance and Racism: John Bull, Johnny Reb, and the Good Templars.* Lexington, Ky., 1996.

Ferrell, Henry C., Jr. *Claude A. Swanson of Virginia.* Lexington, Ky., 1985.

Fischer, David Hackett. *Albion's Seed: Four British Folkways in America.* New York, 1989.

Ford, Linda G. *Iron-Jawed Angels: The Suffrage Militancy of the National Woman's Party, 1912–1920.* Lanham, Md., 1991.

Foster, Gaines. *Ghosts of the Confederacy: Defeat, the Lost Cause, and the Emergence of the New South, 1865–1913.* New York, 1987.

Fox, John, Jr. *The Trail of the Lonesome Pine.* New York, 1908.

Fox, Richard Wightman. *Trials of Intimacy: Love and Loss in the Beecher-Tilton Scandal.* Chicago, 1999.

Franklin, John Hope. *The Militant South.* New York, 1956.

Freeman, Joanne B. *Affairs of Honor: National Politics in the New Republic.* New Haven, 2001.

Friedman, Lawrence J. *The White Savage: Racial Fantasies in the Post-bellum South.* Englewood Cliffs, N.J., 1970.

Friedman, Lawrence M. *Crime and Punishment in American History.* New York, 1993.

——. *A History of American Law*. 1973; rept. New York, 1985.

Friedman, Lawrence M., and Robert V. Percival, *The Roots of Justice: Crime and Punishment in Alameda County, California, 1870 –1910*. Chapel Hill, N.C., 1981.

Friendly, Fred W. *Minnesota Rag: The Dramatic Story of the Landmark Supreme Court Case That Gave New Meaning to Freedom of the Press*. New York, 1981.

Fry, Plantagenet Somerset, and Fiona Somerset Fry. *The History of Scotland*. London, 1987.

Gaston, Paul M. *The New South Creed: A Study in Southern Mythmaking*. New York, 1970.

Gispen, Kees, ed. *What Made the South Different?* Jackson, Miss., 1990.

Godkin, E. L. "The Rights of the Citizen," *Scribner's Magazine* 8 (July 1890): 58 – 67.

Goldfield, David R. *Cotton Fields and Skyscrapers: Southern City and Region, 1607 – 1980*. Baton Rouge, La., 1982.

Goldsmith, Barbara. *Other Powers: The Age of Suffrage, Spiritualism, and the Scandalous Victoria Woodhull*. New York, 1998.

Goodman, James. *Stories of Scottsboro*. New York, 1994.

Goodwin, Doris Kearns. *No Ordinary Time: Franklin and Eleanor Roosevelt: The Home Front in World War II*. New York, 1994.

Gordon, Linda. *The Great Arizona Orphan Abduction*. Cambridge, Mass., 1999.

Gorn, Elliot J. " 'Gouge and Bite, Pull Hair and Scratch': the Social Significance of Fighting in the Southern Backcountry," *American Historical Review* 90 (1985): 18 – 43.

Gramling, Oliver. *AP: The Story of News*. Port Washington, N.Y.: Kennikat Press, 1969.

Grantham, Dewey W. *Southern Progressivism: The Reconciliation of Progress and Tradition*. Knoxville, Tenn., 1983.

——. *The South in Modern America: A Region at Odds*. New York, 1994.

Green, Thomas A. "The Jury and the English Law of Homicide, 1200 –1800," *Michigan Law Review* 74 (1976): 414 – 99.

Greenberg, Kenneth S. *Honor and Slavery: Lies, Duels, Noses, Masks, Dressing as a Woman, Gifts, Strangers, Humanitarianism, Death, Slave Rebellions, the Proslavery Argument, Baseball, Hunting, and Gambling in the Old South*. Princeton, N.J., 1996.

——. *Masters and Statesmen: The Political Culture of American Slavery*. Baltimore, 1985.

Griffin, Larry J., and Don H. Doyle, eds. *The South as an American Problem*. Athens, Ga., 1995.

Grossberg, Michael. *A Judgment for Solomon: The D'Hauteville Case and Legal Experience in Antebellum America*. New York, 1996.

Hairston, L. Beatrice W. *A Brief History of Danville, Virginia, 1728 –1954*. Richmond, 1955.

Hartog, Hendrick. "Lawyering, Husbands' Rights, and 'the Unwritten Law' in Nineteenth-Century America," *Journal of American History* 84 (1997): 67–96.

Hatfield, Sharon. "The Mountain Girl Who Went Modern: The Media's Crusade to Free Edith Maxwell." M.A. Thesis, Ohio Univ., 1991.

Healy, Paul F. *Cissy: The Biography of Eleanor M. "Cissy" Patterson.* Garden City, N.Y., 1966.

Heinemann, Ronald L. *Depression and New Deal in Virginia: The Enduring Dominion.* Charlottesville, Va., 1983.

Herd, Denise A. "Prohibition, Racism, and Class Politics in the Post-Reconstruction South," *Journal of Drug Issues* 13 (Winter 1983): 77–94.

Herringshaw, Thomas W. *Herringshaw's Encyclopedia of American Biography of the Nineteenth Century.* Chicago, 1898.

Hindus, Michael Stephen. *Prison and Plantation: Crime, Justice, and Authority in Massachusetts and South Carolina, 1767–1878.* Chapel Hill, N.C., 1980.

Hines, Garnet, ed. *Radford State Teachers College Handbook, 1930–1932.* NPD.

Hixon, Walter L. *Murder, Culture, and Injustice: Four Sensational Cases in American History.* Akron, Ohio, 2001.

Hobson, Barbara Meil. *Uneasy Virtue: The Politics of Prostitution and the American Reform Tradition.* New York, 1987.

Hobson, Fred. *Tell about the South: The Southern Rage to Explain.* Baton Rouge, La., 1983.

Hughes, Helen MacGill. *News and the Human Interest Story.* 1968; rept. Chicago, 1940.

Ireland, Robert M. "Acquitted yet Scorned: The Ward Trial and the Traditions of Antebellum Kentucky Criminal Justice," *Register of the Kentucky Historical Society* 84 (1986): 107–49.

——. "The Buford-Elliott Tragedy and the Traditions of Kentucky Criminal Justice," *Filson Club History Quarterly* 66 (1992): 395–420.

——. "Homicide in Nineteenth Century Kentucky," *Register of the Kentucky Historical Society* 81 (1983): 134–53.

——. "Insanity and the Unwritten Law," *American Journal of Legal History* 32 (1988): 157–72.

——. "The Libertine Must Die: Sexual Dishonor and the Unwritten Law in the Nineteenth-Century United States," *Journal of Social History* 23 (1989): 27–42.

——. "The Suicide of Judge Richard Reid: Politics and Honor Run Amok," *Filson Club History Quarterly* 71 (1997): 123–45.

——. "The Thompson-Davis Case and the Unwritten Law," *Filson Club History Quarterly* 62 (1988): 417–41.

Isaac, Rhys. *The Transformation of Virginia, 1740–1790.* Chapel Hill, N.C., 1982.

John, Richard R. *Spreading the News: The American Postal System from Franklin to Morse.* Cambridge, Mass., 1995.

Johnson, Charles A. *A Narrative History of Wise County, Virginia.* 1938; rept. Johnson City, Tenn., 1988.

Jones, Ann. *Women Who Kill.* New York, 1980.

Kaplan, Richard. "The American Press and Political Community: Reporting in Detroit, 1865–1920," *Media, Culture, and Society* 19 (1997): 331–55.

Kernan, Thomas J. "The Jurisprudence of Lawlessness," *Reports of the 29th Annual Meeting of the American Bar Association* 29, pt. 1 (1906): 450–67.

Killian, Lewis M. *White Southerners.* Rev. ed. Amherst, Mass., 1985.

Kinney, Martha E. "'If Vanquished I Am Still Victorious': Religious and Cultural Symbolism in Virginia's Confederate Memorial Day Celebrations, 1866–1903," *Virginia Magazine of History and Biography* 106 (Summer 1998): 327–66.

Kirby, Jack Temple. *Media-Made Dixie: The South in the American Imagination.* Athens, Ga., 1986.

——. *Westmoreland Davis: Virginia Planter-Politician, 1859–1942.* Charlottesville, Va., 1968.

Kluger, Richard, with the assistance of Phyllis Kluger. *The Paper: The Life and Death of the New York Herald Tribune.* New York, 1986.

Kneebone, John T. *Southern Liberal Journalists and the Issue of Race, 1920–1944.* Chapel Hill, N.C., 1985.

Kousser, J. Morgan. *The Shaping of Southern Politics: Suffrage Restriction and the Establishment of the One-Party South, 1880–1910.* New Haven, 1974.

Kraditor, Aileen S. *Ideas of the Woman Suffrage Movement, 1890–1920.* New York, 1965.

Kyvig, David E. *Repealing National Prohibition.* Chicago, 1979.

Lane, Roger. *Murder in America: A History.* Columbus, Ohio, 1997.

Larsen, William. *Montague of Virginia: The Making of a Southern Progressive.* Baton Rouge, La., 1965.

Lechner, Ira M. "Massive Resistance: Virginia's Great Leap Backward," *Virginia Quarterly Review* 74 (1998): 631–40.

Lee, Maurice, Jr. *James Stewart, Earl of Moray: A Political Study of the Reformation in Scotland.* New York, 1953.

Lender, Mark Edward, and James Kirby Martin, *Drinking in America: A History.* 2d ed. New York, 1987.

Leonard, Thomas C. *News for All: America's Coming-of-Age with the Press.* New York, 1995.

Lewis, Alfred Henry. "Owners of America II. Thomas F. Ryan," *Cosmopolitan,* July 1908, 141–52.

Lewis, Tom. *Empire of the Air: The Men Who Made Radio.* New York, 1991.

Lewis-Smith, Lanora Geissler. *Radford College: A Sentimental Chronicle through Its First Half Century.* N.p., n.d.

Link, William A. *A Hard and Lonely Place: Schooling, Society, and Reform in Rural Virginia, 1870 –1920.* Chapel Hill, N.C., 1986.

Lombardo, Paul A. "Eugenic Sterilization in Virginia: Aubrey Strode and the Case of *Buck v. Bell.*" Ph.D. diss., Univ. of Virginia, 1982.

———. "Involuntary Sterilization in Virginia," *Developments in Mental Health Law* 3 (1983): 13–14, 18–21.

Lowe, Richard. *Republicans and Reconstruction in Virginia, 1856 –1870.* Charlottesville, Va., 1991.

Lukas, J. Anthony. *Big Trouble: A Murder in a Small Western Town Sets Off a Struggle for the Soul of America.* New York, 1997.

Lule, Jake. *Daily News, Eternal Stories: The Mythological Role of Journalism.* New York, 2001.

Lunardini, Christine A. *From Equal Suffrage to Equal Rights: Alice Paul and the National Woman's Party, 1910 –1928.* New York, 1986.

MacDougall, Curtis D. *Interpretive Reporting.* New York, 1938.

Maddex, Jack P., Jr. *The Reconstruction of Edward A. Pollard: A Rebel's Conversion to Postbellum Unionism.* Chapel Hill, N.C., 1974.

———. *The Virginia Conservatives, 1867–1879: A Study in Reconstruction Politics.* Chapel Hill, N.C., 1970.

Mantiply, Victor Edsel. *A History of Moffett Memorial Baptist Church, Danville, Virginia, 1887–1987.* Lawrenceville, Va., [1987].

Marmon, Lee. *The Measure and Mirror of Men: Generations of the Oak Ridge Estate.* Lynchburg, Va., 1992.

Marquis, Alice Goldfarb. "Written on the Wind: The Impact of Radio during the 1930s," *Journal of Contemporary History* 19 (1984): 385–15.

Martin, Charles H. *The Angelo Herndon Case and Southern Justice.* Baton Rouge, La., 1976.

Martin, Ralph G. *Cissy.* New York, 1979.

Martin–Perdue, Nancy J., and Charles L. Perdue Jr., ed. *Talk about Trouble: A New Deal Portrait of Virginians in the Great Depression.* Chapel Hill, N.C., 1996.

McElroy, Robert. *Jefferson Davis: The Unreal and the Real.* New York, 1937.

McGerr, Michael E. *The Decline of Popular Politics: The American North, 1865 –1928.* New York, 1986.

McGovern, James R. *Anatomy of a Lynching: The Killing of Claude Neal.* Baton Rouge, La., 1982.

McLaurin, Melton A. *Celia: A Slave.* Athens, Ga., 1991.

McMillen, Neil R., ed. *Remaking Dixie: The Impact of World War II on the American South.* Jackson, Miss., 1997.

McWhiney, Grady, and Perry D. Jamieson. *Attack and Die: Civil War Military Tactics and the Southern Heritage.* University, Ala., 1982.

Merril, Boynton, Jr. *Jefferson's Nephews: A Frontier Tragedy.* Princeton, N.J., 1976.
Miller, Wilbur R. *Revenuers and Moonshiners: Enforcing Federal Liquor Law in the Mountain South, 1865–1900.* Chapel Hill, N.C., 1991.
Minutes of 69th Annual Session of Baptist General Association of Virginia. Richmond, 1892.
Minutes of 104th Annual Session of Roanoke Baptist Association. Danville, Va., 1893.
Mitchell, Reid. *Civil War Soldiers.* New York, 1988.
Mitchison, Rosalind. *A History of Scotland.* London, 1970.
Moger, Allen W. *Virginia: Bourbonism to Byrd, 1870–1925.* Charlottesville, Va., 1968.
Mooney, Michael M. *Evelyn Nesbit and Stanford White.* New York, 1976.
Moore, James T. "The Death of the Duel: The Code Duello in Readjuster Virginia, 1879–1883," *Virginia Magazine of History and Biography* 83 (1975): 259–76.
———. *Two Paths to the New South: The Virginia Debt Controversy, 1870–1883.* Lexington, Ky., 1974.
Moore, John Hammond. "The Negro and Prohibition in Atlanta, 1885–1887," *South Atlantic Quarterly* 69 (Winter 1970): 38–57.
Morgan, Ted, *FDR: A Biography.* New York, 1985.
Morton, David. *Off the Record: The Technology and Culture of Sound Recording in America.* New Brunswick, N.J., 2000.
Mott, Frank Luther. *American Journalism: A History of Newspapers in the United States, 1690–1960.* 3d ed. New York, 1962.
———. *A History of American Magazines,* vol. 3, *1865–1885,* and vol. 4, *1885–1905.* Cambridge, Mass., 1957.
Murray, Pauli. *The Autobiography of a Black Activist, Feminist, Lawyer, Priest, and Poet.* Knoxville, Tenn., 1989.
National Cyclopaedia of American Biography. New York, 1901.
Nerone, John C. "The Mythology of the Penny Press," *Critical Studies in Mass Communications* 4 (1987): 376–404 and critical responses, 405–22.
———. *Violence against the Press: Policing the Public Sphere in U.S. History.* New York, 1994.
Nichols, David, ed. *Ernie's America: The Best of Ernie Pyle's 1930s Travel Dispatches.* New York, 1989.
Nisbett, Richard E., and Dov Cohen. *Culture of Honor: The Psychology of Violence in the South.* Boulder, Colo., 1996.
North, S. N. D. *History and Present Condition of the Newspaper and Periodical Press of the United States, with a Catalogue of the Publications of the Census Year.* Utica, N.Y., 1884.
O'Brien, Michael. *The Idea of the American South, 1920–1941.* Baltimore, 1979.
O'Connor, Richard. *Courtroom Warrior: The Combative Career of William Travers Jerome.* Boston, 1963.

Osterweis, Rollin G. *The Myth of the Lost Cause, 1865–1900.* Hamden, Conn.: Archon Books, 1973.

Osthaus, Carl R. *Partisans of the Southern Press.* Lexington, Ky., 1994.

Parker, David S. "Law, Honor, and Impunity in Spanish America: The Debate over Dueling, 1870–1920," *Law and History Review* 19 (2001): 311–41.

Pearson, C. C. *The Readjuster Movement in Virginia.* New Haven, 1943.

Pearson, C. C., and J. Edwin Hendricks. *Liquor and Anti-Liquor in Virginia, 1619–1919.* Durham, N.C., 1967.

Perman, Michael. *The Struggle for Mastery: Disfranchisement in the South, 1888–1908.* Chapel Hill, N.C., 2001.

Peters, John O., and Margaret T. Peters. *Virginia Historic Courthouses.* Charlottesville, Va., 1995.

Pivar, David J. *Purity Crusade: Sexual Morality and Social Control, 1868–1918.* Westport, Conn., 1973.

Pollard, Edward A. *Memoir of the Assassination of Henry Rives Pollard.* Lynchburg, Va., 1869.

Pollock, Edward. *Illustrated Sketch Book of Danville, Virginia, Its Manufactures and Commerce.* N.p., 1885.

Pond, J. B. *Eccentricities of Genius.* New York, 1990.

Pulley, Raymond H. *Old Virginia Restored: An Interpretation of the Progressive Impulse, 1870–1930.* Charlottesville, Va., 1968.

Rabinowitz, Howard N. *Race Relations in the Urban South, 1865–1890.* New York, 1978.

Read, Carl, and May Read. *The Loving Family in America, 1705–1981.* Warner Robins, Ga., 1981.

"Reminiscences of J. J. Kelly, Jr.," *Historical Sketches of Southwest Virginia,* no. 6 (1972): 27–34.

Report of Committee of Forty, Danville Riot. Richmond, 1883.

Rise, Eric W. *The Martinsville Seven: Race, Rape, and Capital Punishment.* Charlottesville, Va., 1995.

Ritchie, Donald A. *Press Gallery: Congress and the Washington Correspondents.* Cambridge, Mass., 1991.

Roanoke Baptist Union Report. Danville, Va., 1893.

Robertson, Rhonda, and Nancy Clark Brown, eds. *The History of the Pound.* N.p., 1993.

Rose, Kenneth D. *American Women and the Repeal of Prohibition.* New York, 1996.

Rosen, Ruth. *The Lost Sisterhood: Prostitution in America, 1900–1918.* Baltimore, 1982.

Rosenberg, Charles E. *The Trial of the Assassin Guiteau: Psychiatry and Law in the Gilded Age.* Chicago, 1968.

Rosewater, Victor. *History of Cooperative News-Gathering in the United States.* New York, 1930.

Rovere, Richard H. *Howe and Hummel: Their True and Scandalous History.* 1947; rept. New York, 1985.

Rubin, Louis D., Jr., ed., *The American South: Portrait of a Culture.* Baton Rouge, La., 1980.

Sayre, Francis B. "Mens Rea," *Harvard Law Review* 45 (1932): 974–1026.

Schiller, Dan. *Objectivity and the News: The Public and the Rise of Commercial Journalism.* Philadelphia, 1981.

Schmeller, Mark. "Liberty of the Cudgel," paper delivered at the 1999 Annual Meeting of the Law and Society Association.

Schudson, Michael. *Discovering the News: A Social History of American Newspapers.* New York, 1978.

——. *Origins of the Ideal of Objectivity in the Professions: Studies in the History of American Journalism and American Law, 1830–1940.* New York, 1990. Originally presented as Ph.D. diss., Harvard Univ., 1976.

——. "Preparing the Minds of the People: Three Hundred Years of the American Newspaper," *Proceedings of the American Antiquarian Society* 100, pt. 2 (1990): 421–43.

——. "Question Authority: A History of the News Interview in American Journalism, 1860s–1930s," *Media, Culture, and Society* 16 (1994): 565–87.

——. "Toward a Troubleshooting Manual for Journalism History," *Journalism and Mass Communications Quarterly* 74 (1997): 463–76.

Schuma, Simon. *Dead Certainties (Unwarranted Speculations).* New York, 1991.

Schuster, Laura, and Sharyn McCrumb, comps. and eds. "Appalachian Film List," *Appalachian Journal* 11 (1984): 329–83.

Schwarz, Philip J. *Twice Condemned: Slaves and the Criminal Laws of Virginia, 1705–1865.* Baton Rouge, La., 1988.

Schwarzlose, Richard A. *The Nation's Newsbrokers: The Rush to Institution, from 1865 to 1920.* Vol. 2. Evanston, Ill., 1990.

Shackelford, Laurel, and Bill Weinberg, eds. *Our Appalachia.* New York, 1977.

Shapiro, Henry D. *Appalachia on Our Mind: The Southern Mountains and Mountaineers in the American Consciousness, 1870–1920.* Chapel Hill, N.C., 1978.

Sherman, Richard B. *The Case of Odell Waller and Virginia Justice, 1940–1942.* Knoxville, Tenn., 1992.

Sherwin, Richard K. *When Law Goes Pop: The Vanishing Line between Law and Popular Culture.* Chicago, 2000.

Shifflett, Crandall A. *Coal Towns: Life, Work, and Culture in Company Towns of Southern Appalachia, 1880–1960.* Knoxville, Tenn., 1991.

Siegel, Frederick F. *The Roots of Southern Distinctiveness: Tobacco and Society in Danville, Virginia, 1780–1865.* Chapel Hill, N.C., 1987.

Silber, Nina. *The Romance of Reunion: Northerners and the South, 1865–1900.* Chapel Hill, N.C., 1993.

Simpson, Benjamin. *Men, Places, and Things.* Ed. Duval Porter. [Danville], Va., 1891.

Smythe, Ted Curtis. "The Reporter, 1880–1900: Working Conditions and Their Influence on the News," *Journalism History* 7 (1980): 1–10.

Stanley, Gregory Kent. "Apology for a Race: The Southern Mountaineer and the Paradox of Progress," paper in author's possession.

Stewart, Frank Henderson. *Honor.* Chicago, 1994.

Stowe, Steven M. *Intimacy and Power in the Old South: Ritual in the Lives of the Planters.* Baltimore, 1987.

Strebnick, Amy Gilman. *The Mysterious Death of Mary Rogers: Sex and Culture in Nineteenth-Century New York.* New York, 1995.

Strode, Hudson. *Jefferson Davis: Tragic Hero, the Last Twenty-Five Years, 1864–1889.* New York, 1964.

Sturgill, Roy L., comp. "The Maxwell Case: Pound, Wise County, Virginia," *Historical Sketches of Southwest Virginia,* no. 18 (1984): 15–24.

Summers, Mark Wahlgren. *The Press Gang: Newspapers and Politics, 1865–1878.* Chapel Hill, N.C., 1994.

Sutherland, Daniel E. *The Confederate Carpetbaggers.* Baton Rouge, La., 1988.

Syrett, John. "Ambiguous Politics: James H. Price's First Months as Governor of Virginia," *Virginia Magazine of History and Biography* 94 (1986): 453–76.

——. "The Politics of Preservation: The Organization Destroys Governor James H. Price's Administration," *Virginia Magazine of History and Biography* 97 (1989): 437–62.

Taylor, William. *Cavalier and Yankee: The Old South and American National Character.* New York, 1961.

Thomas, William G. *Lawyering for the Railroad: Business, Law, and Power in the New South.* Baton Rouge, La., 1999.

Thompson, S. H. *The Life of John R. Moffett.* Salem, Va., 1895.

Thurber, James. "Crime in the Cumberlands: A Reporter at Large," *New Yorker,* Feb. 29, 1936, 39–43.

Tilly, Nannie May. *The Bright-Tobacco Industry, 1860–1929.* Chapel Hill, N.C., 1948.

Tindall, George Brown. *The Emergence of the New South, 1913–1945.* Baton Rouge, La., 1967.

Trigiani, Adriana. *Big Stone Gap.* New York, 2000.

Tucher, Andie. *Froth and Scum: Truth, Beauty, Goodness, and the Ax Murder in America's First Mass Medium.* Chapel Hill, N.C., 1994.

Tyler-McGraw, Marie. *At the Falls: Richmond, Virginia, and Its People.* Chapel Hill, N.C., 1994.

Ullman, Sharon R. *Sex Seen: The Emergence of Modern Sexuality in America.* Berkeley, Calif., 1997.

Umphrey, Martha Merrill. "The Dialogics of Legal Meaning: Spectacular Trials, the Unwritten Law, and Narratives of Criminal Responsibility," *Law and Society Review* 33 (1999): 393–423.

Vandiver, Frank E., ed. *The Idea of the South: Pursuit of a Central Theme*. Chicago, 1964.

Virginia. Richmond, 1937.

Voss-Hubbard, Mark. "The 'Third Party Tradition' Reconsidered: Third Parties and American Public Life, 1830–1900," *Journal of American History* 86 (1999): 121–50.

Waldrep, Christopher. *Roots of Disorder: Race and Criminal Justice in the American South*. Urbana, Ill., 1998.

Wallenstein, Peter. "'These New and Strange Beings': Women in the Legal Profession in Virginia, 1890–1990," *Virginia Magazine of History and Biography* 101 (1993): 193–226.

Waller, Altina L. *Feud: Hatfields, McCoys, and Social Change in Appalachia, 1860–1900*. Chapel Hill, N.C., 1988.

———. *Reverend Beecher and Mrs. Tilton: Sex and Class in Victorian America*. Amherst, Mass., 1982.

Was Rev. J. R. Moffett Murdered? Clark vs. Commonwealth. Richmond, n.d. Copy in Virginia Baptist Historical Society, University of Richmond, Richmond.

Wilkinson, J. Harvie. *Harry Byrd and the Changing Face of Virginia Politics, 1945–1966*. Charlottesville, Va., 1968.

Willey, Malcolm MacDonald. *The Country Newspaper: A Study of Socialization and Newspaper Content*. Chapel Hill, N.C., 1926.

Williams, Cratis D. "The Southern Mountaineer: In Fact and Fiction (Part III)," *Appalachian Journal* 3 (1976): 186–262.

Williams, Frederick Wells. *Anson Burlingame and the First Chinese Mission to Foreign Powers*. New York, 1912.

Williams, Harold A. *The Baltimore Sun, 1837–1987*. Baltimore, 1987.

Williams, Jack K. *Dueling in the Old South: Vignettes of Social History*. College Station, Tex., 1980.

Williams, Lou Falkner. *The Great South Carolina Ku Klux Klan Trials, 1871–1872*. Athens, Ga., 1996.

Williamson, J. W. *Hillbillyland: What the Movies Did to the Mountains and What the Mountains Did to the Movies*. Chapel Hill, N.C., 1995.

Willis, Robert Grant. "Ghosts of 1008 East Clay Street," *Richmond Quarterly* 9 (1987): 32–35.

Wilson, Charles R. *Baptized in Blood: The Religion of the Lost Cause, 1865–1920*. Athens, Ga., 1980.

Wilson, Charles Reagan, and William Ferris, eds., *Encyclopedia of Southern Culture*. Chapel Hill, N.C., 1989.

Wilson, Douglas L. *Honor's Voice: The Transformation of Abraham Lincoln.* New York, 1998.

Wolfe, Margaret Ripley. "Aliens in Southern Appalachia, 1900–1920: The Italian Experience in Wise County, Virginia," *Virginia Magazine of History and Biography* 87 (1979): 455–72.

Woodward, C. Vann. *The Burden of Southern History.* Baton Rouge, La., 1968.

———. *Origins of the New South, 1877–1913.* Baton Rouge, La., 1951.

Wyatt-Brown, Bertram. *The Shaping of Southern Culture: Honor, Grace, and War, 1760s–1880s.* Chapel Hill, N.C., 2001.

———. *Southern Honor: Ethics and Behavior in the Old South.* New York, 1982.

Wynes, Charles E. *Race Relations in Virginia, 1870–1902.* Charlottesville, Va., 1961.

Zimmerman, Joan G. "The Jurisprudence of Equality: The Women's Minimum Wage, the First Equal Rights Amendment, and *Adkins v. Children's Hospital, 1905–1923,*" *Journal of American History* 78 (1991): 188–225.

Index

The American South Series